Civil-Military Relations in the Modern Middle East

Civil-Military Relations in the Modern Middle East

David S. Sorenson

ROWMAN & LITTLEFIELD
Lanham • Boulder • New York • London

Published by Rowman & Littlefield
An imprint of The Rowman & Littlefield Publishing Group, Inc.
4501 Forbes Boulevard, Suite 200, Lanham, Maryland 20706
www.rowman.com

86-90 Paul Street, London EC2A 4NE

Copyright © 2023 by The Rowman & Littlefield Publishing Group, Inc.

All rights reserved. No part of this book may be reproduced in any form or by any electronic or mechanical means, including information storage and retrieval systems, without written permission from the publisher, except by a reviewer who may quote passages in a review.

British Library Cataloguing in Publication Information Available

Library of Congress Cataloging-in-Publication Data
Names: Sorenson, David S., 1943– author.
Title: Civil-military relations in the modern Middle East / David S. Sorenson.
Description: Lanham : Rowman & Littlefield, 2023. | Includes bibliographical references and index.
Identifiers: LCCN 2022037892 (print) | LCCN 2022037893 (ebook) | ISBN 9781538169186 (cloth) | ISBN 9781538169193 (paperback) | ISBN 9781538169209 (epub)
Subjects: LCSH: Civil-military relations—Middle East. | Middle East—Armed Forces—Political activity. | Middle East—Armed Forces—Economic aspects.
Classification: LCC JQ1758.A38 C588 2023 (print) | LCC JQ1758.A38 (ebook) | DDC 322/.50956—dc23/eng/20221107
LC record available at https://lccn.loc.gov/2022037892
LC ebook record available at https://lccn.loc.gov/2022037893

Contents

Acknowledgments		vii
Notes on Transliteration		xi
1	Introduction	1
2	The Military and Society in the Middle East	25
3	The Civil-Military Relations of Middle East Political Transitions	55
4	The Political Economy of Middle East Civil-Military Relations	109
5	Middle East Civil-Military Relations: The Military Dimensions	157
6	Conclusions and Projections	201
Notes		213
Selected Bibliography		299
Index		317
About the Author		323

Acknowledgments

I very much appreciate the efforts of those who have reviewed chapters for this book, include Gabriel Aguilera, Carol Atkinson, Sean Braniff, Stephen Burgess, Evelyn Early, Josh Goodman, Amit Gupta, Chris Hemmer, James Lebovic, Douglas Peifer, Naunihal Singh, and W. Andrew Terrell. I also appreciate the opportunities allowed me by the Air War College, which gave me time to complete the manuscript and funded travel that enabled the interviews and perspectives in this book. Many thanks to Diane Day, who helped greatly with editing. I got tremendous editing assistance from Major Raymond Funke, USAF, who spent much time, effort, and skill correcting my writing. He did it in very short time, and I really appreciate the time he took to make the manuscript better. Jacqueline Plante did a great job copy editing. I also thank the five anonymous reviewers who critiqued the manuscript for Rowman & Littlefield, providing tough and insightful criticism. My editor, Katelyn Turner at Rowman & Littlefield, has been an absolute pleasure to work with, and I deeply appreciate her faith that I could turn what was a too-rough first draft into this book.

I have received useful feedback from the opportunity to present ideas in this book to a variety of forums, including the Army War College Arab Spring Symposium, held in January 2012, where I benefitted from comments by Marybeth Ulrich, Glenn Robinson, and Larry Goodson. I also presented at the conference on "Future Trajectories of Civil-Military Relations in the Midst of the Middle East Crisis," Centra Corporation for US Government Agency, Arlington, Virginia, May 9, 2012, as a panelist on "Contagion Effects and Implications for the Greater Middle East," Workshop on Regional Implications of Political Change in Tunisia and Egypt, State Department Bureau of Intelligence and Research and National Intelligence Council, Army and Navy Club, Washington, DC. I also presented some thoughts on North African civil-military relations on a panel, "North Africa: Reform, Development, and Islamism," organized by the Middle East Policy Council Capitol Hill Policy Conference in September 2007, where I exchanged ideas with Chas Freeman, Reinhold Brender, John P. Entelis, I. William Zartman, and William Lawrence. I have offered previous versions of the chapters in this book at a number of academic conferences as papers, including "Explaining Arab Military Spending: Responding to National Security or Distributive Politics?" (CEEISA-ISA Ljubljana Conference, Slovenia, June 23 to 25, 2016); "Countering the Islamic Appeal of the Islamic State" (Annual National Security Colloquium, University of Texas at El Paso, February 24, 2016); "Civil-Military Relations in Democratic Mexico," co-authored with Gabriel Aguilera (Facultad Latinoamericana de Ciencias Sociales/International Studies Association Joint Conference, Buenos Aires, Argentina, July 2014); and "Reforming the Yemeni Security Sector," co-authored with Ambassador Marwan Noman (International Crisis Group, Center on Democracy, Development, and The Rule of Law, Stanford University, Working Paper No. 137, June 2013). Conference presentations include, "Soldiers on Twitter: Arab Military Use of Social Media" (International Studies Association annual conference, San Diego, CA, April 2012), "The Global Financial Crisis and National Defense Spending: The Cases of United States, Taiwan, and Israel" (American Political Science Association annual conference, Washington, DC, September 2010), and "Civil-Military Challenges for the US as the War on Terrorism Comes Home" (Twentieth World Congress of the International Political Science Association, Fukuoka, Japan, July 2006). At all these presentations, I received valuable criticism on my ideas, and even though I cannot recall all who commented, they have made this a better product. In this book, I draw upon both secondary literatures, on some Arabic language material, and on interviews I have conducted in the Middle East between 1989 and the present. Readers will understand that these interviews often covered sensitive material, so I am careful not to attribute any particular statement to a particular person. To all those who helped, thank you. The errors that remain are my responsibility.

Inspiration also came from former colleagues, some who are now deceased. I learned a lot from Jeffrey Record and Andy Terrell and wish we could continue the always interesting conversations. I started writing this book with encouragement from my wife, Sharon Tyler, who married me while I was still building and racing nitromethane-burning dragsters. After I survived several fiery high-speed crashes, Sharon persuaded me to change gears and go to graduate school, never protesting the spartan life of a graduate student family. As I progressed up the academic ladder, she kept the home fires burning as I traveled the Middle East. I shared many of the ideas in this book with her, and she used her mastery of English to help a former hot rodder craft better words. I lost her in 2017 to Parkinson's, but she lives on in these pages. I also owe a debt of gratitude to my academic mentors, who helped me make the transition from wrenches to books, and ultimately to an academic career. The most important was Barry H. Steiner, who sparked my interest in both international relations and the serious study of politics. I first walked into his classroom fifty years ago, not realizing that he would start my long academic career path. Thank you, Barry, for trusting me to try to live up to your standards.

Disclaimer: The views expressed in this book are of the author alone, and do not necessarily represent the views of any US government agency.

Notes on Transliteration

I employ words and names from Arabic, Farsi, Turkish, and Hebrew. I want to simplify the task of reading unfamiliar languages for readers, so I avoid almost all diacritical marks, though I do spell names with them when I cite an author's work, as I assume that is their preference. I used these conventions even for languages that I am not familiar with, like the Scandinavian languages. I do use the left half ring (ʻ) to mark the Arabic letter ع ("ayn") as it has a distinctive pronunciation, so "ʻAsad," for example. The Turkish ğ in names like "Erdoğan" means that the letter is silent but elongates the following letter. The Turkish ç is pronounced as "ch."

Chapter One

Introduction

Most Middle Eastern countries have an annual "national day" when members of the national elite gather on elaborate grandstands to review passing parades celebrating nationhood. On the dais next to the head of state are the senior soldiers, standing erect with colorful ribbons and badges bedecking their military tunics, eyes masked with aviator sunglasses. Their position next to the head of state is deliberate, as it represents martial proximity to the national political epicenter. These polished soldiers represent one of the most potentially powerful elements in a country, the armed forces, the most powerful state agent in the country, whose guns alone give them tremendous political power. One primary check against this potentially unbridled power is the national civilian leadership.

The bulk of civil-military relations scholarship traditionally focused on how the civilian political arena controls the national armed forces, attempting to maintain a politically neutral military as an effective fighting force. However, Krebs claims that, "The field of civil-military relations is far richer than the classic matter of who guards the guardians, and it should be properly understood as encompassing a wider range of questions about the relationship between the armed forces, the polity, and the populace."[1] Consequently, civil-military relations scholarship also focuses on how the armed forces' spending shapes the economy, and on military participation in the production of goods and services. The field also studies civilian leadership over soldiers in wartime and other military operations. One of the more enduring questions here is whether or not war is too important to be left to the generals, or, instead, whether or not the generals have a right to exercise their war expertise without direction from national political leadership.

While the civil military relations literature is rich with studies into both countries and regions, the Middle East as a region has received less attention until recently. There is now important scholarship on the political role of the armed forces in the Middle East.[2] Recent works by Florence Gaub, Phillipe Droz-Vincent, Caitlin Talmadge, Zoltan Barany, Zeinab Abdul-Magd, Shana Marshall, Robert Springborg, Risa Brooks, and many others have added much to both the overall body of civil-military relations theory and to Middle East civil-military studies. These works have concentrated on the consequences of politicizing a military for wartime performance, the role of militaries in political transitions (like the so-called Arab Spring movements), and the civil-military aspects of military economic activity, to note just a couple of examples. What I add to this research is an expanded application of comparative civil military models to the Middle East. I also extend the coverage of the Middle East to include non-Arab states, Israel, Turkey, and Iran—and Arab North Africa into my mix. The greater Middle East is an accepted field of study, as seen in the various scholarly and political organizations that formed around the area, including the Middle East Studies Association, the Association for the Study of the Middle East and Africa, the Nordic Society for Middle East Studies, the British Society for Middle East Studies, and many more. So, the "Middle East," as I apply it here, aligns to broader practices of regional study.

The one overarching research question that guides this book is: In what ways do national civilian leadership and national armed forces balance power against each other? Their relative positions make civilians and the military natural rivals for influence within the nation state. What are the goals of each party relative to the other? Do they mostly cooperate on policy matters of mutual concern? Or do they jockey for power, trying to gain influence while trying to keep the other in check? To focus this larger question, I concentrate on four Middle East civil-military relations areas: (1) the military and society, (2) the role of the military in political transitions, (3) the military influence on the national economy, and (4) the relationship between national leadership and military policy, which involves the study of, preparation for, and waging of war. I pose four categories of questions of Middle East civil-military relations, which I define in "greater" terms, to include the key Arab countries,[3] along with Iran, Israel, and Turkey. The questions are:

1. How does the military interact with society in the Middle East? Are the armed forces a part of society, or do they stand apart from it? Are they mass-based, or are they a powerful political elite that uses its power to extract scarce goods from the country's population? Why does this matter for civil-military relations? I argue that national society writ large helps to shape and defines institutional power through grants of approval, respect, or disdain.

2. How do civil-military relations affect Middle East political power transitions? While many countries pass power from one elected head of state to their successor with little if any military involvement, in other cases, the armed forces play a role, either as coup maker, or as facilitator of change through "pacted transition" to new rule. In other cases, military officers replace their uniforms with business suits and run for office, using their military connections and their uniformed colleagues to assist them at the ballot box.
3. What is the military role in the national economy, and how do military economic interests compete with civilian economic stakes in Middle Eastern countries? What are the civil-military implications for high defense spending levels, and for military influence in the national economy? When soldiers control portions of the national economy, do they use their position in the strong state to elbow out civilian competitors?
4. What is the nature and scope of wartime civil-military relations in the Middle East, and in military matters short of war? Do political rulers neuter their military forces out of fear of a coup, or do they trust their soldiers as professionals? Do "coup-proofing" measures by insecure national leaders contribute to defeat on the battlefields? What is the relationship between civil-military relations and wartime military performance?

I attempt to deconstruct and clarify the bargaining procedures that shape military access to national power in these issue areas, considering both formal and informal rules that guide the delicate chess match between civil authority, civil society, and the uniformed military. I focus on the modern period for the Middle East, which I define as post–World War II. This forces me to neglect the extraordinarily rich history of civil-military relations in the Middle East that dates back to antiquity. When I occasionally venture into Middle Eastern civil-military relations history, I do so only to show continuity with the modern age.

ADDRESSING THE QUESTIONS

Guidance in addressing these questions should come from *theory*, yet the study of civil-military relations has lacked strong theoretical constructs. James Burk put it cogently, "Only in the loosest sense can we claim to have overarching theories of civil-military relations that explain the widely divergent patterns of conduct that occur throughout this domain under the whole range of imaginable conditions."[4] Owens suggests that what passes for civil-military relations theory is based as much on institution and experience over the formal logic that most scientific theories contain.[5] For Peter Feaver, civil-military relations theory in the American context derived largely from the challenge of a large Cold War military, and thus, "the end of the Cold War has produced something of a crisis in both the practice and the study of American civil-military relations."[6] Matei suggests that while recent scholarship rejects Huntington's model, "nobody has yet come up with a new basis for what is essentially a contribution to normative political theory rather than empirical theory."[7] It is true, however, that other theoretical efforts have been applied to civil-military relations study; for example, Peter Feaver and Deborah Avant have advanced agency theory, Rebecca Schiff developed concordance theory, and Winger applied prospect theory to the 1997 American response to an incident on the Korean border.[8] But thus far, there has not been widespread development nor application of advanced theoretical approaches to the study of civil-military relations.

Much of the initial scholarship on civil-military relations sprung from the American experience, but theories on comparative civil-military relations are in development, and thus there are few truly comparative efforts across regions. The reasons for this are straightforward, as Barany observes, comparative civil-military relations often oversimplifies the relationships because, "the variety of settings, conditions, and explanatory variables stacks the odds strongly against the emergence of power and general theories of civil-military relations."[9] Ratuva notes that Huntington fails to account for militaries that repress their own citizens.[10] While Herspring developed a four-nation study using the lens of "shared responsibility" between civilian and military leaders, the study lacks applicability in countries where the military culture, a key variable in Herspring's study, includes the practice of interfering decisively in national politics.[11] The other missing piece in comparative civil-military relations was that many armed forces had multiple tasks outside of war, contrary to the American-based studies assumption that militaries are devoted mainly to making and executing military policy.

As I approach these questions, I start with a survey of the comparative literature in the relevant civil-military fields. I concentrate in particular on literature from regions that are comparable to the Middle East, including Latin America, South and Southeast Asia, and sub-Saharan Africa, though I also include European and Northeast Asian countries where appropriate. I then offer comparisons, to see what findings from other regions apply to Middle East cases, while taking care to note the multiple differences across regions on culture, economic structures, political environments, and military requirements.

THE VARIABLES OF INTEREST

Many explanatory variables influence the political role of a national armed force: political tradition, existing political conditions, military culture, the type of political system, and the popular imagination of the soldier. These factors may work individually or in concert to influence the politics of national civil-military relations. There are other theoretical approaches that have been a common framework for civil-military studies that I do not employ. As inspired by Barany, I avoid Huntington's *Soldier and the State* explanations, and I do not employ Janowitz's professional soldier conceptualization, as both are not particularly useful for application to the Middle East (I do mention Huntington, though, as that is a ritual for almost every civil-military study).[12] I also do not focus on the role of the military and democracy construction, as there has been very little, if any, efforts to construct democracy in the Middle East, as Barany shows in his study on the topic;[13] almost all the countries he covers are outside the Middle East. My focus is on political tradition, political factors, and military identity and politics.

Political Tradition

Political tradition sets and enforces ideas of place, of identity, of pride (or shame), and pushes informal rules about boundaries between groups, offering either permission or prohibition about crossing them. In Japan, recent reminiscences of political domination by the military before 1945 have kept the Self-Defense Forces far away from the corridors of Japanese political power.[14] Warriors in China were often associated more with banditry and atrocities than with national honor, and consequently few soldiers have ruled China.[15] The relative political neutrality of the American military is reflective of both professional military identity and a general American aversion to a strong central standing army dating back to the time of the founding generation and the debates between Hamilton and Jefferson.[16] In Latin America, the armed forces were often the power behind the scenes, along with the landed and religious elites, but following a series of political transitions that removed them from power, almost all Latin America is civilian governed, and there is little interest in bringing back the man on horseback.[17] In the quest for power competition between civilian leaders and the military, the national economy is a political football that the players can use to influence the other. In some cases, the military vacates the national economic field, but in other cases, politicians offer soldiers a stake in the national economy, either to supplement low military budgets or, more often the case, to keep them in the factories and farms, and thus out of the presidential palace. Once ensconced in the economic sector, soldiers can use their considerable power to crowd out other economic players, often establishing monopolies for themselves.

Political Factors

Sometimes weak or corrupt national leadership invites coups or military intervention in national politics short of a coup, but it is not the only lubricant to such intrusions, as low political institutionalization also facilitates high military participation. Countries with weak political parties, nascent civil societies, few if any independent media, and the lack of embedded public participatory traditions easily fall prey to the man on horseback, who can simply promise to "get things done." Once in a position of political power, soldiers may foil attempts to create viable alternative channels to public power, as such routes would challenge their often-predatory power over the country. Democracy, once institutionalized (a process that can take decades or longer), is often an antidote to military intrusion into political spaces, though weak democracies can result in a swift military takeover. So can the election of populist leaders or parties who marginalize the military and thus sew the seedbeds of their destruction, allowing the generals to rally to "defend" the country from incompetent radicals. Or militarized nationalism may become a part of emerging democratization, as happened in Bismarkian Germany and in Japan in the late 1920s, until the Great Depression derailed the democracy path.[18] In other cases, nationalism can downplay military power, as was the case in Nehru's India, which emphasized neutrality and democratization over war capacity, as was also the case in post–World War II Japan, Germany, and Italy.

Military Identity and Military Politics

National military identity also influences civil-military affairs. Militaries shape their self-image in numerous ways, from a glorified portrayal of their history to self-pity for betrayal by political leadership, to defenders of the faith (religious or ideological, or both), to list just a few examples. *Martial tradition* is usually a source of military identity because militaries often delve into history to tell their stories to justify their existence and their operations. Though most soldiers never see battle, it is what they prepare for. Consequently, martial history and the symbols of tradition often shape the military's organizational ethos. Military bases often contain poignant reminders of past glories, cannons, with cannonball piles in front of them, old tanks on cement platforms, and military cemeteries filled with honored dead. Military education often consists of studying past wars and learning lessons in military leadership from old generals or admirals.

Soldiers usually value order, discipline, obedience, and decisiveness, because such traits are essential for battlefield performance. Partly because they value tradition and stability, military officers tend toward conservative politics, preferring order to the often-chaotic landscape of democratic politics. Such soldiers are thus likely to be more comfortable in authoritarian political systems, and although militaries sometimes initially led revolutionary movements against autocratic regimes, they often simply replaced one autocrat with another, rarely altering leadership methods. While many professional military officers have willingly accepted democratic governance, they usually show a penchant for conservative political parties and conservative leaders that emphasize traditional values (and, sometimes, but not always, robust military budgets). Soldiers may particularly applaud democracy if it prevents radical politics (Marxism, or radical religious politics, for example), though soldiers may also fear that groups advocating radicalism may ride democratic elections to power.

The role of the military in the global march to and from democratic rule is mixed. In some cases, the armed forces have stood aside while democratic forces took command of the country, and sometimes soldiers embraced the change. The Taiwanese military enjoyed considerable prestige and national power under the authoritarian rule of the Kuomintang Party but did not actively resist the coming of democracy to that island country beginning in 1989, and South Korea's armed forces showed a similar acceptance of popular rule after 1987. Most Eastern European militaries similarly stood by as democratic processes superseded Communist Party rule, eager to swap their old Soviet-supplied weapons and doctrine for membership in NATO. As democratic forces swept through most of Latin America beginning in the 1980s, the armed forces, who had often been the political rulers, usually gave way to popular support. Times have clearly changed since the publication of a popular cartoon in Latin America showing a tiny military dictator standing inside a fire alarm box with the caption "in case of democracy, break glass." Even in Pakistan, where military coups have regularly occurred, the military appeared to accept the democratic election of civilian president Asif Ali Zardari in September 2008, and Prime Minister Imran Khan in 2018, even the soldiers remain close on the political sidelines. When Khan lost a vote of no confidence in the Pakistani Parliament in May 2022, he blamed the United States for his fate, rather than the Pakistani military. Sometimes the price for democracy is side payments to the military, including higher military budgets and more responsibility, so military acquiescence to democratization may be more common in countries that can afford to buy military agreement, or to rely on international patrons to buy it for them. The next question is how these observations pertain to the Middle East.

STUDYING CIVIL-MILITARY RELATIONS IN THE MIDDLE EAST

The Middle East provides interesting challenges for students of civil-military relations. First, the region is obviously not homogeneous, as it features a wide range of political structures, from liberal democracies (very few, though) to authoritarian rule. Some countries are overcrowded and economically stagnant (Egypt, Yemen, and Algeria, for example), while some are extremely wealthy and small (Qatar and the UAE). Some have seen relative peace throughout their modern eras (Tunisia, Morocco, and Qatar), while others have known almost endless wars (Iran, Iraq, and Israel). So, one the purpose of this book is to compare Middle East countries on the dimensions of civil-military relations. How are they alike, and how do they differ on the significant civil-military issues? Why do some experience military coups and others do not? Why does the military dominate in some polities and remain politically sidelined in others? Why does the military dominate the national economy of some Middle East countries but stand isolated economically in others? Why do civilian leaders dominate military decisions in some Middle East countries but the armed services make those decisions in other countries? While Egypt's military ran the country after President Mubarak's 2011 ouster and took it over again after the 2013 coup against President Mohammad Morsi, Lebanon's military has very little political power, and is only now beginning to take responsibility for defense matters.

Moreover, civil-military relations have rarely been static in the area. The Turkish armed forces launched several military coups during the life of the Turkish Republic, but the Islamist-oriented *Adalet ve Kalkınma Partisi* (AKP) that came to power in 2002 effectively neutralized the military through mass arrests for both alleged and real coup efforts. The Moroccan national military tried twice to assassinate King Hassan II in the early 1970s but has remained loyal to the monarchy since. The Algerian military thwarted a parliamentary election in 1991, helping to initiate a bloody civil war, and while it remains in the shadows of governance, it has supported civilian rule (though usually rule by retired military officers). It acted quickly in the spring of 2019 to remove comatose President Abdelaziz Bouteflika before he could be sworn to another presidential term when demonstrators showed up to protest. The Algerian generals knew that if they could preempt more demands for Algerian democracy, they enhanced their chances to remain the powers behind the president, particularly knowing that the Algerian civilian authority is divided and often dependent on the military to shape it.[19] Tunisia has enjoyed relatively stable civil-military relations, with its small military concentrated on military professionalism rather than on politics (though there was at least one coup attempt). The army briefly intervened in 2011 against President Zine Abidine Ben Ali when protests against his regime erupted, but then quickly withdrew from politics. Israel's military is politically neutral, but it is not uncommon there to see retired military officers as party heads, and some have become prime minister.

Middle Eastern armies bring their own culture to their profession, though it varies considerably. Some militaries grew from tribal militias, or religious groupings, and their traditions retain fealty to this past, as in Yemen or Libya, for example, where armies hold deeper loyalties to region and tribe over nation. Those identities were one reason why both militaries fragmented into tribal groups after the Arab Spring uprisings ousted national leadership. Other professional officers cut their political teeth in revolution, terminating the old order, and installing a new regime, complete with a new social order. Their tradition as state managers as well as soldiers lingers on. The Algerian, Egyptian, and Libyan armies are examples of "founding" militaries who toppled a monarchy in order to construct a republic and continued to exercise a heavy political hand in politics long after their revolutions succeeded. Colonial administrators developed other Middle East militaries, taking indigenous soldiers to the home country for military training and education, sometimes pressing them into service in colonial armies.[20] That tradition continued after independence, and many officers from countries like Jordan, Morocco, and Lebanon still receive their education in the elite war colleges and military academies of Europe (or the United States), and both retain those lessons and transfer them to their junior officers.

CATEGORIES FOR COMPARISONS

Throughout this book, I develop arguments that I illustrate with examples drawn at the country level. But how to categorize meaningfully? The Middle East has considerable regime type differences. One distinction is between full democracies (in reality, one full Middle East democracy, Israel as Tunisia slipped to partially free in 2022), partial democracies (Morocco, Lebanon, Kuwait, and Jordan[21]) and autocracies. But in reality, there are too few Middle East democracies and too many Middle East autocracies for meaningful comparison based solely on a democracy-autocracy divide. Another way is to differentiate between monarchies and republics, but even that bifurcation is inadequate. Clement Henry and Robert Springborg categorize Middle Eastern countries as (1) bunker states, (2) bully praetorian states, (3) globalizing monarchies, and (4) fragmented democracies.[22] Briefly, "bunker states" are ruled with a bunker mentality, with deeply protected ruling families or clans in power positions. "Bully praetorian states" are ruled on the shoulders of the security apparatus, with ties to both urban and rural elites. "Globalizing monarchies" are kingdoms with few nationalist roots but with close ties to their old colonial mentors. Finally, "fragmented democracies" are countries that have semi-institutionalized political competition, even in the face of antagonistic social forces based on differing ethnicities. Henry and Springborg use their categories to examine how Middle East countries engage in economic development and globalization. I am using these categories, but with some modifications. I am not convinced that the differences between "bully" and "bunker" republics is significant enough, as they have more common than unique features (powerful leaders, a rump parliament at best, and strong regulation of free expression, for example), so I combined them into one category: *bully republics*. Later in their work, Henry and Springborg differentiate between "liberal" and "conservative" monarchies, a category I use here.[23] I retain their "fragmented democracies" category. I am modifying these categories by employing some of Geddes's types, as she breaks out authoritarian regimes into "personalist," "military," "single-party," and amalgams of these types.[24] There are no real examples of true military-run states in the Middle East, but her distinction between *personalist* and *one-party* states is very useful for the Middle East.

I employ these categories with some caution, as Henry and Springborg use them for a different purpose, to compare how Middle East regimes respond to the pressures of economic development and globalization. They focus on how different states treated their capitalists; did new postcolonial regimes empower their capitalists as a source of independence development, or did they replace or marginalize their capitalists with economic managers? Are rent-seeking arrangements emplaced that discourage export-led growth, as happened in bully praetorian Egypt?[25] Do bunker states repress reform, as a threat to entrenched elites, as they did in Syria and Yemen?[26] How militaristic are bunker states? Henry and Springborg claim that Algeria is not a particularly militaristic state, with most of its leaders as civilians, unlike Iraq, Egypt, and Syria.[27] We should expect different civil-military relations patterns between countries that depend on family as opposed to those who run the country through their security forces, though, to be sure, there are overlaps. Democracies should control their militaries through accountable and transparent means, relying on several civilian institutions, including civilian-headed defense ministries and representative bodies. Therefore, I use a combination of the following categories.

Republican Bully Personalist

Republican bully personalist regimes are fully authoritarian, with no serious electoral competition, no independent legislature, or freedom of expression, nor an independent judiciary. The ruler governs as an individual, with little or no party apparatus, and weak state institutions. If there is a political party, the leader dominates it, staffing it with loyalists, and thus lacking a check valve role over the leader. Personalist leaders usually fear their military and engage in coup proofing (discussed in chapter 3), and tend to favor creating a parallel security force, to both lead in military operations, but also to monitor the regular military. Militaries in republican bully personalist states tend to seek economic benefits, more engaged in self-service than in military professionalism. Thus, bully states do poorly in war, or other military operations, compared to countries in the other categories. They are also vulnerable to both the leader's death, and to violent overthrow.[28] Examples would include Libya's Muamar al-Qadhafi or Gamal 'abd al-Nasser's Egypt.

Bully Single Party Republics

Bully single-party republics resemble bully personalist states, but the leaders govern mostly or partly through a party apparatus. That both provides a semi-institutional framework for the state, and also a potential limit on executive power. In strong party states, senior party officials can sometimes dampen the ambitions of the president, though that ability clearly depends on how much the leader has penetrated the party and installed loyalists as party members. In a bully single-party republic, the military has more incentive to work within the party, so coups may be less likely. One limiting factor of this classification is the degree to which a personalist leader has captured control of the leading party, as the case of the Ba'th Party in Syria and the AKP in Turkey suggest—how independent are they from the 'Asad family and President Recep Tayyip Erdoğan? The presence of a party or a legislation does not mean that an autocrat is constrained by such institutions, as Meng shows. Her study of sub-Saharan African cases demonstrates that institutions may constrain an autocrat only if they allow other elite members to access the political system.[29] Yet some categorizations are close calls: Does 'Asad's Syria qualify as a bully single-party republic or a bully personalist republic? I argue that the 'Asad family has such control over the Ba'th Party that it is not a constraint on 'Asad. Algeria's *Front de Libération Nationale*, or FLN, is the dominant party in the country, and exercises a degree of influence, especially over a new president. It must be noted, though, that over the republic's history, retired and active military officers were as much a constraint over the president as was the FLN. Consequently, Algeria is a close call as a bully single-party republic. Turkish President Recep Tayyip Erdoğan's rule over Turkey is probably the best example of a bully single-party Middle East leader, as his party, the Adalet ve Kalkınma Partisi, or AKP, has been the dominant political party for the past decade and more. The AKP is the only party to win six consecutive parliamentary elections in Turkish Republic history.

Liberal Monarchies

Liberal monarchies have a monarch as head of state, with a significant role in national politics. They allow a limited role for a legislature and restrict freedom of expression. Liberal monarchies usually have a parliament, and a cabinet, but the monarch is generally unconstrained much by those institutions and positions, and the primary responsibility of the ministers is to be fired by the monarch when state affairs go badly. Liberal monarchies usually control their militaries by intrusive monitoring, fearing military political opposition, yet needing their armed forces to remain professional, as symbols of the monarchy. Morocco is the best example of a liberal Middle East monarchy, though Jordan also makes the category, though it has ranged from "partly free" to "not free" on the Freedom House rankings (see below).[30]

Conservative Monarchies

Conservative monarchies have some of the tendencies of bully republics, ruling by authority through an extended royal family and permitting little if any opposition. While they may fear their militaries, they are more likely to buy off their soldiers to prevent coups. However, they do rely on alternative security forces, partly to intrusively monitor their regular armed forces. As most conservative monarchies are wealthy, they can provide modern equipment for their militaries, though the professional status of such armed forces varies from country to country. The Arabian Gulf emirates are all examples of conservative monarchies.

Fragmented Democracies

Fragmented democracies allow for relatively open political competition and rely on elections to determine political leadership. There are generally few restrictions on freedom of expression, and both parliamentary and judicial independence is assumed. There are limits, though, on political participation, given that, by definition, such democracies are fragmented, usually by

Table 1.1. Types of Middle East Regimes

Bully Personalist Republic	Bully Single-Party Republic	Liberal Monarchy	Conservative Monarchy	Fragmented Democracy
Egypt	Turkey	Morocco	Kuwait	Israel
Syria	Algeria	Jordan	Bahrain	Tunisia
Libya	Iran (post-1979)		Iran (pre-1979)	Lebanon
Yemen			Saudi Arabia	Iraq (post-2003)
Iraq (pre-2003)			Oman	Iran (1953)
			UAE	
			Qatar	

ethnic divisions (Israel and Lebanon), or by cleavages over religious emphasis (Tunisia). They often enculturate a tradition of apolitical militaries, so military coups are not common. Fragmented democracies usually have either professional armed forces, or a relatively small military that is often engaged in domestic security. Israel is the most obvious example, though Lebanon also fits. I am including post-Saddam Hussein in this category, realizing that Freedom House ranked Iraq as "not free" in 2022. This is a controversial placement, but Iraq has at least some of the makings of a democracy, albeit lacking some desirable parts of it.

The categories are in table 1.1.

As I list the countries, I abbreviate: Bully Personalist Republic (BPR), Bully Single Party Republic (BSPR) Liberal Monarchies (LM), Conservative Monarchy (CM), and Fragmented Democracy (FD). Where it fits, I endeavor to use that distinction, but where the categorization does not fit, I am not going to try to make it fit. These categorizations may aid in making comparisons across countries. One indicator of the type of country is its Freedom House score. In the bully republic category, all the countries in this category are ranked as "not free," making categorization easy. "Liberal" and "conservative" monarchies also differ, as the conservative monarch are all ranked as "not free," while liberal monarchy Morocco is "partly free." However, Jordan, which has varied between "partly free" and "not free" is considered "not free" in 2022. I still rank Jordan in the "liberal monarchy" category, which is bending my own rules, but Jordan, despite its ranking, is more liberal by far than are the Gulf monarchies. I push the limits for post-Saddam Hussein, as even though Freedom House ranks Iraq as "not free," the country has had regular elections which the major players have participated in, and largely accepted the outcomes. The reasons for the categorization of Middle East countries are shown in table 1.2.

Table 1.2. Reasons for Categories

Country	Category	Reason
Algeria	BSPR	Significance of National Liberation Front or FLN
Bahrain	CM	Ranked not free, no viable parliament or judicial system
Egypt	BPR	Dominance of president over party
Iran (pre-1979)	CM	Dominance of Shah Mohammed Reza Pahlavi
Iran (post-1979)	BPR	Dominance of supreme leader over government
Iran 1953	FD	Brief period of fragmented democracy
Iraq (pre-2003)	BPR	Dominance of Saddam Hussein
Iraq (post-2003	FD	Fragmented by ethnicity/religious differences
Israel	FD	Fragmented by ethnicity/religious differences
Jordan	LM	Partly free, partial role of parliament/civil society
Lebanon	FD	Fragmented by ethnicity/religion
Libya (pre-2011)	BPR	Dominance of Muamar Qadhafi
Morocco	LM	Partly free, partial role of parliament/civil society
Oman	CM	Dominance of the sultan
Qatar	CM	Dominance of ruling family
Saudi Arabia	CM	Dominance of ruling family
Syria (1949–1969)	BSPR	Personalist parties
Syria (post-1969	BPR	Dominance of ruling family
UAE	CM	Dominance of ruling family
Yemen	BPR	Dominance of president

Some of the expectations from these categories are unsurprising. I expect that bunker republics will experience much more turmoil in the politics of civil-military relations than countries in the other categories. I expect more coups, partly because republics almost always lack the legitimacy of monarchies, and more military input into the national economy. I posit that bully republics will more likely experience poor performance in war because their leaders distrust their armies and thus are more likely to coup-proof them. I believe that fragmented democracies will generally not experience contested civil-military relations, as their armed forces and their political leadership have reached a modus vivendi that emphasizes civilian control over the armed forces.

The expectations from these categories across issue-areas are shown in table 1.3.

For Arab countries, I compare in several categories, including those listed in table 1.3. One comparison is between Arab republics and monarchies. But Droz-Vincent notes, "Tellingly, the rare studies of the military in the Arab World do not devote many pages to monarchies."[31] I expect to find differences, for several reasons. First, many Arab republics were built on military foundations, as revolutionary groups morphed into national militaries, as in the cases of Algeria, Egypt, Libya, and Yemen, for example. Monarchies,

Table 1.3. Type of Regime Expectations

Regime Type	Coup likelihood	Military economic role	Civil-military type	War performance
Bully Personalist Republic	Relatively high	Rent-seeking	Coup-proofing	Poor
Bully Single Party Republic	Moderate	Rent-seeking	Institutional	Poor/Moderate
Liberal Monarchy	Very low	Insignificant	Intrusive monitoring	Moderate
Conservative Monarchy	Low	High defense spending	Alternative security service	Poor/moderate
Fragile Democracy	Very low	Insignificant	Democratic control	High/medium

by contrast, often feared their militaries, as sources of potential coups, or modernization efforts that might weaken the traditional royal foundations. Militaries often either ruled republics directly or pulled political strings from just outside the presidential palace, whereas monarchies often kept their armed forces under close scrutiny, reserving key positions to princes, or by keeping their armies far from the capital city. There are, of course, important exceptions to these generalizations, as republic leaders, too, often feared their military leaders, while monarchs sometimes relied on their armies in contests against political opponents. Monarchs sometimes actually served in their national militaries, and some became skilled at military operations—as did Jordan's Kings Hussein and Abdullah II. But even in the face of exceptions, the distinction between crown and republic might produce some interesting civil-military comparisons.

I also realize that I am skirting with tautologies in these expectations: Bully republics coup-proof their militaries because their leaders are bullies, for example, and it is difficult to imagine democracies that would permit even a token political role for their militaries. Militaries, by their very nature, are fundamentally undemocratic, as no soldier votes on operations, command trumps consultation, and freedom of expression is strictly limited. Moreover, the professional militaries that are usually found in democratic countries have no real wish to become involved in politics, except to lobby for their resources.

IDENTIFYING THE "MILITARY"

Traditional civil-military relations scholarship tended to concentrate on the active regular military, arguing that reserve or militia forces were not fully professional, or even "military," given their part-time status. However, many developing countries rely heavily on "part-time" armies for their security, unable to afford large full-time forces, and some developed countries also rely on nontraditional militaries because tradition or political preferences prevent a powerful active force. In some cases, regional militias, with greater loyalty to the province or tribe than the nation, have as much influence as does the "national" army. In other cases, religious affinity supports nontraditional militaries, as in the case of Lebanon's Hezbollah militia or the Iran's Islamic Republican Guard Corps.

Why do these distinctions matter for civil-military relations? For one thing, regular armies are usually institutionalized parts of the official government, under a Ministry of Defense, and subject to political and budgetary oversight through institutionalized processes. Their primary mission is defense against external threats, though in the Middle East, they are often used for domestic purposes. The identity that such militaries promote is usually the national identity. But militias that are either attached to a regular army or operate independently have a different chain of accountability, and a different identity promotion. Notes Ardemagni, "sometimes militias, which represent imagined and rival national fragments, exploit nationalist sentiments to promote their strategic interests and ideology."[32] Thus, the Islamic Republican Guard Corps in Iran and the Yemeni al-Houthi are independent of the Defense Ministry in Iran and the Houthi are unconnected to the Yemen government, and both promote a Shiʻa-based national identity. The following section considers the array of militaries found in the Middle East, as a precursor to analyzing civil-military relations.

TYPES OF MIDDLE EASTERN MILITARIES

There is considerable variance across Middle Eastern armies, as there is in every region of the world. Some are huge, consuming around ten percent of the national economy, while others are tiny, spending only a small fraction of the state treasury and fitting almost invisibly into the country. Some armies carry the honor of liberators from either foreign rule or monarchical governance, while others were the occupying force. Algeria's armed forces sprung from national liberation militias fighting against French domination, and thus based their claims for national influence on the argument that they made Algeria possible.[33] Morocco's National Liberation Army (ALN) could make the same claim about its role in Morocco's 1956 independence from France, a claim carried over into Morocco's national army as King Hassan II folded elements of the ALN to the regular military. The Jewish militias who won the 1948 war and became the Israel Defense Forces can claim that there would not have been an Israel had they lost. During the "Arab Spring" period, some Arab militaries took credit for helping remove an unpopular autocrat, as they did in Egypt and Tunisia (and a year later, the same Egyptian army took credit for installing another autocrat). Yet other Arab militaries turned their full force against anti-regime demonstrators, fearful that they would see their regime-granted privileges disappear should democracy replace the king or president-for-life, as in Syria and Bahrain.

Some Middle Eastern countries have armies with performance standards worthy of NATO membership (which Turkey holds), while in other countries, soldiers wile away hours collecting rents from their privileged positions. Some state treasuries are so limited that militaries ration such things as fuel or training time (on average, Syrian fixed wing aircraft pilots flew only thirty hours a year before the Syrian civil war), compared to hundreds of hours flown by NATO pilots annually). Some soldiers lay in wait for battles that rarely if ever come, biding their time by maintaining their machinery, holding parades, shining boots, ever engaged in the practice of looking busy. Some militaries have a long legacy of battle, and proudly display captured enemy tanks at their military museums. Others can barely maintain their own tanks.

One argument that I make in this book is that military typology shapes civil-military relations. There are clearly different types of militaries across countries, but typologizing them is problematic. The most common distinction is between *professional* soldiers, and *praetorian* military members. It is a useful distinction, though it is also incomplete.

Samuel P. Huntington did not originate the notion of military professionalism, but he used it to structure of his concept of *objective control* of the military. Contrasting objective control with *subjective* control, where the state assimilates the military, Huntington's notion of objective control stressed *expertise, responsibility* and *corporateness* as cornerstones of military professionalism.[34] The professional soldier seeks corporate autonomy to develop and hone military expertise, while avoiding politicization. Gaub argues that objective control includes constitutional constraints including the civilian responsibility to declare war, civilian control over military budgets, and civilian monitoring of military activities.[35]

From this, it is to be expected that professional, institutional soldiers will remain relatively neutral in politics, focusing instead on the profession of arms. The operative term is "relative," as a number of Huntington's critics note. Brooks notes that not only do professional officers have political views but also tactics to air those political views: public appeals, resignation in protest, or alliance building with political supporters outside of the military.[36]

For some civil-military relations scholars, the other end of the military identity spectrum is the *praetorian* officer, whose responsibility is to defend the regime, not the country.[37] But that is too narrow a concept, as armies on the other side of military professionalism are more than just protectors of the palace. The members of such armies view the military as a personal opportunity, more than a profession. For such soldiers, the military is a means to exercise domestic political control. It is a source of prestige, in countries where wearing a military uniform brings respect. It is business opportunities, or access to corruption. Military service brings training opportunities (also true for professional militaries), or it provides social opportunities, such as better marriage chances when in the military, for example. I label such militaries *rent-seeking* militaries. Though the term is imperfect, it does differentiate between professional soldiering, for a common good, with professional standards, and militaries that emphasize personal, rather than professional, rewards to their members. The concept of *rent* has ambiguous meanings, but for this book, *rent* is understood as the return on artificially constricted commodities through state actions. *Rent-seeking* is "the process of expending resources to capture artificially created rents"—the use of the political arena to extract personal or organizational returns from rents.[38] Rent-seeking is often portrayed as involving corrupt activity for self-enrichment, but legal and semi-legal practices can also be included in the general term, including placing restrictions on import licenses to benefit a particular party, for example.[39]

The notion of military rent-seeking is not intended to be negative. There are many countries without a serious threat on their borders. There are many countries that have a domestic security force to handle internal security threats. Wars have been few for many decades in most of South America, and many African countries have not fought wars with a bordering country for a very long time. So, militaries in such countries occupy their time with holding parades, running businesses on the side, and sometimes compensating for a low military budget through private business activities.

Eva Bellin develops another useful distinction on military types, between an *institutionalized* military, where merit-based performance determines recruitment and promotion, and a *patrimonial* military, which is linked to regime elites through family or clan, and cronyism determines military recruitment and advancement.[40] While not all rent-seeking militaries are patrimonial, many are, as ties to the regime usually open the doors to the spoils of office.

Fred Lawson summarizes the professionalization requirements for the military by listing four variables that characterize militaries:

1. Whether or not the military is well institutionalized or penetrated by non-military actors,
2. Whether the military is staffed by universal conscription or through volitional recruitment,
3. Whether the military focuses its attention on military affairs, or engages in sustained activity in other areas,
4. Whether or not the armed forces provide a substantial proportion of the country's political leadership.[41]

Based on this scholarship, I use the following categories for Middle East militaries: (1) institutionalized, (2) transitional (somewhere in between institutionalized and patrimonial), and (3) patrimonial. The pairing of countries with their military type is listed in table 1.4.

Regular

Regular armies best fit the Weberian understanding of the state as holding a monopoly over armed violence, which under most countries is trusted to the regular armed forces, with both full-time and reserve components.[42] Usually the ministry of defense, or some similar state agency, controls the regular armed forces, charging them with external defense.[43] The locus of military

Table 1.4. Military Categories

Country	Regime Category	Military Type
Algeria	BSR	Patrimonial
Bahrain	CM	Transitional
Egypt	BPR	Patrimonial
Iran (pre-1979)	CM	Institutional
Iran (post-1979)	BPR	Transitional
Iraq (pre-2003)	BPR	Patrimonial
Iraq (post-2003)	FD	Transitional
Israel	FD	Institutional
Jordan	LM	Institutional
Lebanon	FD	Institutional
Libya	BPR (pre-2011)	Patrimonial
Morocco	LM	Institutional
Oman	CM	Institutional
Qatar	CM	Institutional
Saudi Arabia	CM	Transitional
UAE	CM	Institutional
Yemen	BPR	Patrimonial

professionalism, for Huntington, lies in the regular forces, since preparation for and waging of war is their sole duty, whereas reserve forces consist of individuals and units for which war and its obligations are only a part-time responsibility.[44] When the term "military" appears in this book, it refers to regular armed forces unless I indicate otherwise.

Eleonora Ardemagni has developed a useful typology to identify Middle Eastern military relationships with other societal members, with the first being armies existing with or complemented with militias, the second is armies complemented by militarize police or elite units, and the third as armies serving as the sole supplier of defense.[45] Middle East militaries have generally been of the second type, as most states built both a professional military charged mostly with defense against external threats, complemented with an internal military unit for both internal threats and as a monitor for the regular military.

TYPES OF MIDDLE EAST MILITARIES

Distinctions across military types are important for civil-military relations. Based upon the categories in the previous section, Middle East military types may be categorized as follows.

Regular Military

Regular militaries are the backbone of national military forces in almost all Middle Eastern countries except Iran, where the regular *Artesh* competes with various Islamic-oriented militias for political influence and resources. Control of most Middle East armies belongs to the civilian Ministry of Defense, usually headed by a defense minister.[46] Usually the defense minister may have expertise in security matters (some are retired military officers), but others do not.

Many Middle Eastern militaries have dual missions: defense against foreign threats and internal missions. The militaries of Israel, Iran, Iraq, Syria, Egypt, and Jordan have participated in interstate wars against state-based threats, while other militaries have engaged in combat against terrorist groups like the so-called Islamic State, or ISIS, with forces from the United Arab Emirates, Egypt, and other countries deploying outside their borders to fight ISIS. Other militaries fought in Yemen against the Shi'a-linked al-Houthi. Other militaries have fought inside their borders. So, for example, Syrian, Libyan, Bahraini, and Yemeni militaries joined state security in quelling anti-government demonstrations in their countries following the "Arab Spring" movements. Oman's military has internal security and customs collections as a part of their regular missions.[47] Bahraini armed forces dispatched tanks into the Manama streets in concert with police forces to disperse demonstrators during that country's "Arab Spring," thus protecting the minority Sunni regime from a population where three of every four or five people are Shiʻa.[48] Saudi Arabian and other Gulf Cooperation Council forces joined Bahraini forces to maintain Bahraini stability.

State Security Forces

Not many Middle Eastern armies follow the American model where the *posse comitatus* restricts US federal military action in domestic policing.[49] The French model is more common, with a regular military focused on external threats and a *gendarmerie* that conducts national policing and is normally housed in the Ministry of Interior. But in the Middle East, state militias range from relatively well-trained forces loyal to the state, to informal groups that often reflect state weakness. In other states, the militia may have stronger ties to the regime, but, in Robert Springborg's words, they often function as a "deep state," sometimes funded by predatory means, and exist largely to remind the population that they, and not the citizenry, hold sovereignty.[50] There is sometimes ambiguity between the regular military and security forces, because in many Middle Eastern countries, the military join domestic security forces in policing domestic dissent, or civil war.

Morocco's King Hassan II placed his paramilitary forces, including the national police, under military command.[51] The military also dominated the state security forces under the reign of Shah Muhammad Reza Pahlavi (1941–1979). The line of command went from the Shah to the army, which partially controlled the internal security apparatus known as SAVAK (*Sazman-I Ettelaʻat va Amniyat-I Keshwar*, or State Organization for Intelligence and Security). The director of SAVAK and its senior officers and enlisted were from the army, as were the commanders of the gendarmerie and the national police.[52] The Turkish military actually direct the Turkish gendarmerie, even though each organization is nominally separate. Reforms in 2008 placed it under the Ministry of Interior, with wartime control reverting to the Turkish General Staff. Reforms also made the gendarmerie commander subordinate to the Interior Ministry, allowing it more civilian control.[53] The Turkish gendarmerie performs a variety of domestic duties, including special forces operations that it carries out against insurgents, often in collaboration with the regular Turkish forces. Saudi Arabia has a National Guard force along with forces assigned to the Ministry of Interior, which are responsible for critical infrastructure protection. The Syrian security services include the General

Intelligence Directorate, the Political Security Directorate, the Air Force Intelligence Service, and the Military Intelligence Service (*Mukhabarat*).

Militias

The precise definition of "militia" is illusive, but generally the term refers to irregular forces that fight alongside, or independently of, state military forces to defend the population against insurgents.[54] Sometimes militias affiliate with political parties or non-party political organizations, like Lebanon's Hezbollah, or the multiple quasi-military forces in Iran, like the *Basij* militia, loosely tied to the Revolutionary Guard Committees. Sometimes the state accommodates or even encourages such informal militias,[55] as Iran's ruling clerics did the Basij when it violently suppressed protests connected to the disputed 2009 national election.[56] The Lebanese state, of which Hezbollah is a part, has had to acquiesce to Hezbollah's contention that it, more than the regular Lebanese army, is the true defender of Lebanon against Israel, which was a claim strengthened by its performance in the 2006 war against Israel.[57] That claim raised the question as to whether Hezbollah should integrate with the Lebanese Armed Forces. But such integration faced strong obstacles, including the inward orientation of Lebanon's military, the American funding that it receives, Hezbollah's sectarian orientation, and its pan-revolutionary ties to Iran.[58]

Lebanon also had numerous militias tied to its various sectarian and family factions. The Lebanese Forces were a predominant fighting group formed from a Phalange coalition of Maronite Christian families.[59] They became more militarily powerful, with superiority in both troop numbers and equipment, than did the regular Lebanese Military Forces, with superiority in both troop numbers and equipment.[60] Israel also supported militias in south Lebanon, with the South Lebanon Army (SLA) as the best known. The SLA was unable to remain in the area without the protection of Israeli forces, so it melted away when Israel withdrew its forces in May 2000.

Libya also had militias during the Qaddafi years, such as the People's Militia and the Revolutionary Guard, the former counted more than forty thousand members and the latter had around thirty.[61] Qaddafi favored these forces over his regular military, and sometimes installed his relatives to command them.[62] They performed shadow missions, and their relations to the regime were never clear. After the 2011 popular uprisings, they appeared to either disappear or blend in with the militias fighting for parts of Libya. Qaddafi also relied partly on outside militia forces to quell domestic protests during the 2011 revolution. Iraq, under Saddam Hussein, had numerous militia groups in its state structure, operating alongside non-state militias with local roots, such as the Islamic Army of Iraq (once tied to Al-Qaeda), and the *Jaysh al-Mahdi* (Mahdi Army) of Muqtada Al-Sadr. In Israel, the military incorporated settler's militias into the Territorial Defense, empowering their members to police Palestinian villages adjacent to their settlements, and blurring the distinction between the regular military and the state armed forces.[63]

The lines between private and state militias are often fuzzy. Iran's *Quds* force, a militia special forces unit, is an example of a unit not technically a state organ, but an arm of the Islamic Revolutionary Guard Corps, with direct ties to Supreme Leader Ali Khamenei. Compounding the identity problem is the nature of the Iranian state, which has both formal structures and individual and group power centers. While a part of the state, these structures appear to be in conflict with each other. A similar situation exists in Iraq, where Shi'a militias developed before Saddam Hussein's fall in 2003, but quickly became significant players in post-Saddam Iraq. The Lebanese Hezbollah militia fits here too, as a supplemental militia that claims to defend not only the Lebanese Shi'a but the country itself. The indistinct line between state forces and militias also existed in Syrian during the Syrian civil war, as the 'Asad regime used militias as replacements for killed and defected soldiers from the regular Syrian army. Some militias were incorporated into the praetorian National Defense Forces, while the Syrian Air Force Intelligence Directorate operated the Tiger Forces (*Quwwat al-Nimr*) and the Desert Hawks (*Suqur al-Sahra'*), with militia forces with possibly over 140,000 troops, or more.[64]

Permit me to add a couple of notes at the end of this introduction. Since I started this book some years ago, much new scholarship has enriched Middle East civil-military relations. Some of this scholarship has reinforced my original arguments, but some has also caused me to question my original positions. A welcoming trend is that women have done much of this scholarship, including Risa Brooks, Florence Gaub, Caitlan Talmadge, Zeinab Abul-Magd, Dalia Ghanem, Amy Austin Holmes, and Shana Marshall, to name just a few.

I am also aware that some of the analysis I do in this book might subject me to charges of "orientalism." Generally, orientalism involves the application of "Western" standards of modernity to other parts of the world. I am also aware of the charges of "military orientalism," levied most recently by Hashim, who argues that "the West has distorted, in many ways deliberately, the ways of war in the Middle East, just as it has in the larger entity, the Orient."[65] I try to avoid such distortions, as I do not compare "oriental" militaries to the West, nor do I apply "Western" standards to the Middle East. I ask what the goals of Middle Eastern military campaigns were, and how civil-military relations affected them. Moreover, Hashim's broad-brush bundling of "Western" scholarship is not useful, especially his closing statement that "The West looks at how others fight through a peculiar lens, military orientalism as the academic literature would have it." I have tried to be as objective as I can, which is my obligation as a scholar. I am not applying value judgements to the cases I present. Thus, coups are neither "good" or "bad," and my purpose is to study them, not value them. My analysis of the performance of Middle East militaries may draw similar criticism, but again my purpose is to explain, not criticize.

Chapter Two

The Military and Society in the Middle East

Most countries have a "Memorial Day," with solemn ceremonies to commemorate the sacrifices of their soldiers, often centered at tombs of unknown warriors. Such memorials are one reminder that soldiers come from society and that connection remains even after the military takes its soldiers, isolates them from their communities, and inculcates them with the values of soldiering and service, to make them different from the civilian neighborhoods where they came from. The military relationship to national society is complicated; the military serves the nation, but also stands apart from it, remotely located in bases and seaports, in order to concentrate on its deadly craft without much civilian interference. Even its cemeteries are located separately from civilian burying grounds.

The scholar Zoltan Barany notes that "The societal side is at time neglected in writings on military politics, even though it is obvious that there can be no state nor army without society."[1] Stephen Peter Rosen notes that militaries come from societies where fissures can weaken military performance.[2] Specific country studies illustrate how societal practices influence military behavior, as does Agyekum's study of Ghana, and Forster's examination of the covenant between the British army, state, and society.[3] Soldiers carry values from society into their armies, and societal values may well determine the limits of military activities. Thus, this chapter seeks to explain the military role in modern Middle Eastern societies and ways that societal norms and behaviors influences their armies.

The chapter starts with the organization and sociological contexts of Middle Eastern civil-military relations. Then it considers the sociological conditions that influence civil-military relations, and then offers other conditioning factors like military cohesiveness, military religiosity, military service attractiveness, and the degree to which the military is an integral part of national society. These factors are included here because they are essential explanatory factors in the military role in politics; thus, this chapter concludes with a section on the political role of the armed forces that attempts to locate reasons for the relative strength of the soldier in Middle East political life. The political variables that I highlighted in the first chapter are appropriate here, including *political tradition*, which the military often uses to establish its societal place; *political factors*, as the military and civilian leadership compete for political influence in national society; and *military identification*, where the military can balance from being a part of, and from, society, but also standing apart from it.

THE MILITARY AND SOCIETY

Clausewitz first argued that civil-military relations have three components: the military, the government, and society. Owens notes that American civil-military relations constitute a bargain between the people, the government, and the military institution.[4] Rapp crafts the Clauswitzian triangle, presented in figure 2.1, showing this relationship.[5]

Line 2 gets the most attention in civil-military relations, but line 1 is also significant. The military ultimately draws its identity, its resources (including recruits), and its legitimacy from the citizenry. While public accountability over the military in an autocracy is not the same as in a democracy, societies in autocracies still hold values toward their armed forces, ranging from pride in (often rare) military victories in war, the employer of last resort, or the baker of bread during famine, or to fear and resentment of the military's privileged position in society.

How does society value its military? Does it fear its army as a parasitic force that threatens societal rights and privileges, or is the military an honored institution? Or do citizens give it much thought at all? This question matters

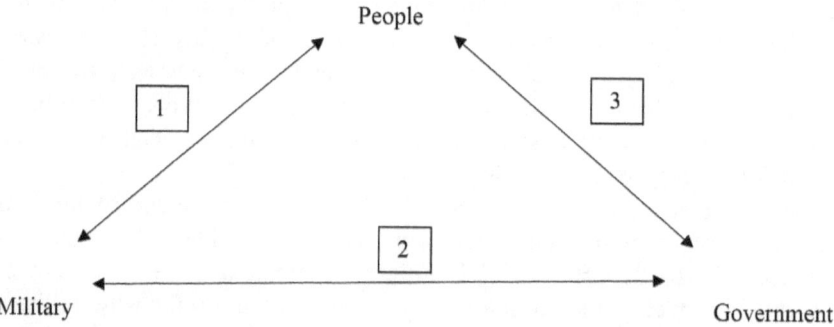

Figure 2.1. The Civil-Military Triangle

because institutions that hold valued places in the hearts and minds of citizens may fare better in contests for power and influence. High public respect for the military may enable the armed forces to avoid or minimize public criticism, as Urben and Golby note about the United States.[6] A common public/military narrative may motivate the military to intervene in politics to protect democracy, as was the case of the "People Power" movements in the Philippines.[7] Barracca finds that positive public support for military rule was a factor in coups in Venezuela, Pakistan, and Thailand.[8]

The distance between political and martial spheres varies considerably, from the military junta to the state with no formal military. Among the variables that help determine this space is the historical position of the armed forces, which can range from honored creator of the nation-state to despised former rulers. Indonesia's armed forces were the vanguard of the independence movement, and this status partially assisted them when General Suharto ousted President Sukarno in the 1960s.[9] Pakistan's military justifies its frequent forays into national politics on its status within the nation, which Pakistani officers often compare to the disdain felt for the often-corrupt civilian politicians.[10] In comparison, Argentina's military now bears the shame of inefficient governance during its dictatorship period, which bequeathed a legacy of the "disappeared" opponents and the humiliation of the Falklands/Malvinas Islands defeat. The Japanese Self-Defense Force is highly restricted in both military and political affairs because of the lasting memories of its role before and during World War II. Many Japanese museums do not include World War II in their presentations. The Myanmar (Burma) armed forces, known as the Tatmadaw, rule every aspect of the country, especially after their February 2021 coup. Consequently, the public, even under extreme repression, has continued to express its disdain for their armed forces as they plunge the country into ruin.[11]

It is tempting to argue that relative closeness to national society empowers the armed forces politically, either enhancing their ability to capture a disproportionate share of national treasure, or to exercise political power, either directly or behind the scenes. Brooks argues that when the military forms alliances with key societal members, they gain influence within the state.[12] Yet evidence that militaries take advantage of a high positive image in the public eye is mixed. For example, the Russian military builds on popular Russian mythology that it was primarily responsible for saving Mother Russia during World War II. Yet the Russian military suffered dramatic budget cutbacks after the Cold War ended.[13] Concerned about the need to imbue Russia's armed forces with public support, Russian President Vladimir Putin has launched a campaign to militarize Russian society.[14] How well that move was working in the face of the 2022 Russian invasion of Ukraine was difficult to determine, though, as Russian polls showed very mixed reactions to the invasion.[15] The British case is also instructive; "The British public has traditionally maintained a distant relationship with its armed forces, partly because they set themselves apart from society. In contrast to other militaries, the British armed forces have never had those deep ties with their society that derive from being used as a means to earn citizenship or as a tool to inculcate national values."[16] In Japan, the Samurai tradition noted earlier has not given the Japanese Self-Defense Force access to political power nor increased the defense budget above one percent of Japanese GDP. This may be due to, as Samuels argues, "The balance of public opinion valued protection from, over protection by, their military."[17]

The Military and Society in the Middle East

The power, composition, and identity of militaries in the Middle East vary considerably across countries. Some armed forces are content to operate within a strictly martial realm, recruiting, training, and equipping their forces and serving to protect the realm and carry out its military interests. Other militaries are either deeply involved in national politics or are in a position to intervene should they view political decisions as threats to their interests or to their vision of national identity and purpose.

Focusing on Arab armies, Droz-Vincent states that, "Arab armies have cultivated their cultural and social 'embeddedness' and their untouchable image, also an ideational power and often a source of propaganda. The imagery of the Arab officer is contested and has been for centuries.[18] Salamé puts it elegantly:

> On the one hand, there are the glorious conquests and the great military leaders, such as Khalid ibn al-Walid, Uqbah ibn Nafi, and Tariq ibn Ziyad . . . conquests stretching for Khurasan to Andalusia. However, this bright image of the Arab military was to a large extent replaced by another: the image of foreign mercenaries who, though the adoption of Islam, were able to become an integral part of authority and consequently transformed the Caliphate into a formal instrument in their hands.[19]

The warrior class exists in ancient Jewish mythology, and the army and military service became a cornerstone of Israeli identity after the 1948 war, "The IDF was organized on the basis of mass compulsory recruitment, which under the auspices of the ethos of statism (*mamlachtiyut*) tied a Gordian knot between soldiering and citizenship"[20] Now, according to Bar-On, the tales told to children and the markers that dot the Israeli landscape are particularly laden with the symbolism of 1948 in particular, and the warriors who won it.[21]

Most Turkish rituals, from early Ottoman times onward, incorporate warrior traditions.[22]

The armed forces are often the best-positioned national agent to claim the right to rule, or at least the right to be the paramount source of political influence, because they are the most skilled at advancing the national narrative of liberator, defender, and protector of the national image. Sometimes the army was the core of liberation movements before independence or soldiers ushered in a new modern era after humiliation and defeat. Algeria's military led the fight against France,[23] and the Israeli and Turkish militaries have a legacy of prideful nation building after the tragedy of the Holocaust and the humiliation of the last days of the Ottoman Empire. Thus, the army has a ready-made storyline for taking and retaining power, particularly in times of turmoil. Henry and Springborg put it well:

> For the moment, the military . . . possess substantial resources. The institution is central to the didactic nationalist historiography that has been propagated in school textbooks and by museums, national holidays and even the sporting events that the military sponsors throughout the country. Hundreds of thousands of ex-conscripts learned their trades in the military's economic enterprises, which employ additional hundreds of thousands. It provides patronage to scores of politicians in the form of military enterprises located in their constituencies.[24]

Social Distance between Civilians and Soldiers in the Middle East

In some ways, the military must exist separately from civilian society to preserve its autonomy, meeting its need for maneuver and requirements for secrecy, and to separate soldiers from the corruption that they fear runs rampant outside their barracks. Thus, military separateness is usually a feature of most Middle East countries.

Physical and social barriers vary considerably from country to country, with differing results. In Tunisia, the armed forces are visibly separate from society, with bases located in relatively remote areas, partly because founding president Habib Bourguiba believed in a correlation between military physical separateness and an apolitical military. In Israel, most bases are some distance from urban areas, but more because of operational concerns (noise, for one thing). Though the Israeli sea forces are located in close proximity to other coastal civilian activities, IDF soldiers readily mix with civilians outside of bases, and it is a common sight in Israel to see uniformed men and women hitchhiking home from their bases in the afternoons. Egyptian military bases are usually located away from populated areas, though Cairo is home to many officer's clubs, and military headquarters, that accord a degree of mixing with the civilian population. The Hashemite monarchy in Iraq kept its military stationed away from Baghdad, gave them little ammunition, and, fearing that the military was one of the greatest threats to Hashemite rule, planned to blockade the city from a possible military coup.[25] In the liberal monarchies of Morocco and Jordan, most of the military bases are distant from cities, requiring a long helicopter ride to reach them.

The other social distance is historical; early Muslim rulers often recruited their soldiers from Christian, Black African, Kurdish, or Circassian populations, who collectively became *Mamluks* (literally "owned" or "slave" in Arabic). Housed separately from the host population, they were a class that knew only war and, in Vatikiotis's words, "only those who bore arms seemed to have any political rights."[26] While the Mamluks themselves have long disappeared, the military separateness that they embodied continues in many countries that formerly had Mamluk troops. Chaney traces an alliance of Islamic soldiers and religious leaders back to the ninth century.[27] Chaney argues that this alliance, enforced initially by Mamluk soldiers and the Sunni religious leadership, survived the Ottoman conquest through Napoleon's Egyptian invasion in 1798.[28] In Turkey, as one official put it, during the Ottoman Empire, others (Greeks and Jews, for example) did the commerce, Arabs did the administration, and the Turks did the military, so when the Empire went away in 1918, the Turks were left with just the military.[29]

In the Arab world, the relationship between the military and the nation's political and social forces was usually marked by mutual suspicion. Droz-Vincent puts it well: "Role beliefs prevalent among officers tended to consider civilian rulers as incompetent, ineffective, and corrupt, and endowed the military with a sense of guardianship and a highly positive self-image. Conversely, civilians were fearful, or very reluctant to address military topics, hence explaining the lack of civilian (societal) counterweights to the military institutional weight."[30]

Social distance between the national military and society and its leaders is hardly static, and political trends can obviously alter it. As Droz-Vincent cogently states, "The armed forces were pulled out of their torpor (in 2011) as status quo actors or satisfied stakeholders in most cases, either self-chosen and/or cultivated by regimes, only as a result of mass civic mobilizations."[31] Turkey and Egypt provide examples.

Turkey (BSPR)

In Turkey, the Kemalist republic swept out the religious power centers that were part of the Ottoman glue. As Sunar and Sayari note, the most powerful elements in the new Turkish republic were the military, the Republican

People's Party, and the bureaucracy.[32] The old banker and rich artisan class that had allied with religious elites lost power, while the military gained considerable influence in the Second Constitutional period, after losing power in the Committee of Union and Progress ("Young Turk") period.[33] The question for current affairs is whether the popularity of the Turkish military is supportive of Turkish democracy. An indication that support for Turkish democracy and the Turkish armed forces is found in Sarigil's observation that public support for democracy and trust in civilians does not reduce trust in the military. He states that "This result seems to suggest that most Turkish citizens regard the military as 'part of the democratic process' or as 'the ultimate guardian of the democratic system of rule.'"[34] The fact that the military that the military overthrew elected governments but then departed politics still helps the image that the Turkish military is a protector of the Turkish democratic system,[35] but the fact remains that the military overthrew elected governments. Still, outside of coup politics, some argue that Turkish military pressure and preferences actually enhances Turkish democracy. When the Republican People's Party moved to left-of-center after 1965, the military gravitated to the Justice Party of Demirel. Argues Dodd,

> At this juncture Bülent Ecevit, now leader of the Republican People's Party, made it clear that the party was henceforth going to avoid being linked in the popular view to the military and was going to appeal to the people. An historic alliance was broken. . . . This break must be regarded as a gain for Turkish democracy. With no party now in intellectual harmony with the military, the latter was better able to distance itself from politics.[36]

Perhaps, but the military did not reduce its distance from politics all that much and it remained capable of interfering with democratic results when it saw fit, as it did in 1997, and threatened to do so afterward, until the September 2010 referendum that modified its 1980-drafted constitution. The 2010 amendments, pushed by the AKP, changed the structure of the Constitutional Court and the Supreme Board of Prosecutors and Judges (along with strengthening the rights of children and women), won the support of 58 percent of Turkish voters.[37] Since the Constitutional Court in particular was a venue of influence for the Turkish military, the referendum was yet another indicator that the Turkish public wanted reforms that reduced military political influence. That shift was also underscored by the 58 percent approval of a referendum in September 2010 which limited the jurisdiction of military courts and allowed for the trials for officers accused of crimes and rescinded the immunity of officers responsible for the 1980 coup.[38]

The Turkish military has maintained a long-standing opposition to Islamist-oriented political parties. However, shortly after the AKP came to power, it appeared to be less an Islamist party than a modernizing movement aiming to advance both democracy and international connections. Additionally, Dagi claims that,

> By seeking integration into the EU, the AKP is pushing for a structural transformation of Turkey that means turning away from Islamization. By pursuing EU membership, the AKP leadership, despite its pro-Islamic background, would seem to have abandoned the idea and ideal of establishing an Islamic government in Turkey, as EU membership almost certainly would eliminate such a possibility.[39]

Yet the AKP began to reverse course as Erdoğan drew closer to his initial Islamist roots. As his initial political popularity waned after the first few years of his rule, he responded by increasing the funding for Islamic schools, demanded public prayers from the mosques, and insisted that high interest rates fueled inflation, citing Islamic opposition to usury. He also constructed a giant mosque in Istanbul's Taksim Square and permitted the head of the Diyanet to introduce elements of Shari'a law into Turkish society.[40] Interest in joining the EU then faded. The strategy was successful, as the AKP's 34 percent of the vote in 2002 grew to 45 percent in 2007 as Erdoğan used the increase in party support to rebuff the military's effort to curb his power.[41] The military never overcame this and other AKP efforts to marginalize their power (see chapter 4). It is paradoxical that the military was once the greatest barrier to Turkish democratization. The European Union recognized this in its critique of Turkish efforts to subordinate the armed forces to democratic control.[42] Yet Turkish political neutralization of the military occurred at the hands of an autocratic president, and not because of an incipient requirement for Turkish democracy.

Egypt (BPR)

The Egyptian Free Officers who launched the independent republic in 1952 came mostly from humble social origins and did not gravitate toward radical or social belief systems. The consequences for governing were important, as Cook states:

> Although the Officers rigged Egypt's institutions to serve their interests, they were never able to embed in the minds of Egyptians a set of ideas around this political order. The Officer's distinct lack of ideological convictions or anything but the most rudimentary guiding principles made them vulnerable to other political forces selling more comprehensive, emotionally satisfying notions of what Egyptian society and politics should look like.[43]

Thus, the Free Officers, after squelching opposition from less political rival military factions, undertook a reorganization of Egypt's political and economic order by using socialist ideas to capture most elements of the Egyptian economy.[44] However, defeat in the 1967 war reduced both the army's social popularity as well as its political and military role.[45] That military loss also contributed to President Anwar Sadat's restructuring of the economy,[46] though there were multiple reasons for economic liberalization.[47] One contributing factor was the military role in economic ownership and management which, according to some estimates, was a high as 20 percent of the economy's total value (see chapter 4 for details). The military's interest in protecting its economic stake became apparent in the events following the "Arab Spring" events, as they withdrew support for President Mubarak, partly because Mubarak's son, Gamal, and his wealthy civilian associates threatened to privatize the military share of the Egyptian economy. The armed forces apparently hoped that their candidate for president, former general Ahmed Shafiq, would win the subsequent election, however he lost narrowly to the Muslim Brotherhood's candidate, Mohamed Morsi, in June 2012. While Morsi was careful not to jeopardize the military's role in state and society, one of his advisors offered to send Egyptian forces into the Syrian conflict without consulting the army.[48] Preferring a less belligerent approach, Morsi also pushed back on the military's eagerness to engage militarily in the Sinai insurgency issue.[49] Morsi also tried more Islamification of Egyptian society, and declared that he was not subject to constitutional restrictions. Thus, Egypt's military took advantage of the turmoil Morse caused, and joined protestors in deposing him a year after his election. The armed forces initial disappointment in electoral politics turned to success when Field Marshal Abdel Fattah al-Sisi won the presidency in June 2014. Unsurprisingly, al-Sisi has advanced the military's position in Egypt allowing it to not only increase its share of the Egyptian economy (see chapter 4), but also to be the controlling arm of Egyptian politics. Article 200 of Egypt's constitutional amendment gives the army the right to, "preserve the constitution and democracy, protect the basic principles of the state and its civil nature, and protect the people's rights and freedoms,"[50] an extraordinary power gift. Granting such power enabled the Egyptian army to perform social services, such as disaster relief, the construction of low-income housing, donation of food, and providing education and other public services.[51] Lust-Okar chronicles the Cairo and Alexandria riots in 1968 protesting the lenient sentences given to military officers held responsible for Egypt's defeat in the 1967 war.[52] The army knew that supporting President Anwar Sadat's request to establish order during the January 1977 food riots would be unpopular, so the generals demanded that the president roll back the price increases before they acted.[53]

So, the military adjusted to changes in the political order, but in both cases, support for "democracy" was replaced by a military preference for a return to autocracy. However, this may well have reflected an inherent military preference for order, and not just the categorization of "bully state"—which would be tautological in any event.

MILITARY PUBLIC APPROVAL

Public support for the national military represents the most tangible connection between the populace and the armed forces. High public approval of the military can lead to more military resources, more willingness to join and serve with the armed forces, and, in democracies, more political support for the military. While there are many ways to evaluate the impact of public opinion and the military, the most common way is to use public opinion samples.

In the United States, the Gallup organization asks annually the question, "How much confidence do you have in the following institutions?" followed by a list of both public and private organizations, including the news media, Congress, big business, and the Supreme Court. In 2021, the military received the second highest comparative ranking, with 69 percent of respondents giving the armed forces a "great deal" or "quite a lot" of confidence.[54] In a 2002 VTsIOM poll, the Russian military ranked third in the "most trusted" category, just behind the president and the Orthodox Church.[55] A 2017 Russian poll revealed that the Russian military was second only to the Office of the President, and above the Orthodox Church.[56] A 2020 poll of Russians ages fourteen to twenty-nine showed that trust of the military was only below trust of the president, with 44 percent of the respondents giving the armed services the two top marks.[57] In contrast, the Japanese Self-Defense Forces ranked low in status during much of the post–World War II period, with members often shedding their uniforms when in public, though its status improved to a positive public image of 55 percent in 2006.[58] The Thai military, with its history of coup involvement, has tried to capitalize on its flood relief work in 2011 to improve its public image, even launching its own Facebook page, "We Love the Thai Military," with more than seventeen thousand followers.[59] A survey of public institutional support in eight European countries in 2018 found that, in all cases, public trust in the military far outranked trust in parliaments, banks and financial institutions, and the news media.[60]

Public Approval of Middle East Militaries

In the Middle East, public confidence in the national military has traditionally been high (where it has been measured). Historically, as Halpern argues, "Because of historical circumstances, Middle Eastern armies often produce more able, honest, and decisive leadership than any other institutions." In many Middle Eastern countries, that comparison probably remains true.[61] Gaub notes that surveys taken in 2012 found that 77 percent of civilians expressed a great deal or at least some trust in the military.[62] In a July 2007 poll, the Moroccan public expressed higher trust of the Moroccan military than for any other institution. Combining "great deal of trust" and "fair amount of trust" into "total trust," the military received 72 percent trust, followed by "religious authorities" at 67 percent, and political parties at the bottom with 24 percent, while Llewellyn observes how the Lebanese army gained "enormous popular respect across the population" by taking on militant Palestinians in the Narh el Bared refugee camp in 2007, which helped army commander Michel Suleiman win the 2008 presidential election.[63] A later survey found the military receiving a 70 percent approval rating from Lebanon's population, compared to just 4 percent for that country's parliament.[64] That approval rate continued into 2021, as the Arab Barometer ranked Lebanon's military as that country's most trusted institution.[65] That is not surprising, as Lebanon's military has led the country in reconciliation after the tragic civil war and has refused orders that would threaten Lebanon's very fragile stability.[66] Lebanon's military became involved in policing the anti-regime protests in 2020, going so far as to try arrested civilians in military tribunals.[67] The Lebanese army also enforced lockdowns during the coronavirus (COVID-19) epidemic.[68]

Egypt's military regularly got public approval ratings around 90 percent, though its behavior since the 2011 transformation has also drawn criticism.[69] A 2014 Pew poll showed that public approval for Egypt's armed forces had dropped considerably since the 2011 timeframe, while a majority of the public (56 percent) continues to say the military has a good influence on the way things are going in Egypt, 45 percent say the military's influence is bad. And support for the armed forces is considerably lower today than it was just last year, when nearly three-quarters said the military had a positive impact (73 percent).[70] The Egyptian militaries relative popularity may be high partly because of the competition, the brutality of the Interior Ministry security forces, and the local police, coupled with the corruption and rent-seeking behavior of the small coterie around the Mubarak regime made the military look positively moral compared to the competition.[71] Egypt's armed forces initially gained popular appeal after their defense of the Tahrir Square demonstrators, though they lost it when they remained to police post-Mubarak Egypt. They remained the most popular element in 2012, though that affection was relative: "no one is very popular now," quipped one US observer.[72] The Egyptian military retained top spot in a survey conducted by the Pew Charitable Trust in April 2011, with 88 percent saying that the military is having a good influence on "the way things are going in Egypt," compared to 81 percent who say the same things about religious leaders.[73] This reaction likely sprang from the role that the army took in eliminating the Mubarak regime. However, for many Egyptians', support for the military as a governing body lessened over time. *Al-Jazeera's* "Vote Compass" showed around 51 percent of Egyptians saying that they distrusted the military.[74] A November 2011 poll asked the question: "Do you think that the military authorities are working to, (1) advance the gains of the revolution, or, (2) slow or reverse the gains of the revolution?" Of the respondents, 43 percent agreed that the military was trying to slow or reverse the gains of the revolution, while 21 percent believed that the military was advancing the gains of the revolution.[75] Still, when Egypt's Islamist-dominated parliament opened in January 2012, Speaker Saad Al-Katatni, of the Muslim Brotherhood's Justice and Democracy Party, and deputies of the Salafist-oriented Al Noor Party, praised the military for Mubarak's departure and for the transition to democracy, a considerable concession to the institution that had repressed Islamists for over six decades.[76] Yet when the military-dominated election commission rejected the presidential candidacies of several leading contenders in April 2012, including the Freedom and Democracy Party's Khariat al-Shater, Al-Noor Party candidate Hazem Salah Abu Ismail, and former Mubarak Vice President Omar Suleiman, the public reaction was denunciations and the threat of more demonstrations. However, as noted earlier, General Sisi's overwhelming election to Egypt's presidency in 2014 demonstrated how much the military still had Egyptian public support.

Sometimes the military attempts to raise their public status by claiming the national and moral high ground. The language of former Egyptian President Hosni Mubarak on the fiftieth anniversary of the Egyptian revolution captures this image: "The graduation of this new batch of military academy cadets coincides with the fiftieth anniversary of the glorious July Revolution that was carried out by a group of loyal sons of Egypt, Armed Forces officers who were motivated by the strong patriotic feelings and lofty loyalty to the people to make their blessed revolution."[77] His words echoed Nasser's language, who claimed that the Egyptian revolution, led by his army "forced us to restore the lost dignity of moral values."[78] The Egyptian military tried to capitalize on these sentiments in 2011, when it ultimately sided with protesters, and a year later when it ended Mohammed Morsi's presidency. Said one analyst, "the dismissal of President Mohamed Morsi and the declaration of the roadmap to the future were the product of full and close cooperation and coordination between the military establishment and the youth, especially the *Tamarod* (Rebel) movement, and then all other political forces and movements."[79]

However, military service itself may also result in negative moral constructions of both the military and the state that supports it. Recent reports state that Egyptian military salaries have fallen below private sector pay and that soldiers have fallen out of favor with the other sectors of Egyptian society.[80] Osman reports on consequences of military service for the often-poor Egyptian young who engaged in it:

> More than a million young Egyptians had returned from the (1967) war front to towns and villages all over Egypt . . . a majority had spent more than six years (some almost a decade) in a harsh military environment, detached from the life of a changing society. The stressful military experience bred in many cases aggression and a predilection to violence, which were exacerbated by the wider social anger. Many of the returning soldiers described themselves as a "defrauded generation": they claimed that "the spoils of peace" had gone to the regime's cronies, not to the people or "those who spent years away from home, under fire."[81]

Egypt's armed forces tried to project a positive image outside of battle partly to overcome the public negativity from wartime experiences, as when they initially sided with anti-Mubarak demonstrators in 2011 (see the next chapter for details). However, any gains that they might have achieved quickly faded as the military, who took command after Mubarak departed, turned violent and arrested almost twelve thousand citizens and discoveries of military corruption by anti-Mubarak activists only worsened the military's reputation.[82]

Turkey's armed forces historically draw considerable positive public support, which is unsurprising given its ties to Kemal Atatürk. Says Akkoyunlu, the Turkish military "is generally thought to be the only highly successful institution in Turkey" and because the other Turkish institutions pale in comparison to the Turkish army.[83] That support was particularly evident in 1997 as the military resumed its traditional defense of secularism during first, albeit, brief stay of an Islamist-oriented government. Two years later, a poll revealed that 81 percent of the public held the military in high trust, while just 17 percent held politicians at such a level.[84] A 2014 Pew poll showed that around 52 percent of the survey found that the Turkish military is "having a good influence on the way things are going," while 37 percent said it was having a "bad influence."[85] The positive attitude toward the Turkish military extends to Turkey's Armenian community (around 1 percent of the total population), where around 52 percent score the Turkish military as the most credible and trustworthy institution in Turkey.[86] This level of support had important consequences for the United States; when American military forces arrested eleven Turkish special forces troops in the Iraqi town of Sulaymaniyah in July 2003, the resulting images of the event, showing the Turkish military bound and hooded, was a contributing factor in a significant rise of anti-Americanism in Turkey.[87]

Caution must be exercised in calculating Turkish public support for its armed forces; Aydinli argues that public trust of the Turkish army dropped considerably after its 1997 "velvet coup," which ended the Islamist Necmitten Erbakan government.[88] This implies that the public supported the army more for its ability to defend Turkey from outside threats than for the military claims that it was a barrier to the Islamization of Turkey. The tepid public reaction to the "Ergenekon affair" and the 2011 decision to put the 1980 and 1997 military plotters on trial seems to reinforce the limits of Turkish public approval of its armed forces.[89] Additionally, the mass turnout after Diyanet officials issued mobilization calls during the failed July 2016 coup cemented the sense that the public had lost confidence in Turkey's military.

The Omani military reportedly carries substantial prestige inside the country. Although their combat roles have been small, they have considerable responsibility for internal security, including the policing of religious groups and smuggling control, but also engage in civic operations in communications and education.[90] The Omani public appreciated the military role the military played in the aftermath of a 2007 typhoon, which did considerable damage to the Omani coastal areas.[91] The Royal Jordanian armed forces also carry similar prestige, and, according to one official, membership in the Jordanian military is a particularly good way to develop *wasta*, or influence.[92] An interesting indicator of the popularity of the Royal Jordanian military is that, according to one official, the military is so respected even among regime critics that when the military shows up at anti-regime demonstrations, the demonstrators leave of their own accord.[93]

According to Michael, a 2003 poll showed that the Israeli Defense Forces earned the highest level of trust of all Israeli institutions.[94] 73 percent of respondents held the IDF in "high trust," while an additional 21 percent said they "trusted" the IDF. However, the degree of trust in the IDF trended moderately downward from 90 percent in 2000 to 79 percent in 2009.[95] Public confidence in the IDF dropped after its controversial performance in the 2006 Lebanon war but rose again after "Operation Cast Lead," which sent IDF troops into Gaza after Palestinian rocket attacks against Israel. After the 2006 conflict, as Ben Meir and Bagno-Moldavsky document that 46 percent of Israelis polled decreased their confidence in the IDF, 46 percent were unchanged and only 8 percent reported increased confidence in the military.[96] However, after the "Cast Lead" operation, 48 percent had increased confidence in the IDF, 48 percent unchanged, and only 4 percent stated decreased confidence. Public trust in the military continued to increase, and by 2013 Israeli Jews gave some of the highest confidence marks to the IDF, with 91 percent giving it "high trust," compared to 37 percent for political parties.[97] A 2021 poll showed that 80 percent of Jewish Israelis gave the IDF approval for operational capacities, and 77 percent for "ethical conduct in combat." However, only a third of Israeli Palestinians gave the IDF positive marks for ethical conduct.[98]

Yet while the Israeli public holds a relatively positive attitude toward the Israeli Defense Forces, that does not mean that civilians do not challenge the military ethos, or the societal standing of the IDF. Arian notes that while Israelis generally hold a positive attitude towards the security sector, there is cynicism and questioning just below the surface, with a significant minority wondering if security decisions reflect military self-interest as well as national defense.[99] Rosenhek, Maman, and Ben-Ari note that the growing controversy of the IDF's operations since 1973, and particularly in Lebanon after 1983, have produced a growing willingness to question the very principles upon which the IDF exists:

> that the diminution of the legitimacy of the IDF and the weakening of the consensus about "national security" and its broad socio-political meanings have led to an accelerated acceptability of publicly challenging and disputing things military in Israel . . . one important consequence of these internal conflicts and struggles appears to have been a significant erosion in the almost sacred status once enjoyed by state institutions-especially the military-among the majority of the Jewish population. A central assumption now being questioned by many groups is that of the centrality of the military in society and in definitions of "Israeli-hood" and full citizenship.[100]

Still, Maoz notes that the high public esteem for the IDF allowed it to develop and execute military operations with little challenge from other Israeli political agents.[101] That confidence remained in 2020, as while the COVID-19 outbreak in Israel dampened public confidence in most Israeli institutions, public confidence in the IDF was 80 percent.[102]

Other militaries face similar situations, which are particularly common in poor countries like Syria and Yemen. The Syrian army often conscripts soldiers against their will and requires them serve under bad conditions. Noted one report:

Syrian infantry units tend to be made up of young men from heavily Sunni regions that are poor, rural and knit together by clan. These are the same kinds of areas that have produced the largest protests against President Assad's government. Soldiers say they often have little more than bread, potatoes, and ghee to eat; they earn only about $10 a month. A well-known saying in Syria underlines the miserable life of many soldiers. "A soldier takes care of himself," the proverb goes.[103]

The implications in the Arab world, in particular, for high public approval of the military has some potentially interesting implications for Arab civil-military relations. Partly as a consequence of the coronavirus outbreak, and partly due to laggard economic growth, many Arab publics have lost confidence in their civilian state institutions while military approval has grown. A 2018 Arab Barometer survey showed that in Algeria, Egypt, Iraq, Jordan, Lebanon, Saudi Arabia, Tunisia, and Yemen, public support for the military exceeded that for other public institutions.[104] While Arab world coups are now less frequent than in previous years, still, as Lotito argues, the, "unprecedented public trust in military institutions, reaching 81 percent in 2016, according to the Arab Barometer. By contrast, trust in civilian governments continues to decline—from 54 percent in 2010 to 38 percent in 2016—creating a trust gap that threatens the region's delicate civil-military balance."[105]

RELIGION AND THE ARMY

Religion is one of the factors that can shape the army's societal and political role and, consequently, civil-military relations though the connection is not always obvious. Most militaries prefer unified ranks, as the more uniform the military, the less likely it will divide into tribes during the stresses of battle. Moreover, the military would like to choose its own soldiers, that fit military needs, thus the armed forces leaders tend to resist civilian efforts to interfere with its processes for recruiting. Moreover, military fealty is almost always first to the state; most military uniforms feature the national flag, and marching soldiers carry the national flag, thus symbolically minimizing religious identity.

Religious affiliation affects military recruitment as members of some faiths reject military service or insist that the militaries that they join make particular accommodations to their religious practices. Other sectarian tenets emphasize martial values, or endorse violence as a way to protect faith, sometimes emphasizing faith over nationhood as the highest value. Other faiths reject the military as antithetical to pacific values and their members refuse to serve in it.

While many militaries have a tradition of prayer before battle, modern armies are generally secular, existing for nation over faith. Militaries usually try to restrict religious appeals, partly because religious faith can conflict with the nationalist underpinnings of the armed forces, and because many militaries are multi-faith organizations where appeals to one faith will fracture unit cohesion. Moreover, religious obligations may clash with a military steeped in order and regulations, as faith-based requirements ranging from dietary mandates, to pacificism, to a requirement to kill those of the same faith can conflict with military duty and order. Still, militaries may use tenets and images of religion to motivate troops, or build cohesion among like-minded soldiers, or to erect ties to religious groups for political support. Sometimes religious elements can infiltrate militaries, sowing dissent or worse; as it has in Nigeria's and Pakistan's armed forces.[106] This motivated the Indian military, which includes members of Hindu, Muslim, and Christian faiths, to ban religious shrines on its bases and casts its missions through nationalist language. The US military avoids religious messaging, though in 2014 the American military relaxed regulations on the display of religious identity. Thus, militaries try to isolate themselves from civilian pressures to adopt sectarian identities.

ARMIES AND RELIGION IN THE MIDDLE EAST

Middle Eastern military culture is also relatively secular, yet in most Muslim Middle Eastern countries, such culture includes homage to the prevailing faith, and usually codes of conduct emphasize defending Islam, or in Israel's case, Judaism. War college instruction includes lessons from great wars in Islamic, Jewish, or Persian history.[107] Soldiers weave religious imagery into their collective identity, as Israeli soldiers wear the Star of David and Saudi Arabian officers have "there is no God but God and Muhammad is his Messenger" on their shoulders. Examples from Turkey, Egypt, Israel, and Iran illustrate the various ways that the military incorporates religion into its folds.

Turkey (BSPR)

The Turkish War College (*Harp Akademileri Komutanlığu*), once the umbrella command of the Turkish war colleges before President Erdoğan closed it in 2016, had a curriculum filled with Ottoman and early Turkish Republic military images though the Islamic heritage was muted because of the Atatürk influence. For Gürbey, the Turkish military fulfils the Kemalist message that Islam is a province of the state,[108] standing guard over the

Kemalist constructions as arbitrators, because their identity aligns with that of Atatürk; religion belongs in private spaces, and public displays or embraces of faith are highly discouraged. Still, the army is careful not to tread on Islam. The leader of the 1960 coup, General Cemal Gürsel, claimed that, "Those who blame religion for our backwardness are wrong. No, the cause of our backwardness is not our religion but those who have misrepresented our religion to us. Islam is the most sacred, most constructive, most dynamic and powerful religion in the world."[109] Tachau and Heper make an interesting argument specific to Turkey, but applicable to other predominately Muslim countries:

> In the most general sense, the Turks are heirs to Muslim culture which recognizes and accepts the legitimacy of the military as an arm of the community. It may be recalled that Islam was initially disseminated through the Mediterranean basin in the wake of military conquest. Moreover, the Koran declares that those who are martyred in defense of the community of the faithful are guaranteed automatic and immediate access to eternal paradise.[110]

It is particularly interesting that Atatürk would impose strict limitations on public Islam after his establishment of the Turkish Republic, but the point remained that the army remained central to Turkish life until the 1950 election and part of the purpose of the coup ten years later was to reinstall that connection. Periodic coups since then serve as a reminder of the secular military foundations, until the AKP won such an overwhelming victory in 2002 that the military could no longer challenge the Islamist political tilt after that election (see chapter 4).

The Turkish military developed ties to Islamic groups to further its own ends, as have other Middle Eastern armies. The Turkish armed forces actually pushed for Islamic education—General Kenan Evren, Chief of Staff, argued in favor of mandatory religious education in Turkish public schools, arguing that a person without religious knowledge would more easily be led astray by religious extremists.[111] Moreover, during the 1960s through the 1980s, Turkish senior officers believed that strengthening Islamist groups would counter the appeal of leftist political groups, particularly those linked to Kurdish or Alevi factions, as well as limit the appeal of radical Islam, reflecting a more general tendency of Turkish regimes from Atatürk forward.[112] After the 1980 coup (see chapter 4), the Turkish armed forces created the "Turkish-Islamist Synthesis," where the military agreed to not harass members of "mainstream" Sunni Muslim organizations that, in turn, the military expected support in military political affairs, to include coups where necessary. The "synthesis" backfired for the military, though, because it created space for moderate Islamists to grow politically, leading to the rise of the Welfare Party and its successor, the AKP.¹¹³ The ultimate irony for the Turkish armed forces came in 2011–12 when the Islamist party leaders empowered by the "Turkish-Islamist Synthesis" arrested many top members of the armed forces and charged them with a variety of political crimes (see chapter 3).

Egypt (BPR)

Egyptian military cadres initially found common cause with Egypt's Muslim Brotherhood after 1948, which had resisted the Farouk monarchy and held it responsible for Israel's victory in the 1948 war.¹¹⁴ The newly empowered officers gave amnesty to Brothers jailed by the previous regime and invited Islamist thinker Sayyid Qutb to speak at their officer's club; an address attended by Gamal 'abd al-Nasser shortly before he assumed the presidency.¹¹⁵ Earlier, Anwar Sadat, Egypt's future president, developed a relationship with Hassan al-Banna, founder of the Muslim Brotherhood, hoping that the Muslim Brotherhood would cooperate with the military in overthrowing the Egyptian monarchy.¹¹⁶ Even as the Free Officers began to move away from the Islamists, they continued to embrace Islam as a legitimizing influence, creating the Islamic Congress under direct presidential supervision, and initially headed by Sadat.¹¹⁷ The honeymoon between the Brotherhood and the Free Officers quickly ended as the military leaders began to regard the Brotherhood as competitors for the national ideal,¹¹⁸ and the Nasser regime hanged Qutb in 1966 after charging him with crimes against the state. The effort to maintain religious neutrality in the Egyptian military continues, and most observers regard it as secular and non-ideological, with no evidence of Muslim Brotherhood activity within the ranks.¹¹⁹ This is hardly surprising as it was Muslim extremists (though not Muslim Brothers) who had infiltrated the army and assassinated President Sadat in 1981. The disparity in pay and responsibility between the senior and junior ranks could lead to an increase in the appeal of the Islamist platform to those junior members.¹²⁰ When the military joined other security forces in terminating the Muslim Brotherhood-affiliated Mohamed Morsi regime in the summer of 2013, military concern about possible religious defections also grew. The Egyptian military enlisted Muslim preachers and scholars to defend the argument that it was the Muslim Brotherhood, and not the military, who had departed from Islamic teachings, and thus the soldiers had a duty to punish them. One scholar, formerly a mufti appointed by the Mubarak administration said in a video produced by the military's Department of Moral Affairs: "If a person wanted to rebel with arms against the military, what would the situation be? Kill him. I hereby say it again. Those who rebel against the Egyptian military or police deserve, according to Shariah, to be killed."¹²¹

Israel (FD)

Israel is truly a fragmented democracy, with a mix of sectarian communities that tend to disagree on the role of the military, and their roles in it, among many other things. Around 80 percent of Israel's population is Jewish, and 20 percent Palestinian Arabs (mostly Muslim). The Jewish population is further divided, into the Ashkenazim, those from Europe, mostly, the Mizrahim, immigrants from mostly Arab countries, but some of mixed origin, many from Russia or Ethiopia. They vary widely by identity—some identify primarily as "Jewish," while others as "Israeli."[122] Israel also presents a particular challenge to military identity, as the State of Israel is not a religious state governed by religious law, though its identity is contested, to put it mildly.[123] Founding Prime Minister David Ben Gurion insisted on de-politicizing the army to divorce it from the sectarian belief systems of its founding militias, which some Israeli officers objected to,[124] and former IDF commander Yigal Allon resigned, claiming that military professionalization would undermine the pioneer spirit of the early kibbutz and erode its commitment to service of Israeli society.[125] Even the conscription of women became a religious issue; conservative Jewish and Arab Knesset members tried to persuade Ben Gurion not to conscript women. While the prime minister agreed to exempt Arab Muslim women, he insisted on drafting Jewish women,[126] while exempting *yeshiva* students in order to replace Torah scholars lost in the Holocaust.

Conscription exists for all men and women upon reaching their eighteenth birthday, except for Muslims and religious students, but some observant Jews do serve their military time out of a sense of duty to the state. The IDF excludes most ultra-orthodox males and all ultra-orthodox women, and does not conscript Israeli Palestinian citizens, though Druze and Circassians are subject to compulsory service,[127] and Israeli Palestinians, Arabs, and Bedouin may volunteer for military service but are exempt from conscription. Israel conscripts officers for forty-eight months, and enlisted for thirty-six months of active duty, then transfers non-career personnel to the reserves where they serve until age forty-one, or for some specialties, at fifty-four.

The exemption for religious students was a point of contention among those Jews who bear the brunt of military duty, and save for the Haredim, it was clearly not popular across the broad Jewish spectrum. But, as Cohen and Cohen argue, the issue is complicated, to say the least:

> Neither mizrachiyim (who comprise roughly 50% of the Jewish population) nor the national-religious (14–17%) subscribe to the haredi stance of resistance to military service. Nevertheless, until recently, even males in both groups played subsidiary roles in Israel's armed forces. During the first decades of its history, the IDF's most prestigious combat formations were principally staffed by sons

of the secular and predominantly Ashkenazi (European) bourgeoisie, who also dominated Israel's political, economic, and cultural life. But that is no longer the case. Male scions of the old elites are now demonstrating greater reluctance to perform frontline duty, which many shirk by resorting to quasi-legal ploys.[128]

The issue of Haredim exemptions came to a head in February 2012 when the Supreme Court held that the exemption for yeshiva students was unfair to secular Israeli Jews who had to serve their military time. In March 2014, the Knesset voted to phase out the exemption over a three-year period but allowing students a choice of civilian or military service.[129] Former Prime Minister Benyamin Netanyahu wanted to preserve the exemption, but when former Defense Minister Avigdor Lieberman insisted on ending it, Netanyahu lost his potential Knesset majority and in May 2019 had to call for new elections. The elections of June 2021 replaced Netanyahu as prime minister, which meant that the ultra-orthodox parties that were a part of that coalition, and supporters of the yeshiva exemption, lost power as they were not included in the replacement government. The new coalition government included parties headed by Yair Lapid and Avigdor Liberman, both opponents of the yeshiva exemption, though the coalition did advance a bill offering a choice to those students between military service and work.[130] This choice is available to women from religious Zionist backgrounds, though these women are increasingly finding that the high-tech aspects of national service are more attractive career choices, rather than the military.[131]

Despite efforts to move the IDF beyond Jewish identity, religious symbolism is common and has been for decades, as noted in one symbolic text, portraying Yitzhak Rabin as telling King David about the great victory of 1967: "alongside the fighters were those from Masada, from Bar Kochba, all those murdered because they were Jews."[132] The symbolism of military Judaism was strong in the markings of the Revisionist Zionist Herut Party that merged with Likud in 1988; a photograph shows future Likud Prime Minister Menachem Begin standing behind a map of Israel with the Herut symbol of a bayoneted rifle on it.[133] The expansion of Jewishness in the IDF is also symbolized by the considerable expansion of the Rabbinate, which is now thoroughly integrated in all IDF levels.[134] Levy tells of a growing religious sentiment in the IDF, with a growing body of soldiers coming from religious schools and maintaining those ties once in service to the point where they have refused to engage in settler removal when ordered to do so, on religious grounds.[135] Others have protested when they believe that the military fails to observe their sometimes-strict observance of Jewish law, so in the Israeli navy, observant males protested when required to serve with women, for example.[136] Says Cohen: "The heavy representation in that cadre of a group that is particularly sensitive to the emergence of the new field of *hilkhot tzavah u-milchamah* (religious laws relating to war) in all its nuances, could well exert a profound influence on the tenor of IDF operations as a whole."[137] Should that occur, it gives greater authority to the religious scholars who interpret such laws. Religious civil society has also attempted to influence IDF policy toward women serving in the ranks, though women's civil society groups have taken much less interest in shaping military policy on women.[138] Still, the IDF remains a professional military whose primary focus is on addressing threats to the Israeli borders, and the observant Jews who serve in its ranks are reasonably well integrated into the force.[139] That is helped by the fact that more Israeli Muslims are joining the IDF, indicating that Israel's military more reflects Israeli identity as a fragmented democracy.[140]

Iran (BPR)

Iran's armed forces are another manifestation of the nexus between religious identity and military service. Article 144 of the Islamic Republic Constitution states that military members must be Muslim believers who accept Muslim commands. The military requires its soldiers to take courses emphasizing Shi'a religious texts, and religious "commissars" insure Shi'a religious fidelity at all army levels.[141] While Sunni members are permitted to join the military, non-Muslims (except Bahais) with college educations could serve as officers during mandatory service but could not become career officers. The lengthy and bloody Iran-Iraq war demonstrated that such fidelity is vital to the Iran's military performance. Ideas of martyrdom and sacrifice replaced strategic and military planning, and spiritual zeal was to combat Iraq's technical superiority.[142] It is also a force that Iran's ruling clerics use to partially marginalize the regular *Artesh* military in favor of the Republican Guard militias, whose religious fervor better reflects the belief systems of the ruling cast than does the professional army. The IRGC itself purged senior members of the Artesh, arguing that their lack of religious passion was responsible for the early losses following Saddam Hussein's 1980 invasion of Iran.[143]

Iran's revolutionary leaders created rival militias, as they distrusted the regular Artesh, even after purging its ranks, The *Quds* force is an example. It is not technically a state organ, it still has direct ties to Supreme Leader Ali Khamenei, and is an arm of the Islamic Revolutionary Guard Corps. Thus, when reports tied Quds to an assassination plot against the Saudi Arabian ambassador to the United States, the question was whether the Iranian government orchestrated the plot, or if it was carried out by contesting organs of that government.[144] The lines of authority for the army and the IRGC appear to connect to different sources, as Artesh reports to the executive under the president, and the IRGC to the supreme leader. Thus, it was noteworthy when the commander of the IRGC, General Mohammad Jafari, obliquely criticized President Hassan Rohani by complaining that Iran had become infected by "Western doctrine" in late 2013. When both Rohani and Ayatollah Ali Khamenei suggested that the IRGC should not become involved in politics, Jafari countered by stating "The main threat to the revolution is in the political arena and the Guards cannot remain silent in the face of that"[145] Rohani's anti-corruption efforts also threatened the IRGC's major business interests, as noted in chapter 4.[146]

MILITARY COHESION

Military cohesion is a key ingredient in understanding civil-military relations, for several reasons. The more cohesive the military is, the more powerful it can be relative to civilian authority. The most common metal that welds militaries together is national loyalty, and the most loyal military adherents are found in countries with relatively homogeneous populations. So civil authorities may insist on divided armed forces as a mechanism for coup-proofing. Or civilian authorities often view the national army as a way to build more national cohesiveness, so they use the military as a melting pot for a divided country.[147] Raw military recruits are expected to learn loyalty to country and service early in their socialization process. The stark and dangerous requirements of war alone mandated that warriors must stay in combat and fight, bleed and die if necessary for their fellow troops, for crown and country, or for whatever symbols they are told they are fighting for.[148] Most other government agencies do not have such requirements, so while agricultural or customs inspectors may feel a certain kinship with their fellow inspectors, they are rarely told to die for their service. For soldiers, loyalty is one of the most important assets that they take to both the battlefield and in contests for national power. From Hirschman, "loyalty holds exit at bay and activates voice," where loyalty is just a preference to remain a customer or a staff member and to work with some structure to attempt change (or preserve the status quo).[149] But loyalty, as Hirschman himself realizes, usually involves something more than a shift in demand curves, for example, because the penalties for defection are usually very high, and complete escape is not possible.[150] For soldiers, the choices include obeying orders (loyalty above all else), complaining privately, or exit via resignation or coup.

Regimes can affect military loyalty through competing preference systems. McLauchlin offers several choices, including favoritism through ethnic preferences or through incentive program (expensive officer's clubs, shares in private investments, for example). Such choices have consequences:

> Military favoritism that can help to engender the social cohesion of ethnic out-groups increases the likelihood of rebellion among the lines of discrimination. In particular, it may reduce the start-up costs of rebellion since an ethnic out-group has been branded as disloyal by the regime anyway; it stands to gain very little from preference falsification. . . . In contrast, in an incentives system, the selection bias runs the other way. Open rebellion should occur only when the participants believe that there is a good chance of success.[151]

Differing social origins may challenge military cohesion, for obvious reasons. For some traditional militaries the officer corps came from the aristocracy like the German *Junker* class, with their dueling traditions and polo pastimes. When such officers commanded enlisted troops from working or peasant class origins, cohesion could suffer, though class-consciousness sometimes dictated almost absolute obedience to the "superior" class members. Yet other military distinguish their proletariat roots and link more with the lower rungs of society's economic ladder. Members of the People's Liberation Army officer corps were mostly of peasant or worker origin, reflecting a Chinese tradition that the elite became bureaucrats or artisans while peasants joined the military, often as a last desperate effort to stave off famine in hard times. Very few patrician Russians joined the combat brigades in the Czar's imperial army.[152] The Japanese military has not only been a separate structure from general society since 1868 but also a ladder of succession to members of the lower classes.[153] A study of British officers serving in the Indian army revealed that a large number of cavalry soldiers and engineers came from the upper classes, while the infantry came from the lower income classes.[154]

Military cohesion has a significant impact on war outcomes. Simonsen argues that, "On a lower level homogeneous units in a country whose population is diverse and divided could threaten to splinter off to follow commanders, either from within the army itself or from outside, who exercise authority over the soldiers."[155] Similarly, weak states or states lacking strong nationalism make it even more challenging for their militaries to build the kind of cohesion required to succeed in war. Rosen cites numerous examples where military cohesiveness was a critical factor in combat performance, as in the case of the German army versus Soviet forces in World War II, whereas Italian armies were split between autocratic officers and common soldiers.[156] Lyall's massive study of centuries of warfare comes to a clear conclusion: "Successful armies are inclusive; unsuccessful ones largely die by their own hands, wracked by the poison of inequality that kills them, sometimes slowly, sometimes quickly from the inside out."[157]

Military Loyalty and Military Cohesion in the Middle East

In the Middle East, some militaries show a very high degree of internal cohesion, staying tightly together either in combat or in campaigns for budget shares or other domestic matters, including supporting its regime.[158] As McLauchlin notes, the ʿAlawi-dominated military units in Syria ultimately triumphed in the Sunni Muslim Brotherhood in the 1977 to 1982 revolt because ethnic cohesion within the army ultimately held the forces together.[159] Some Syrian soldiers who defected to the "Free Syrian Army" appeared to come from central and northern Syria, away from the Damascus center of support for the ʿAsad regime and the defectors appeared to come from populations outside of the minority ʿAlawite, which is the backbone of the ʿAsad rule.[160] Similarly, the Jordanian military quashed the so-called Black September revolt in 1970 and protected the monarchy from several coup efforts by relying on the Bedouin core of the Royal Guard after defections by Jordanian troops of Palestinian ethnicity.[161]

Yet in other instances militaries split asunder; they lose faith in national leaders, or national purpose because they were recruited more for remunerative purposes than for national defense, because cleavages open up between younger and older officers, or for a host of other reasons. Sometimes soldiers feel that they must choose between loyalty to leader versus loyalty to the national ideal. While most leaders claim they represent the nation, military officers sometimes differentiate national as opposed to family or personal rule, and thus may choose one or the other, with significant consequences. Rent-seeking militaries are most prone to rupture. Following the 2011 Arab transitions, significant numbers of soldiers defected from the Libyan, Yemeni, and Syrian militaries, partly because they lost faith in the mission of protecting a dictator, but also because of initial weak cohesion. Five generals and more than 120 officers left Qaddafi's army before the dictator died in rebel hands.

In some cases, even relatively cohesive military forces may become fragmented. Jordan's King Hussein's decision to abide by the Anglo-Jordanian Treaty generated nationalist-oriented military opposition against the king's seemingly pro-British position, including a 1956 coup effort, as I note in chapter 4. A combination of military grievances against Morocco's King Hassan II generated bloodier coup efforts in the early 1970s. In other cases, moral arguments may divide militaries, as was the case in Israel during both the Lebanon War of 1982–83 and the policing of the Palestinian *Intifada* where some reserve forces refused combat orders and a small number of this group received prison sentences for their disobedience.[162] The incentives-based reward system in the Pahlavi dynasty-era Iranian military did not prevent defection in large numbers (up to one thousand troops per day) immediately prior to and during the 1979 Iranian revolution.[163]

Internal military cohesion is also an issue in many Middle Eastern countries. There may be stark differences across ranks, as Ahmad noted about the Turkish military in the early twentieth century.[164] The rank-and-file were the largest and least important, easily influenced by demagogues and officered by politically infused Hamidian military college graduates. As the senior officers were determined to create an army free of political influence, they formed the Group of Savior Officers (*Halâskar Zabitân Grubu*) seeking to destroy the power of the Committee for Union and Progress (the "Young Turks") in 1912, demanding at the same time the withdrawal of the army from politics.[165] More recently, schisms appeared between the upper and lower ranks of the Egyptian army with some lower ranking officers critical of the senior ranks, claiming that they were infested with self-serving generals who valued loyalty over military skill.[166] Yet in general, Arab military cohesion was generally good, and sometimes outstanding, with the exceptions usually occurring during retreats.[167] However, the post-Saddam Hussein Iraqi military faced considerable unification problems for the military and as unification attempts aimed to join militias from the differing ethnic groups into a national military, loyalty between tribe and nation was tested. In 2007, more than three thousand Kurdish militia soldiers were incorporated into the newly unified Iraqi national army and sent to Baghdad for operations. While the hope was that this operation would help foster national unity by demonstrating that soldiers from one ethnic group would operate outside of their home territory, the Kurdish troops deserted in large numbers to avoid serving in Baghdad, reflecting the reality that, for Simonsen, "the desertions reflected the critical fact that the soldiers in question, like Iraqi army units in the Kurdish areas in general, came from the Kurdish *Peshmerga*, a militia army whose loyalty is to the Kurdish homeland and the regional government."[168] The Iraqi army also suffered because Sunni officers dominated its leadership before 2003, though Shi'a troops were usually the foot soldiers. In many cases, Shi'a officers replaced the Sunni officers who held their jobs because of loyalty to Saddam, creating friction in a country that has a significant Sunni minority.

Conscription, as noted above, exacerbates the cohesion challenges for Israel. Israel already had obvious cleavages, which Prime Minister David Ben Gurion hoped to mend partially by universal military service. However, as Peled notes, quick opposition by leading Jewish politicians to Arabs serving in the Israeli military and demands for religious exemptions for Jewish Yeshiva students threw roadblocks into Ben Gurion's aspirations.[169] While Druze, Christian, and Circassians serve as conscript soldiers (Arabs can volunteer), the Yeshiva students drew increasing ire from secular Israelis because they avoided the often-dangerous role of military service. The Israeli Supreme Court, though, offered a potential solution when it ruled in February 2012 that the Yeshiva student military exemption was unfair to secular Jews who had to serve in the IDF. The ruling might have allowed the IDF to fill Ben Gurion's dream of national integration through military service, but the fragile nature of Israeli politics intervened, and Israel remains a fragmented democracy.

The so-called Arab Spring political uprisings in 2011 tested the cohesion of several national militaries, and some held together relatively well, while others splintered. Tunisia's military unified against the Ben Ali regime in late 2010 and early 2011, deciding to resist orders to fire on anti-regime demonstrations, and remaining cohesive throughout the turmoil.[170] Part of the reason for this internal cohesion was high professionalism, and part of it was a lack of Tunisian tribal identity.[171] The Yemeni armed forces appeared to disintegrate as the spring 2011 protests ultimately drove President Saleh out of the country. Officers not only split the upper ranks, but also split from their own services. Noted one report about the commander of the Yemeni Air Force, General Muhammad Salih al-Ahmar distributed weapons meant for his own force to pro-regime thugs: "The sources also stated that Major General Al-Ahmar fears providing the Air Force with arms. The relationship between the Air Force personnel and Al-Ahmar is not good since he mistreats them, according to their assertions. Furthermore, they repeatedly defy orders to carry out air strikes against civilian targets."[172] This disunity partially reflects Yemen's tribal divisions, as General Ahmar feared that weapons might wind up in the hands of rival tribe members in the air force. Reportedly, some younger officers in the Egyptian army favored more participation by the Muslim Brotherhood in the post-Mubarak era, forcing a change in the decision by senior officers to ban the group from competing in the scheduled elections. During the Syrian civil war of 2011 onward, some Syrian units defended the national leadership, while others defected to form the core of the rebel Free Syrian Army. As Droz-Vincent observed, the ʿAsad regime "deployed only a fraction of its military forces out of fear of mass defections; clearly, it did not trust its armed forces in general."[173] The Bahraini military, dominated by Sunni officers in a majority Shiʿa country (and a military with foreign Sunni recruits), defended the Sunni regime, because its identity is less Bahraini than Sunni.[174] In the post-Saddam Hussein Iraqi military, which the US attempted to weld together into a cohesive force that would bridge sectarian differences, has devolved into what one report labeled "a hodgepodge of Shiite militias more interested in marginalizing the Sunnis than in protecting the country's sovereignty. Across the country, Shiite flags—not Iraq's national flag—fluttered from tanks and military vehicles, evidence, many said, of the troops' sectarian allegiances."[175] Lebanon's supposedly nonsectarian army largely disappeared during that country's civil war, fracturing into religious or clan-based militias.[176] It was also highly politicized during the first Michel Âoun, who injected his own politics into the Lebanese armed forces, ultimately using them to battle a rival Maronite militia in February 1983.[177]

It would appear from the above that military cohesion is at least partly a function of the nature of the military and the state: Weak states with rent-seeking militaries are much more likely to suffer low military cohesion and loyalty than are states with professional armies. While this is certainly an expected finding, its importance spills over to larger elements of military behavior, because fragmented militaries are more likely to launch coups (because they are one way to get more because of dispossession), more likely to fragment when challenges erupt against leadership (because autocratic leaders usually rely on a single base of support, thus militaries outside that base are likely to defect), and much less likely to perform well in combat, for reasons shown in chapter 5.

CONCLUSIONS

This chapter sets out definitions and ideas to support the remaining chapters in the book. It defines terms like "military," and grapples with distinctions over military force types, as some militaries serve to provide armed protection of the nation-state, while other military roles are to soak up unemployment, or to provide economic rewards to senior military officers. There are distinctions between the national military and militias that are not really "military forces" because they do not report to the defense ministry, but nevertheless play a significant role in the political and security affairs of the nation, as does the Lebanese militia Hezbollah and the Iranian Islamic Republican Guard Corps.

The chapter also probes the relationship between the military and society because this relationship can impact civil-military relations either enhancing or degrading the military role depending on how the public perceives the national armed forces. If those forces are seen as heroic defenders of the nation, distinguishing themselves in battles for the country's survival or honor, then the military benefits in ways that it cannot if society sees it as just another state agent with its nose in the public trough.

Does regime type explain differences in the military's relationship to society, as well as for military cohesion and loyalty? In bully personalist republics like Egypt, the army may be seen in two forms: either an employer of last resort or a parasite on society, though memories of its brief success in 1973 still get celebration now. But in Iran, memories of both the Artesh and the

IRGC in combat against Iraq still resonate though the growth in the IRGC's political influence is deeply troubling to many Iranians, as many blame it for the economic malaise that has engulfed the country.[178] This places them in the same category as the Egyptian military. The Israeli situation, under a fragmented democracy, shows the military as both more respected and cohesion appears to not be impacted by the increase in non-Jewish members and of the Jewish Haredim among their ranks.

The roles that the armed forces play during political transitions, particularly in autocratic countries, is partly shaped by the society-military relationship. But many other factors influence how Middle East militaries take in political transitions, which is the focus of the next chapter.

Chapter Three

The Civil-Military Relations of Middle East Political Transitions

The so-called Arab Spring that began in late 2010 drew considerable attention to the varying actions of Arab armies in Arab world political transitions. Such engagements varied considerably; sometimes soldiers emerged as heroes of the people, protecting demonstrators from internal security forces protecting the embattled regime. In other cases, the military pushed out an unpopular leader, and then stepped aside to allow elections. Yet in other cases, soldiers defended the regime against popular demonstrations with particularly disturbing scenes of army troops beating protestors and stripping the clothing off a woman in Cairo's Tahrir Square or dropping "barrel bombs" filled with shrapnel on Syrian civilians. The opposing pictures suggested that the reality of the military in Middle East transitions is quite complicated.

This chapter considers the dynamics of military involvement in Middle East political transitions. "Transitions" are transfers of power from one leader or one party, or both. In some Middle East countries, transitions occur through the ballot box, but the lack of Middle East democracy makes those transitions rare. More likely are transitions through military coup, or the death of a monarch, or, in many cases, no transitions, as Middle East rulers tend to rule for decades. The discussion on Middle East political transitions begins by focusing on the military coup and then moves to military-leveraged political transitions. The "pacted transition" is particularly important to understanding some of the bargains struck between the armed forces and the political agents of transformation. The chapter considers how those bargains unfolded especially after the surprising events following the "Tunisian Revolution" of 2010 as it spread beyond Tunisian borders.[1] The purpose of this chapter is to explain why Middle Eastern militaries act as they do in transitions; why they launch coups, why they engage in particular bargains during pacted political transitions, and what the likely transition military end states might be. The political variables of interest outlined in chapter 1 are pertinent here, as *political tradition* is sometimes involved in the roles that militaries take in political transitions, as is *political factors*, including the relationship between the military and the varying regime types introduced in chapter 1. *Military identity* and *military politics* is particularly important, as the soldier's identity as guardians of the nation are often a motive for either a coup or a pacted transition.

FACTORS INFLUENCING MILITARY TRANSITION ROLES

What influences the variation in military behaviors exhibited during political transitions? The traditional civil-military literature suggests that "type of military" should be a determining factor in the type of role militaries chose when faced with political transitions. Thus, from the previous chapter's discussion, categories like "professional" versus "rent-seeking" military suggest that a professional military will either stand aside during political change or work to stabilize the results, while a rent-seeking army will either fight to save its regime or push it out and replace it if the existing government has paid insufficient military rewards. The state types, modified from Henry and Springborg, typologize (1) bully personalist republics, (2) bully single party republics, (3) liberal monarchs, (4) conservative monarchies, and (5) fragmented democracies might also explain the variance over military behavior in regime change.[2] We should expect that bully personalist republics will experience more coups, and more pacted transitions, because the leadership lacks legitimacy and because as it pays rents to its militaries, it can fuel military greed for more rents. Bully single party republics could experience fewer coups, as they may hold more legitimacy through the governing party. Patrimonial militaries are more likely to be enmeshed in political activity than are institutional militaries, given that the former lives off its political ties to the regime. Liberal monarchies often rely on the legitimacy of the crown to keep militaries obedient, while conservative monarchs are more able to pay enough rent to buy military acquiescence. Fragmented democracies, however divided, offer the best protection against coups or pacted transitions. This is because a peaceful transfer of power, and the lack of concentrated political power can reduce military political power, and thus persuade the armed forces to engage in political change.

The degree of military autonomy is also a likely predictor of military political response. Barak and Miodownik propose a definition of military autonomy as "the military's autonomy as its ability to set an agenda independently of the state's political leaders, despite being formally subordinate to them the (actual) capacity of the military to make decisions rather than its (formal) authority to do so that is indicative of the military's autonomy vis-á-vis political leaders."[3] They further argue that an autonomous military can play a balancing role in a political crisis (including transitions crises) but a nonautonomous military in a similar situation will be unable to play such a role.[4]

The remainder of this section concentrates on the forms of political transition common in Middle East countries, beginning with the coup d'état.

THE MILITARY COUP D'ÉTAT

The term literally means "strike of state:" a military takeover of the state government. Jonathan M. Powell and Clayton L. Thyne define a coup as entailing "illegal and overt attempts by the military or other elites within the state apparatus to unseat the sitting executive."[5] Notes Naunihal Singh, "Every military coup is primarily a struggle for power within the armed forces that, if successful, grants the victor control over the state."[6] Normally, the military objective in a coup is not just a removal of the chief executive but also a voice in choosing the new chief executive.[7] The Cline Center at the University of Illinois defines a coup as an "organized effort to effect sudden and irregular (e.g., illegal or extra-legal) removal of the incumbent executive authority of a national government, or to displace the authority of the highest levels of one or more branches of government."[8] De Bruin puts it simply: "The aim of a Coup d'état is to seize executive authority within a state."[9]

Military coups d'état were once a worldwide phenomenon, particularly in developing countries. Quinlivan documents fifty-five developing country coup efforts between 1949 and 1980, half of them successful.[10] Singh finds that 471 coups occurred between 1950 and 2000.[11] Europe also experienced coups, in Greece in 1967 and Portugal in 1974, and members of the *Guardia Civil*, Spain's gendarmerie force, staged a brief but unsuccessful coup in 1981.[12] Sub-Saharan Africa experienced ninety-nine coup attempts between 1970 and 1989, though this number did drop to sixty-seven between 1990 and 2010,[13] many fueled by anger over corruption and the belief that Africans instead of expatriate Europeans should lead African armies.[14] In March 2012, Malian soldiers overthrew the government of President Amadou Toumani Touré, complaining that his regime had not prepared them to fight Islamist rebels armed with weapons taken from Libya. The resulting power vacuum allowed the rebels to over much of northern Mali, resulting in a temporary self-proclaimed Islamist state in northern Mali whose members committed significant human rights abuses.

While the number of coups is less than it was in the 1960s and the 1980s, they still occur, and the number of coups is rising. Between 2005 and 2010 there were only eight coups.[15] According to a January 2022 report, between 2015 and 2020, there were never more than two successful coups a year, but eight coups occurred over the twelve months before January 2022.[16] There have been nine military coup attempts since January 2021, of which six—in Myanmar, Sudan, Chad, Guinea, Mali, and Burkina Faso—were successful.[17] Earlier coups outside the Middle East included the Thai armed forces coup in May 2014, and an earlier coup in Burkina Faso in September 2015. In February 2021, the Myanmar military ousted the de facto government headed by Aung San Suu Kyi, however, the military was already the most powerful political force in the country.

An understanding of coups is important, not only because of their frequency but also due to their historical impact. As Singh explains, the Soviet Union might not have fallen if a military coup attempt had succeeded, and rebellious Portuguese troops ushered the "Third Wave" of democracy with a 1974 coup.[18] Some of the bloodiest twentieth-century dictators, Saddam Hussein and Idi Amin of Uganda, both came to power through coups. The 2016 Turkish attempted coup effort led to mass arrests and a clampdown on Turkish political actors that resulted Turkey being reduced from "partly free" to "not free" by Freedom House. Some argue that the January 6, 2021, insurrection in the US Capitol amounted to a failed coup effort. Coups, in short, matter.

Coups appear to be more likely in sub-Saharan Africa and Southeast Asia. In April 2021 soldiers overthrew the government of Chad, and in September 2021, soldiers removed President Alpha Conde of Guinea and took over the country. Sudanese soldiers launched a coup a month later, which only added more political chaos to a country paralyzed after the 2019 ouster of President Omar Hassan al-Bashir. However, these are exceptions; outside of a failed coup attempt in Venezuela in 2002, and a January 2000 military-joined regime ouster in Ecuador, Latin America has been free from government military capture for decades. The same is true in Asia, aside from the examples of Thailand and Myanmar, coups are rare; although there were rumblings of a coup attempt in Pakistan in late 2011, and Bangladesh officials claimed to have thwarted one in early 2012.

One likely reason for the decline of military coups globally is the growth of democratic governance, as that process allows for an alternative means of regime replacement. Because successful democracy requires a deeper set of controls over military political participation, constitutions establishing democratic rule usually contain provisions that place soldiers, military budgets, and other parts of the military establishment under civilian control. It is important to note that "civilian control" not only means control by elected state leaders, but also by a civilian headed ministry of defense, a civilian Parliament or Congress, a civilian judiciary, and nongovernment organizations such as human rights groups and the media.[19] Globally, democracy is in retreat,[20] thus, it is possible that coups will occur with increasing frequency.

The rationale for a coup may be evaluated by placing them in the following categories: (1) economic class, ethnic, or power struggles; (2) coups "for the nation"; and (3) coups that occur "with a little help from our friends," with assistance from entities outside the country. Of course, the coup perpetrators often hide their true coup motives, particularly if they involve self-interest; it is much better to argue that the coup is for the good of the nation instead of to fatten some general's bank account.[21] Moreover, many coup perpetuators have multiple motives, thus caution must be exercised when attributing the grounds behind a coup.

Coups as Class or Ethnic Struggles

This is one of the most common reasons for coups, particularly in former colonial countries. As colonial powers departed the former colony, they rarely left viable political institutions behind, so soldiers often filled political vacuums. Since many of these soldiers came from lower income backgrounds, they had little incentive to defend regimes constituted from the wealthy oligarch classes that the former imperialist powers often left behind. In some cases, lower-ranking officers overthrew such oligarchs to usher in revolutionary politics.[22] This was noticeably true in Panama, for example, during the 1968 coup by the Panamanian National Guard whose leaders empowered the lower economic classes and attempted a transition from an agricultural to a service-based economy.[23] It also explained the outcome of some West African coups as Kandeh implies, where military subalterns from the lower ranks and thus from the lower classes, as evidenced by the coup attempts of flight lieutenant Jerry Rawlings of Ghana in 1979 and Master Sergeant Samuel Doe in Liberia in 1980.[24] Such coups often resulted in political turmoil as underclass officers tried to rearrange the political and economic order through the creation of large parastatal enterprises.[25]

Ethnic conflict is a common coup factor, as either majority militaries launch coups to protect their status, or minority military leaders launch putsches to protect them from the majority.[26] Such coups are more probable when the regime either favors an ethnic group or does not prevent or minimize discrimination against a particular ethnic group. Both the instigators of the Ibo coup in Nigeria in 1966 and the Hausa-Fulanis coup that followed it feared disproportionate promotions favoring a rival group.[27] Ethnicity cleavages were also a factor in the 1987 Fiji coup,[28] and in other sub-Saharan African countries.[29] Harkness documents the practices of "ethnic stacking" in many sub-Saharan African countries as a form of loyalty manipulation by leaders, often leading to ethnically based coups.[30] Khuri and Obermeyer argue that military intervention in political spaces is more likely in peasant-based societies such as Syria, Egypt, Algeria, and Iraq and less so in tribally organized societies like Jordan, Saudi Arabia, and the Gulf emirates.[31] They also argue that peasants are more likely to be integrated within new states than are those relatively tribal members and thus use their military ties to affect social change.

Coups for the Nation

The military is the first line of defense of the country, and thus guards its ability to perform that vital role. Should the armed forces believe that national leadership has denied them the ability to use their arms successfully in war, and there are no other avenues of recourse, the coup becomes an option. Geddes states that "officers agree to join coup conspiracies only if they believe that the civilian government prevents the achievement of their main goals, and that many, in fact, will only join if they believe that the military institution itself is threatened."[32]

Soldiers often argue that their patriotism is stronger and deeper than for civilian politicians, as the military, at least theoretically, are willing to die for their country, unlike most civilian politicians. Thus, the military status as self-appointed protectors of national virtue is often the motivational factor when soldiers believe that civilian rule has so corrupted the national core values as they define them that a coup is the only solution. The military can also be the conservers of conservative politics, and thus efforts by civilians to usher in government control or intervention in the national economy or introduce a religious message in the national political narrative can serve as ammunition for a coup.[33]

Members of the Brazilian army, described by Nordlinger as having a "high level of professional expertise"[34] exercised a coup in 1964 partly to end President Joao Goulart's nationalization of key economic sectors.[35] The Thai military periodically established a tutelary democracy where military-inspired constitutions limited party formation.[36] Shah states that "although Pakistan's army is professional, it has no respect for the political system. . . . As an institution, it deeply distrusts politicians and sees itself as the only force standing between stability and anarchy, intervening in politics whenever it decides that the politicians are not governing effectively."[37] Such an operational code allowed the armed forces to easily displace civilian politicians,[38] to claim a significant share of national resources, and to push an Islamic identity to the point of radicalization in order to sustain its position.[39] General Idi Amin made similar claims after launching his 1971 coup in Uganda, though the blood bath that followed was more a result of Amin's crass brutality than it was an effort to save Uganda from its supposed problems, including the economic influence of its "Asian" population.[40] The Chilean army overthrew President Allende in 1973 because they feared that his arming of leftist militias threatened both the country and the military power base.[41] Bangladeshi officers launched several coups in the 1970s, inspired by their disagreement with the country's post-independence politics.[42]

A sub-set of nationalist coups are "honor coups," which may occur if military officers believe that they have been denied victory in some campaign or theater or robbed by civilian authority that, in the officer's minds, do not understand the significance of defeat. Thus, elements of the French military launched an unsuccessful putsch in April 1961 against President Charles DeGaulle. For Kelly:

> By 1958, and even well before the coming of the de Gaulle regime, the French Army, long trained to submit to civilian command and operate discreetly within a penumbra of silence, had not only discovered language but the gift of speaking with many tongues. The *grande muette* of former times had become an incorrigible *grande bavarde*, spewing its pent-up feelings about politics, doctrine, and, above all, Algeria at an insouciant public, a scandalized regime, and a restricted but fascinated international audience.[43]

The deep traditions of civilian control, imbued since the Dreyfus Affair [44] had weakened over the defeats in Algeria and French Indochina, something that, for many French senior officers, represented not only losses against the perceived communist menace, but also the loss of territory where their troops had shed blood. There were also dimensions of honor lost in the failed August 1991 Russian coup attempt by former Soviet officers dismayed by the loss of empire under Gorbachev. One of the reasons for the 1989 military coup against Paraguayan dictator Alfredo Stroessner Mattiauda was military dismay at Paraguay's international isolation because of its dismal human rights record.[45] The 1974 left-wing officer's coup in Portugal had similar elements, as Portugal was losing status as a NATO European country because of its colonial policies.[46]

Coups "With a Little Help from Our Friends"

Coups are frequently more than national events planned and executed by national forces. Sometimes they have help from outside countries eager to replace an out-of-favor regime. There are some real advantages in the use of covert actions over overt intervention for outside countries. As Poznansky states, "The range of outcomes associated with covert action are often less volatile and extreme. In the best-case scenario it helps states topple or rescue a foreign regime without betraying their sponsorship. Even if their cover is partially blown, plausible deniability may still shield them from the most severe risks."[47] In other situations, the negative actions of foreign patrons' coups may in turn inspire coups with officers eager to terminate excessive dependence on outside countries. Yet in other cases, the outside country itself either conducts the coup, or finds groups in the country to execute it. During the Cold War, both the US and the former Soviet Union jousted for influence globally by sponsoring coups. The US assisted in instigating coups in Guatemala in 1954,[48] against the Chilean leftist Allendé in 1973,[49] and against the Diem government in Vietnam in 1963,[50] among others, usually to preclude a communist government, or at least a government that might include communists or suspected leftists. The US appeared to share responsibility with France for a 1964 coup in Mali.[51] The "help" may be indirect, because while the US did not directly support the 1964 Brazilian coup, it rewarded the resulting military government with massive foreign aid, thus legitimating it[52] and acted similarly in Argentina after the 1976 coup.[53] The former Soviet Union also launched or supported a military coup in Afghanistan in 1979 against President Hafizullah Amin,[54] and encouraged coups in Somalia in 1969,[55] and Ethiopia in 1977[56] though the Soviets preferred to cheer leftist coups from the sidelines, as they did in numerous African countries in the 1960s.

Outside help supporting coups may be direct, as it was in the cases above, or it may be indirect and even unintentional. Foreign military training, which is sometimes designed to foster the values of the training country on its students, can actually increase coups. Savage and Caverley find that participation by international officers in the American Foreign Military Training (FMT) program actually increases the likelihood of coups by students when they return to their country. One reason for Savage and Caverly is that FMT graduates will be more professional and thus less invested in the survival of the regime.[57]

Coups: The "Velvet Shove"

More commonly referred to as "bloodless coups," or "soft coups," the "velvet shove" is a military replacement of an existing government by using largely non-military means. Its foundation is a military strong enough to use military force, usually, which thus makes just the mere threat of using armed force enough to effect regime removal. Sometimes a monarch is used by the military to pressure the head of government to resign, as occurred in the 1981 Spanish velvet shove.[58] As Doxey notes, a velvet shove is also designed to avoid the usual international condemnation that often follows a hard coup.[59]

There are multiple reasons for coups, and, moreover, there is rarely a sole reason for any coup. Coups are a gamble, with many failing and their plotters often facing a firing squad or the noose. Consequently, the decision to initiate a coup is often a desperate one, with multiple motives driving the instigators. The examples below of Middle East coups try to identify the primary reason for each.

Middle Eastern Military Coups

Middle East military coups were once regular occurrences, as Hurewitz counts the overthrow of seven Middle East civilian regimes after 1949, including a series of coups in Iraq and Syria.[60] A fuller picture shows that at least twenty-seven coup or coup attempts occurred in nine Arab countries between the 1930s and 1990s,[61] while Quinlivan counts fifty-five coup attempts between 1949 and the end of 1980, half of them successful.[62] A list of post-1945 Middle East coups is listed in table 3.1.

Table 3.1. Successful Middle East Coups Since 1945

Country/year	Regime Type at Coup Time
Yemen 1948	CM
Syria, 8/1949	BSPR
Syria, 12/1949	BSPR
Egypt, 1952	CM
Iran, 1953	CM
Iraq, 1958	CM
Turkey, 1960	FD
Yemen, 1962	CM
Iraq, 2/1963	BSPR
Syria, 1963	BSPR
Iraq, 11/1963	BSPR
Algeria, 1965	BSPR
Syria, 1966	BSPR
Iraq, 1968	BSPR
Libya, 1969	CM
Syria, 1970	BSPR
Turkey, 1980	FD
Algeria, 1992	BSPR
Turkey, 1997	FD
Egypt, 2013	FD

The list includes only those coups that actually removed the existing regime, as there were dozens of unsuccessful efforts, ranging from close-to-successful to those involving only a handful of disgruntled soldiers. The list includes only military coups, so the 1979 overthrow of Iran's Shah Mohammed Reza Pahlavi nor the 1987 overthrow of Tunisian President Habib Bourguiba are included. Nor are the inter-family quarrels in the UAE or Saudi Arabia included.

For the past twenty years, successful Middle East coups are now rare, except for the 2013 Egyptian coup. Part of the reason for the decline in coups is that autocratic regimes learned to stabilize their relationship with their officer corps, including the use of military networks to expand their power.[63] Certainly, the lack of coups is *not* related to the spread of democracy, because democracy in the Middle East is declining, as the 2009 Freedom House count of seven "partly free" countries is down to four as of 2022 (Morocco, Lebanon, Tunisia, and Kuwait), with only one, Israel ranked "free." As I will argue below, the most likely reason is that the "velvet shove" as the softest but most effective modern coup has replaced the tank-led coup. In the sections that follow, I apply the types of coups given above to the Middle East.

Coups for the Nation: Egypt (BPR)

Egypt's first modern occurred in July 1952, when a clique of Egyptian officers ended the reign of King Farouk I, the last member of the Muhammad Ali Dynasty. The officers' justification for the coup ranged from Farouk's lavish lifestyle (he owned hundreds of expensive cars and a large pornography collection, among other assets) to the mismanagement of the Egyptian forces during the 1948 war with Israel. Herb notes that the Egyptian military of the 1950s was composed largely of middle-class officers who had little loyalty to monarchial regimes with wealthy patrons and roots in the imperial past.[64] The soldiers believed that Farouk's regime had failed them militarily and because Farouk continued to emphasize that the primary mission for the Egyptian army was internal repression.[65]

The 1952 Egyptian coup also ended the continued British presence in Egypt and the privileges of the landed elite whom the army blamed for impoverishing the peasantry.[66] However, the subsequent military rule shifted Egypt from a liberal era with a constitution, a relatively free press, and civil society, to an autocracy.[67] The successful coup plotters quickly coup-proofed their regime, fearing a countercoup, purged thousands of officers from the military ranks, and created a republican guard to defend the military rulers from the military.[68] The military-led regime quickly redistributed land to the peasants and centralized economic power under the state, a move partly reflecting the lower and middle-class backgrounds of the Free Officers.[69] The military also took command of a considerable portion of the Egyptian economy, as noted in chapter 4, so in addition to distributing much of Egypt's economy to the disenfranchised, they retained some of it themselves.

During the 2011 "Arab Spring," the Egyptian military somewhat reluctantly gave President Mubarak the velvet shove largely to preserve its position in Egyptian political and economic spaces, and to minimize harm to Egypt, rather than because it wanted to open a democratic door.[70] The army waited until it became obvious that Mubarak had lost political support, and that further delay in removing him would only hurt the military.[71] After Mubarak's ouster, the army created the Supreme Council of the Armed Forces (SCAF) and ran Egypt as a military dictatorship in the interim period before presidential elections in June 2012. During this time, military courts tried more than seven thousand Egyptians for a variety of protest activities, and women protesters found themselves subject to "virginity inspections" by military police.[72] Bowing to both internal and external pressure for elections, however, the SCAF disbanded in the hopes that its favored candidate, former vice president (and retired air force general) Ahmed Shafi would win the June 2012 election.

However, Islamist President Mohammad Morsi, an American-educated engineer, and Muslim Brotherhood member won the presidency in 2012 over Shafi, though Morsi's inexperience and hubris quickly evaporated his limited legitimacy. Morsi dismissed senior generals, announced that he would not be bound by the rulings of Egypt's judicial system, and presided over an economy that shrank precipitously. The military initiated a campaign with potential protesters to help destabilize Morsi's grip on power.[73] In July 2013, crowds once again gathered in Tahrir Square to express their dissatisfaction with Morsi's governance. Ready to move after months of prepping the opposition, the Egyptian military arrested Morsi, moved him to an undisclosed location, and swiftly took control of Egyptian politics.[74] When angry Morsi supporters set up encampments in Cairo, security forces attacked them, resulting in hundreds killed. In late 2012, the army installed former Supreme Court chief justice Adly Mansour.[75] Then the military nominated one of their own, General Abdel Fatteh al-Sisi, to run for president. The armed forces first promoted Sisi to Field Marshal, and then allowed him to resign the military. For Holmes, Egypt's military shove of Morsi and elevation of al-Sisi was not technically a military coup, but what she termed a "coup from below."[76]

In May 2014, Sisi won a barely contested presidential election, cementing the military hold on Egyptian politics for the near future, and also assuring Egypt's armed forces that they would protect their percentage of the Egyptian economy, as noted in chapter 4. Sisi has ruled without opposition since, and a 2019 referendum passed with little opposition, which, among other power grants to Sisi, contained Articles 200 and 204 that state that the armed forces will "safeguard the constitution, democracy, civil life, the rights and individual freedom and maintain state foundations."[77] With that power grant, and one of their own in power, Egypt's armed forces had little incentive to try another coup.

Coups for the Nation: Syria (BPR)

In Syria, coups began shortly after Syria gained independence from France and continued until the ʿAsad family put an end to them with a combination of reforms and draconian military oversight. The first coup plotters, led by army commander Husni Zaʿim, launched their operation in March 1949, drawing on festering military anger over poor government support for the army in the 1948 war.[78] President Shukri al-Quwatli further angered the military when he cut the military budget after the 1948 war, implicitly shifting the blame for defeat to the army.[79] The officers arrested Quwatli and most of the cabinet, and then Zaʿim installed himself as Syria's new president.[80] His rule lasted barely a year as Zaʿim became increasingly erratic and brutal, consequently inspiring yet another coup in August 1949. A rival group of officers led by Colonel Muhammad Sami al-Hinnawi took control, assassinated Zaʿim, and invited civilians to form a new government.[81] Al-Hinnawi's rule was even briefer than was his predecessor, though, as Colonel Adib Shishakli and his fellow officers orchestrated a coup in December 1949. During his five-year rule, Shishakli, concerned with his long-term governance prospects, established a cult of personality around him, setting the precedent for other rulers like Hafiz ʿal-ʿAsad to follow.[82]

Occasionally the military allowed elections to be held, as happened in December 1961, yet Nazim al-Qudsi's election returned much political power to Syria's traditional elites, which resulted in another military overthrow in March 1962. This coup, led by Colonel Abdel Karim Nihlawi and Major General Abdel Karim Zahreddin did not have complete military support, though, and other officers dismissed the coup-makers, bringing back Qudsi as prime minister. A subsequent government purge of the military stimulated yet another coup in March 1963 that initiated the Baʿthification of Syria by bringing in Baʿth theorist Salah al Din al-Bitar as prime minister.[83] The contest for influence in Syria (and particularly in the army) between Baʿthists and Nasser-inspired officers resulted in yet another coup effort in July 1963 by Nasserist officers, and as Baʾathist officers crushed the attempts, Baʿth strength grew.[84] The power base of two Baʿth generals, Salah al-Jadid and Hafiz al-ʿAsad grew, and in February 1966 they, along with Nureddin Atass, launched yet another violent ouster of the government. This is how members of the minority ʿAlawite came to power in Syria in 1966, supported by their Druze allies.[85] However, the Druze, once allies with the ʿAlawi, feared that they would be excluded in an ʿAlawi-dominated regime. Consequently, a Druze officer, Colonel Salim Hatum, attempted a coup in February 1966 that quickly failed.[86] A final 1970 coup brought the Baʿth Party, and ultimately the al-ʿAsad family to power, as Hafiz al-ʿAsad, another ʿAlawite, "cleansed" the regime to take power himself. The Syrian-Israeli 1967 war debacle gave Hafiz al-ʿAsad justification to elbow aside Syrian leader Salah Jadid to take power himself, purging numerous Jadid loyalist officers in the process.[87] The Syrian military had the dubious distinction of orchestrating fourteen coups between 1949 and 1970.

The Syrian armed forces, initially politicized by their 1949 coup, had favored the Ba'ath Party with its appeal to nationalism and socialism, but even by the mid-1950s, the Ba'ath had been weakened by divided leadership, and thus, as Kaylani astutely observed, "The Ba'athist *raison d'etre* was gradually but irretrievably lost and radical praetorianism was ushered in. These were the seeds that were sown in the 1950s, germinated in the 1960s and left in full bloom today."[88] Almost fifty years later, those words remain true, as the ʿAsad family has ruled Syria since that time, and the Syrian military has assumed a praetorian role in keeping the ʿAsad family in power before and during the Syrian civil war.

Class resentment apparently was a partial driver for Syrian coups, particularly in the late 1940s and early 1950s. The officer corps, drawn mainly from poor or minority religious groups (usually ʿAlawite or Druze) wanted to break control over the Syrian economy by the mostly Sunni Muslim civilian political and economic elite.[89] Thus, after the 1970 coupe, the military-influenced Ba'ath expropriated land from the elite and nationalized it, paradoxically driving the old landlord gentry to support the anti-Baʿth Muslim Brotherhood in places like Hama in the 1970s and 1980s.[90]

Like other coups covered in this chapter, other factors besides "for the nation" shaped dynamics of the Syrian coups. They were also carried out by rent-seeking rivals to the officers at the top of the military power pyramid. Should the rent distribution among the ranks be seen as insufficient, as Mbaku argues, then excluded military groups will use coups as an avenue to rents.[91] Syria's religious and ethnic factions were also a major factor in coup dynamics. In almost every coup since independence, Syria's religious and ethnic divides played key roles. As Sunni officers tried to maintain their grip on military power, they were responsible for most of Syria's coups, which also involved Sunni machinations against minority officers. To take just one example, Sunni officer "Adib al-Shishakli. After rising to power, the colonel quickly dispatched Druze and 'Alawi officers to far-flung assignments away from the capital and filled their vacant positions in Damascus with Sunnis. In 1951, al-Shishakli had thirty-five Druze officers and soldiers arrested on charges of espionage for Israel; several officers were later found guilty and executed.[92]

Coups for the Nation: Libya (BPR)

After independence from Italy, Libya struggled to achieve national unity as historically it comprised three regions, Tripolitania, Cyrenaica, and Fezzan. The country gained independence under the Sanusi Monarchy headed by King Idris al-Sanusi. However, more than forty to fifty thousand Italian settlers who held the best land, remained after independence. At independence, Libya had an illiteracy rate of 90 percent and an infant mortality rate of 50 percent.[93] Idris was a feeble leader ruling over a weak country who neglected the Royal Libyan Army and relied instead on his praetorian guards, the Cyrenaica Defense Force and the Tripolitania Defense Force to protect his reign. Yet Idris's security forces distrusted the monarch, and they remained neutral as the King's end came in September 1969.[94] In that month, a group of Libyan officers, led by then-major Muamar Qadhafi, overthrew the Sanusi Monarchy. Included in their list of complaints about the Sanusi monarchy was its continued ties to western nations, including the presence in Libya of the US Air Force's Wheelus Air Force Base, which, Qadhafi complained, he once tried to visit but US officials denied him entry.[95] The remaining Italian settlers, and the economic distortions posed by the rapid growth of the oil economy helped the officers to justify their coup.[96] After some post-coup deliberations, the officers chose twenty-seven-year-old Qadhafi as its leader.

Qadhafi mercurially ruled the country for decades, abolishing formal state institutions, invading or threatening Libya's neighbors, and eliminating all who disagreed with him. As Qadhafi developed his theories on Islamic governance as published in his "Green Book," ideological differences emerged within his small military coterie. As a result, a few senior officers attempted a coup in August 1975, though it failed and they went before a firing squad.[97] Yet attempted coups continued, as senior Libyan officers, displeased and disheartened by poor Libyan military performance in Chad, and in brief encounters against the US military, attempted more coups against Qadhafi in 1983, 1985, and 1993.[98] Information on these efforts remains scant, but Qadhafi ordered a number of military executions following the Chad debacle, to deter further coup attempts. When oil revenues were high, they enabled Qadhafi to pay his military well, but reduced oil monies and the failures in Chad may also have been factors in the coup attempts.[99] Soviet-supplied East

German advisors reportedly protected Qadhafi from a 1980 coup attempt, and possibly from earlier efforts as well.[100]

In October 2011, angry anti-Qadhafi demonstrators accomplished what Libya's military failed to do, as hastily organized militias drove him from Tripoli and killed him before he could flee the country. By some estimates, over half of the military defected, as the force shrank from fifty-one thousand to somewhere between ten and twenty thousand.[101] But old coup habits die hard, and in May 2014 retired Libyan general Khalifa Haftar joined forces with the head of Libyan special forces and an air force unit to storm the Parliament.[102] It was difficult to understand exactly what they were trying to seize, as Libya had no central government and was in the process of swearing in its fourth prime minister since 2011. Possibly the officers wanted a return to the rewards that once benefitted military loyalists though their rhetoric focused on combatting Islamist militant militias. In May 2017, the Libyan Government of National Accord named General Haftar as chief of the armed forces though not all of the militias that were part of the GNA welcomed the appointment.[103] Haftar was appointed commander of the "Libyan National Army," a militia force, which he used to push Islamist militants out of Benghazi in 2016, and three years later, directed it against Tripoli in April 2019. His efforts at conquest were sometimes thwarted by opposition forces, but he appeared to retain his objectives, to rule Libya as a military dictator. According to a 2016 interview with analyst Jonathan Winer, Haftar "wanted to take Libya by conquest. He does not really want to participate in the political process. He does not want to be subject to anyone else."[104] Hafar over-reached, though, and his Russian and UAE-backed forces suffered defeat at the hands of the Turkish-backed GNA, with cease-fire declared in October 2020. And Haftar retained control of much of the country, and his self-styled "Libyan Arab Armed Forces" (LAAF) appeared determined to dominate state institutions in eastern Libya, thus making unification all the more difficult.[105]

Coups for the Nation: Yemen (BPR)

In February 1948, Yemeni military officers, fueled by a numerous grievances (including distrust of foreign-educated soldiers) assassinated Imam Yahya Hamid ad-Din and replaced him with his personal advisor Abdullah al-Wazir. Al-Wazir took the Imam's title and appointed a largely civilian cabinet; however, the coup did not sit well with other tribal leaders, who sent Al-Wazir and the military coup leaders to face the firing squads. A month later, a different set of military officers, angered over lies about Yahya's death (the coup leaders claimed Yahya died naturally despite more than fifty bullet holes in his Cadillac) captured the palace and installed Amir Ahmad.[106]

In 1962, Colonel Abdullah al-Sallal ousted Imam Mohammad Al-Badr, the last heir to a Zaydi imamate that had lasted for centuries in Yemen.[107] Al-Badr escaped the initial coup and fled to north Yemen, where he formed a tribal confederation to fight against the republican coup makers.[108] Egypt joined the republican side while Saudi Arabia supported the Al-Badr royalist faction. Al-Sallal had been inculcated with republican notions after he was sent for training in Iraq, and he returned to Yemen hoping to rid the country of what he described as "backward and dirty rule."[109] The officers established a republic, terminating the imamate, but they did not accomplish their objective of eliminating or reducing "backward and dirty rule." But their intervention did trigger a civil war with Egypt backing the insurgents (and quiet support from the US, as noted below), while Saudi Arabia tried to protect the former royals.

Coups for the Nation: Algeria (BRSP)

Following its independence from France in 1962, Algeria experienced several coups, most stemming from debates within the ruling circles about what Algeria's post-independence state and society would become. The new state was divided among elites, including the intellectuals, the military, and the revolutionaries with most power divided between the latter two groups.[110] These groups were never really homogeneous, though, as the military was divided into the *wilaya* guerillas and the professional army, which became the basis of the *Armée Nationale Populaire* when the guerillas disbanded.[111]

The first National Assembly elections in August selected Ahmed Ben Bella, a revolutionary, to form a government. Ben Bella used that grant to expand his powers and by 1963 he was president, secretary general of his party, and head of government.[112] Yet for all those positions, Ben Bella underdelivered on his promises to his multifaceted constituency. Ultimately one of Ben Bella's former allies, Army Chief Houari Boumediene, who objected to Ben Bella's Marxist orientation, his marginalization of Islam, and Algeria's continuing development problems and overthrew Ben Bella in June 1965. Algeria's new leaders found, though, that governing was more difficult than ending a government, and the country continued to struggle with both internal and international challenges.[113] There were fewer coups, however, partly because each president from Boumediene on was a former military officer, thus allowing the armed forces a significant role in Algeria's political and economic life. Relative political stability set in, interrupted only by a brief coup attempt by Chief of Staff Tahar Zbiri in December 1967, which other military forces quickly crushed.[114]

In the early 1990s, The Algerian military feared that the Islamist *Front Islamique du Salut* (FIS) Party's majority in the 1991 parliamentary vote would tilt the country in ways that ran counter to their Algerian nationalist image. They also feared that the FIS could challenge their corporatist interests, as they owned key sectors of the Algerian economy. The officers seized power in early 1992, suspending the subsequent electoral rounds, and forcing President Chadli Benjedid to resign.[115] This was the stated reason, but the military also distrusted the FLN leadership as well, demanding that Chadli fire his prime minister, Mouloud Hamrouche, for gerrymandering the 1991 election and forcing the army to quell the resulting large public protests.[116] Chadli had also engineered political reforms that had increased individual rights while downgrading the status of the military.[117] Yet the December 1991 election that resulted in a FIS majority was partly a consequence of the military stopping Hamrouche's election rigging. The military demanded that Chadli step down, which he did in January 1992. So, while the coup was "for the nation," like so many other coups, it was really for a very specific military vision of "the nation." One of its instigators varnished the reasons as: "I said that if the PNA (Popular National Army), especially since 1992, has more or less involved in politics, it was because of a need for national destiny on the republican character of the state and sustainability of the Algerian nation."[118]

The military claimed that they were defending the constitution and sovereignty of Algeria through their coup, but, as Sadiki argues, "With the benefit of hindsight, it can be argued that the armed forces lacked any real commitment to disengaging from politics."[119] The generals dismantled the existing political structures, replacing the presidency with a "High Council" that they dominated, dissolving Parliament, and justifying their actions by claiming that Algerian voters made "the wrong choice."[120] Then confronted with the outbreak of a bloody civil war as the "Armed Islamic Group" replaced the FIS as the most powerful Islamist power in Algeria and began massacring all Algerians who did not accept the GIA, as dictated by its new leader, Antar Zouabri. More than two hundred thousand Algerians died as a result.[121] The civil war gave the military the chance to justify a "state of emergency," allowing them to rule at will through 2004, when the presidential election in that year indicated that President Bouteflika had gained the upper hand over the military.[122] However, the military remained politically powerful, and thus able to derive considerable rents from Algeria's petro-economy. That led the military adopt extreme means, including assassination of reformers, to protect their nest eggs.[123] Still, President Bouteflika periodically reminded the armed forces that he had the power to fire senior officers, as when he dismissed the Chiefs of the Air Force and the Territorial Air Defense Forces in September 2018.[124] Whether or not Bouteflika feared a coup or was looking for scapegoats because of public discontent over corruption is difficult to discern.[125] But the military got the last move in against Bouteflika, when in March 2019, chief of the Algerian Army, General Ahmed Gaid Salah, urged the president to step down, not necessarily because of his incapacity but because large crowds were gathering in the Algiers streets demanding that Bouteflika step down.[126] Bouteflika complied, and the army quickly named a replacement, upper house speaker Abdelkader Bensalah, as they were likely fearful that elections would reduce their power. The protestors prevailed though, and in April 2019, the acting president set July 4 as the date for a presidential election. Unsurprisingly, no candidates chose to run for the presidency, and thus the generals scrapped the July 4 date, and continued to manage Algeria with no electoral mandate.

Coups for the Nation: Jordan (LM)

In the 1950s, members of the Jordanian military were becoming receptive to the appeal of Arab nationalism, which was rising as a function of the 1948 Israeli-Arab war. King Hussein sensed the rising nationalism and tried to counter it by appointing General Ali Abu Nawwar as chief of staff, hoping to gain his loyalty. However, as Lust-Okar notes, Abu Nawwar himself chose Arab nationalism over fealty to the Hashemite Crown and brought in fellow nationalists to power, forcing the monarch to call for new elections in October 1956 and bringing left-wing nationalists to power.[127] Tensions over Arab nationalism between some military units and the monarchy grew until military units stationed in al-Zarqa threatened a coup against King Hussein in April 1957.[128] Both the king and other loyal officers thwarted the coup, as Hussein drove to al-Zarqa to confront the potential mutiny. He walked into the troop gathering, confronted Abu Nawwar, and ultimately exiled him from the country. As Robins notes of the army, "The Jordanian army contained genuine Nasserite sympathizers. Perhaps more importantly, it also contained ambitious and self-regarding figures prepared to exploit the turbulent regional situation for their own personal ends."[129] While the Jordanian military is one of the more professional armies in the Middle East, some Jordanian officers seemed to believe that a Nasserist foundation was a preferential option to supporting the Hashemite monarchy, though a majority of senior Jordanian officers felt otherwise and doomed the coup. Since that time, there have been no additional coup efforts.

In April 2021, a "palace coup" reportedly led by Prince Hamza, who had been Crown Prince until King Abdullah removed him in 2004. The details of the event remain murky but there is evidence that the chief of staff of the Royal Jordanian armed forces, Major General Yousef Huneiti, talked Prince Hamza out of his actions and thus cementing the professionalism of the Jordanian military.[130] Barak and Miodownik would likely argue that the relative autonomy of the Royal Jordanian military allowed it to play a balancing role in the political crisis.¹³¹

Coups for the Nation: Turkey (BSPR)

Turkey is one of the more coup-prone countries in the Middle East, as actual and attempted coups are a part of the historical landscape. What makes this remarkable is that the Turkish armed forces are among the most professional in the region, while their actions support the argument above that professional militaries can and do engage in the execution of coups, they are more likely to carry them out "for the nation."

Following the creation of the Turkish Republic in 1923, President Kemal Atatürk kept the Turkish military out of power during his rule, fearing it as a rival power center.¹³² The Turkish military acquiesced to civilian control under both Kemal Atatürk and his successor Mustafa İsmet İnönü. In 1950, democratic elections swept in new civilian leadership. Prime Minister Adnan Menderes initially promoted military officers based on personal loyalty to him rather than on merit. Fearful of yet military coup by the military loyal to Atatürk's Republican People's Party, Menderes purged all of Turkey's top military commanders.¹³³ Those military fears only grew when Menderes additionally fired sixteen generals and 150 colonels based on rumors that they had pledged fealty to İnönü on election night.¹³⁴ That action kept the soldiers in their barracks for only another decade. Menderes then used Turkish infantry units to suppress domestic anti-Menderes demonstrations.¹³⁵ These demonstrations were in response to a progressive deterioration of internal security, as Menderes's Democrat Party cracked down on the political opposition. The military disliked the retreat from the laïcité republican ideals, as Menderes had allowed the return of public prayers in Arabic and government funding of the construction and rebuilding of mosques.¹³⁶ Moreover, according to Lerner and Robinson, the military viewed the Democratic Party's civilian leadership as weak because it leaned on the military for support, blocked promotion channels for Turkish officers, and alienated the civilian intellectual elite that the military depended on for ideas.¹³⁷

These conditions, along with a deteriorating economy, inspired some members of the Turkish armed forces to take matters into their own hands.¹³⁸ In May 1960, soldiers led by General Cemal Gürsel, arrested Turkey's national leadership, suspended the constitution, declared martial law, and took control of the country, and installed General Gürsel as Turkey's fourth president. The coup leaders claimed noble motives: "In throwing the office-holding rascals out, the soldiers claimed that they were performing the highest duty to the nation. They were cleansing the country of corruption, tyranny, and selfish interests."[139] The relative poverty that the Turkish military had sunk into following the 1950 election which empowered an economic elite at military expense was one of the explanations for the 1960 coup.[140] Military fears also inspired the uprising, as some officers believed that Menderes was about to abolish Atatürk's party which his successor, İsmet İnönü, led.[141] Menderes was also disliked by the military, as he silenced them on matters of foreign and security policy.[142] The 1960 putsch leaders hanged Menderes and the finance and foreign ministers.[143] In October 1961, the coup leaders returned Turkey to civilian rule, as General Gürsel transferred the reins of power to İnönü.

The military coup participants were not of one mind on their political role, as some wanted to swiftly return to democracy while others wanted to remain in power. So, while İnönü called for early elections in 1960, a radical military faction opposed that move, and thus Colonel Talat Aydemir attempted coups in 1962 and 1963. However, those efforts failed when senior military officers refused to support him.[144] Moreover, the 1960 coup taught Prime Minister Süleiman Demirel a lesson as he tried to appease the senior officers by cracking down on radical violent political movements.[145] According to Sakallioğlu, one development in the aftermath of the 1960 Turkish coup was Demirel's abandoning efforts to bring the military under civilian control and instead granting them autonomy.[146] Moreover, institutions created by the military after the 1960 coup remained in place, including the National Security Council (*Milli Güvenlik Kurulu*, or MGK) and the military court system.[147] This allowed the military to continue to influence state political decisions neither through praetorian identity or by undermining democracy or infiltrating civilian institutions, but through military institutions.[148]

In March 1971, the army returned to the political realm, this time through a "velvet shove" memorandum ordering Demirel to resign because "terrorists" from both the left and right were threatening to take Turkey into a civil war. There are differing reasons for this "coup," however. Some argued that the officers who authored the memorandum were hesitant to intervene and did so largely to declare martial law to end the episodic internal violence.[149] Others argue that the Turkish senior officers launched the coup to halt a pending coup by junior officers.[150] The latter explanation may be closer to reality, as the officers returned the resilient Demirel to the prime minister post. However, the coup clouds were brewing again as the extreme right and extreme left continued to battle for influence. Moreover, Demirel again failed to appease the Turkish army because of a combination of poor economic performance and his wooing of the Islamist-oriented *Milli Selamet Partisi* (National Salvation Party) and its leader, Necmitten Erbakan.[151]

In September 1980, the Turkish military again took power after the centrist forces in the two major parties failed to compromise, and minor parties (including the Islamist National Salvation Party) gained more power. The resulting logjam allowed extreme forces to fragment Turkish political life.[152] This time, soldiers arrested Demirel and his cabinet, suspended Parliament, and named retired Admiral Bülend Ulusu as prime minister. Arrests of union and party leaders and political activists followed. Soon more than fifteen thousand civilians languished in Turkish military jails[153] by one estimate, by another, 650,000 persons wound up in military custody.[154] The coup followed a long period of disorder and the military quickly restored order with a combination of violence, arrests, and pleas for order. Then, after drafting a new constitution, the military returned to its quarters with its reputation largely enhanced by its actions, according to Cooper.[155] While the coup had many justifications, Tachau and Heper note that,

> What may be significant, however, is that the coup occurred immediately after a highly provocative political rally organized by the National Salvation Party, during which brimless headgear (still legally prohibited) were abundantly evident, and during which a significant number of those in attendance refused to stand for the playing of the national anthem. It is noteworthy that the organizers of the 1980 coup appear to hold the image of Atatürk in exceptionally high esteem and that they particularly value the principle of secularism.[156]

Yet Eligür claims that the 1980 coup was aimed more at Turkey's political left, with the coup driving a wedge between the center-right and the center-left and thus creating political space for the Islamist-oriented *Refah Partisi*, or Welfare Party.[157] Thus, the urban poor, who traditionally had voted for the Turkish left-wing parties turned their loyalties to the Islamists as a substitution.

In 1997, the Turkish military intervened again to overturn the results of the 1995 election, which brought the Islamist-oriented Welfare Party to power and elevating its head Necmettin Erbakan to Prime Minister.[158] The armed forces regarded Erbakan as a challenge to their vision of a Kemalist Turkey, objecting to the inclusion of an Islamist party in the governing coalition. Again, the public and key civil society groups seemed to support their actions.[159] In a later piece, Demirel argues that "the 1997 incident showed once again that center-right parties, which did not accept the military version of secularism, were prepared to accept military encroachments into civilian domains so long as their core interests remained unharmed."[160]

Yet the military may have harmed its standing with lower income Turks by forcing out the Erbakan-led government.[161] Support for Islamist parties was highest among lower-income Turks, whose support formed the backbone of the 2002 election victory of the Islamist *Adalet ve Kalkınma Partisi* (AKP) led by Recep Tayyip Erdoğan, the former mayor of Istanbul. The AKP, the heir to *Refah Partisi*, won a majority of parliamentary seats for the first time in Republican Turkish history, a victory large enough to probably deter Turkey's armed forces from yet another coup attempt against Turkish political Islam. Thus after 2002, a new tacit bargain emerged between the military and the AKP, with the party recognizing the autonomous role of the military in national security, while the army recognizes the primacy of the government in domestic matters as long as it pursued secular politics. The AKP reformed the MGK, reducing its political power, though the reforms did not curb military power as much as the reformers had hoped.[162] The AKP also put defenses in place to prevent further military incursions into their space and thus Harris argues that the reason AKP wanted to continue Turkish policy of applying for European Union membership was to prevent military political moves.[163] There were reasons for this push, as the Turkish military would have had to reform its relationship with political leadership. Thus, while military officers desired the modernization aspects of EU membership, the more conservative members feared that EU membership would empower Turkish political Islamists.[164] The AKP's most robust coup defense was to go on the offense against the armed forces.

In February 2008, Turkish civil police initiated mass arrests of senior military officers because of supposed coup plotting, later encapsulated under the term "Engenekon," after the alleged name of the gang.[165] Press accounts suggested that the Engenekon plotters were a band of right-wing extremists, criminals, civilian business exectutives, and military officers (the so-called deep state) who had secretly organized in the 1990s, but had its cover blown when the police raided a house belonging to a high-ranking special forces officer in the Eskisehir neighborhood of Istanbul and found weapons and explosives. Then the charges grew, to include assassination attempts and other nefarious activities, spawned in part by the liberal and Islamist press[166] and, according to Jenkins, supporters of the Fethullah Gülen Movement.[167] The arrests started with retired general officers (including the former commander of the Turkish gendarmerie and the former commander of the First Army of Land Forces. As the arrest list grew, so did the accusations, including mass killings of Kurds, collaboration with Turkish Hezbollah, and penetration through illicit means by military organizations like Özel Harp *Dairesi* (Special Warfare Unit, or ÖHD) that dated back for decades.[168] Many of the claims in the charges brought against the accused appeared fanciful and supported with spurious evidence, yet the trials moved forward. In January 2009, two more retired generals joined the list of detainees, driving Chief of Staff General İlker Başbuğ to complain about the arrests, which ultimately ended with the subsequent release of the retired generals by the prosecutor.[169] But Prime Minister Erdoğan supported the Engenekon investigation in the face of criticism that politics was driving the query. In January 2012, security forces arrested General Başbuğ himself, charged with "founding or directing an armed terrorist organization" and "inciting the overthrow of the government of the Turkish Republic or the prevention of it fulfilling its duties."[170] In August 2013, a court sentenced General Başbuğ to life in prison, though an appeals court eventually overturned his conviction in March 2014.[171]

Engenekon was not the only reported coup attempt; others included *Balyoz* or "Sledgehammer," a 2011 military coup effort supposedly disguised as an exercise, but whose real purpose was to bomb mosques and shoot down a Turkish civilian airline, then blaming it on Greece. The alleged rationale behind this attempt was to justify a government takeover by the military.[172] After Turkish authorities announced their discovery of the "Sledgehammer" case, they arrested more than 250 officers, including fifty active duty generals and admirals.[173] In July 2011, the entire top echelon of the Turkish military resigned, angered at the arrests and arrest warrants issued for many senior Turkish officers. Then the AKP-dominated regime in a resolute show of political strength, arrested over a tenth of Turkey's remaining senior officers. General Isik Kosaner, the chief of staff, complained bitterly that the reason for the arrests "is to create the impression that the Turkish Armed Forces are a criminal organization," and that the climate under AKP rule "has prevented me from fulfilling my duties to protect the rights of my personnel and thereby rendered me unable to continue this high office I occupy."[174] As the charges against the military mounted, a senior American official familiar with the case stated that "Sledgehammer" was nothing more than an exercise and not a coup plan.[175]

After these dramatic shifts in Turkish civil-military relations, Turam stated "the cooperation between the AKP and the military is still fragile. As always, maintaining the sensitive fine balance takes constant work, communication, and mutual compromise."[176] Yet the relationship evolved in yet another unexpected direction, when reports spread in late 2013 that AKP cabinet members and Erdoğan's sons were under investigation for corruption. Erdoğan counter-charged that the prosecution and the police were actually working under the direction of Gülen. However, when Erdoğan began to eliminate Gülenists from his party in 2011, Gülen turned on Erdoğan, charging his ministers and his family with corruption.[177] Apparently fearful of the charges, Erdoğan turned back to his former rival, the Turkish military, offering to retry some initially found guilty, but the brief interlude would not last long. Erdoğan feared that Gülen supporters had infiltrated the military, paradoxical as Erdoğan used the Gülenists to purge the military, as noted earlier. Thus, Erdoğan began to purge military units where he believed Gülen influence lay, and apparently some of these units decided to preempt.

On July 14, 2016, units of the ground forces, air force, and some gendarmerie forces launched a poorly coordinated coup, taking control of some bridges in Istanbul, along with Turkish CNN, while bombing the Parliament building and attempting unsuccessfully to capture Erdoğan, who was on vacation. However, the coup effort did not have the support of Turkey's military leadership, and the plotting officers badly bungled the operation. Erdoğan managed to get to a television station, from which he urged Turkish citizens to oppose the putsch, thus taking full advantage of the AKP's authoritarian control of both the mass media and the mosques.[178] The coup attempt ultimately ended in defeat, with the fighting killing more than 240 people. While only 8,600 soldiers out of an army of 500,000 participated (some may have been deceived into joining) the military itself suffered greatly, as it lost prestige and public support.[179] The Turkish Air Force, which was a central participant in the failed putsch, saw the purge of more than three hundred F-16 fighter pilots, thus decimating that force of experienced aviators.[180] Later a court sentenced the chief of the Turkish Air Force, General Akin Ozturk, and 151 other military officers to life in prison for their alleged role in the attempted coup.[181] The consequences of the coup beyond the arrests were severe for the military beyond the arrests, as military schools closed, and the Higher Military Council was civilianized, with ten civilian members outnumbering the four military members.[182]

The Justice and Development Party started to dramatically reduce the power of the Turkish armed forces before 2016, and even more draconian measures followed the failed putsch. As Demir and Bingöl aptly put it, "over the last century, the status of Turkey's military has evolved from military tutelage under a 'praetorian' or 'guardianship' model to one of 'absolute civilian-control.'"[183]

Coups "For the Nation": Lebanon (FD)

From its founding in 1945 onward, Lebanon's small military largely stayed out of politics, though its loyalty, from 1958 until the civil war of 1975 to 1990, was with the country's Maronite president.[184] There was a brief coup attempt at the end of 1961 stemming from military discord with President Fouad Chehab, but it failed for a variety of reasons.[185] The coup effort was a stunning disappointment to President Chehab, as he had founded and professionalized the Lebanese military himself when he was a general. However, the army fragmented into militias during the civil war, losing whatever political neutrality it might have had. It is therefore not surprising that several of its leaders tried coups during and after the war. General Aziz al-Ahdab announced his coup effort in March 1976 as Lebanon's civil war was rapidly escalating, appearing on Lebanese television and demanded the resignation of the cabinet and the president.[186] General al-Ahdab's coup failed to gain support from Lebanon's major political players, including Syria, whose defense minister lampooned al-Ahdab, and the general then faded into retirement. A second, bizarre coup occurred in September 1988, when Lebanese army chief of staff, General Michel Âoun, a Maronite Christian claiming to represent the Lebanese army, demanded and received the resignation of President Amin Gemayel, who had replaced his assassinated brother Bashar, and of the interim prime minister, Selim Hoss. Âoun then got Gemayel to sign an executive order appointing Âoun as Lebanon's president. While in power, Âoun engaged in a large-scale politicization of the Lebanese Armed Forces, choosing his favorites for promotion, and ultimately pushing Lebanon's military to battle with the Lebanese Forces Phalangist militia.[187] However, when Hoss refused to depart his office, Lebanon suddenly had two governments,[188] a duality which ended only when Hoss's replacement, Elias Hrawi, ordered Âoun to abandon his rival presidential claim, and Syrian forces ultimately drove him from his palace to exile in France in 1990. He would return after the 2006 Israeli war to form a political party, align with his old enemy Hezbollah, and join the governing coalition, suggesting that his motives for the coup and after were largely personal. In October 2016, Âoun became the President of Lebanon, finally realizing his long-held dream.

Coups for the Nation: Iraq (BPR)

The first successful modern coup in the Arab world occurred in 1936, when Brigadier Bakr Sidqi and his followers shot their way to power in newly independent Iraq, hoping to end the political instability and parliamentary weakness that marked King Faisal's post-independence rule.[189] A rival faction assassinated Sidqi the next year, setting in motion a pattern of coup after coup. The organizers justified their actions through the flimsiest of complaints ("failure to support the revolt in Palestine," for example), and thus the various military factions went to war jockeying for national power.[190] General Nuri al-Said emerged from the coup turmoil as foreign and prime minister, taking on considerable powers, and entering into negotiations with both British and Nazi representatives during World War II to choose the best partner for a favorable postwar outcome.[191] An April 1941 coup interrupted al-Said's influence when a group of pro-Nazi officers led by General Rachid 'Ali al-Kailani took power, thus giving Britain a reason to invade the country, with support from General al-Said, who clearly wanted his job back.[192] While the motives were complex, some of the plotters were anti-British and hoped that Nazi Germany would defeat Britain and thus end British imperialism.

However, the British succeeded in driving al-Kailani from Baghdad and restored Nuri al-Said to the premiership.

Iraq's next coup occurred in July 1958 launched by General Abdel Kerim Qasim and his follower against King Feisal II's Hashemite monarchy. This was due partly because the officers, largely from middle-class backgrounds, wanted to terminate an upper class-dominated regime in favor of something closer to their own status.[193] The rebels may have killed Feisal because the soldiers did not want him to become the rallying point for resistance to the new republican regime.[194] Coup after coup attempt followed; four alone in 1958, and a July 1959 army mutiny in Kirkuk that led to swift repression of Iraq's communists, who were believed to have been behind it. In February 1963, Baathist operatives finally succeeded in executing Qasim after he survived an early assassination attempt by a rebel group of officers, including Saddam Hussein, who peppered his Chevrolet sedan with bullets.[195] General 'abd as-Salam Arif launched another coup against Iraqi Ba'ath leaders in November 1963 because of the poor Iraqi military performance against Kurdish insurgency,[196] which deposed General Abdel Rahman Arif, the brother of one of the 1963 plotters. There was another failed coup effort in 1965, led by pro-Nasserist Brigadier Aref Abdul Razzaq, who snuck back into Iraq in 1966 after the regime exiled him, to try yet another coup. The coup plotters finally succeeded in July 1968 when General Ahmed Hassan al-Bakr ousted President Arif, but in June 1973, Colonel Nazem al-Kazzar, the director of internal security, attempted to overthrow the Hassan al-Bakr regime (Saddam Hussein was then vice president). However, Saddam foiled the plot and ordered the execution of al-Kazzar and his followers. Saddam Hussein then seized power and quickly liquidated most of his rivals in a televised trial. He was apparently not thorough enough, as he faced several coup attempts from his officers, which may have been a function of Saddam's demilitarization of the Ba'th Revolutionary Command Council (RCC) between 1968 and 1986. Saddam replaced most of the military members of the RCC with loyalists, including a number of Shi'a and Kurdish party members. By 1986, military members of the RCC had almost disappeared.[197] The consequences of Saddam Hussein's communal coup-proofing strategy became more apparent only after Saddam was toppled by the US in 2003. As Kiyani finds, the dissolution of those forces led to those forces committing extreme civil violence and partnering with *Daesh* because they had become so dependent on the communal rent that Saddam paid for their loyalty.[198] Coups also occurred because of military dismay over the bumbled 1990–91 Kuwaiti invasion, including an effort in 1992 by a Republican Guard brigade that Saddam's internal security forces appeared to have interrupted in its first stages.[199]

While the US-led invasion of 2003 ended Saddam's reign, it did not end coup politics in Iraq. In 2014, embattled Prime Minister Nuri Kamel al-Maliki deployed Iraqi forces around Baghdad after Iraq's Parliament elected an ethic Kurd and former communist Fuad Masoum, as president. Maliki, who, like Saddam, kept his military under tight reins, apparently ordered them to mobilize, fearing that Masoum would not reappoint Malaki to a third term.[200] However, after a day of uncertainty, Maliki issued this command to his generals, "Prime Minister Maliki urges commanders, officers, and individuals to stay away from the political crisis and to commit to their military and security duties and tasks to protect the country, and not to intervene in this crisis. Leave this issue to the people, politicians and justice."[201] Whatever other flaws Maliki may have had, the statement revealed that coups were not an answer for Iraq's troubled political system, no matter what reason might have justified them.

Coups "For the Nation:" Morocco (LM)

Morocco has a tradition of military professionalism, bolstered by its Berber troops, who had joined the military before independence and carried their professionalism into Moroccan military ranks[202] The military operates a professional war college (the Royal College of High Military Studies), modern equipment, and emphasizes professional norms.[203] The Royal College curriculum and faculty are quite comparable to war colleges in the US.[204] Morocco's military operate modern equipment, including French and American-made combat aircraft.[205]

Morocco's armed forces initially pledged their loyalty to King Hassan II, which the crown needed during the turbulent 1960s, but by 1971, senior officers revolted and twice attempted to assassinate Hassan.[206] He survived both attempts and the plotters either went to prison or to the gallows.[207] Military greed, fueled by royal favoritism, trumped military loyalty as the soldiers sought even more power and wealth.[208] Howe claims that military anger over the corruption of key ministers, and possibly Nasserite sympathies, triggered the coup attempts.[209] Both Willis and Damis reaches a similar conclusion, noting the reported military revulsion at official corruption (high government officials taking bribes from foreign firms for hotel contracts and secret Swiss bank accounts).[210] There was a certain irony that some of the very officers who plotted the first coup, including General Mohammed Medbouh, had become wealthy themselves through royal favors before the coup attempt. General Mohamed Oufkir, the leader of the second plot, may also have been concerned about corruption, though he may also have feared that the King planned to kill him.[211] Thus, while there were elements of both professionalism and rent-seeking motives for these coup efforts, the military seems to have acted more out of professional concerns about the direction of the country.

MIDDLE EAST COUPS "WITH A LITTLE HELP FROM OUR FRIENDS"

"With a Little Help from Our Friends:" Syria (BPR)

The US reportedly assisted several coup attempts in Syria. The first occurred in March 1949 as two US CIA operatives worked with Military Chief of Staff Husni Zaʻim to overthrow the Shukri Quwatli regime because of its alleged pro-Soviet leanings and its refusal to allow the then-Saudi Arabian/American oil company ARAMCO to build a pipeline terminus in Syria.[212] The CIA role is disputed, and evidence indicates that while the agency may have assisted, it was Zaʻim himself who took the initiative.[213] The second effort took place in August 1957, as American CIA agents again tried to topple the Quwatli regime in Syria, apparently getting an agreement from former President Adib Shishakli to lead the coup.[214] The project, code-named "Operation Straggle," was intended to support the Syrian Social Nationalist Party. It failed, and the CIA and British intelligence partnered with another plot, the Preferred Plan, designed to foment border incidents.[215] Both plans failed, as the Syrian security apparatus quickly discovered the first plot, purged senior army ranks of any suspects, and expelled three US Embassy staff members. There is evidence that Jordan and Turkey, concerned about the growing Soviet influence in Syria, cooperated in the coup effort.[216] The net effect of the coup effort was not only to increase enmity between the US and Damascus, but also to increase the influence of Moscow as Syria's leaders had even more reason to need Soviet assistance, given the threats from the US and their neighbors.

"With a Little Help from Our Friends:" Yemen (BPR)

The 1962 coup also had "a little help from our friends," in that Egypt's Nasser actively encouraged the plotters in an effort to woo a new republican Yemen into his imagined "United Arab Republic."[217] The outside interference would continue into the late 1970s, as the former Soviet Union got into a dispute over foreign policy between Rubayi Ali, the president, and Hafez Ismail, the leader of the National Front, Yemen's only political party. In a twist of events suitable for a movie plot, in June 1978 an agent from Ismail brought a briefcase supposedly containing papers asking for North Yemen's president Ahmad al-Ghashmi's support into a meeting with Al-Ghashmi. The agent detonated the bomb inside the briefcase once he got into al-Ghashmi's office, killing both. Ismail, who had Soviet backing, blamed president Rubayi for the assassination, and got him dismissed.[218] However, Rubayi launched a countercoup, using loyal military units to arrest Ismail and his associates, but Ismaili loyalists launched yet another countercoup by attacking the presidential palace. Rubayi and some of his colleagues met the usual fate for Yemeni presidents in those turbulent days—the Ismail forces executed them, an act that triggered yet another coup attempt by Rubayi's troops. However, Cuban troops flown in from Ethiopia prevented a repeat performance.[219] In July 1978, Major Ali Abdullah Saleh assumed the presidency, escaping an assassination attempt in September and yet another coup attempt the next month when four military units in Sana'a tried to take advantage of his absence from the country, but a loyal military unit thwarted their efforts. In November the firing squads again took their toll with nine officers and twelve civilians going against the wall, though outside sources reported over a hundred executions and more than seven thousand arrests.[220]

Yemen's armed forces largely broke apart during the anti-Saleh movement starting in 2011 but some units that remained loyal to Saleh were reportedly ready to remove his successor, 'abd Rabbo Mansour Hadi.[221] As Hadi removed some senior officers seen as too loyal to Saleh, the rumored coup attempt might have been an effort to restore previous perks for those officers. Saleh himself switched sides twice, once shifting loyalty to the Houthi and then abandoning them, a decision that cost Saleh his life in December 2017, from an al-Houthi attack on his car. After Saleh's death, his loyalists chose to realign with the surviving Hadi regime, while maintaining some autonomy. Hadi institutionalized the Southern Transitional Council forces, which got support from by Saudi Arabia and the UAE, leaving a polyglot national military in place of the former state armed forces. Thus, Yemen has several militaries, all relying on informal structures and still fueled by patronage, though arranged through local warlords and tribal leaders.[222] But most of the fighting in Yemen now is done by either the Houthi or by foreign militaries, along with militias that are the remnants of Yemen's military. It is hard to imagine a unified Yemeni military again, as it is hard to imagine a unified Yemen.[223] Hadi himself appeared to have only political spin left to cover up his failure to govern Yemen from his perch in Saudi Arabia, in an interview, he claimed that Yemen has nearly restored a lot of its security and stability, adding "that does not mean risk has totally ended. Armed groups, especially those are supported from external sides, still make a threat against Yemen's stability. Any party has weapons must realize that they will never be stronger than the State, even if they thought it is weak. Hadi also stressed that 'Yemen can be patient, exercises caution and avoid using force since the victims from any party will be Yemenis.'"[224]

"With a Little Help from My Friends": Iran (FD)

Iran has a history of coups with outside assistance. In 1921, Reza Khan, with some help from the British, seized power over the failing Qajar Dynasty, and established the Pahlavi Dynasty in its place.[225] Iran's politically powerful military dominated the state security forces under the reign of Shah Mohammad Reza Pahlavi (1941–1979). The Shah had political use of the military, as the line of command went from the Shah directly to the army, which also controlled SAVAK (*Sazman-I Ettela'at va Amniyat-I Keshwar*, or State Organization for Intelligence and Security). The director of SAVAK and its officers and enlisted were from the army, as were the commanders of the gendarmerie and the national police.[226] When Mohammad Mosaddeq won the post of prime minister in April 1951, he tried to curb the power of those forces partly by reducing their budget.[227] When Mosaddeq nationalized Iran's petroleum industry after unsuccessfully trying to get Britain to increase oil prices, the United States Central Intelligence Agency and British MI-5 worked with elements of the Iranian armed forces to engineer Mosaddeq's ouster in August 1953.[228] Britain played a role, using paid Iranian operatives to pose as Communists, threatening anyone who opposed Mosaddeq, and, additionally, bought off some members of the Iranian military. Mosaddeq aided his ultimate demise by rigging elections to suspend Parliament.[229] After Mosaddeq retaliated by dismissing Parliament the army finally moved against him.[230]

The Shah retook the Iranian reins of power and held them until 1979, when the 1953 coup became one of the justifications used by Ayatollah Ruhollah Khomeini to mobilize a revolution against the Shah, very much to the detriment of US policy for decades to come. After Khomeini took power, the Carter administration contemplated the use of the Iranian military to embark on a coup. Carter sent American general Robert Huyser to instruct Iranian military leaders to support the Shapour Bakhtiar regime that had replaced the Shah's rule against Ayatollah Ruhollah Khomeini, but the Shah departed the country and Khomeini arrived before the plotters finalized their plans.[231] The Shah had lost whatever legitimacy he once had with the armed forces as his increasingly weak and paranoid ruling style severed military support from the regime, and the soldiers could hardly resist the massive pro-Khomeini crowds, which were largely peaceful.[232]

SYNTHESIZING THE REASONS

Coups "for the nation" are the primary reason for military power takeovers. Soldiers who were fed up with what they saw as incompetent, venal, and self-serving regimes decided to terminate them. Their primary complaint was that the old regime failed the country militarily, partly because of embedded regime corruption and misrule that indirectly affected its armed forces. The second reason for coups reflected ethnic and economic class differences in the country, where the military either took over to advance their own ethnic or economic interests (e.g., Syria and Iraq), or to prevent another group from exercising political influence (Islamists, communists, or minority religious groups, for examples). This reason does overlap with coups "for the nation," as sometimes the coup plotters claimed that their ethnic or religious group was better at governing the nation than was the group in power. Both the Turkish and Egyptian armies justified their respective coups against Islamist parties because they argued that their nationalist visions were better for their countries than was religiously inspired rule. It must also be said that these findings do not nullify the desire for power that is often a secondary motive behind coups. As noted in chapter 4, the Egyptian armed forces enjoy considerable economic benefits from their proximity to state power, and while the Turkish military does not have comparable economic interests, they do benefit from generous retirement and other benefits.

Coups are much more likely to occur in bully republics, which is hardly surprising, given their nature. The orientation of the bully state does not seem to matter, as coups occurred in both single party and personalist bully states. The only two coups attempted in liberal monarchies failed, partly because both monarchies rely on Islamic identity (the kings of Morocco and Jordan both claim descendance from the Prophet).[233] But they most likely also failed because not enough of the military accepted the reasons for the coup efforts, and thus retained their loyalty to the throne.

MIDDLE EASTERN COUP PROOFING

The violent military coup is becoming more of a rarity in the region for a number of reasons. First, where democracy has taken root, coups are much more unlikely—there has never been serious talk of a coup in Israel. And in Freedom House's list of "partly free" countries, coups were not attempted in Morocco, Kuwait, Lebanon, and Tunisia after those countries improved the quality of governance and moved into Freedom House's "partly free" list (and, for Tunisia, gaining "free" status in 2015, but losing it in 2022). This reflects a global trend that as democratization increases, the likelihood of military coups declines.[234] But the primary reason that coups are less common in the Middle East is that many autocratic regimes have found methods to coup-proof their regimes.

In nondemocratic Middle East countries, regimes have adopted a variety of strategies to make themselves less vulnerable to coups, dismissing officers of questionable loyalty, appointing loyalists, stationing troops far from the capital, or paying military rent, to name just a few examples. As Quinlivan finds, the swiftest mechanism for coup-proofing is simply to fire officers suspected of political ambitions.[235] Thus, Saddam Hussein, Gamal Abdul Nasser, and Hafiz al-'Asad, King Hassan of Morocco, and others cleaned out the ranks of their militaries, often leaving loyalists in the place of professionals, as noted above.

The flip side of relying on an alternative security force is that even rival security units may choose to attempt overthrows of national leadership should that leadership not meet their expectations. Alternatively, the counterbalancing forces may place their trust in the family but not the principal head-of-state family member. Heads of state in Egypt, Syria, Yemen, Libya, and Tunisia created special forces or "counterterrorism units," which were assigned to spy on the army.[236] In Iran, the post-1979 clerical regime replaced existing members of the armed forces with officers with family ties to clerical leaders, though as Talmadge notes, "The result was an officer corps supportive of the new regime, but even more poorly situated than its predecessor to handle the challenges of interstate war."[237] Muamar Qaddafi used similar methods, first creating the "Revolutionary Committees" and later "Deterrence Battalions" as praetorian units designed specifically to prevent coups.[238] Libya's Muamar Qaddafi created alternative militias, including the People's Militia and the Revolutionary Guard, the former with more than forty thousand members and the latter with around thirty thousand.[239] Qaddafi favored these forces over his regular military and sometimes hired his relatives to command them.[240] Qaddafi also relied on his projections of charisma to extend his rule, increasingly relying on opera-like uniforms and plastic surgery to enhance his appearance as he aged.[241]

In addition, where other methods may fall short, the power of money is another tool to purchase loyalty, as I note above. Wealthy Arabian Gulf countries commonly pay their armed forces lucrative salaries. In Saudi Arabia, rival princes control various military forces, assuring that patronage money flows readily.[242] Mohammed Reza Pahlavi regularly sent royal gifts to his military commanders, always reminding them that the return on those presents was military loyalty.[243] But as noted earlier, rent-seeking, when done by communal coup-proofing, can lead to increased violence against civilians should those forces lose access to their booty after regime change.

Preferences for coup-proofing can also be partially explained by regime type. For example, rent-seeking regimes are more likely to fragment their security forces than are other non-democratic regime types as they charge parallel military units to monitor each other. This is partly because such regimes lack formal political institutions and monitoring ability, whereas traditional monarchies rely more on loyalties and are thus more likely to staff their militaries with loyal tribe members. Party-based regimes are more likely to rely on existing institutions for coup-proofing.[244] Thus, Saddam Hussein relied more on the creation of a parallel force, the Republican Guards, while the Syrian 'Asad regime based its coup-proofing more on Ba'th Party oversight. The monarchies in the Arabian Gulf tended to populate top military positions from loyal tribes and family members.

Coup-proofing has its limits though, as it may build loyalty to the *regime* rather than the *incumbent*. If the regime chooses only the top officers for loyalty, that may not stop defections of lower-ranking officers; as happened during the Syrian civil war.[245] Moreover, coup-proofing through increasing the military budget may satisfy *combat* officers, but not *elite* officers who, unlike their combat brethren, can be members of the authoritarian ruling coalition. High military spending may deter elite officers from coups; but for combat officers who benefit from high *social* spending, political reforms may be better at keeping them in the barracks than more military money.[246] Finally, Albrecht finds that coup-proofing is only partly successful in preventing coups, and that potential coup plotters adapt to coup-proofing measures.[247]

When the result of a coup is a bloody civil war of the kind that wracked Algeria in the 1990s, the military rulers may ultimately compromise with the very factions that they used to justify the coup. General Liamine Zeroual, who assumed the presidency in 1994 (and won an election to the post in 1995), began a process to include the FIS in order to split it from its more violent and radical Islamist rival, the Armed Islamist Group (GIA), a policy continued by Zeroual's successor, Abdelaziz Bouteflika.[248] In April 2019, the chief of the Algerian military removed the ill Bouteflika as public opposition to his presidential re-appointment grew, replacing him with Senate head Abdelkader Bensalah, and thus continuing the pattern of military-selected Algerian presidents.

A Turkish court under the influence of President Erdoğan may have found another way to prevent military coups: punish those responsible for previous coups, even if they happened over thirty years previously. In April 2012, the Twelfth High Criminal Court in Ankara opened a trial of two of the aging generals who orchestrated the 1980 coup, Kenan Evren, chief of staff, and Tahsin Şahinkaya, then head of the Turkish Air Force. The prosecutors, perhaps mindful that the 1980 coup was publicly popular because it ended a period of domestic violence, accused the coup perpetuators of not only the coup, but of instigating the violence through massacres of both left-wing and Alevi demonstrators prior to the coup.[249]

Despite the conspiratorial nature of the charges, the message was that the post-Atatürk Turkish state would reach into the "deep" part of that state to remind the military that coups would never go unpunished should they happen in the future.[250] And, just to make sure that the military got the message, in mid-April 2012 Turkish prosecutors ordered the arrests of four retired generals and charged them with the "semi-coup" of 1997, which terminated the governing coalition that included the Islamist-related Welfare Party. At the time of the arrests, Foreign Minister Ahmet Davutoglü stated that the point was to ensure that Turkey would not experience any more coups.[251] However, some units of the Turkish armed forces did attempt a coup in July 2016, which was probably a desperate effort by the engaged units to avoid the government purging them because of alleged ties to the Gülen movement. It was noteworthy, though, because Turkey's senior officers seemed to learn from earlier coup-proofing efforts and refused to join the putsch effort. As Kandil argues, had the corporate interests of the Turkish military been at stake, more might have joined the failed effort, but the Turkish military leadership instead opposed the coup attempt.[252] The limited participation, though, did not stop further coup-proofing measures, however. The Erdoğan regime dismantled the Turkish Armed Forces command system, removing them from the chief of staff's jurisdiction to that of the Ministry of Defense and the Ministry of Interior, and added a new security unit that reported directly to the president.[253] But after a failed coup in 2016 attempted by some military units, the Islamist-oriented ruling AK Party cleaned out the military senior ranks, jailing or dismissing thousands of officers, fearful that the military was attempting to thwart the AKP's challenge to the *laïcité* policies of Kemal Atatürk, which the army had pledged to uphold. In 2018, additional changes further marginalized the Turkish armed forces after President Recip Tayyip Erdoğan won a new presidential term and a majority coalition in the Turkish Parliament.[254]

Perhaps ironically, a decision by a regime vulnerable to coups to send its armed forces into interstate war is also a coup-proofing method. Piplani and Talmadge employ a large data set study that finds that as interstate war actually reduces coup risks. Specifically, regimes that were engaged in an interstate war lasting longer than a year were more likely to remain in power than otherwise would have been the case.[255] There is evidence that Jordan's King Hussein's decision to intervene in the 1967 Arab-Israeli war was partly motivated by his fear of a coup from some of his pro-Nasser officers, who had first tried to unseat the King in 1956.[256] And there is reason to believe that some of Nasser's war decisions were at least partially based on coup-proofing. Gat argued that, "Nasser had always preferred a weak and highly politicized army preoccupied with in-fighting that would pose little or no threat to his regime. Nasser's decision to send Egyptian forces into Sinai was a political one, which the armed forces were unable to execute."[257] The alternative view, though, is that if Nasser purposely sent his military off to a war, he knew they were likely to lose, he might be even more vulnerable to a coup.

Coup-proofing has been a strategy of certain outside powers, though different outside powers have produced different results. Casey notes that no Soviet-backed regime fell to a military coup, partly because the Soviet assistance included the formation of political commissars and security services directly embedded into the client's armed forces.[258] But Western-supported regimes reflected the ambivalence of those countries toward their client states, as they were unwilling to take extraordinary measures to coup-proof autocrats.[259] So, while the Soviets protected regimes in Egypt, Algeria, Iraq after 1958, and Syria, US-backed regimes in Turkey, Morocco, and Jordan either faced a coup or at least an attempted coup.

But the US and the European Union have also employed measures to make coups less likely. Both the US Congress and the European Union adopted measures to punish coup efforts, thus reducing the incentives for military officers to execute coups.[260] If a military overthrows a regime and then is denied military weapons by either the US or a member of the EU, then the choices for weaponry become narrower. But such restrictions can run afoul of weapons producers and have produced mixed results. The US did cut off arms supplies to Sudan after its army overthrew the government in October 2021, but those supplies were very small in value. The US also briefly suspended F-16 sales to Egypt after the 2013 "coup," but those sales were quickly restored. Several select examples of Middle East coup-proofing follow.

Egypt (BPR)

Egyptian President Nasser quickly coup-proofed his military after his own 1952 takeover, purging or reassigning thousands of officers considered potentially disloyal.[261] Nasser also had his army chief of staff, 'abd al-Hakim Amir, create the Office of the Commander-in-Chief for Political Guidance whose official responsibility, issuing political guidance to the military, masked its real purpose, monitoring suspicious activities.[262] Egypt's leaders lavishly funded military economic projects (see chapter 4) hoping that the senior military would be satisfied with the rents from commercial practices and thus less interested in a political takeover.

Egyptian President Mubarak removed several suspect officers, including Minister of Defense Abdel Halim Abu Ghazala. His successor, Abdel Fattah al-Sisi, having come to power in a coup himself, has fired or jailed a number of senior officers who challenged his presidency.[263] Even as he consolidated his power, Sisi continued his purge of senior military and civilians, removing 130 since 2017, including the army chief of staff, firing even those like Mohamed Farid Hegazi, the chief of staff of the armed forces, and Mamdouh Shahin, who had joined Sisi in the 2013 government overthrow. As Al-Shamahi notes, "The persistent shake-ups have ensured that few figures in the military and intelligence have the ability to build up a power base that could potentially threaten el-Sisi in the future."[264] Partly to protect the executive, The Egyptian Directorate of Military Intelligence exists partly to watch the rest of the military for signs of disloyalty.[265]

Yemen (BPR)

Yemen's president Abed Rabbo Mansour Hadi, who replaced Abulazziz Saleh in 2012, quickly purged Yemen's military of leaders who were loyal to Saleh, fearing that they might launch a coup to re-install him. Thus, General Mohammed Saleh al-Ahmar, the head of the Air Force (and Saleh-s half-brother) and General Tariq Mohammed Abdullah Saleh, Saleh's nephew, got walking papers only weeks after Hadi took the presidential oath of office.[266] But other Saleh relatives remained in high places, as brigadier general Ahmed al-Saleh, the former president's oldest son, remained in command of the Yemeni Republican Guards though under orders from General Mohsen through President Hadi to restructure his units to make them more professional.[267] Qatar's Crown Prince Hamad ibn Khalifa al-Thani overthrew his father in 1995 to assume the Emirship, and a counter-coup failed when the former Emir failed to show up at the airport. Earlier, Qatari security arrested over seventy military officers in 1983 and charged them with orchestrating a Libyan-supported coup,[268] and reports surfaced of Qatari coup attempt in 2009, led by General Hamad bin-Al-Attayah, this time supported by Saudi Arabia.[269] However, because most Arabian Gulf ruling families have deeply penetrated their small militaries by installing family members as military leaders, and because most Gulf leaders keep their armed forces well supplied with arms and training, coups in those countries are very rare there. Turkish Prime Ministers fired coup-advocating Generals Talat Aydemir in 1962 and Cemal Tural in 1969.[270]

Coup-proofing strategies also include actions taken by coup-fearing regimes to limit the very military capabilities that enhance military effectiveness. Talmadge argues that such essential military skills as training and decentralized command communications can also build coup-making abilities, so insecure regimes restrict military training and centralize military communications, which shows just a few of several coup-proofing measures that can result in combat failure.[271] Other coup-proofing mechanisms involved the dispersion of military power though injecting militaries with political loyalists, from the ruler's tribe, or community, for examples. In Saudi Arabia, founding monarch Abdul-Aziz al-Saud forged links to almost all major tribes, often through marriage so that national loyalty extended from the seat of government to tribal groups.[272] Saudi Arabian military leaders stationed military units in the periphery of the country to keep them away from Riyadh and the Kingdom supplied them with weapons from different national suppliers to limit operational coordination against the regime.[273] Herzog noted that in Saudi Arabia, "The military was perceived as the most dangerous section of the new bureaucratic stratum, but the peril of a takeover was contained through institutional and geographic fragmentation of the armed forces, which were moreover shot through with dozens of princely officers. A coup attempt in 1969 did not get far."[274] After that failed coup, Saudi Arabian authorities arrested hundreds of officers, especially from the Royal Saudi Arabian Air Force. Unlike previous military purges that resulted in jailing and executions, the incarcerated officers were mostly released, as the monarchy shifted tactics to buy-offs.[275] During the Yemeni war of the 1960s, the Saudi royal family feared, correctly, that some Saudi Arabian military units were sympathetic to Egypt's Nasser. They suffered the defection of Saudi Arabian air force pilots then, resulting in the grounding of the Saudi air force for a time.[276] Saudi Arabian leadership has transferred oil revenues into payments for military fealty,[277] a practice they repeated in 2011; the Crown gave each member of the Saudi Arabian military a promotion and a pay increase in 2011, as concerns about the spread of the Arab Spring grew in Riyadh.[278] As Saudi Arabia's military enjoys a large military budget and a relatively free hand in its fight in Yemen, it is likely to remain loyal to the Saudi regime. Such loyalty is also reinforced by the short leashes that the Crown Prince, Mohammed bin Salman, gives to his generals.[279] Yet the danger of military fatigue remained, as the Saudi Arabian military found itself fighting multiple opponents, and increasingly isolated, as its former partner, the UAE, announced that it was departing the fight.[280]

Syria (BPR)

Hafiz al-'Asad maneuvered other groups in Syria out of the way after the 1969 Ba'th coup to assure that his minority 'Alawi group has dominant status in Syrian political space.[281] 'Asad used several tools to accomplish the task, including establishing parallel security forces to safeguard his regime. The Syrian security services include the General Intelligence Directorate, the Political Security Directorate, the Air Force Intelligence Service, and the Military Intelligence Service (*Mukhabarat*). The latter two institutions report to the Ministry of Defense, thus pairing the military and the non-military security services to share domestic intelligence information and to partner in policing internal security matters. They also can, and sometimes do, police each other. For example, getting the army back to the barracks after its 1954 coup required the separation of the security forces from the army, and their incorporation into the Ministry of Defense, to create a counterweight to the military.[282] Hafiz al-'Asad increased the power of this force after his accession to power, using it partly as a counterweight to the regular army then commanded by his brother, Rifat. Hafiz made sure that the paramilitary force came equipped with enough firepower to challenge the conventional army, and, as a further measure to prevent army coups, the paramilitary force was the only force permitted within the capital.[283] Despite this move, units loyal to Ri'fat al-'Asad may have picked him over his brother in a family dispute that possibly spawned a coup attempt against Hafiz.[284]

'Asad may have had such a deep fear of coups that even the creation of a parallel security service was not enough coup protection. There is good evidence that 'Asad kept the regular military weak and divided, and not only keeping the 'Alawi officers in top positions, but also allowing the military equipment and conditions to deteriorate. The Syrian military operates obsolete Russian equipment, for the most part, which is subject to frequent breakdowns, and military education is sparse, so many Sunni Syrian officers suspect that this is simply coup proofing.[285] That allowed Hafez 'Asad to rule post-coup until his 2000 death, though, the personal charisma he tried to project may also have contributed to his long tenure.[286] His son Bashar al-'Asad, added to the list of Syrian state-sponsored militias when the regime created the National Defence Force (NDF), which first publicly appeared in 2013 to augment the Syrian military in fighting for the regime in the Syrian civil war. The NDF had only loose ties to the 'Asad regime, as it was composed of local tribe members, slackly organized, and funded partly by businesspeople loyal to the regime.[287]

Hafiz 'Asad created "Defense Companies" commanded by his brother Ri'fat that performed similar functions, and again their loyalty was to the ruler rather than to the state. Syria's complex security architecture reflected deep concerns about coup prevention; Hafez 'Asad also created multiple agencies to oversee each, thus before the 2011 anti-regime uprising, there were four security force branches: Military Intelligence and Air Force Intelligence under the Defense Ministry, the Political Security Directorate under the Ministry of Interior, and the General Intelligence Directorate, which had no ministry affiliation. After the July 2012 bombing that killed four top regime leaders, Bashar Al-'Asad consolidated control of the security forces, giving more authority to Military Intelligence, the *Shubat al-Mukhabarat al-Askariyya*, shortened to *Mukhabarat*. There is growing evidence that the ʿAsad regime is using the feared *Shabiha*, ʿAlawi criminal gangs who appear to target Sunnis.[288]

The creation of counterbalancing forces, like republican guards, presidential guards, interior forces, or even militia groups, is another coup-proofing method. De Bruin's masterful study of coup prevention through counterbalancing demonstrates that it decreases the risk of coups by presenting incentives to alternative forces to resist the coup.[289] Thus, rulers like Saddam Hussein and Abdul Aziz Al-Saud created republican or national guards to police not only internal parts of the country but also, where necessary, the national military. While Saddam's Baʿthist predecessors employed coup-proofing measures, Saddam built upon them when he created his "Popular Army" in 1970, as a counterweight to the regular Iraqi military.[290]

Kiyani adds texture to the parallel military coup-proofing strategies by noting that the likelihood of loyalty or defection may depend on the type of communal structure of the military. She states that

> Communal coup proofing is divided into three types: a-communal, communal, and partial-communal. Under a-communal coup proofing strategy, no communal group is honored in the security apparatus and the armed force structure reflects the demographic structure of society. In contrast, under a communal coup proofing strategy the leader recruits most of the security apparatus personnel from trusted communities and aims to unite the political and military elites, such as in Syria under Hafiz al Assad or Bashar al Assad. In a partial communal coup proofing strategy, a small portion of security apparatus is based on communal ties, as in Yemen under President Ali Abdullah Saleh. Among these types, a communal coup proofing strategy increases the cost of defection.[291]

PACTED TRANSITIONS AND THE ARMED FORCES

The military may choose remedies beyond a coup to address their political disagreements with the existing government. Such remedies might include a "pacted transition," a bargain between soldiers and the potential new rulers and parties, seeking to replace the previous order. Such pacts usually take the form of an exchange of pledges: the old elite depart peacefully as its guardians promise to eschew violence and to respect rights as negotiated. Note O'Donnell and Schmitter:

> The basis of an extrication pact might well be the following: in exchange for restoring basic individual rights and tolerating some civic contestation over policy, the leader obtains an agreement from notables and/or moderate opponents

that they will neither resort to disruption or violence, nor seek sanctions against military officers for "excesses" committed under the aegis of the authoritarian regime.[292]

In countries with low institutionalization and high politicization, the military may adopt Stepan's "moderator" model of civil-military relations.[293] Here the military becomes a referee in the political arena, called upon to moderate political activity, while not necessarily directing political changes. The model is not dependent on a formal set of controls, but rather a set of norms that both civilians and the armed forces may tacitly agree upon.[294]

Authoritarian regimes try to maintain military loyalty through pacting, offering the officers a *protection pact* emphasizing shared threats, or a *provision pact* where the regime buys off the military in exchange for its fealty.[295] Such payments are either direct, or indirect, which can involve allowing the military to take bribes,[296] or putting them in positions to extract side-payments in places where they are based. Unsurprisingly such transitions often result in flawed democracies, with weak institutions, less accountable public officials, and apathetic citizens.[297]

When popular unrest grows beyond small groups to include a significant percentage of the total population, military activism in support of the rulers can obviously cast the military in a negative public light. Thus, the military sometimes has to walk a fine line between using force to suppress public uprisings or either sitting silently on the sidelines or in some instances joining the protests. The Indonesian military had previously intervened to protect President Suharto, who then used the army's *Sekretariat Bersama Golongang Karya* as a political platform, turning it into a powerful platform for his rule.[298] As his regime tottered under widespread public protest, Suharto did not call up the military to rescue him—the armed forces themselves were not predisposed to do so had he called—and thus he resigned in May 1998. Abdurrahman Wahid, who challenged the military on several fronts, won the subsequent election so unsurprisingly, when Wahid asked the military to intervene to save his own regime, it refused. As a result, Wahid lost out to new president Megawati Sukarnoputri, who quickly forged an alliance with the very military who had ousted Megawati's dictatorial father, Sukarno decades earlier.[299]

In both South Korea and Indonesia, angry protests against autocrats forced the military in those countries to choose between the ruler and the street, and they chose the latter, allowing for elections (the first South Korean elected president was a general, but those following him have been civilians). Indonesia's generals took less than a year to schedule elections and allow the political return of the previously banned Islamist parties.[300] Both countries are now largely free of military political influence and Freedom House ranks

South Korea as "free" and Indonesia "partly free" as of 2022. The February 1986 decision by key Filipino generals to withdraw support from President Ferdinand Marcos and pact with the political opposition came as both the Catholic Church and the United States withheld their support for the dictator after evidence of electoral fraud became apparent.[301] The Philippine military has remained largely outside of political space since that time, though it disliked the abrogation of the US-Philippines basing agreement and the "People Power II" movement of Joseph Estrada's presidency.[302]

In these cases, as elsewhere in transitioning countries, the military may simply want to distance themselves from the old autocracy, because:

> Many military officers would prefer to disassociate themselves from the authoritarian legacy. The failed policies and immoral practices of military governments in South America directly harmed the military institutions themselves. Military incompetence, self-aggrandizement, and repression while in office contributed not only to an unprecedented repudiation of the profession by civil society but also to a crisis of identity among many in the officer corps as well.[303]

Military officers may conclude that they lack sufficient skills to manage a troubled political and economic system. Therefore, instead of opting for direct military rule, military officers are more likely to indicate where their red lines lay, for instance, no penalties for previous military misbehavior, no empowering of groups that the military thinks are deleterious to their vision of "national interests," and an agreed-upon share of the national budget. Thus, Chilean president Agusto Pinochet demanded a high price for transition: permanent office for military chiefs, protection of the "prestige of the military," and continuing amnesty covering possible political crimes committed in the years 1973 to 1978, among other items.[304]

The "Velvet Shove"

As militaries consider coup alternatives, they may decide to simply refuse to support an embattled government, or by offering to let the governors leave the capital (or the country). Officers either publicly or privately notify the political leadership that the soldiers will march on the palace, mobilize popular forces, or simply withhold cooperation should the regime not get the appropriate message. Sometimes this may take nothing more than a phone call to the presidential quarters, to announce that military has ended its regime support. This was the situation in Ecuador in January 2000 when a coalition of lower-income indigenous nationalities massed in Quito in opposition to the Jamil Mahuad presidency. Counter to the crowd's expectations, the military supported them, with Mahuad fleeing the country after the military chief of staff demanded his resignation.³⁰⁵ The head of Indonesia's military, General Wiranto, decided to cease support for President Suharto in 1998 after public impatience with a severe economic climate.³⁰⁶ In December 1989, Romanian dictator Nicolae Ceausescu's military refused to protect him from angry demonstrators, and soldiers ushered in those demonstrators to Ceausescu's palace, while shooting at his security police who were trying to protect him. While the end was not really "velvet" as a military firing squad dispatched both Ceausescu and his wife, the army pushed him out first, siding with his opponents.³⁰⁷

Pacted Transitions in the Middle East

As noted earlier, the Middle East lags behind most of the world in democratic governance. Consequently, short of engineering coups, the militaries in those countries had little experience in political transitions to democracy before 2011. Yet as the "Arab Spring" movements evolved, the armed forces in countries faced with political protest movements had to decide whether to protect the regime, side with the protesters, or sit on the fence. This section concentrates on the comparative military role of political transition relative to other state actors in the Middle East. Those roles range from the armed forces taking the lead in political transitions to being a relatively silent bystander as the parade of political change marches by them.

The Velvet Shove: Tunisia

Tunisia's founding president, Habib Bourguiba envisioned Tunisia as a modern Western-style country and thus marginalized his military to keep them out of politics.³⁰⁸ Bourguiba favored the Tunisian gendarmerie, while limiting military power, keeping generals out of civilian positions, and restricting the military budget.³⁰⁹ Bourguiba had reason to fear his army, as eight military officers (including one of his bodyguards tried to assassinate on his life in December 1962.³¹⁰ When Islamists and other political groups began to threaten his rule, Bourguiba initially used his military against the demonstrations, causing considerable resentment among its leadership.³¹¹ The military pushed back on further demands that it suppress political demonstrations, resulting in military budget cutbacks and military frustration that its military was no match for the revolutionary Libyan military next door.³¹² Thus, Bourguiba turned to former military general Zine al-Abidine Ben 'Ali in 1986 to power up the Interior Ministry with its own forces, which Ben 'Ali used effectively after assuming power in 1988.³¹³ Ben 'Ali, like his predecessor Bourguiba, had feared that Tunisia's armed forces could become politicized and, thus, marginalized them and allowed them to focus on professionalism, though they were also poorly funded. Ben 'Ali also targeted the military as he purged what he claimed were members of the banned al-Nadha Party, which appeared to get the military to avoid criticizing his policies as much as it was intended to rid the armed forces of Islamists.[314]

In January 2011, angry demonstrators took to the streets of Tunis, agitating for President Zine Abidine Ben Ali's removal following the self-immolation of a peddler in south Tunisia, Mohamed Bouazizi, who set himself on fire after being disgraced by police who stole his wares and slapped him when he protested. Compounding public anger were high food prices, corruption, and unemployment, and their numbers grew to include middle-class non-religious participants, fueled partly by Tunisia's relatively widespread social media. While internal security forces initially fired weapons on the crowds, reports indicated that the head of Tunisia's armed forces, General Rachid Ammar, personally intervened to protect the protestors and then to persuade Ben 'Ali to depart the country.[315] Later Ammar proclaimed support for the revolution: "Our revolution is your revolution. . . . The army will protect the revolution."[316] However, the army had earlier stood by while the security forces repressed demonstrators (as it had during mining violence in 2008), ultimately siding with the protests only in the final days of the revolt.[317] What happened next is a matter of dispute. General Ammar did demand that Ben 'Ali leave the country, a clear "velvet shove." Some argued that the military returned to its barracks, calculating that they probably did not have the forces to successfully challenge the growing anger of the anti-Ben 'Ali movement.[318] Brooks argues that General Ammar became the primary power broker in Tunisia, and in that guise facilitated the transition to Ben 'Ali's prime minister, Mohammed Ghannouchi.[319] For Brooks, the military abandoned Ben 'Ali not because they were apolitical, but because he had badly marginalized them and saw their corporate interests furthered by his elimination.[320] Panchon argues that many of the internal security forces also defected from supporting Ben 'Ali.[321] When those internal security forces had previously refused to crush protests, the Tunisian military did, implying that arguments about its unique status as an apolitical military must be taken cautiously. Finally, Masri argues that both the internal forces and the military coalesced into removing Ben 'Ali,[322] and Croissant and Selge note that a majority of the military conscripts shared grievances with the demonstrators and would have held ranks had the military not fired on them but would have likely defected had the army opened fire.[323] As Barany argues, "When Ben Ali had to turn to the soldiers as a last resort—the other security forces were incapable of suppressing the massive demonstrations—he was doomed."[324] Sarihan also argues that the decision to not support Ben 'Ali was due to the orientation of

Tunisia's military as pro-*statist*, acting "in the interests of state rather than its own individual sake, because there have not been any important benefits that have emerged for the military in the post-Ben Ali term other than some promotions and wage increases."[325] But Jebnoun argues that following both attacks from Libya-based rebels and internal terrorist strikes, the Tunisian regime did dramatically increase military spending.[326] That increase might accompany an increase in the Tunisian military role in politics, though. The executive had to rely on Tunisia's armed forces to assist in COVID-19 vaccinations, but, more importantly, the military collaborated with the internal security services in arresting several regime opponents, and some worried that the faltering Tunisian civil institutions would weaken civilian control over Tunisia's soldiers.[327]

The Velvet Shove: Egypt (BPR)

The clearest example of a pacted transition through the velvet shove occurred in Egypt in early 2011, after the uprisings that had eliminated Ben 'Ali in Tunisia invigorated large crowds in Cairo's Tahrir Square demanding the resignation of President Hosni Mubarak. The regime initially seemed surprised by the rancor in the square and after a few efforts by the interior security forces at quelling the demonstrations, many of the poorly paid and trained security police either joined the demonstration or refused to act against the crowd. The army rolled some of its tanks into the square, and several Egyptian fighter planes flew low over the city, but the army refused to join the fray with some soldiers and their leaders declaring their fealty with the demonstrators.[328] While soldiers cited their loyalty to the nation of Egypt, they were also concerned about protecting their large economic holdings threatened by Gamal Mubarak's push for privatization, which would have included some of the military's share of the Egyptian economy,[329] as noted more in chapter 5. Mubarak, apparently fearing that the military would oppose his plans to transition the presidency to Gamal Mubarak, increased police power at the expense of the military, while increasing the police budget by sevenfold, whereas he only doubled the army budget while limiting military access to the presidency at the same time.[330] The military also had reason to fear that if the protesters got their way, they would demand changes to the military economic sector, as both protests and strikes targeted the military sector.[331]

Mubarak initially rebuked the protestors in a defiant speech that only added fuel to their anger but eventually departed Cairo under pressure after submitting a resignation and appointing military intelligence director General Omar Suleiman as vice president, thus canceling the presumed succession of Gamal Mubarak to the presidency. Air Force commander General Ahmed Shafiq became prime minister and created the Supreme Council of the Armed Forces (SCAF) to run the country for an unspecified interim period. The process and participants that generated this temporary succession was illustrative of the power of the military outside of formal government circles—a rump council of "wise men," including Arab League Secretary-General Amr Moussa and business leader Naguib Sawiris recommended that General Suleiman take charge of the interim government structure.[332] The military still sat on the political fence until thugs apparently ordered into Tahrir Square by Mubarak supporters savagely attacked the protestors in early February 2011, and at that point the Egyptian military took control of Egypt and demanded Mubarak's departure.[333]

Mubarak's ouster in January 2011 allowed the generals to fill the power vacuum. The military were initially unwilling to reverse Mubarak's limited political participation policies, as Martini and Taylor argue: "The generals now hope to create a system of carefully shaped democratic institutions that will preserve their power and reduce the chances that any single political group can challenge them."[334] The inactions of the Egyptian military leadership raised questions about whether the armed forces would prefer a political realm that emphasized the status quo and protection of their material interests,[335] or if they would yield to demands for fundamental changes. General Suleiman seemed to prefer the former, as a supporter of Mubarak's general orientation toward the West, peace between Israel and the Palestinians, and enmity toward Iran.[336] As Kandil observes, the SCAF refused to consider any revolutionary changes to Egypt's political system, unlike the Free Officers after the 1952 coup.[337] Yet other analyses argue for the military striving to retain its position while also craving political change. Osman notes that the Egyptian armed forces have received an influx of younger Egyptians who want, on the one hand, to keep military privileges yet, as representatives of Egypt's middle classes, also seek change from the decades-old status quo.[338] That view got support from US embassy cables stating that mid-level officers were dissatisfied with their senior leadership and thus more sympathetic to the protest movement.[339] It appears that the senior officers cooperated enough with both the Mubarak opponents and the regime to negotiate Mubarak's departure, the exodus of his cabinet (save the Ministry of Military Production, see chapter 4), and the arrest of some key Mubarak officials (including some in the state security services) through a pacted transition. However, their willingness to go beyond regime removal and pave the Egyptian political road with a plan for democratization appeared limited by military tradition and comfort zones. Noted one analyst commenting on the renewed ferment in Cairo's Tahrir Square after weeks of little political movement following Mubarak's removal, "I think they are incapable of understanding the extent to which the revolution wants to change things in the country. To them, removing the president was enough."[340]

The SCAF suspended the constitution, granted itself a six-month rule, dissolved the national Parliament, and gave itself the power to issue laws during the six-month period (and ultimately beyond it). The initial SCAF positions reflected the senior officer's preference for something as close to the status quo, absent Mubarak, as they could engineer.[341] The SCAF ordered the arrest of more than twelve thousand civilians, imposed "virginity tests" on women who claimed that soldiers raped them, and cracked down in particular on Coptic demonstrators, killing twenty-six who were protesting outside a radio station.[342] While there were promises of future elections, the military gave such promises largely to pacify public anger over military rule.[343] The SCAF announced that it would choose eighty of the one hundred constitutional drafting committee members, and that they were under no obligation to select a prime minister and cabinet from the winning political parties.[344] Moreover, the SCAF originally promised to return power to civilians by September 2011, but September came and went with the generals still in control. They then reneged on their pledge for early presidential elections, stating in November 2011 that there would be no presidential elections at least until 2013.[345]

The reaction was significant, as the crowds returned to Tahrir Square in late 2011; this time turning their anger toward the very military they had previously saluted for removing Mubarak. Under duress, the SCAF allowed for parliamentary elections in January 2012, in which the two leading Islamist parties, the Muslim Brotherhood's Freedom and Justice Party and the more radical Al-Nour Party, won more than 70 percent of the vote in a large turnout. Yet General Mukhtar al-Mulla, speaking for the SCAF, said to a gathering of American and British reporters (no Egyptian reporters attended), "So whatever the majority in the People's Assembly, they are very welcome, because they won't have the ability to impose anything that the people don't want," because, the general argued, the election results did not reflect the true will of the Egyptian people: "Do you think that the Egyptians elected someone to threaten his interest and economy and security and relations with international community? Of course not."[346] In June 2012, the military-influenced Supreme Constitutional Court dissolved the Parliament elected in the previous January, contending that over of third of the members were improperly elected. The court also dismissed the constitutional drafting committee appointed by that Parliament. The court's ruling, coming a day before a runoff election, solidified the old political guard that the military was part of, leading one analyst to comment that "This is an all-out power grab by the military."[347] Yet in July, the army at least symbolically handed power to

Morsi, as Field Marshal Tantawi stated, "We will stand with the new president, elected by the people," and gave him a military fly-over and an honor guard parade.[348] The generals also made President Morsi an honorary lieutenant in the Egyptian military. However, the quarreling between Morsi and the military continued, as Morsi challenged the military-influenced Court's closure of Parliament. This came after Tahani al-Gebali, deputy president of the Supreme Constitutional Court announced that she had advised SCAF members to dissolve Parliament.[349] The court refused the challenge, calling it "aggression against the nation, the judiciary and the people."[350]

Still, the SCAF and the Muslim Brotherhood needed each other because neither had a clear monopoly on power, and thus both sides had incentives to continue the pacted transition. Akl put it well, "Compromise will serve the Brotherhood's interests and secure its position as the dominant political force. SCAF, ever with an eye on a safe exit strategy, sees compromise as a way to facilitate continued military dominance over the political scene while maintaining the necessary democratic façade."[351] In late March 2011, the Muslim Brotherhood appeared to be gaining power at the expense of the young demonstrators whose activism had toppled the president. Observed Elijah Zarwan, "There is evidence the Brotherhood struck some kind of a deal with the military early on. It makes sense if you are the military—you want stability and people off the street. The Brotherhood is one address where you can go to get one hundred thousand people off the street."[352]

Yet under pressure from both internal and external sources (particularly the US), the military temporally relinquished the political floor to a democratic process. In early December, Egypt held the first round of parliamentary elections, and Field Marshal Tantawi assured voters that the army would protect voters and insure against voter fraud. Soldiers guarded ballot boxes, and the Egyptian military even provided aerial transportation to move ballot boxes from isolated villages to Cairo.[353] These movements suggested that it is likely that the military knew what it could *not* do, to govern, as Karawan argued, "It has no solutions for Egypt's external indebtedness, social tensions, sectarian eruptions, youth unemployment, and complex relations with the United States."[354] From the military point of view, it was preferable to let civilian governance at least grapple with these and other Egyptian problems, because long-run army governance failure would only reduce the army's role as a political backstop.

The first round of presidential elections was in May 2012, with the military backing retired General Ahmad Shafiq while the Muslim Brotherhood–linked Freedom and Justice Party nominated Mohamed Morsi. Shafiq and Morsi were the top winners in the first round, and in the runoff held in mid-June 2012, Morsi prevailed with a narrow 51 percent victory margin. The military reaction was to issue a decree that reduced the president's power considerably, before the SCAF stepped down. It was another indication of the "soft coup" power of the armed forces, which continued as the SCAF sent representatives to meet with Muslim Brother official Khairat al-Shater, to negotiate presidential powers.[355] The pact, though, proved to be temporary as a year later, accompanied by growing public resentment against the Morsi regime the army again joined protesters and ousted Morsi in July 2013. They sponsored a limited-participation election reminiscent of those that elected Mubarak, and in May 2014 Field Marshal Abdel Fatteh al-Sisi received more than 95 percent of the presidential vote. Since that time, Egypt has returned to "not free" in the latest Freedom House rating, and al-Sisi, like his military predecessor, has clamped down hard on political opposition. He has also surrounded himself with military officers, staffing his cabinet with General Mohamed Ahmed Zaki as defense minister, Lieutenant General Younis Hamed al-Masri, the minister of aviation and Major General Mahmoud Sayed Abdel Hamid Sha'arawi as minister of local development after having served as chief of national security.[356] Rutherford argues that these moves imply a shift by Sisi from the Mubarak-era *provision pact* to a *protection pact*, as discussed earlier in this chapter.[357] In exchange for loyalty, Egypt's armed forces are now protecting both Sisi and themselves from what both understand to be the most significant threat to their existence; political Islam.[358] But the protection pact has flaws, particularly as is reduced the power of civilian elites, and thus giving the military even more political power.[359] Sisi is also moving toward a more rent-seeking style to control his military, as he is increasingly staffing senior positions with family members. However, he has yet to create new military units under his kin, as has happened in Syria and other rent-seeking regimes.[360]

Algeria (BSPR)

Another example of pacted transition is the Algerian bargain struck in 1999 between military leaders and President Abdelaziz Bouteflika. The armed forces had toppled the government in 1992 to prevent an Islamist-dominated Parliament, forced President Chadli Benjedid to resign, banned most Islamist parties, and governed with increasingly harshness as civil war gripped the country. However, military-dominated rule had become increasingly unpopular as the armed forces became associated with the massacre of large numbers of civilians in addition to violent Islamists. Thus, Bouteflika was able to maneuver the soldiers from power, but only after negotiating an amnesty from prosecution for human rights violations and a round of new military equipment for the officers.[361] The soldiers also demanded that Major General Khalid Nezzar become a member of the newly created "High State

Council," thus assuring the armed services a voice at the top of the power pyramid.[362] While Bouteflika succeeded in retiring some senior officers after his election, some of them continued to serve as power brokers in new positions (General Larbi Belkheir became Algerian ambassador to Morocco, for example) yet others retained access to patronage networks.[363] Bouteflika was able to do this only after his successful 2004 re-election (his first election in 1999 was uncontested as all six other candidates withdrew). Algerian soldiers also received some unspecified economic privileges for their abandoning the political stage. The military also reserved the right to veto presidential choice of a defense minister, as they did in 1999, and expressed their continuing influence by influencing the head of the Party of the National Liberation Front (PFNL) to run against Bouteflika in 2004.[364]

Algeria's military benefitted from this pacted transition in several ways by obtaining a large increase in military spending whose lack of transparency allowed many officers to enrich themselves, and by the lack of meaningful political checks on their power, as both the Chamber of Deputies and the Senate are "little more than echo chambers."[365] While the government disbanded the powerful Department of Intelligence and Security in an effort to restore public faith in Algeria's armed forces, some less-than-successful efforts to combat internal terrorism have not done much to rebuild such faith.[366] The reported professionalization of the military also has not seen a proportionate withdrawal from politics. Said one analyst:

> Professionalization does not necessarily mean becoming less politicised. The professionalization of the army is a fact. The People's National Army (PNA) invested in quality training, reduced military conscription from eighteen to nine months. It also invested in women's training and their integration. But again, it does not mean that they are withdrawing their political arena. Their influence remains intact.[367]

Such influence would clearly meet the preferences of the military, as 45 to 50 percent of Algeria's soldiers preferred a role as political referee, whereas only 30 percent of Algeria's civilians preferring such a role.[368]

The military demonstrated the power of their influence again in 2019, when thousands of demonstrators demanded the resignation of Bouteflika after it became clear that he was incapacitated by a 2013 stroke.[369] Fearful of a possible "Arab Spring," Chief of Staff General Ahmed Gaid Salah called for Bouteflika to resign, which he (or someone representing him) did several days later. That allowed the military to guide the transition, placing Bouteflika ally Abdelkader Bensalah in as acting president before an election could take place.[370] While General Salah, who became the public face of Algerian political leadership after Bouteflika's departure, promised elections, he also busied himself with removing military rivals, thus paving his way to assume the presidency.[371] Yet Salah was cautious; while denouncing the idea of Algerian democracy ("poisonous ideas"), he also locked up many of Algeria's business and political elite, though that was not enough to pacify Algerian street protests.[372] However, the Algerian military may have just been biding time until the protesters tired as they traditionally held the keys to power, and showed their unwillingness to yield it through their actions in the bloody civil war. As Yolcu argues, Algeria's military has consistently demonstrated its power to dominate the civilian polity through its domination of political parties and its organization.[373] In December 2019, the military engineered yet another power placement by installing Abdelmadjid Tebboune in the presidential office, thus guaranteeing the armed forces protection of their corporate and political interests.[374]

DEFENDING THE REGIME

For armies whose primary mission is to protect the regime because it pays their rent, the choices are stark—boot out the government and face public wrath, lose rents, and possibly face a firing squad, or stand and defend it. Bellin puts it cogently, "With its back against the wall of potential ruin, the security elite is more inclined to repress democratic reformers."[375] Soldiers must also weigh the costs, because, again from Bellin, the cost of shooting civilians can badly damage the military's reputation as defender of the nation.[376] However, when the demonstrations are small (as they were in Algeria in 2011), or armed (as they were in Syria in the 1982 Muslim Brother revolt), or associated with a national enemy (as in Bahrain when the military associated Shi'a demonstrators with the Iranian threat), or when the army defends its patrimonial ties to a favored regime (as the ʿAlawi-dominated military defend the ʿAlawi-dominate ʿAsad regime) the military can and will pull the trigger on anti-regime remonstrations.

For Bellin, authoritarian rule has become entrenched in the Middle East because the "coercive apparatus in many states has been exceptionally able and willing to crush reform initiatives from below."[377] Bellin cites numerous reasons for the power and persistence of coercive institutions, including robust shares of the national budget (see chapter 4), support from outside (including the US), the threat from inside (usually Islamist movements) and the power of palace-made appointments (where loyalty is rewarded over competency).[378] Saddam Hussein routinely appointed family members, including his son-in-law, Hussein Kamal, to high military positions,[379] as did Muamar Qadhafi, whose sons commanded elite military units before Qadhafi's demise in 2012.

In other Middle East cases, militaries either fracture during uprisings or accept the new reality after the leader is all but gone, as in the Yemeni and Libyan cases. The rent-seeking militaries in both those countries fought initially to protect the regime, but a combination of military defections and determined resistance (and, in Libya's case, NATO intervention) ultimately finished off the leader. Neither the Libyan nor the Yemeni army appeared to be interested in returning to the political realms that they had both dominated and, at least in Libya's case, sometimes resisted. However, both countries are badly ruptured after transition, and the dilemma for both their militaries is at what point they try to reassert national unity without generating the same popular opposition against them that drove both Qadhafi and Saleh from office.

Syria (BPR)

The 'Asad regime worked to assure the loyalty of Syria's praetorian forces by developing a few select units to protect the regime, the Fourth Armored Division, the Third Corps, and the Republican Guard, for example, to protect the regime. 'Alawi officers, chosen for their ties and indebtedness to the 'Asad family, mostly led these elite units, to assure their loyalty.[380] Droz-Vincent also notes that 80 percent of the officer corps, and 90 percent of the generals in the Syrian military were 'Alawi's.[381] For the Syrian army, the 'Alawi-dominated Bashar 'Asad regime is its only source of rent, and most senior officers understand that they were not only protecting their income and status but also their lives, given the likely death sentences they would receive if a new order emerged to replace 'Asad. Thus, the Syrian army joined with internal security forces to violently suppress the anti-regime uprising that originated in southern Syria in 2011 and spread to the entire country by the end of the year. Not all Syrian senior officers appeared to agree with the harshness of the crackdown; apparently General Ali Habib Mahmoud, the defense minister, disagreed with some aspects of the counter-protest operations, and the president replaced him with General Daoud Rajha, a Greek Orthodox, who continued to preside over operations until his death in a suicide bomb attack in July 2012. Other Syrian officers could not accept the brutality of the clampdown and defected, including senior pilots and general officers, including the son of former defense minister Mustapha Tlas. Even the general in charge of preventing defections, Major General Abdul Aziz Jassem al-Shallal, head of the military policy, defected in December 2012.

Despite the defections, most of the Syrian army remained to defend the regime against a variety of civil war militias during the civil war. Given the weaknesses caused partly by defections, Syria's armed forces had to depend on Iranian ground units and Russian airpower to keep it in the fight, and thus it can be expected to ask for a role in the post–civil war ʿAsad regime. Yet Syria's military showed little interest in the military reforms that its Russian supporter tried to implement, because such reforms would institutionalize and depoliticize the Syrian armed forces, as well as to de-sectarianize them. However, such changes would remove the ʿAsad regime informal control mechanisms and resist the administration's efforts to actually add more ʿAlawi troops to the existing force.[382] Thus, even though the military's war performance continues to be abysmal, ʿAsad prefers a military he can control to a professional force that might threaten his rule.

Bahrain (CM)

In early 2011, Bahraini armed forces dispatched tanks into the Manama streets in concert with police forces to disperse demonstrators during that country's Arab spring "fulfilling its mission "as a fighting force of Sunni Muslims who are charged with protecting a Sunni ruling family and Sunni political and business elites in a country . . . where three of every four or five people are Shia."[383] While Bahrain's military has an aura of professionalism (its air arm operates modern combat aircraft, for example, and it receives significant US funding), its military does not reflect Bahrain's demographics as around 70 percent of its population is Shiʿa. In comparison, a majority of the military (and the government and business leaders) are Sunni.[384] The regime is Sunni, which faced the shortage of Sunni military by importing Sunni citizens from Pakistan, Yemen, Syria, and Jordan to fill out Bahraini military ranks[385] while excluding most Shiʿa from the ranks. When protests in Bahrain broke out in early 2011, the regime got support from its Sunni-majority neighbors by portraying the rebellion as a Shiʿa movement likely inspired by Iran. So, the Bahraini military, joined by Sunni-dominated Bahraini police and some forces from other GCC countries, effectively crushed the rebellion.

Yemen (BPR)

The Yemeni military initially clamped down on protests against President Ali Abdullah al-Saleh protests in Sanaʿa and elsewhere, but then demonstrated the fragile unity of the Yemeni army when the military fragmented, with units fighting other units. Some troops under the command of General Ali Mohsen al Ahmar, Saleh's half-brother, fought to take over half of Sanaʿa,[386] while forces loyal to Saleh held the other half, making the fight a family affair as much as a civil-military relations conflict.[387] Then the bulk of General al Ahmar's military defected and sided with the protestors.[388]

Part of the reason for the military breakdown into family-led factions is that training standards, operational procedures, and equipment readiness are very low in the Yemeni armed forces. Post-Saleh Yemen suggests that the politicization of Yemeni security forces continues, as each of the large competing factions, the GPC and Islah, accuse each other of recruiting their followers into the army,[389] thus the Army's considerable political role will continue in support of its highest bidder. The Yemeni military, with some US support, went on the offensive against Al-Qaeda forces and reportedly captured Jaar from them in June 2012.[390] Yet victories were rare, as the al Houthi militia swept through the country from their northern stronghold, taking a large swath from the north down to Taiz in the south. They allied with Saleh, who was a member of their faith, the Zaʻidi (followers of the Shiʻa Fifth Imam), until the Houthi turned against Saleh and killed him in December 2017. That opened the door for more military participation against the Houthi by the army, as they no longer had to worry about loyalty to the late president. Thus, Army Chief of Staff Taher Ali al-Auqaili (himself a Zaʻidi), was able to advance a campaign against the Houthi, as well as weaken its ties to Islah, which was distrusted by the Saudi Arabian and UAE forces also fighting against the Houthi.[391] If the army ultimately succeeds in reducing or eliminating the Houthi power base, it will position itself to hold a strong hand in a post–civil war Yemen. But as of 2022, that seemed very unlikely, as Saudi Arabia sought a way out of the conflict, and the Yemeni military remained badly divided.[392]

CONCLUSIONS

In this chapter, I dissected a complex set of military-induced or influenced Middle East power transitions, arguing that military orientation helps us to understand why officers launch coups or engage in negotiated transitions from authoritarian governance. The evidence here suggests that the military in Middle East countries does not usually hesitate to oust leaders who have failed the military test of proper governance, which varied in the cases studied here. They generally acted out of either a belief that they were protecting the state, or on behalf of an outside party, but not for personal or institutional gain. Once the ruler was safely ousted, the military tended to return to their duties, though they sometimes left behind a revised constitution or a new institution (the Turkish National Security Council, for an example). This pattern tended to hold whether or not the military engaged in an actual coup or measures short of a coup—the velvet shove.

The second finding in this chapter, which is consistent with the findings from other regions as well as the Middle East, is that most armies are *political* armies as much as they are *professional* armies; they engage in politics to the extent that contingencies and leaders permit. The American, Japanese, Chinese, NATO Europe, and most Southeast Asian models do not apply in the Middle East, nor, for that matter, do some of the cases in Latin America or sub-Saharan Africa. Most militaries, except for Tunisia, have at least some influence in national politics; influence that goes beyond military and national strategic areas.

Do the categories listed in the introduction help to explain the differences across military forces as they act in political transitions? Bunker republics have seen the most "coups for the nation," whereas liberal monarchies (Jordan and Morocco) and fragmented democratic republics have rarely had successful coups, and few attempted ones. While this is interesting, it is hardly surprising. It is also unsurprising that no regime type saw its military work a transition to shift the political direction from autocracy to democracy. As Henry and Springborg note about globalization, political elites, including military elites in Middle Eastern countries facing a non-democratic transition fear democracy because like globalization, it could sweep them away.[393] It is certainly not surprising that all the successful "coups for the nation" happened in bully republics, as the nationalist narrative has been an essential part of regime legitimacy in such countries, as leaders embraced the national story to justify their rule, and to push back on competing stories, ranging from Marx to religion.

In some Middle East countries, military influence extends to the national economy, due in part to military political power. Thus, the next chapter examines the political economy of civil-military relations in the Middle East.

Chapter Four

The Political Economy of Middle East Civil-Military Relations

The giant Abu Za'bal Tank Repair Factory stretches over many acres south of Cairo, where it has been building American-designed M1-A1 main battle tanks since 1987. The Ministry of Military Production (MMP) operates the factory, which turns out around eleven tanks per year. The connection to the MMP was obvious; tanks are military machines. Yet other factories under MMP purview had less of a noticeable military connection, as they produced garbage bags, washing machines, auto parts, and a host of other goods and services intended for civilian markets. The range of economic endeavors managed by the Egyptian military suggested that its orientation was something more than defense of the homeland. Instead, the patterns of military ownership and management indicated that senior officers could earn rents while also serving in the military, which not only gave them more lucrative incomes but also presented more challenges for national civil-military relations. Military management in the national economy provides a gateway into national politics as officers who own factories, farms, and other enterprises have a stake in advancing those interests through the political system, manipulating it to provide them with contracts, influence, favorable regulations, and, in some cases, the ability to squeeze out civilian business rivals. Military managers of the economy may become essential to the national political life, but not because they are the defenders of the country. Instead, they are the providers of bread during a bread crisis, of national infrastructure, or of jobs, such as those to dig an extension of the Suez Canal.

While most of the focus of civil-military relations concentrates on the *political* dimension between civilians and the military, there is a critical *economic* component to civil-military affairs, which has clear political implications as well. This chapter considers the nexus between the military and the national economy in the Middle East. It starts by considering the power of the military in shaping their budget share of the national economy. All militaries need state funds to support their task of applying military force to national purposes, but in numerous cases, military budgets are highly disproportionate to national military requirements. Countries with no obvious enemies can spend considerable sums from their budgets on national militaries, who buy weapons they will never need, justified by foes that do not exist. More commonly, soldiers exaggerate threats, both internal and external, to help themselves to disproportionate shares of the national treasury, enabled by close ties to national leadership. The second set of questions involves the impact of soldiers moving away from their traditional role as guardians of the country through war preparation to running farms and factories for profit. Does the military compromise its mission when military officers refocus their attention from soldiering to entrepreneurship? This is one of the variables listed in chapter 1, as *political tradition* has normally placed the armed forces in a state protective roll, not as business executives. What happens to military professionalism when the primary focus of the military is running businesses for profit? The *political factors* variable also matters here. Why does the state empower such entrepreneurial activity by its armed forces? Is this a form of subjective control? Or is it coup-proofing, designed to buy the loyalty of soldiers by enabling them to become wealthy with the state's permission? There are also questions about how the impact of military business ownership affects private business. Do military officers have an advantage over potential competitors as they are agents of the state, and can employ state resources to empower themselves at the expense of private owners (the *military identity–military power* variable)? These questions will guide the remainder of this chapter.

SOLDIERS AND THE STATE

One of the most perceptive writers on civil-military relations, Samuel E. Finer, observed that: "the military proved incapable, by their training, of ruling in any sense wider than putting the economy of the country on a 'care and maintenance' basis."[1] There are similarities between business and military skills, to be sure, as leadership and management skills are required for both professions, but Finer is largely correct; military professionalism and especially military education rarely includes economic management, economic planning, investment planning, market assessment, marginal rates of return, or any of the other arcane concepts that business leaders are supposed to know. Operating a battalion or a ship squadron requires a different approach than does the management of a company. The often-delicate calculations of how much product to plan for in a finely tuned market would be perplexing for a general whose method of accomplishing a mission is to fire as many artillery rounds as it takes to obliterate a target. The nuanced methods used by advertisers to sell skin cream or diet pills would be difficult to implement for a colonel used to barking orders to get troops to take a hill or fly a dangerous mission.

Military influence over the national economy can be subtle but important. Senior military officers often have influence with state organs—including the head of state—that gives them leverage over the non-military elites. They can direct parts of the national economy to work on their behalf, insisting, for example, on more control over national petroleum or computing assets for military purposes. Moreover, the impact of defense spending on national economic health is an issue for civil-military relations, because where it might accelerate economic growth, the military may take credit as a boon to national well-being. However, if defense spending crowds out more robust economic endeavors, or becomes destructive through side effects like inflation or government debt, then the professional military may appear to be more a predator than an economic savior, and opposition to higher defense spending may rise to trim military budgets. Defense spending may pump up the economy but, like many government spending programs, it may lack economic efficiency, denying the opportunity for more efficient spending.

Military political power ultimately rests on economic power: "The ability of the military to act as a political coalition partner often depends upon the extent of its own economic base."[2] That economic base may include its share of the national budget, industries that supply it with guns, bread, shoes, and millions of other consumables and durable goods. The military has strong influence over the national defense budget making process, and thus the ultimate size and trend of military budgets. While defense budgets have rarely climbed above 10 percent of total GDP in most countries (Oman was highest at 8.8 percent in 2019, which is the latest figure in the 2022 CIA World Factbook edition), they can still exercise considerable influence over the national economy, though that influence remains debated. Some argue that military spending serves as a brake on non-military economic activity as it represents wasted opportunity to spend in more economically productive ways.[3] Others argue that defense spending serves as a government stimulus to accelerate short-term economic growth and in the longer term generates infrastructure and technology to serve as a platform for sustained economic expansion.[4]

Theorists of civil-military relations from Lasswell forward have argued that when the military become managers of a state, they will take over its economic system and eliminate, among other things, unemployment: "In the garrison state, there must be work—and the duty to work—for all. Since all work becomes public work, all who do not accept employment flout military discipline."[5] Unemployment in the garrison state is to be abolished through state-run labor projects and soldiers will manage the economy, and economic pump-priming will come partly from war production: "The elite of the garrison state will have a professional interest in multiplying gadgets specialized to acts of violence. The rulers of the garrison state will depend upon war scares as a means of maintaining popular willingness to forego immediate consumption," warned Lasswell many years ago.[6] While this now seems extreme, Lasswell could be describing the economies of a number of Middle East countries.

THE CIVIL-MILITARY RELATIONS OF DEFENSE SPENDING

The armed forces influence national economies in several ways. The most obvious is direct defense spending, usually measured as the percent of the national GDP devoted to national defense. The traditional presumption is that through civilian control of defense spending, civilian politicians can regulate the amount of money earmarked for the military and thus regulate military activities. From the dawn of American history, the constitutional framers drew from British experience to place control of the military budget with a civilian Congress.[7] European democracies, as well as Japan also stress civilian control of military spending.[8] Thus, debates about the size of military budgets are, in some sense, debates over civilian control of the military, as Defense Comptroller Ferdinand Eberstadt noted in 1949, "The budget is one of the most effective, if not the strongest, implement of civilian control over the Military Establishment."[9] Sometimes it becomes a one-sided debate, however, because the military usually controls military expertise, and thus civilian politicians find it difficult to challenge military claims for funding levels.

THE SIZE OF MIDDLE EAST MILITARY SPENDING

For decades, some of the largest military spenders have been Middle Eastern countries. Currently the Middle East still dominates global defense spending as a percentage of GDP, though the numbers fluctuate, as of 2022 the Middle East as a region is still at the top of the list of military spenders.[10]

In states with weak political institutions, the military usually gets what it wants, and often more. In such countries, there are rarely questions about how the most powerful sector plans on using the funding, and a lack of transparency in the budget approval process almost assures that the armed forces will benefit, to the detriment of other budget claimants.[11]

Civilian Control of the Defense Budget

The power of any national organization lies in its ability to control access to budget shares, an arena where the military has particular leverage. Its claim to be the defender of a country facing either external or internal threat is difficult for other agencies to match, and in weak democracies or autocracies, the army can often just help itself to the national treasury. As Giraldo indicates, democratic defense budget control includes the primacy of democratic determination of spending choices (primarily national and military strategy making), and full transparency of the process from start to finish.[12] That usually means that elected legislatures have the power to determine military budgets. The US Congress holds multiple hearings annually to scrutinize all elements of the military budget, though most European parliaments do not give their national defense budgets the same oversight. In some political settings, cabinets determine, or at least deliberate budgets as rival agency heads, pitting relative requirements against each other in competition for monetary shares. In autocracies, the head of state has primacy over defense budget-making, though such control varies from situation to situation.

CIVILIAN CONTROL OF MIDDLE EAST DEFENSE BUDGETS

Military spending is a significant part of the political and economic life of the Middle East, though the amount as a percent of GDP varies considerably. The size and growth of Middle East defense budgets in the 1970s was record-setting, as Lebovic and Ishaq observe: "While absolute regional military spending (between 1973–1982) was phenomenal, the military also controlled a greater percentage of the central government budget in the Middle East and twice as much of the national output as in other developing countries or in the world as a whole. Middle Eastern defense accounted for one-third of the military spending of developing countries and almost one-half of world arms imports."[13] The high-end spenders have often topped the list of global military spending countries for decades. In 1965, Iraq devoted 12.7 percent of its GDP to defense, and Jordan 12 percent, while Saudi Arabia spent 8.6 percent of its total economy on military force.[14] After the 1967 war, Israeli defense expenditures began to rise, and by 1975, defense consumption was 32 percent of its GDP.[15] That war devastated the Egyptian military, and the cost of rebuilding it damaged the Egyptian economy, as Waterbury noted, the quality and quantity of other economic services deteriorated during this time.[16] So, while Egyptian military spending declined for a long time, other Middle Eastern countries continued to devote high levels of their GDP to defense even as the Cold War wound down. While factors like the price of petroleum and the 2007 global recession did impact Middle East military spending, it remained high relative to other parts of the world and increased again in 2017 after a slight decline in 2016.[17] In 2021, the Middle East led the list of high spenders with twelve of the top twenty in the Middle East. In the Arab world, military spending increased by 8.2 percent of GDP in the 1970s and 1980s, while global military spending increased around 5 percent over the same period. Norlén argues that, "Most MENA countries are heavily militarized. In contrast to the rest of the world, military budgets in the Middle East rose as a proportion of GDP in most Arab states over the past decade, a "phenomenon that is often correlated with both conflict incidence and recurrence, and corrupt and autocratic governments."[18]

Both authoritarian and democratic countries have processes to approve defense spending, partly as a control over military power. The level and scope of this budgetary scrutiny is a partial indicator of the political power of the military relative to the rest of the state. In the Middle East, control over the defense budget varies with type of political system, to a point. Parliamentary systems usually exercising more control of the budget size and impose more limits on how it may be spent, though there are few functioning Middle East parliaments (Turkey and Israel, for example), and these parliaments do not always scrutinize military spending; their oversight rarely approaches that of the United States.[19] As the following cases below indicate, military power is quite considerable.

Turkey (BSPR)

Turkey's military budget has varied over time. In 1993, Turkey's defense budget reached around 40 percent of the total government budget, in comparison to the 10 percent devoted to education and 3 percent to health,[20] largely because of the campaign against Kurdish insurgency. But in 2021, it was only 1.6 percent of the total GDP.

In Turkey, civilian defense budget control is almost absent. Hen-Tov observes that "in contrast to most Western democracies, Turkish military expenditures are almost never the subject of parliamentary debates and Turkish military demands are not scrutinized. The Turkish military devises its defense budget and procurement policies (within fiscal limits) without ever encountering opposition in parliament."[21] Demir states that "Although any spending from the central budget is subject to parliamentary approval, in practice defense budget is the only item that passes without any discussion or criticism in the parliament despite the fact that it accounted for at least 14% of the budgetary (non-interest) expenditures during 1998–2008."[22]

The erosion of Turkish democracy since 2003 (the year the *Adalet ve Kalkınma Partisi* [AKP] took control of the Turkish Parliament) the Turkish defense burden shrunk to less than two percent of GDP in 2008,[23] rising to 2.3 percent in 2012. That trend reversed though, as by 2020, the Turkish defense budget grew by more than 86 percent in the decade preceding 2019.[24] There was a particularly steep increase in Turkish military spending between 2017 and 2018 of 27 percent, while the increase between 2018 and 2019 was 5.8 percent."[25] The 2020 military budget increased to 145 billion liras ($19.7 billion), around 13 percent of total government spending.[26] The 2018 increase was 24 percent over the previous year and the largest increase among the top fifteen military spenders.[27] Turkish military spending increased again for 2022, by almost 30 percent.[28]

It is noteworthy that as Turkish defense spending rose, Prime Minister/President Erdoğan increased his political power at the expense of both the Turkish Parliament and the Turkish military. Some of the defense increases could well have gone to support Erdoğan's ambitious goal of expanding Turkish power beyond Turkish borders. Erdoğan sent Turkish forces into northern Syria, and into Libya to assist the Government of National Accord against rebel militias. Turkish-built Bayraktar TB2 drones were effectively destroying Russian tanks in Ukraine in 2022. Erdoğan also lavished funds on Turkish defense industries, pushing to develop and build a range of weapons, from military drones to combat ships. This may also have been Erdoğan way to keep a wary eye on the Turkish military, given its historical role as guardian of the Atatürk legacy, and one way to keep his soldiers in the barracks was to lavish more military money on them.

Israel (FD)

The Israeli Knesset must approve the entire state budget, which it usually scrutinized thoroughly. But, as Ben Meir notes, "The Knesset . . . is as reluctant to exert control over the defense budget as it is to impose restraints on executive action in the field of defense,"[29] and Shiffer argues that "it (the Knesset) is . . . a marginal actor in the process."[30] Moreover, "the army has a central, if not decisive, influence on the budget."[31] Arian argues that "One of the important myths of Israeli political life is that checks and balances exist within the system. This is simply not so."[32] But this may miss the point; the main debate is usually at the ministerial level—the finance and defense ministries are often in disagreement over the amount of funding.[33] Despite the perceived threat from Iran, and three campaigns against Hamas, the then-Israeli Finance Minister Yair Lapid wanted to cut the 2014 budget by almost 6 percent, drawing predictable opposition from Defense Minister Moshe

Yaalon.[34] But as has been the case, the debate was very public and robust, suggesting that both transparency and checks and balances do exist in the Israeli defense budget system. Yet the military has generally had the upper hand in budget debates, as shown by the mid-2015 proposal to reduce defense spending by around 14 percent. At the behest of then—Prime Minister Binyamin Netanyahu, retired Israeli Air Force General Yochanan Locker, issued a report arguing that the size and service requirements for the IDF could be reduced to accommodate the 14 percent cut in military spending. The IDF fought back, successfully, it would appear, as no member of the cabinet except the defense minister would even meet with General Locker's committee. After one general complained that the report was "a bullet between the eyes," Netanyahu deleted the cut from the proposed budget.[35] The IDF also got a win in 2020 when it resisted Finance Ministry efforts to cut its NIS 3.3 billion ($964 million) increase over the 2019 budget. The IDF has previously canceled a large exercise, allegedly due to lack of funds, which some analysts saw as a political pressure tactic.[36] Such tactics were most likely successful, adding to the normal political clout of the military. Thus, the 2021 IDF budget simply carried on the budget approved in 2018, showing no decline due to the budgetary pressures imposed by the COVID-19 outbreak.[37] Still, in December 2021, the Knesset granted a 7.4 billion shekels ($2.4 billion) supplementary defense budget increase, supposedly to bolster Israeli plans to strike targets in both Syria and Iran.[38] The 2022 Israeli defense budget made it through a fragile political coalition, partly by adding funds for medical treatment and scholarships for wounded veterans.[39]

Syria (BPR)

Countries with perfunctory parliaments tend to give the defense budget little independent scrutiny. Noting, for example, the debate in Parliament over the 1951 Syrian military budget, Torrey finds that the army almost never got objection to its request, and that "Parliament had become little more than a puppet whose strings were pulled by the army command."[40] During the 1980s, the Syrian economy suffered considerable setbacks, from drought, high inflation, balance of payments shortfalls, and the overall problems inherent in a centrally planned economy. Though the military budget continued to grow as other budget elements were pared down (by more than 5 percent in real terms), the defense budget remained robust, taking more than 40 percent of the total state budget, posing "a heavy burden on the economy."[41] Perthes also argues that because Syria's defense budget is not dependent on domestic bargaining, it could be used freely for infrastructure development, bureaucratic expansion, and "served to increase both the autonomy of the state from its citizens and its penetration of and hold on society."[42]

With Syria in the throes of civil war that began in 2011, the "defense budget process" has disappeared, replaced by individual "defense budgeting," as military commanders turn to corruption and thievery to raise money for both their units and themselves. The ʿAsad regime, once the beneficiary of large sums of aid from the Gulf Arab regimes, found itself having to rely on smaller aid amounts from Iran (whose economy continued to struggle from low oil prices and international sanctions), and donations from the global Shiʿa community. When much of the country was lost to insurgent forces, the ʿAsad regime thus lost much of its tax base, as the rebel groups took it over and used it to fund their own activities, thus providing Russia and Iran with an opportunity to supplement Syrian defense funds with their funds, and thus increasing their Syrian influence. Even though Syrian forces, aided by Russian and Iranian military assistance gained back much territory initially lost to insurgents, the key petroleum areas remained outside of the ʿAsad regime's control, and thus its tax base.[43] Given its dire budget situation, the ʿAsad regime was unable to pay its military more than a few dollars a month in almost-worthless Syrian currency,[44] there was the prospect that the Syrian soldiers would simply help themselves to parts of the Syrian economy. The decline in the overall government budget from around $9 billion USD in 2020 to $5.3 billion USD in 2022 only increased the likelihood that Syrian soldiers would have to depend on their firearms for just economic survival.[45]

Egypt (BPR)

Historically, the Egyptian military budget escaped public or legislative scrutiny during the Nasser through Mubarak presidencies. During the brief Mohammed Morsi rule of 2012–13, one defense official claimed that: "Egypt's military will remain a red line. Details of the military budget should be kept strictly confidential."[46] As parliamentary power grew after Mubarak's departure, some the military leaders feared that their budget would come under parliamentary scrutiny, thus in November 2011, the army tried to get a constitutional amendment passed by Parliament to shield their budget from oversight, but the amendment failed.[47] The Islamist-dominated Parliament had little stomach to take on the powerful armed forces, and the suspension of that body by the military after the Morsi arrest in 2013 and the "election" of former general al-Sisi all but guaranteed that there would be no legislative scrutiny of Egypt's defense budget. And that has clearly happened; a recent report noted that "Much about the Egyptian military's role in the economy is unknown—its budget is secret."[48] Abul-Magd, Akça, and Marshall note that the Egyptian military economy is "characterized by a general immunity from independent auditing or public accountability."[49]

Iran (BPR)

Iran's Shah Mohammad Reza Pahlavi embarked on a military spending binge that probably contributed to his fall in 1979. In 1972 and 1973, when oil prices rose steeply because of the OAPEC oil embargo, the Shah pumped up Iranian military spending by 29 and 11 percent, respectively.[50] Says Moran:

> The high priority given the military in Iranian public spending (together with the waste, corruption, and inefficiency of Iran public spending in general) seriously drained the resources and the attention that Iranian authorities could have devoted to heading off the wave of political dissatisfaction, including frustration among those groups that traditionally had been the bedrock of support for the monarchy, especially the peasantry, rural migrants, and lower middle classes in the cities.[51]

Iranian defense spending on the regular army decreased after 1979, and the budget distribution probably reflect a loyalty reward by the current Islamist government, which favors the Islamist-based paramilitary forces under the Islamic Republican Guard Corps (IRGC) over the regular Iranian armed forces (*Artesh*). While the Artesh has the normal divisions into land, sea, and air forces (and a separate air defense unit), so does the IRGC, with the Ground Resistance Forces, Navy, Aerospace Force, and the Quds Force (special operations). Those units may be better paid and organized than the Artesh.[52] The Artesh, which were once the backbone of Shah Mohammed Pahlavi's power, remain distrusted by the religious Iranian leadership, which prefer the Islamist militias whose loyalty can be acquired by their elevation over the regular forces. For 2020, the Artesh got only 13 percent of the total defense budget, while the IRGC got 34 percent.[53]

The Iranian economy grew after the 2015 Joint Comprehensive Plan of Action (JCPOA) reduced some economic sanctions, but when President Donald Trump withdrew American participation from JCPOA and re-imposed sanctions on Iran, the national economy tumbled. As a consequence, political leadership imposed sharp cuts on defense spending, with the formerly favored IRGC taking a 17 percent budget cut, while the Artesh took a smaller 10 percent slice,[54] possibly reflecting the weakening of the clerical power that once favored the IRGC. However, the IGRC has off-the-books revenues from the companies it owns or controls,[55] and none of these monies are seen by anyone other than IRGC leadership. That was one likely reason why former Iranian President Hassan Rohani criticized the IRGC's business operations, calling it a "government with a gun" that scared away the public sector.[56] But Rohani's defeat in the 2021 elections and replacement by conservative President Ibrahim Raisi also increased the fortunes of the IRGC, with a 930 trillion rial budget for 2022, up sharply from 2021's figure of 380, and a bonus of 4.5 euros worth of oil for the IRGC to sell on international markets.[57]

THE ECONOMIC IMPACT OF MILITARY SPENDING

Part of the civil-military debate on military spending is its potential impact on the national economy; because if military spending harms national economic prosperity, civilian pressure may arise to curb defense budgets. But if national defense spending accelerates economic growth, civilians may accede to larger amounts because it provides economic, and thus political, stability in a region where significant economic reform may be rare. Thus, military power relative to civilian authority is partly a function of the effect of defense spending.

Some argue that military spending has a positive effect on national economic growth; the classical "military Keynesian" model. The seminal work is Benoit, who concludes that "the simple correlation between defense burdens and growth rates was strongly positive: countries with high growth rates tended to have high defense burdens, and vice versa."[58] Other studies, however, found fault with Benoit's arguments and conclusions, with little evidence of such relationships in a universe of developing countries.[59] Using data from seventy countries from 1960 to 2017, Desli and Gkoulgkoutsika find that the correlation between military spending and economic growth was negative, but perhaps surprisingly, there was no effect in low or lower-income countries.[60] On the other hand, Churchill, and Yew find that military spending produces positive economic growth in developed countries, more so than in developing countries.[61]

Studies on particular regions also generate differing results for the impact of military spending on national economies. DeRouen and Heo test the proposition about the accelerant effect from military spending on select Latin American countries and conclude that, not unsurprisingly, it varies across countries, with military spending having a negative impact on economic growth in thirteen countries and but four showing a positive relationship. Thus, in general, "Military spending . . . has thwarted (economic) growth."[62] Goldsmith, using data for 1886 through 1989, finds "economic growth is positively associated with the defense burden. New resources in the economy seem to go disproportionately to defense, whereas a declining economy leads to a reduction in the defense burden."[63] In sub-Saharan Africa, Dunne and

Mohammed, examining thirteen countries between 1967 and 1985, find "A strong and important result that emerges from the analysis is that there is no evidence of military spending having a positive economic effect in our sample, with the aggregate results and individual country results suggesting that there are substantial costs."[64] At a broader level, Dunne and Tian, using data from 1960 to 2014, find no relationship between military spending and economic growth, for ninety-seven countries.[65] In a study of seventeen OECD countries using data from 1960 to 1980, Cappelen, Gleditsch, and Bjerkholt find that "When applying economic growth data which are both longitudinal and cross-sectional, the overall picture seems to be that military spending does not stimulate economic growth in the industrialized West, but rather the opposite. Thus, conversion of military spending to areas that would stimulate investment is likely to increase economic growth in the developed countries."[66] Leontief and Duchin arrive at a similar conclusion using input-output analysis across a variety of countries, from high to low income: "All regions would appear to benefit (as measured by increases in GDP and per capita consumption) at given regional levels of military spending if client regions continued to reduce their reliance of these (military) commodities by accelerating domestic production."[67] Knight, Loayza, and Villanueva also find that defense spending reductions correlate with positive economic growth, while increases in defense spending crowds out non-military investment.[68] Yet in a study of five industrial countries—the United States, Germany, Russia, Great Britain, and France—found no conclusive evidence of a strong relationship between defense expenditures and economic output between the years 1870 and 1939.[69] Yet a study of China produces a different result, as Su, Xu, Chang, Lobont, and Liu find that defense expenditure stimulates economic growth, and, reciprocally, economic growth stimulates defense spending.[70]

While poverty rates constitute only one indicator of national economic health, a study by Brady on poverty rates in eighteen Western countries found that while social security transfers, social wage, and public health expenditures significantly reduced "state-mediated" poverty rates in these countries, military spending and public employment were insignificant.[71] Luqman and Antonakikis find in the Pakistani case that military spending has a negative effect on both economic growth and human development.[72] Finally, examining the US, Taiwan, and Israel, Sorenson finds that "The trends do not show significant adjustments to the American, Taiwanese, or Israeli defense budgets, which appear to be relatively impervious to dramatic change."[73]

In authoritarian countries, it is reasonable to expect that the military should have more power relative to civilian institutions relative to governmental budget shares. Soldiers, after all, are often the pinnacle of state power under non-liberal regimes, serving under a former colleague as head of state, or at least a regime that needs the point of the military sword to remain in power. In Africa, Dunne and Mohammad find that military governments are high military spenders compared to civilian regimes.[74] Zuk and Thompson find that between 1967 and 1976, military regimes spend proportionately on defense than do civilian regimes.[75] Thus, transitions to democracy should show a relative shift where military budgets decline relative to civilian budgets. In short, money for tanks and training and such should decline in favor of civil education, health care, and welfare spending. This has happened in Latin America, as Lebovic concludes, "The effect of democratization was to increase civilian relative to military shares of countries within the region."[76] Blum has a similar finding, noting that democracy's "third wave," using the period from 1972 to 2013, produced an average 10 percent decrease in defense spending per GDP.[77] Clardie finds that for the period of 1967 to 1999, countries that transformed from central rule to democracy lowered their military expenditures as a percent of the national economy.[78] More generally, democratic states allocate fewer resources to national defense than do autocratic states, other things being equal.[79] South Korea's defense burden dropped from 4.3 to 2.7 after democratic transition, thought it later rose by 7.5 percent in 2019.[80] In democracies, citizens tend to prefer transfer payments over defense budgets, as Eichenberger and Stoll find in the United States and select European countries.[81]

Military economic interests also shape national economies through indirect means. In many countries, the armed forces have an interest in preserving and developing economic sectors to supply them with a wide range of goods and services. Officers can extend their influence into national planning by supporting policies that enhance national economic capacity even though the consequences may not enhance overall national economic health. An example is military support for nationalist policies like import-substitution industrialization (ISI), which some governments implemented as a way to free their countries from import dependence, and to fuel domestic growth, although sometimes such policies ran counter to economic efficiency. Chudnovsky and López note that the Argentinean military pressured the regime to adopt ISI support for aluminum, iron and steel, and petrochemicals, even though "This obviously introduced noneconomic elements in decisions on the approval of investment projects and probably disregarded microeconomic efficiency."[82] Some of this ISI was for the military, to continue an industrial base in order to supply the army with its requirements. It is interesting to note, however, that in some democratic transitions, the armament sector actually rose in value and scope after the transition, possibly as a side payment to keep the officers from returning to politics. The arms industry in Brazil and Spain actually grew after those countries' transition to democracy, though Stepan argues that military relative satisfaction with the state of arms production may deny them at least one excuse for taking back the government, and thus protecting democracy.[83]

THE ECONOMIC IMPACT OF MIDDLE EAST MILITARY SPENDING

As noted above, military spending may stimulate economic growth or, conversely, may retard prosperity. Alternatively, it may be neutral, showing little if any effect on economic growth. Relative impacts vary by country, of course, but it is less clear that they vary by type of political system or military. Lebovic and Ishaq, as noted above, examine the non-oil producing Middle East states between 1973 and 1982 and conclude that higher defense budgets suppress economic growth, in contrast to Benoit.[84] Gaub also finds that Arab states with high levels of military spending suffer a loss in economic growth, noting: "Had the Arab states adjusted their military budgets to European levels in 1990—and maintained them—their economies would have grown by between 2 and 3 percent a year, and generated output levels more than 50% higher than at present."[85] And while Abu-Bader and Abu-Qarn generate a similar finding for the "front-line" Arab states aligned against Israel (Egypt, Jordan, and Syria), the results were barely significant, and not causal, suggesting that other variables besides military spending probably contributed more to variance in economic growth.[86] Pan, Chang, and Wolde-Rufael examine the relationship between economic growth and defense spending in ten Middle East countries (Bahrain, Egypt, Israel, Jordan, Kuwait, Lebanon, Oman, Saudi Arabia, Syria, and Turkey) and found that military spending played an important role in economic growth only in Turkey and Israel.[87] Yet Saba and Ngepah find a positive correlation between levels of defense spending and economic growth in the Middle East and North Africa, while also observing that, defense spending "is still needed for security purposes, to ensure and encourage some level of economic and developmental activity."[88] And while their study ranges beyond the Middle East, Yildirim and Öcal studied 128 countries over the period of 2000 to 2010, and found that there is not only a positive relationship between military spending and economic growth but also that such military spending induced growth also spills over into neighboring countries.[89] Applied to the Middle East, the finding suggests that higher defense spending in the Gulf Arab countries might support economic growth in some of the lower-income countries (assuming, of course, that borders would allow such a spillover).

Increases in defense spending may depress other portions of government budgets, the "guns versus welfare" tradeoff, which may have an indirect impact on overall economic growth. Yet Coutts and his fellow authors do not find a relation between military spending and other non-military programs: "we find no evidence that increased security needs as measured by the number of domestic terrorist attacks are complemented by increased military spending and thereby 'crowd out' and reduce government expenditure on key public goods such as health care."[90] However, Ali finds that in Egypt, increases in defense spending crowds out health care spending, but not education or food subsidies.[91] More generally, Noble finds that Egypt alone accounted for more than half the eastern Arab military spending in the early 1960s, yet Egypt's population had the second lowest per capita income of any member of this system ("eastern" Arab means the Arab world minus North Africa).[92] While this comparison is hardly causal, it does suggest that high levels of defense spending depress the non-defense economic sector. Yet a study of the Jordanian economic impact from military spending from 1970 to 2015 finds a positive relation, as defense budgets did increase employment.[93]

Most oil-producing Middle East countries are rentier states, meaning that they derive much of their national income from rents derived largely from raw material exports, whose gains flow back to the state. In 2010, Saudi Arabia derived almost 61 percent of its GDP from petroleum rents, Qatar 60 percent, and Iran around 30 percent.[94] Ten years later, that figure remained high despite diversification efforts, averaging 40 percent though the UAE dropped to 30 percent (Kuwait was close to 60 percent).[95] As Bellin argues, the rentier status of many Middle Eastern countries helps to sustain the armed forces.[96] Thus, Middle East rentier states are more likely to feature high defense spending levels relative to other state budgets and the overall economy because rents are easy tools to buy military loyalty. Some of the top military spenders relative to GDP are Saudi Arabia, Yemen, Qatar, and Oman, all with rentier state characteristics. Algeria and Libya, also rentier states, saw sharp increases in military spending after military-inspired or led coups. Libya's defense spending rose to 40 percent of total government spending after the 1969 coup, and the Algerian military is also a beneficiary of rent receipts: "In 1992, the army acted to preserve the Algerian state and prevent its collapse. Whether this decision was based on ideological values or a plot to keep its access to oil rents is unclear, but what is clear is that the army wanted to remain in power."[97] Willis notes that the Algerian military, through government support, was able to grab most of Algeria's import sector with revenues they obtained from oil and gas sales.[98] Algeria's military also used their economic access to engage in numerous corrupt practices,[99] along with investments in import markets like wheat, sugar, pharmaceuticals, and automobiles.¹⁰⁰ Algeria, along with Angola, ranks among the African countries with the highest levels of military corruption.¹⁰¹

In 2021, despite the continuing Middle East tensions and fights, defense spending did decline in a number of countries, including rentier states. Saudi Arabia's 2021 military budget was 27 percent lower than its 2017 level in real terms (adjusted for inflation), while Oman's defense spending was 28 percent lower than its 2015 peak, again in real currency.¹⁰² Yet in other Middle East countries, military spending was up, in Egypt with 3.6 percent annual growth since 2019, Kuwait by 21 percent over 2020, Tunisia, with its 2021 defense budget higher by 24 percent over 2017, and Morocco by 21 percent for 2021 over 2020.¹⁰³

There is another significant implication to military influence in the economies of Middle Eastern countries: the importance of protecting a military economic stake from popular uprisings. Lawson observes that since large-scale violence is a direct threat to military-held companies, the military leadership will take steps to crush armed opposition by any means necessary.¹⁰⁴ This could well have been a part of the Syrian military reaction to the first blossoming of the "Arab Spring" in early 2011, and the Egyptian armed forces violent suppression of the post-Morsi demonstrations in Cairo and elsewhere in 2014. Protection of investments is also one reason why the Algerian army reacted violently to the Islamist movements in the 1990s.¹⁰⁵

The following section compares select Middle East countries on the impact of their military spending on the economy. As always in making comparisons, it is essential to note that comparisons do not usually factor in the different ways that countries spend money on national defense. Some invest the bulk of their defense budgets on weapons, not only buying firepower but sometimes also the loyalty of their military, who prefer fancy equipment over the more mundane elements of training and maintenance, for examples. Other military budgets sometimes go to fund civilian projects (bridges, roads, and water projects, for examples). Yet other regimes lavish money on pay and benefits, which both can enhance the quality of their military and also possibly buy military loyalty, and so comparisons must be read with caution.¹⁰⁶

Israel (FD)

There is intense scholarly debate on defense spending impacts in Israel. Shiffer argues that military spending and military demands have had a positive impact on some sectors of the Israeli economy: "military demands have apparently contributed considerably to the development of high-tech industries in Israel, and, in particular, to the rapidly growing Information Communication Technology (ICT) sector."¹⁰⁷ Yet Rivlin argues that defense spending was ultimately harmful to Israeli economic prosperity: "High and rising levels of defense spending were one of the main causes of economic slowdown and crisis in the late 1970s and early 1980s"[108] because of the size of the defense burden noted above. Of course, a single variable rarely explains much variance in GDP, but when defense spending rose by as much as 64 percent after the 1973 war, it is likely to constrain the non-defense sector. Many jobs depend on military largesse, with Israeli Aerospace Industries providing more than sixteen thousand jobs.

Israel's defense spending shows dramatic cycles of increase and decline, topping 30 percent of GDP during the pre–Camp David period (before 1979). However, it did drop from around 36 to 16 percent by 1986,[109] and as of 2018, is around 5.6 percent. These swings allow comparisons of the decline of the defense budget with measures of economic growth, to assess the impact of the defense burden. Cohen, Stevenson, Mintz, and Ward find that "The trend since 1979 (and especially since 1985) in Israel is that a shrinking defense burden has been accompanied by a strong, growing economy. The evidence suggests that defense spending and economic growth are tied together through some type of equilibrium dynamic—one that exhibits a negative correlation between defense spending and growth."[110] Moreover, according to Mintz and Ward, military spending is the most significant mechanism for stimulating economic growth, and thus political leadership uses its simulative effect to influence electoral outcomes.[111]

Seliktar offers a different argument, that Israeli defense expenditures squeeze resources from the non-defense state spending sector, generating protests from both lower-income Israelis and the Israeli "Peace Now" movement, which complained about harmful economic effects on those Israelis who depended on the non-defense public sector.[112] If this is correct, Israel may be able to support dramatic increases in military spending politically by increasing non-defense spending at the same time to keep non-defense political constituencies supportive. Israeli defense expenditures as a percentage of GDP rose dramatically after the 1967 war, exceeding many developed countries at over 30 percent. However, a part of the increase did not draw on Israeli resources, as the United States provided a considerable portion of this increase, supplying foreign aid and grants to cover more than 60 percent of Israeli military imports.[113] Total US aid amounts to around $3 billion annually, on average. For fiscal year 2020, Israel received $3.3 billion, with an additional $850 million budgeted for missile defense, under separate line items.[114]

There is usually an annual fight over the Israeli military budget between the defense minister and the finance minister, which can become acute when the Israeli economy falters. Beinin observes that Israeli capital growth suffered as military spending increased dramatically after the 1967 and 1973 wars; "the cost of military expenditures is directly responsible for the sluggish growth of the Israeli economy in the last decade."[115] The economy slumped again in 2003 because of security issues during the second intifada, and political pressure grew to cut defense because of declining national revenue grew, yet the armed forces wanted additional funds to combat the insurgency in the Occupied Territories. As Peri writes, the military felt that the cuts demanded by the finance minister were affronts to its status and power, yet the cuts also reflected an agreement by Minister Shaul Mofaz, who had agreed to the cuts to keep in the good graces of the cabinet.[116] Such a bargain did not endear Mofaz to the uniformed personnel, who used the cuts to justify the security barrier between Israel and the territories as a less expensive means to prevent terrorists from slipping over the border. In 2015, Finance Minister Moshe Kahlon and then–Defense Minister Moshe Yaalon agreed to constrain military spending, but in 2018, Netanyahu called for defense to rise to 6 percent of the Israeli GDP, while arguing that such an increase would actually boost Israel's economic growth.[117] For 2020, Netanyahu asked for an additional 3.3-billion-shekel ($966 million) defense budget increase, despite the budget pressures stemming from the COVID-19 pandemic.[118] But if the post-Netanyahu coalition of 2021 holds together, it has such a broad representation of the Israeli political spectrum that it cannot do much but agree to the one thing that all members want: infrastructure spending. That may require a cut in Israeli defense spending.

Turkey (BSPR)

There is evidence that Turkish defense spending may repress economic growth, as Tekeoglu first finds a negative correlation between Turkish defense expenditures and economic growth in the years 1969 to 2004, and concludes that the Turkish economic growth would become more robust with defense cuts, a finding supported by growth rates at around 8 percent in 2010–11 accompanied by defense reductions.[119] Supporting evidence of a negative effect from Turkish military spending, Ozsoy finds that it suppressed education and health expenditures between 1925 and 1998,[120] and Elveren's evidence confirms a negative relationship between military spending and Turkish income inequality between 1963 and 2007. The years between 1924 and 1996 saw a negative trade-off between Turkish defense spending and health spending, though they also saw a positive trade-off between defense and education spending.[121] A 2020 study by Usman and Habimana shows a significant negative relationship between military expenditures and GDP per capita growth.[122] That finding was similar to research results by Jülide

Yildirim and Selami Sezgin that found that long-run changes in Turkish GDP provide more robust explanations of changes in Turkish military spending—the level of military spending actually decreases as GDP increases.[123] Karadam, Yildirim, and Öcal find positive effects for low levels of military expenditure but negative growth impacts for high levels of defense spending for Turkey between 1988 and 2012.[124] Using a different approach, the augmented Solow growth model, Töngür and Elveren find no relationship between Turkish economic growth and military expenditures for 1963 to 2008.[125]

The impact of military spending may ultimately depend on where the military spends its money. When military funds go to buy locally produced food or housing, or rifles, then the money has direct benefits, but when military budgets go to purchase foreign-produced goods such as weapons, training, or services, then the result can be a drain on national resources. In Turkey, when the armed forces purchase American-made weapons, including tanks, fighter planes, and tanker aircraft, money flows out of the country, creating opportunity costs that otherwise might benefit the Turkish economy.[126] Partly for this reason, the Turkish government arranged for co-production agreements allowing some Turkish aircraft to be produced in the Turkish Aircraft Industries plant north of Ankara.[127] This was also a key justification for Turkish production of the American-designed F-35 "Joint Strike Fighter" aircraft, originally scheduled to start in 2015.[128] The F-35 program mattered for the Turkish economy, as Turkish Aircraft Industries employs more than three thousand in its Ankara plant. The joint Kale Industries–Pratt and Whitney engine plant in Izmir, Turkey, employed another five hundred workers.[129] However, in 2019, the US suspended Turkish F-35 participation because of the Turkish decision to purchase a Russian-made anti-aircraft missile system, leaving in question what would happen to the employment created by that program.[130] But Turkish military and defense planners have responded with a wide array of new weapons, including several naval warship programs, military land vehicles, and the Bayraktar drone series that has proven very effective in use by both the Turkish and Ukrainian militaries.

When the Turkish economy declines, tax revenues sharply decrease because the level of tax avoidance rises quickly, and thus the Turkish budget deficit ballooned by 2009.[131] The budget shortfall generated opposition to Turkish military spending levels within both the government and civil society, partly because the armed forces budget exceeded the Turkish education budget. However, possibly due to this opposition, the ratio reversed in 2010,[132] supporting the point above that an increase in democracy may result in reduced military spending in favor of other more popular public spending. The deficit increased ten years later again, as recession drove more government spending, rising 70 percent just in 2019,[133] yet defense spending increased by 27 percent in 2018 and an additional 5.8 percent in 2019.[134] There are also complaints from some Turkish civilian sectors that the Turkish defense budget lacks sufficient civilian political oversight, along with insufficient transparency in the military-operated Turkish defense industries.[135]

Turkish budget allocators appear to try a balanced approach to budget tradeoffs. Günlük-Şenesen summarizes the over-time ratio of defense-to-welfare expenditures in Turkey:

> the trend of defence expenditures with respect to basic welfare expenditures . . . is more or less stable . . . during 1980–1986. There is quite a sharp decline, down to 50%, during 1987–1993, recovering thereafter . . . (but) a considerable recovery of education expenditures during 1988–1993 reverses the trend in this period. Increasing defence expenditures combined with declining education expenditures then led to an increase in the share of funds allocated for defence expenditures in recent years.[136]

In short, Turkish economic conditions seem to partially explain changes in Turkish military spending, indicating that the military is sensitive to its impact on the national economy, and foregoes spending increases when the economy lags, or, conversely, civilian budget makers keep a tight reign over military spending, benchmarking it to economic progress.

Egypt (BPR)

The 1979 Camp David agreements that ended the state of conflict between Israel and Egypt promised that lower military budgets would lead to higher economic growth for both Egypt and Israel. War spending can deprive countries like Egypt of the resources needed to sustain its population. Whynes concludes that "Egyptian war casualties in 1972 were . . . around 11,000 in a year in which defence spending accounted for approximately 20 percent of GNP. In the same year, nearly 250,000 Egyptians died of diseases of the respiratory and digestive systems. The moral is clear—guns kill in more ways than one."[137] The Camp David Accords, which Makovsky credits for allowing the Egyptian budget to shrink from around 20 percent of GDP in 1976 to around 2 percent in 2009, and "allowed Cairo to reallocate military funds to economic development projects."[138] But Maher and Zhao find that military expenditure has a significant negative impact on the short-run GDP growth rates.[139] This finding may be attributed to a considerable reduction in military budgeting after the 1979 treaty. Unsurprisingly, following the 2012 "coup" and the election of retired general Abdel Fattah al-Sisi as president, the military role in the economy grew, with the army taking a leading role, supporting showy new projects like a second Suez Canal,[140] as noted below. Yet Egypt's defense budget remained low in relative terms, taking 1.2 percent of GDP in 2019, making Egypt 103rd in the world. It thus showed a considerable contrast with other Middle East countries, like Saudi Arabia and Oman, which invested over 8 percent of their GDP on their militaries.

Paradoxically, the low levels of military spending may have contributed to increases of political violence. Maher and Zhao find a significant negative impact on GDP growth and political violence in Egypt for the years 1982 to 2018, which they partially attribute to Egypt's declining defense spending during those years.[141] This low amount is particularly significant as Egypt faces serious security issues on all of its borders, to include a civil war in Libya, Jihadist forces in Sinai, and the opening of Ethiopia's "Grand Renaissance Dam" on the Blue Nile. President Sisi is demanding that Egypt's military modernize, and it has expanded purchasing of international-made equipment while building up its own domestic capacity to produce weapons.[142]

Jordan (LM)

While Jordan is a small country, its defense budget is relatively large, prompting vindications of its size by relatively pro-monarchy outlets. The *Jordan Times* was blunt about the positive impact that Jordan's military budget had on the Jordanian economy,

> In order to examine this issue comprehensively, it needs to be mentioned that the military is a major employment agency, hiring thousands at a time when unemployment is still a major problem in the country. Those employed by the military and security agencies, and their families, enjoy medical insurance and, for the most part, are assisted with their housing, education, social security and other expenses that give them a more favourable status than that of the rest of citizens. At the same time, thousands of practising physicians, engineers, computer technicians and others working in badly needed professions were trained by the military. In other words, the heavy expenditure of the military and security helps not only the security but the national economy as well. That is money well spent.[143]

The Jordanian military earns rent by sending its officers to Gulf Arab countries where salaries are higher than in Jordan, similar to how the Syrian army accrued rent in Lebanon.[144] In Jordan, foreign assistance and rents earned by Jordanian oil laborers working in Arab oil countries allowed the government to pay generous subsidies to a broad swath of its population,[145] offsetting what funds went to defense spending. More significantly, the Jordanian military budget became an engine of economic growth during state formation;

the army was the largest employer of Jordanian males after agriculture, and around 50 percent of village men had jobs in the army in the 1960s, by 1997 10 percent of the labor force worked in the military.[146] Jordan's military spending for 2021 was 5 percent of its GDP, ranking twelfth in the world. Additionally, Jordan has received almost $1 billion in American security assistance since 2015.[147] That supplements Jordan's regular defense budget, which for 2021, was the second largest item in the state budget, taking over 27 percent of it.[148]

Saudi Arabia (CM)

Saudi Arabia (CM) has had high levels of military spending relative to GDP, even after arms sales tapered off in the 1990s.[149] For 2014, Saudi Arabia increased its defense budget from the previous year by 14 percent. This increase surpassed the United Kingdom, France, and Japan, countries with much larger populations, ranking it fourth in the world.[150] Yet by 2021, Saudi Arabia announced a 4 percent decrease in its defense budget,[151] perhaps reflecting the long-run decline in petroleum prices, and an emphasis on non-military infrastructure. Still, Saudi Arabia remained close to the top of the big spenders list. While there are multiple reasons for Saudi military expenditure levels,[152] one explanation for their largess is rent payments to senior officers, an explanation consistent with the bargain that the Saudi state struck with its military in 2011 to give all a promotion and a pay increase. While the Saudi Arabian military does not operate a military industrial base, its retired officers do have considerable opportunities to run their own businesses, along with generous retirement benefits.

DEFENSE INC.: THE ECONOMICS OF MILITARY BUSINESS RENTS

Militaries are well organized to seek rents compared to other national agencies, because they can wrap their claims in patriotism, fear, or national pride. When they are close to the political centers of power, rent-seeking opportunities are considerable. Soldiers can also take advantage of their armed status to bully their way into power and influence.

A number of militaries have owned and operated businesses that span an opaque divide between military necessity and commercial profit seeking. North Korean generals hold vast interests in North Korea's export business to China, including the sale of coal, iron ore, and other raw materials.[153] Pakistan's military not only has charge of a considerable portion of national infrastructure (highways, transportation facilities, warehouses, and the like), which squeeze out potential private competition, but also ran a number of trusts that funded some of Pakistan's largest industries: fertilizer, cement, electric power, and banking, among other activities.[154] By one estimate, the "for profit" Pakistani military enterprises are worth over $100 billion US, more than a third of the national GDP.[155] The military in Myanmar runs holding companies, including the vast Union of Myanmar Economic Holdings, Ltd., owned jointly by active-duty military personnel and the Directorate of Defense Procurement, which controls the countries gem trade, among other activities. The Northeastern Command runs vast farms and uses its military muscle to keep chicken farming out of its province, thus granting itself a monopoly.[156] The biggest banks, breweries, and hotels in Myanmar are operated by the military.[157] Soldiers also allegedly run opium poppy farms in cooperation with criminal gangs.[158] The Sri Lankan armed forces grow vegetables for sale on commercial markets, as well as build roads, bridges, and cricket stadiums, as well as operate restaurants and luxury hotels.[159] The army grew during the long civil war, but national leaders were reluctant to disband some of it because of the consequent unemployment levels, and thus they receive "development work" for what are largely political reasons. Lissak observes that the Indonesian armed forces gained control over former Dutch property holdings in 1957 in what was to be a temporary takeover, but the army clung to its seized assets and marketed their commodities, gaining both foreign currency and considerable national power from their economic privileged position.[160] Gibbons notes that the Haitian military found itself in an ideal rent acquiring position through its ability to control the black market in embargoed fuel, using the proceeds not only for personal wealth but also to fund its own military activities in a poverty-stricken country.[161] Mexico's armed forces have increasingly moved into the civilian sector, building and operating a railroad though the Yucatán Peninsula, along with other economic projects, like running ports, and running a bank to dispense cash to the needy.[162] Said the head of a Mexican construction organization, "The Defense Ministry has more contracts than the biggest construction companies in the country."[163]

Seeking rent through business engagement may also be an alternative method to fund the armed forces so that they may adequately carry out national missions. Should the national budget be insufficient to meet the requirements soldiers need to do the nation's business of defense, they may attempt to raise the necessary resources themselves. Thus, when the People's Republic of China cut its defense budget in the 1990s, the Chinese People's Liberation Army added "business" to its list of competencies—running hotels, casinos, and other enterprises to raise military funds.[164] The Indonesian army started businesses to generate revenue for its independence movements in the 1940s, when it was rebelling against Dutch rule; more than sixty years later, business involvement continues.[165]

Rent-seeking can generate revenue while at the same time reducing military overall costs, as individual soldiers can supplement their often-meager pay through side-employment. Lambeth described Russian military pilots who spent weekends performing manual farm labor just to get by, though he also noted that Russian officers managed to pocket as much as $65 million through the corrupt sales of military property that they controlled.[166] Pion-Berlin details conditions in Argentina where defense budget cuts under President Raúl Alfonsín were so severe that soldiers left their bases at mid-day to work in the private sector to supplement their meager pay and benefits.[167] Ecuador's armed forces sometimes rent out their security services to private firms as well.[168]

Rent from Defense Industries

The relationship between the armed forces and national defense industry varies considerably from country to country, but in almost all situations, the military has considerable control over the arsenals that produce its weapons and equipment, either owning them outright or developing dependency ties to private ownership. The mass production factories that industrialized warfare began in Europe and North America in the nineteenth century[169] grew dramatically during World Wars I and II, and continued to produce weapons and equipment during the Cold War. In the former Soviet Union, the military industry developed close ties to the military that strengthened after that time, particularly under Leonid Brezhnev. However, while that industry churned out massive weapons amounts in a splurge that lasted into Gorbachev's time, Cooper argues that the uniformed Soviet military was rarely happy with industrial performance or responsiveness, because sometimes the result was poorly built aircraft, tanks, submarines, and other military systems.[170]

In some countries, the military actually own and operate national defense industries. In both Chile and Brazil, the military operated large sectors of the industrial economy in both countries during authoritarian years, benefiting from the military's ability to bully opponents of its military production into silence.[171] The Chinese People's Liberation Army (PLA) operated much of China's defense sector, using it not only to produce goods for the army but also to provide employment for military dependents and retired soldiers. Facing budget cuts, the PLA moved into the commercial sector to offset state budget cuts, entering the hotel and commercial food markets, and using its uniform factories to produce and sell civilian clothing, along with running its own airline.[172] This industrial sector allowed the Chinese to both modernize their military and their economy, as the PLA could rely on their industries to both supply their forces and to transfer innovation to civilian firms, thus facilitating overall national economic growth.[173]

RENT-SEEKING MILITARIES IN THE MIDDLE EAST

Middle East military rent-seeking may take many forms and may be driven by multiple motives. For example, some members of the Lebanese armed forces transfered weapons to conservative Christian militias during Lebanon's numerous militia wars.[174] As the army disintegrated during the civil war of 1975 to 1989, Christian army units in particular transferred armored personnel carriers, guns, and communications systems to Christian militias, gaining both money (and presumed gratitude) from their fellow Christian militia fighters. The Moroccan military attempted two coups against King Hassan II in 1971 and again in 1972, as noted in chapter 3, at least partly because the monarch had rewarded them with enough goods to fuel their desire for even more wealth and prestige.[175] While the regime either executed or jailed some of the coup plotters, Hassan decided to secure military loyalty through the grants of large land tracts for those officers not involved in the putsch.[176]

Though soldiers join and stay in the military for multiple reasons, a main reason is pay. Soldiers who serve for rent may be motivated by the ability to extract higher shares of the budget, particularly when their services are essential to the survival of the regime. Bellin notes that when regimes lose their ability to pay their troops or avail themselves of military equipment, the regime weakens from within and their coercive power deteriorates.[177] This may be why the ʿAsad regime gave its armed forces hefty pay increases during the large anti-regime protest days of 2011, even though the economy was deteriorating because of the demonstrations.[178] As the Syrian civil war intensified, the Syrian economy teetered on the brink of collapse, leaving less money to pay regular Syrian military units, thus forcing the ʿAsad regime to both shift tactics and personnel. These tactics included increasing the use of aircraft (often dropping "barrel bombs" on civilians to weaken the opposition) and the use of Lebanese Hezbollah and Syrian "*Shahbiha*" criminal gang members as alternative military forces.[179] As the war dragged on, Syrian government resources dwindled and the military had only ten to twenty thousand personnel available for offensive operations out of a total force of one to one hundred and fifty thousand total troops—most poorly trained conscripts who could not be deployed outside their local regions.[180] However, the elite Syrian army units were paid very well, both for service in Syria and as mercenaries. Syrian troops fighting in Libya can earn more than thirty-seven times the salary of the Syrian vice president, for example, and even new Syrian military recruits get one hundred and eighty times the starting salary of a public sector official.[181]

The bargaining over control of Iraqi government ministries post-Saddam provides evidence of military rent-seeking. Noted one political figure: "If the government allocates $7 billion to the Ministry of Culture today, tomorrow it will become a sovereign ministry. Everybody is after the money. Nobody cares about the ministry itself."[182] This is not surprising as the Iraqi army has historically served to protect the regime rather than the borders.[183] More evidence of military rent-seeking was evidenced by the mass defections of leaders and soldiers alike when the Islamic State attacked across much of northern Iraq in June 2014. Around four divisions, accounting for more than thirty thousand soldiers, melted away rather than fight; so many that the Iraq defense ministry tried to woo them back, knowing that they were in it for the pay: "Most of those interviewed said they were joining primarily because they badly needed the pay, not out of any sense of loyalty or desire to fight."[184] It is true, however, that a reconstituted Iraqi military performed well in the recapturing territory from ISIS, though their ranks were supplemented with Shi'a militia and Kurdish fighters. Still, a 2020 report by Anthony Cordesman indicated significant weakness remains in Iraq's military, and the government has not undertaken the necessary reforms to construct a viable fighting force.[185]

Middle East Military Industries

Henry and Springborg provide a useful spectrum of military business involvement in the Middle East, starting from a high level (Egypt and Iran, with economic activities spanning almost the entire national economy), through a middle level (Syria and Sudan, where military business activity is restricted mostly to military business), to a lower level (Algeria, where the military prefers the hidden world of side-payments rather than direct economic involvement), to the lowest level of involvement (some GCC countries and Tunisia).[186]

While the primary purpose of national defense–related industries is to supply the armed forces with necessary equipment (and free them from foreign dependence), they also serve as an instrument of economic power for the armed forces. Such industries can capture resources from other sectors and are often isolated from market forces because of their perceived critical missions. They can generate foreign trade earnings for their country, but they can also generate economic (and thus political) power, for their managers. The following cases illustrate the influence of Middle East military enterprises.

Egypt (BPR)

The Egyptian military has a larger role in the Egyptian economy than anywhere else in the Middle East; a role that dates back to the 1952 revolution that brought a series of generals to the head of the Egyptian power structure. In the years since 1952, retired colonels and generals have served as Egypt's president for all but two years, 2012 and 2013. The military started doing land reclamation after the revolution and later rebuilt the damaged infrastructure from the 1967 war.[187] The military's economic role accelerated under President Sadat, who needed to protect himself from military layoffs after Camp David and to give the armed forces economic benefits in exchange for political neutrality.[188] Egypt's armed forces shifted to rent paying, as Egyptian soldiers actually begged to be sent to Yemen during Egypt's involvement in the Yemeni civil war in the 1960s because of the large material rewards offered for service.[189] One consequence was that the war led to the emergence of a corrupt privileged officer corps that enjoyed wealth and access denied to Egyptians who did not serve in that conflict.

The military rule that followed the 1952 Free Officers coup accorded officers preferred access to the Egyptian economy. But while the military leaders did attempt economic modernization through industrialization, they paid insufficient attention to the needs of Egypt's peasants—failing, for example, to plan for sufficient consumer goods and agricultural products such as insecticides and agricultural implements.[190] Egypt's armed forces' business involvement was borne from the desire to provide jobs for the thousands of Egyptian troops demobilized after the 1979 Egypt-Israel peace treaty.[191] President Sadat, declaring that the 1973 war would be Egypt's last war, redirected the military's activity toward economic development projects; creating the National Service Projects Organization (NSPO) in 1978 to facilitate that shift.[192] Sadat also created the Arab Organization for Industrialization (AOI) in 1975, as a means to draw financing from Saudi Arabia, the UAE, and Qatar into Egypt's military industries.[193] That involvement grew considerably; consequently, Egyptian armed forces have a permanent and powerful role in that country's economy.

Samir Shehata considered the implications for the Egyptian military role in the Egyptian economy: "The military as an institution, the high-ranking officer corps, certainly has vested economic interests that could be changed or could be put in jeopardy. If the military was completely removed from politics, then there is no question that these interests would be put in jeopardy."[194]

There was seemingly no activity beyond the scope of Egyptian military involvement; it has had influence in arts, letters, and education since Nasser, and used these vehicles as a way to disseminate Nasser's brand of Arab nationalism.[195] These avenues also offered rent for the military, including government-run publishing houses, among other sources of revenue.[196] The Egyptian military allows their soldiers time off to work extra jobs because military pay is too low for them to survive economically. So, the Egyptian army brings in troops from the ranks of the poor to simply provide jobs at very low pay,[197] and then lets them work in the afternoons.[198] These conscripts provide cheap labor for Egyptian military-run enterprises, and the firms also benefit from subsidized land, fuel, and electricity, not to mention the protection of military production facilities by soldiers.[199]

While such enterprises appear to provide rent to military owners and operators, one Egyptian official put a different spin on it: "We help the Egyptian people, because the defense budget is lower because we earn some of our own funds."[200] The Egyptian military enterprises claimed to reduce prices, with 60 percent reduction in construction costs and a 10 to 25 percent claimed reduction in food prices in military-operated supermarkets.[201] The Egyptian military also argued that their economic activities supplement other bureaucracies in order to help "institutionalize" the state.[202] Other defenses had a similar ring; the Food Security Division of the Egyptian armed forces claimed that it had entered the farming and food sector to allow self-sufficiency for the military food supply (understandable for a country that has imported almost half of its food supply for decades); but the thousands of hectares have not only earned the military considerable sums of money but also allowed for partnerships with Egypt's private sector through the buying and selling of land. Notes Springborg, "the military favors the private sector, not only because it perceives it as more dynamic and possessing superior resources, but also because of its ability generously to reciprocate favors granted."[203]

Egypt's military economic empire has its own factories and its own personnel.[204] The AOI itself claims to employ fourteen thousand workers; overall, the military industry states that it provides work to more than forty thousand Egyptians, though other sources claim twice that number.[205] Droz-Vincent claims an employment number of between eighty and one hundred thousand persons. While many of these jobs stem from government spending, which may crowd out other more permanent or efficient forms of job creation, they also create dependencies that are difficult to curb.[206] By one estimate, a significant majority of Egyptian companies are headed by retired officers.[207] Egyptian officers run malls, a bottled water factory, air conditioning and refrigeration companies that sell to the civilian consumer sector, among other enterprises; and probably employ more than fifty thousand workers.[208]

Military factories have expanded into the civilian sector; producing washing machines, clothing, food, medical services, automobiles, and other items.[209] Other military-run enterprises include the National Co. for Batteries, the National Co. for Fisheries, the Egyptian National Co. for Pharmaceuticals, the Arab Renewable Energy Company (ARECO), Egyptian Black Sand, and many more.[210] These enterprises have an abundant stock of workers as Egyptian soldiers essentially provide free labor to these and many other industries.[211]

Outside of the formal military industrial structure, the military also has influence, as many retired senior officers get a piece of the Egyptian economy as a reward for loyalty. For example, General 'abd al-Halim Abu Ghazala, former President Mubarak's classmate in the Egyptian Military Academy, and one of the most powerful military officers under Mubarak (until his 1988 firing), persuaded the US to transfer funds to the Egyptian Passenger Car Company in 1986; apparently because Ghazala wanted an engine plant for his military vehicles.[212] Like the Egyptian Passenger Car deal, much military production is co-mingled with civilian work through the AOI; so military vehicles and sewer pipe production coexist in the same bureaucracy, which may help efficiencies but also maintains a degree of opacity over the real role of military industries and their beneficiaries. These activities gained public support when former President Mubarak ordered the Egyptian army to use its bread factories to bake bread during the grain shortage of 2008.[213] The MMP lists a variety of military-owned businesses, including the El-Nasr Company for Services and Maintenance (75 percent owned by the military, and the rest private ownership by retired generals) with more than seven thousand employees working in child care, automobile maintenance, and hotel administration.[214] Al-Toraifi notes that the scope of Egypt's military business is so large that the armed forces could offer the government a one-billion US dollar loan; indicating the size of the undeclared monetary surplus it has earned from its enterprises.[215] By some estimates, Egyptian military industries has constituted between 5 and 15 percent of the Egyptian economy by 2011.[216] Other analysts suggest that the real number is closer to 30 or 40 percent, though some dispute this estimate.[217] Those numbers include the military management of almost one-quarter of all housing and public infrastructure spending, close to $24 US billion.[218] The Ministry's reach into almost all sectors of Egypt is pervasive; from partnering with Chinese firms to convert busses to natural gas,[219] through automobile production,[220] to manufacturing solar panels.[221]

These military corporations neither pay taxes on their incomes, nor do they have to deal with the bureaucratic morass that often entraps the private sector.[222] They can borrow money easily, from the MMP, thus they are able to circumvent the private banking system.²²³ It is noteworthy than when state-sector privatization began under Sadat and continued under Mubarak, privatization did not include the military industrial base. Political efforts also protected that base from foreign competition,²²⁴ and the military can take advantage of privatization laws to acquire private firms.²²⁵ The sheer size of military enterprises has sometimes driven out the competition; Egypt's cement industry being one example. The military-owned Al Arish Cement Company produced so much cement that it drove the state-owned National Cement Company out of business.²²⁶ In other cases, the military simply steals the competition. When the Juhayna dairy refused to sell a controlling share to the military, the state accused its owner of "terrorism" and incarcerated them. When an electronics manufacturer declined to share his technology with the military, they canceled contracts with his company, and then also accused the owner of terrorism and locked him up. When the military stood up a new company, Silo Foods Industrial City, the jailed owner of Juhayna offered to run it for the army, but they refused.²²⁷

If military-run businesses can exercise such power, foreign investors may well be reluctant to partner with non-military Egyptian enterprises.²²⁸ Egypt's military businesses also take advantage of cheap and compliant labor, as much of the work in Egyptian military enterprises is performed by low-paid military conscripts who receive harsh military punishment for mistakes, accidents, or work stoppages.²²⁹ One serious consequence of the dominance of these military businesses is that they are driving out investment in Egypt's private sector. As Diwan notes: "In Egypt, as the army's involvement in the economy rose, private investment has fallen to 6 percent of GDP, less than its level under former president Gamal Abdel Nasser in the 1970s."²³⁰ Another consequence is when the state removes production risks, and is immune to market forces, industry stagnates. This is clear with Egypt's military industries, as they routinely lose money, refuse to innovate, and produce generally shoddy goods and services.²³¹

Probably knowing that their role in the national economy would draw scrutiny and criticism, the officers involved defend their business stakes by arguing that the projects, run through the NSPO would resolve income inequality and foster economic development.²³² They also recognized that a private economic role would make the military less dependent on the national budget for its resources; as a lack of a viable Israeli threat and demands for budget austerity from international lending agencies placed political demands on the military to seek less from the national treasury.²³³ Egypt's Sovereign Wealth Fund contributed to the perception of military budget independence when it partnered with the NSPO in 2020 to fund more NSPO-affiliated companies.²³⁴ The development of the Sovereign Wealth Fund may have led to a perception that the state was trying to curb the military industries; however, a closer look indicated that it was just another source of funds for those businesses. Notes Kaldas: "the military may have found a way to access their parked capital and further intertwine their interests. The goal is not simply to accumulate wealth, but rather to control how and by whom wealth is accumulated."[235]

In August 2014, President Sisi announced a series of mega-projects around the Suez Canal, including a second canal, a road network, and an air terminal—all at a total cost of over $200 billion USD, with thirty-seven Egyptian companies and "with the army in overall charge."[236] Joining these projects were massive land reclamation ventures that would dramatically increase the habitable area of Egypt from 5 percent to 20 percent, through a series of canals, new cities, and irrigation schemes, along with investment in tourism and industry; all to be managed by the armed forces.[237] Despite serious questions about the viability and cost of these projects, they served to enhance the political and economic power of Egypt's military class.

The Egyptian military has done better in business than in battle. As a 2020 article notes: "Egypt's army is wary of foreign wars, a caution that dates back to its ill-fated intervention in Yemen in the 1960s. . . . Instead it has fought jihadists on the Sinai Peninsula, overthrown a president, and built an economic empire that stretches from luxury hotels to cement."[238] Pollock documents the many Egyptian military failures from the 1948 war on. The reasons for these Egyptian disappointments are complex, but one may be its choice to emphasize business over military affairs.[239]

Jordan (LM)

The case of the Jordanian Aeronautical Systems Company is instructive; it is a part of the Royal Jordanian Air Force. It also has private partners and is a profit-making company.[240] The King Abdullah II Design and Development Bureau (KADDB), which produces equipment and offers training to the Jordanian military, with a good portion of its business coming from Gulf militaries in particular.[241] So, is military participation in and ownership of a for-profit firm rent-seeking or just controlling the company that maintains military aircraft?

Jordan's defense industry has entered into partnerships with a number of international defense firms. Marshall finds that KADDB received numerous tax and other incentives from the Jordanian government that allowed it to become a favorable international partner.[242] So, KADDB produces the Desert Iris, a light armored vehicle, with a British company, and partners with South Africa to produce additional military vehicles.[243] The company has also moved into non-defense business sectors.[244] This suggests interesting parallels to the Egyptian case; where the armed forces used their defense firms to merge with private sector firms, and thus expanding Egyptian military rent opportunities.

Jordan does face corruption challenges in its defense sector; as Transparency International notes that Jordanian defense industries may be owned by military members, and that there have been no audits of them by the Audit Bureau. Nor is there any parliamentary oversight of the military industries, which are under the sole control of the monarch.[245]

Saudi Arabia (CM)

Saudi Arabia, long dependent on petroleum revenue for most of its income, has attempted to diversify its economy in recent years; including the development of a defense industry. In Saudi Arabia, Abdullah al-Faris Company for Heavy Industries manufactures the al-Fahd Infantry Fighting Vehicle and the Al-Faris 8-200 Armored Personnel Carrier, along with the Ashibl 1 and Ashibl 2 armored vehicles.[246] Under the direction of Crown Prince Mohammed ibn Salman al-Saud, Saudi Arabia consolidated its various military enterprises into the Saudi Arabian Military Industries (SAMI) conglomerate; which aspired to create more than forty thousand direct jobs and $3.7 billion to the Saudi Arabian economy.[247] As Barany notes, SAMI was also a way for Saudi Arabia to get around foreign arms embargoes for its Yemen policies.[248] Outside of SAMI, international firms formed partnerships with Saudi interests, such as American firm Oshkosh Defense's partnering with Al Tadrea Manufacturing Company in the production of armored vehicles in the Kingdom.[249] However, concerns about Saudi Arabian human rights, both domestically and internationally, threatened this and other international partnerships. SAMI developed plans to sidestep any sanctions against the Saudi defense industry by seeking partnerships with the UAE and, potentially, China.[250] To facilitate cooperation with the UAE, SAMI signed an agreement in February 2021 with NMIR, an Emirates-based defense firm, to produce light armored vehicles.[251] The emphasis on "localized content," where Saudi Arabian firms are the primary producers, rose to 8 percent in 2021, with a goal of 50 percent by 2030.[252] This hope reflected the continuing concern that Saudi Arabia was not adding enough jobs for its youthful population, to wean the market from jobs held by international labor. Saudi Arabia also expressed a determination to engage in research that would enable the Kingdom to produce equipment of its own design, as scientists at the King Abdulaziz City for Science and Technology were developing laser-guided bombs and short-range ballistic missiles to be produced in the Kingdom.[253]

Iran (BPR)

Iranian military rent-seeking began before the 1979 revolution; under the reign of Shah Muhammad Pahlavi. In 1963, when the Shah tried to inject a dose of competition into Iran's flaccid economy, the decision drew immediate opposition from numerous rent-seekers, including senior military officers; among them General Karim Ayadi, the Shah's physician, who controlled the import of military supplies and equipment.[254] Gasiorowski observes: "Most senior officers in the security forces were loyal to the Shah, mainly because their careers and opportunities for personal enrichment depended upon his approval."[255] Skocpol implies that Shah Muhammad Pahlavi managed a divide-and-conquer strategy over his bureaucracy, in essence de-powering them as a threat to his reign. She notes: "The Shah personally made all major decisions—about official appointments, about military procurement, about major state economic investments. . . . Military officers, for example, lacked the corporate solidarity to displace the Shah in a coup and save the state at his expense."[256] Instead, it was the centers of Shi'a opposition who led the 1979 Iranian revolution and many of Iran's soldiers perished before revolutionary firing squads.

Post-revolutionary Iran continued its rentier status; creating "another sort of rentier state: a populist, welfare-oriented rentier state, with the ulama passing out alms in return for moral conformity on a grander scale than ever before. Unemployment and underemployment could continue at high levels in a stagnant national economy."[257] The Iranian Revolutionary Guard Committees (IRGC) and its offshoots have attained a privileged position in Iranian political and economic space, particularly after the Iran-Iraq war. Now, the IRGC alone may control either up to one-third of Iran's economy,[258] or 15 percent, according to Khajehpour (2017).[259] The economic arm of the IRGC, the *Khatam-al Anbiya,* employs around 1.5 million workers, including contractors.[260] The IRGC owns and operates factories, farms, oil and gas development, construction companies, along with the very firms that are supposed to be auditing them, and a network of docks and terminals that are believed to facilitate up to 60 percent of the illegal imports that flow into Iran each year and provide substantial income to IRGC members.[261] The IRGC has also received more than half the petroleum contracts allocated by the Iranian Oil Ministry,[262] and is the sole contractor for Iran's natural gas industry.[263] Their engineering arm, Khatam al-Anbia, received more than 750 oil and gas contracts.[264] By one count, the IRGC operates more than three hundred companies, including some state companies that the regime "privatized."[265] Some argue that this total ownership of the Iranian economy by the IRGC could range from one- to two-thirds, including firms in oil and gas, transportation, construction, and telecommunications.[266] The IRGC range of ownership is difficult to assess, though, as it apparently holds many companies under the guise of private sector enterprises.[267] As Saadati says, The IRGC dominates Iran's economy and acts as the regime's financial and military artery.[268]

The IRGC benefits from the religious trusts (*bonyads*) that operate independently from the state.[269] It also appears that the IRGC uses *bonyads* under its control to facilitate weapons procurement along with financial support for the Lebanese Hezbollah and other revolutionary forces.[270] There was plenty of rent-seeking in Iran's defense industry as well; as various defense industries took considerable funds to develop what they claimed were new developed weapons when in fact they were either former American systems with fake parts attached, or complete fakes, like the "Qaher-313," a supposed fifth-generation fighter.[271]

The IRGC has also used its political muscle to push out international competition for the provision of economic services; as demonstrated when the Turkish cell phone provider Turkcell initially won a contract to operate in Iran, and a Turkish-Swiss consortium initially won a contract to operate Khomeini International Airport. In both cases, the IRGC pressured to replace the international operators and take the contracts itself.[272]

As these IRGC activities were squeezing out the private sector, then-President Hassan Rouhani asked that their share of Iran's economy be pared back.[273] As their political power stems from their close association to the supreme leader, Rouhani's request went unanswered. In 2018, he again attacked these interests publicly: "A number of semi-state entities belonging to military, religious and revolutionary foundations represent a different layer of overlap between political and business interests. . . . Consequently, major embezzlement cases were facilitated and even tolerated as part and parcel of a culture of opacity."[274] It may have been that Rouhani's message, combined with a more general trend away from military economic ownership, that reduced the role that both Artesh and the IRCG now play in Iran's economy.[275] But after the 2021 elections, won by the conservative Ebrahim Raisi, it is likely that Rounahi's efforts will be pared back.

Yemen (BPR)

Yemen is the poorest country in the Arab world; and with a large army that faces both internal and external threats, it is not surprising that there has long been military rent-seeking. The armed forces were often vessels to be filled with soldiers who joined for salaries and the opportunity to collect rents on the side.[276] Yemen's military was considered so corrupt that when the US pressured for increased coastal patrolling, Yemen (with US support) established a new coast guard rather than expand the traditional navy.[277]

The Yemeni military also has its hands in the business sector. As Clark documents, the Military Economic Corporation, headed by the top military brass, initially provisioned the Yemeni military with military basics.[278] It then quickly expanded into producing bathroom fittings, shower curtains, and other clearly non-military items; along with expansions into oil-producing land and other real estate options. Other army leaders have shares in telecommunications and oil companies, and the Ministry of Defense manages private enterprises for the benefit of senior officers.[279] The military also runs hospitals, also sources of graft and price-gouging, in collusion with civilian aid workers.[280]

Yemen's armed forces have exclusive ownership of the Military Economic Corporation (MECO), now known as the Yemen Economic Corporation (YECO), which used to distribute commodities of all kinds to local communities. As subsidies dried up, YECO moved into land purchasing (allegedly for military use, but in reality, for military profit), and has built enterprises on military-owned land ("Tourist City" in Sana'a, for example), pocketing the profits.[281] YECO expanded into multiple civilian enterprises, including commercial fishing, pharmaceuticals, tourism, and real estate.[282] In the post-Saleh era, Yemeni leadership is attempting to ferret out military corruption; partly by giving military payments directly to the soldiers rather than running them through senior officers, along with efforts to remove the members of the Saleh family who still control military units.[283] Because the corruption also ties into the traditional tribal identities of Yemeni military members, reducing it will be difficult until tribal identity itself is more integrated into Yemeni national identity. This was illustrated by the al-Houthi takeover of much of Yemen after Saleh's suspension of oil subsidies in response to the need for international loans. However, the military had benefited from the subsidies and from the smuggling of diesel fuel; after Saleh terminated them, many Yemeni military units surrendered to the Houthi in protest, allowing them to sweep through much of Yemen.[284]

Yemen's ongoing brutal civil war has enabled corruption, especially military corruption, as whatever enforcement mechanisms before the war have disappeared with the formal Yemeni state. As in the Saleh era, military commanders remaining with the fractured Yemeni military pad their payrolls with "ghost soldiers," and have created an economic enterprise by selling their arms and equipment, usually provided by Saudi Arabia or the UAE, for cash.[285]

Turkey (BSPR)

Beginning in the 1960s, the Turkish military carved out independent access to economic resources, partly to ensure that it never had to depend on civilian rule to support its requirements. It created an independent holding company, the *Ordu Yardımlaşma Kurumu* (OYAK, or Armed Forces Trust and Pension Fund), which operates shopping centers, officer's clubs, cement factories, banks, and recreational facilities.[286] A 2012 report using 2009 data showed that OYAK employed almost thirty thousand persons with net assets worth more than $15 billion USD, with interests in sixty companies and some twenty-eight wholly owned by OYAK. These companies had a wide range of activities, including joint ownership of a Renault factory that had produced more than four million automobiles.[287] In 2013, OYAK's total assets were around $20 billion USD, making it one of the five largest conglomerates in Turkey.[288] By 2017, OYAK's total value had dropped to $13 billion USD[289] but recovered and grew to $20 billion by 2020.[290] What is remarkable, as Abul-Magd, Akça, and Marshall note, is that while the AKP has dramatically reduced the power of the Turkish military (see chapter 3), OYAK has continued to prosper; with its total assets jumping from $668 million in 2001 to $19.6 billion in 2017.[291] OYAK also partnered with a number of international corporations, including Austrian Chemson and OYAK Renault Otomobil Fabrikaları, which produced 308,568 motor vehicles and 431,337 engines in 2020.[292]

Turkish Law 205 of 1961 established the Army Mutual Aid Association, which is a type of insurance corporation offering subsidized mortgages and other loans for officers and civilian employees of the Defense Ministry. Because the Army Mutual Aid Association invests its funds in domestic firms, the military has a strong interest in the health of these large companies.[293] Consequently, the military has a significant interest in maintaining Turkey's economic status quo. When the Islamist Refah Party proposed economic reform and the development of new economic ties to Turkey's southern neighbors in the early 2000s, the policy "was clearly a challenge to the military's core economic interests."[294]

In 2010, the Turkish armed forces encouraged Turkey to adopt the International Monetary Fund's austerity package that was intended to push the country toward a true market economy. Paradoxically, it empowered the Islamist business class, among others, which, according to Eligur, would weaken the comparative political power of the armed forces. Turkey's military may have been simply recognizing the obvious; the AKP was clearly curbing its power and it could either resist or capitulate to reality. The IMF move suggests the latter.[295]

Turkey has been building a robust defense industry for decades, partially reflecting a suspicion that the US and other NATO allies would be reluctant to share advanced military technology with Turkey as it was not a reliable NATO partner.[296] The military industrial growth also reflected the power of the Turkish military, which was able in the pre-AKP days to draw considerably on state funding to invest in military production. That resulted in some sophisticated weapons systems like the Bayraktar TB2 and TAI Anka military drones that may be among the best in the world.[297] The Turkish defense industry was also involved in developing a new main battle tank, a series of unmanned ground vehicles, and the "Siper" air defense system.[298] The Turkish-built Bayraktar TB2 drone, at a cost of around $2 million, has been used by several countries in the Middle East, and by Ukraine after the March 2022 Russian invasion, garnering decisive results against Russian forces.[299]

Cook provides evidence that the Turkish military role in defense production is shifting to a higher level of civilian control.[300] This would hardly be surprising, as President Erdoğan is deeply suspicious of the Turkish military. Erdoğan wants Turkey to be completely independent of foreign military equipment requirements by 2023, and thus is investing heavily in modernizing Turkish military industries.[301] But the military has largely been excluded from the expansion process.

Israel (FD)

Israel's defense sector is a significant part of the Israeli economy; consisting of more than six hundred companies, employing more than forty-five thousand workers, and generating more than $10.3 billion in revenue in 2017.[302] Plants, large and small, scattered all over Israel, often contribute to employment in largely rural areas. They also contribute not only to Israel's defense but also to Israel's trade balance, as they export much of what they produce.

The Israeli defense sector grew considerably during the 1970s and 1980s, and its relative power extended beyond the economy itself. According to Mintz,

> The relative growth of the defense-industrial sector in the economy and the increase in the number of senior officers holding key policy-making positions has already been translated into a prominent rise in the complex's influence in several spheres, including: the conduct of foreign policy through use of arms exports as a political tool; decision making on such fundamental issues as initiation of war, resulting in a broader involvement of the military sector in determining policies; intensified activities in the administered territories, resulting from support of government policy by senior military officials; supply of social services, a function of the IDF's extension to the spheres of education, social welfare, health, and other areas.[303]

This may be a bit of an exaggeration of the power of the Israeli defense sector and its military overseers; still, as the largest employer in the state of Israel, it does have considerable influence. Moreover, its structure, managed heavily by the IDF due to the relative weakness of the Ministry of Defense, has allowed the Israeli defense industry to resist necessary reforms. Notes Lewis, "The inability to reform the defense industry significantly has been attributed to the interconnections at the highest levels of the public sector, the IDF, and the defense firms."[304] Rivlin notes that monopoly and oligopoly are widespread in the Israeli defense industry, and that "prices are often either controlled by the government or strongly influenced by it."[305]

The size and scope of Israel's military industry is considerable; Israeli Military Industries, a maker of small arms, has opened a subsidiary in the United States.[306] Israel Aerospace Industries (IAI) is not wholly owned by the Israeli military, but its primary Israeli customer is the Israeli Defense Forces (though it also produces commercial aircraft). IAI also has a North American subsidiary, headed by retired US Air Force general Robert Fogelsong, which gives IAI access to the US defense market as well. That is helped by a big selling point for IAI, because one of its slogans is "As used by the IDF," thus its relationship with the IDF is critical to this marketplace, says the CEO Yair Shamir, son of the former prime minister.[307] Elbit Systems produces some of the world's most sophisticated weapons systems, and has numerous international partners, including the United States on the F-35 and Bradley Fighting Vehicle.[308] Elbit's international presence is considerable, as it derives 80 percent of its revenues from sales outside of Israel.[309] The US Army has purchased "Iron Dome" missile defense components from Rafael Industries[310] Israeli defense exports topped $8.3 billion in 2020, up 14 percent from the previous year. Israeli defense officials continue to seek new markets; asking the government to suspend compliance with the Missile Technology Control Regime so that they can sell more unmanned aerial vehicles on the international market.[311]

Syria (BPR)

Syria has a large military-operated industrial complex under the Syrian Organization of Military Factories, a producer of spare parts and small arms, along with co-production of imported weapons. It produces very few weapons or support systems of Syrian design.

The Syrian military used its privileged position to amass resources for its diverse industrial holdings, which expanded outside of military production to include civilian industry, agricultural production, bottled water, furniture, and other commodities. The range of its activities was signified simply by the titles of the organizations under the umbrella *Mu'assatat al-Iskan al-'Askari*: the Constructions Organization, the Medical Industries Organization, the Military Social Organization, and the Military Housing Organization—all under the Ministry of Defense.[312] Rivlin notes the nexus between the Syrian military and its ties to the national economy: "the military complex has spread into other sectors of the economy, especially construction and trading. This military industrial complex has to be supplied and appeased when policy is made, and this has economic as well as political costs."[313] It may be that the more lucrative (at least before 2011) civilian market drove Syrian military companies to produce civilian goods at the expense of military hardware, which, given the state of the Syrian state budget, probably did not earn much for its military entrepreneurs. Still, there were ample opportunities for side payments to officers involved in the form of kickbacks and commissions on the side.[314] Following the Syrian civil war, which devastated Syria's economy, military officers found a new source of rent: the production of illegal Captagon, an addictive drug similar to methamphetamine. The Fourth Armored Division of the Syrian Army, an elite unit commanded by Maher al-'Asad, the Syrian president's younger brother, controlled both the manufacture and distribution of the drugs.[315] The Fourth Armored Division, which had the responsibility of suppressing the protests when the Syrian civil war began, not only protected President 'Asad's regime but also furnished it with rent, while taking shares for themselves.

Given how badly the regular Syrian military disintegrated after the start of the Syrian civil war, Russia stepped up efforts to professionalize the military, including a reform of the military-run defense industry. Progress was unclear, as Russian influence was offset by a 2018 agreement between the 'Asad regime and Iran that gave Tehran the right to rebuild the Syrian defense industry.[316]

Algeria (BSPR)

Algeria's military industry reflects the military's desire to become independent of both Russia and the West, though it has ties to both. Its defense industry capacity ranges from the small, such as bullets, to the significant, such as military ships (including corvettes and frigates) along with armored vehicles.[317] The industry co-produces armored vehicles with Germany, along with Mercedes trucks, allowing the military to spend money for its political benefit. Italian analyst Marco Di Liddo stated: "Military spending nourishes the power of the armed forces at a time when they are in competition with the civilian government for influence and as the country's president is seeking to strengthen politics at the Army's expense."[318] By 2021, the Ministry of Defense-operated Mercedes plant was delivering thousands of vehicles throughout Algeria.[319]

Sons of senior Algerian military officers run some of the industries that supply the armed forces, providing such goods as sugar and butter; and there have been allegations of corruption stemming from their favored status.[320] While Algeria's armed forces do not own and operate the country's defense facilities, those plants produce side payments to the army and the senior officers gain significant wealth from their service. Notes Slyomovics, "decades of formal and *de facto* military rule has resulted in a military establishment that directs the country's resources with the result that many individual high-ranking officers have amassed great wealth."[321] This was but a part of a larger involvement in the national economy by Algeria's military elite, as Dilman observes: "Some military elites became pseudo-private actors, importing through their own companies, taking commissions on imports, or facilitating access by private companies to import contracts."[322] Resulting from a 1995 regulation that allowed officials to manage foreign exchange transactions on behalf of traders. Moreover, again according to Dilman, military officials joined other state bureaucrats in benefitting from rents stemming from the privatization of the state-run pharmaceutical sector through the establishment of joint-venture enterprises that gained an oligopoly over drug imports.[323] This is a part of a more general trend where the Algerian armed forces use their influence to bend other agencies to their will for rent-seeking, as Elguettaa observes:

> the civilian state bureaucracy is a source of privileges and income. At the national level, military elites negotiate with national ministers and general managers to benefit their real estate ventures, reduce tax liability, facilitate business, and ease bureaucratic restrictions. Through family businesses, military elites also win national tenders and strike agreements with the defense and other ministries. At the regional level, a network of interests forms between influential military figures and governors, in which regional military leaders and traditional civilian regime elites (often belonging to the ruling party) play a central role.[324]

RENT-SEEKING CONSEQUENCES

Military rent-seeking challenges both military professionalization and, beyond that, the national economy and its connection to the military. The first issue is clear: when soldiers are managing business enterprises instead of performing their military professional requirements, military professionalism suffers. That may be insignificant in countries without a real outside threat, which is true for some Middle East countries, but not for most, as security threats are high in most parts of the region. It is sometimes true that the motive for operating business enterprises is to generate more funding for military activities when the state has cut the military budget; still, efforts devoted to making business decisions are efforts not devoted to military activities. When this happens, the military just becomes another bureaucracy, with interests that can be bought off in a clientelist structured system. As Herzog notes about the Saudi Arabian system: "The incredibly rapid growth of the Saudi bureaucracy has led to the clientele's employment of many mid- and low-level bureaucrats with few qualifications and limited motivation. In this environment it did not take long for jobs to be seen as an entitlement. These entitlements have been tied to the broad patronage of individual princes as Sultan in the vast Ministry of Defense or Abdallah in the National Guard."[325] While it was not clear whether Herzog was describing civilian employees or military personnel in the MOD, the argument is applicable to many officers in rentier states where payoffs include plum appointments, foreign travel, access to modern weapons, and side jobs. Davidson observes that the UAE has purchased billions of dollars of new highly-sophisticated military hardware, but "closely connected to the rentier pathologies discussed earlier . . . there is a fear that given their privileged backgrounds and their status as members of an elite groups in receipt of distributed wealth, there is little likelihood that UAE nationals employed by the UAE Armed Forces would actually stand their ground in the event of combat."[326] Despite Davidson's argument, UAE forces have fought well in attacks against the so-called Islamic State, with one raid led by a woman fighter pilot. UAE forces have also fought against the al-Houthi in Yemen. American officials now regard the UAE as their most capable partner in the entire Central Command structure.[327] Barany argues that the UAE military is the "most professional and ambitious military in the Gulf States." The same cannot be said for the Egyptian military, whose rent-seeking may have damaged its already limited war-making capability. Since the 1973 Suez Canal crossing, Egypt's armed forces have rarely succeeded in combat. They did little in the 1990–91 Gulf war and have struggled to contain jihadists in the Sinai."[328] The limited range of Egyptian military power has prevented Egypt from challenging Turkish-backed forces of the Government of National Accord in neighboring Libya.[329]

There are other civil-military consequences for military businesses, as privatization of state enterprises threatens military commerce. Military commercial operations do not usually pay taxes to the state, and often benefit from conscripted labor (soldiers working at low military wages in commercial factories, for example). The state often provides free land and other production factors. Privatization reduces or eliminates such privileges, and thus senior soldiers are usually opposed to it. Moreover, as senior armed forces took charge in the wake of President Hosni Mubarak's departure from Cairo, there were reports that the officers were purging advocates of economic reform from the cabinet; including Finance Minister Youssef Boutros-Ghali and Trade Minister Rachid Mohamed Rachid, who suddenly faced allegations of corruption.[330] The military-led removal of President Mohammed Morsi in July 2013 was also partly aimed at protecting their vast business interests; demonstrated by Morsi's retiring more than seventy generals, who thus lost part of their own business returns.[331]

MILITARY CORRUPTION

Corruption eludes precise definition, because one person's corruption may be another person's price for navigating a byzantine political system. Generally, corruption is the use of state resources for private gain by an individual or group, or the payment for goods and services that violates or skirts the lawful exchange system. Corruption includes the payment of bribes to gain an advantageous position, the use of public funds for private gain, the falsification of data to hide personal indiscretions, and other such behaviors that not only violate national laws but also public trust. Succinctly: "Corruption conventionally is understood as the pursuit of self-interest through misdirection of organizational resources."[332] National armed forces often consume larger percentages of the government budget, and thus soldiers have the means to use cash transfers to buy their way into either organizational or personal gain. Sometimes this leads to corruption; the violation of national laws regulating what and how government officials and agents dealing with such officials may do relative to transactions.

Military corruption is often more prevalent when soldiers actually control the state or are close to the corridors of power.[333] Thus, rent-seeking militaries are much more likely to engage in corrupt practices than are professional soldiers. Rent-seeking soldiers may easily offer bribes of military supplies, shares of the defense budget, or access to military personnel by those willing to pay for it; primarily because the army needs political allies in national power struggles, or because of simple greed. Because developing countries often do not have institutional protections against corruption, the problem is often worse as it is compounded by the reality that the military budget as a share of GDP is usually larger than in developed nations. The lack of civil society, an independent judiciary, and the relative political power of the military only increases the opportunities for military corruption. An example of this is found in1970s Nigeria: military members reportedly pocketed $3.6 million from an illegal C-130 aircraft sale and equipped themselves with expensive tanks and aircraft even though its primary threat was from low-intensity ground conflict.[334] Nigeria also provides an example of the seriousness of military corruption on security, as military funds diverted by military corruption meant that Nigeria's forces were under-manned and ill-equipped to fight Boko Haram insurgents.[335] Ulrich observes corruption at the Soviet Ministry of Defense during the 1990s. Some generals may have converted as much as $65 million for their personal use, and that the shift from a state-controlled economy the private sector only increased the opportunities for military enrichment.[336] Defense cutbacks have only made this system worse. Military bribery has also been rife in the Russian military, as apparently only 9 percent of military purchases goes through the legal processes There also are widespread reports of Russian soldiers selling their weapons and fuel to the enemy (in Afghanistan and the Caucuses, for example), among other diversions of military resources for private use.[337] "Ghost" soldiers, fictitious names carried on military rosters enabling supervising officers to pocket pay allocated to these "soldiers," are a common problem in many militaries. Recently, Russian cyber-military units stand accused of using cyber technology for criminal purposes.[338] Li argues that the separation of civilian and military elites fostered a climate of military corruption in post-Mao China.[339]

Military corruption, as a preventative against coups, is often a partial function of civil-military relations. Weak or fearful leaders will sometimes not only turn a blind eye toward corruption, but quietly encourage it as a reward for troops remaining in their barracks. If such leaders are going to countenance their militaries to operate businesses and earn rents from them, why not go a step further and let them engage in corrupt practices? It is also likely that, as the military's role in national politics grows, so will its ability to practice corruption. Siddiqa finds that Pakistan's armed forces, also with government acquiescence, engaged in considerable corruption in league with other Pakistani bureaucracies.[340]

MILITARY CORRUPTION IN THE MIDDLE EAST

In some Middle Eastern countries, members of the military stay out of the economy. Their professionalism does not allow for such activities, other elements do not allow them in, or because their military salaries and benefits are large enough to satisfy their needs. Yet political conditions in other countries encourage military participation in the national economy. In some instances, military remuneration is inadequate to provide even a basic living, and so soldiers sometimes hold a second job to boost them above poverty lines. In other cases, the demands of military service are not enough to preclude time spent in a second occupation or profession. After duty hours, military dentists may drill civilian teeth, and soldiers build furniture in small shops. There is a long-standing tradition that bolsters such activity. Parker, examining the post-2003 Iraqi military, states: "The culture of graft leads to crippling inefficiencies and dangerous gaps: commanders pad military pay rolls with soldiers who do not exist, military officers and ministry officials receive kickbacks on contracts for everything from food supplies to defense equipment, and senior officials create skeleton companies to pilfer money from the Treasury."[341] Similar military corruption in Morocco may have been the consequence of King Hassan's decision to provide economic privileges to the military after their 1970s coup attempts, allowing senior generals to earn lavish profits from fishing rights and arms sales.[342] As the cases below illustrate, sometimes corruption is endemic, impacting military performance, and public confidence in the armed forces. Though the Israeli military is seen by the Israeli public as at less corrupt than other Israeli institutions, but military corruption does exist.[343] The Indian military banned an Israeli arm of the military, Israeli Military Industries, from selling arms to India for ten years as the result of an investigation that reportedly revealed that the firm bribed Indian officials to purchase its products.[344]

Yemen (BPR)

The Yemeni military exists largely to protect the regime and expects payment to fulfill its tasks. A 2006 report commissioned by the US embassy in Sanaʻa found: "There are five main elite groups that profit from the structure of corruption in Yemen. The two most important are also the two with the most overlap: tribes and the military-security establishment. Leaders of key tribes constitute the lion's share of top military and security officers."[345] Despite reports of widespread Yemeni regular military corruption, the US funneled millions of dollars (almost $68 million in fiscal 2009) to Yemen to purchase military equipment and military training. Yet inadequate monitoring produced the obvious result: "much equipment was unaccounted for. There were also significant discrepancies between . . . data on the quantity that had been provided and that which was in the Yemeni forces' inventories."[346] The weak central state empowered para-states in Yemen's regions, with five military regions commanded by a Yemeni general officer. General Ali Mohsen al-Ahmar's defection from President Saleh in March 2011 highlighted his reported involvement, along with the other four regional commanders, in transferring funds for development to residents. He also withheld funds to punish disloyal citizens, a power that earned General Al-Ahmar the description of a cross between a warlord and a business oligarch.[347] Yemen also drew Clarke's attention as she reported that in Yemen approximately one-third of Yemen's soldiers are actually "ghost soldiers," those who show up only on the rolls of the commander, who then pockets their salaries and sells off their equipment;[348] a finding echoed by a 2006 report on Yemeni corruption.[349] By 2020, that had apparently changed, as one researcher found: "70% of the Yemeni army was fake and that the efforts of the Arab coalition and its funds are simply wasted."[350] The level of military corruption was bad enough before Saudi Arabian and United Arab Emirates poured funds into Yemen in order to combat the Iran-supported al-Houthi after the Yemen uprisings of 2011. Reports indicate that Saudi Arabia alone is paying the salaries of more than fifty thousand anti-Houthi fighters, which has resulted in not only more "ghost soldiers" but also sales of Saudi-supplied weapons on the black market and, paradoxically, to Houthi fighters.[351]

Corruption levels in Yemen are so high, particularly in the navy, that US advisors established a new Yemeni coast guard in 2002 because the navy was too corrupt and unprofessional to carry out Yemeni coastal defense, as noted above. The new coast guard, equipped with western-supplied vessels and training (and $1.1 million in US aid), now is responsible for Yemeni maritime security. As a result of these measures, there are reports that commercial traffic transiting Yemeni waters has finally returned to normal following two terrorist attacks on commercial ships from Yemen.[352]

Saudi Arabia (CM)

The Saudi kingdom usually suppresses stories of military corruption, though it is rumored to be high. It also has serious consequences. Notes Barany, "Throughout Arabia, the practical upshot of widespread corruption associated with military affairs has been that a lot of kit simply 'disappears' and often finds its way to the arsenals of ISIS, Al-Qaeda, or the Houthis."[353]

Sometimes corruption comes out only when foreign partners are involved, as it did on the *Al-Yamamah* Saudi arms purchase from British producer BAE. The deal, which involved large numbers of British military aircraft, had a side-payment that also entailed dropping a previous British investigation into corruption involving Prince Turki bin Nasr,[354] along with charges of US side-payments to former Saudi Arabian Ambassador to the United States Prince Bandar.[355] A sweep in March 2020 saw a number of arrests of public officials, including both active and retired military officers, although the crimes or the names were not given.[356] In September 2020, King Salman bin Abdul-Aziz fired the commander of Saudi Arabian forces in Yemen, Prince Fahd bin Turki bin Abdulaziz Al Saud, as commander of joint forces in the Saudi-led coalition fighting in Yemen along with his son, Prince Abdulaziz bin Fahd, as deputy governor of al-Jouf region.[357]

Egypt (BPR)

Egyptian military corruption accelerated after Anwar Sadat inherited power from Nasser in 1970. Anxious to construct a military loyal to him, Sadat apparently turned a blind eye toward military corruption: "From their positions of power, the senior officers were able to trade on their influence, pocket kickbacks on everything from citrus exports to arms purchases, and to acquire property and income through appropriations of management of sequestered properties. There were no checks and balances against any of these abuses."[358] In 1988, Egyptian field marshal Abdel-Halim Abu Ghazala disappeared from public life amid rumors of an illegal arms transfer scandal involving an Egyptian officer acting on Ghazala's orders. The story involved the attempted import of rocket material from the US to Egypt, which resulted in the arrest of an Egyptian officer and an American defense contractor, though the full details of the case remain unclear.[359] What little that is known about the case does not suggest that wrongdoing occurred for personal gain, nevertheless the Egyptian regime decided to quietly purge Marshal Ghazala, who otherwise had an exemplary career. Egyptian cases suggest military corruption does benefit senior Egyptian officers, like the use of US-made Gulfstream VIP transports for personal use. Said one retired US officer familiar with the programs about the transfer of funds from the sales of goods built in Egyptian military-run factories to senior generals: "How much goes back from the actual sale to the military so they can buy other equipment? I don't know . . . I do know that a fair amount goes back to the senior officers that are in charge of these particular factories."[360] Charges that an Egyptian Air Force general received kickbacks in excess of half a million US dollars for steering contracts also surfaced.[361] Similar charges surfaced earlier; when senior officers, some associated with former President Sadat's brother Ismat, stood accused of overcharging for American-made arms after the 1979 Camp David Accords. Others also took bribes from a Canadian company to purchase its aircraft.[362] US military assistance also produced side-payment deals for senior military officers, who kept their illegal proceeds in overseas bank accounts.[363]

The end of the Mubarak administration in 2011 opened the door for military corruption investigations, as the new Morsi government reportedly found out that the general in charge of rooting out military corruption was actually covering up illegal dealings by his military cronies. General Mohamed Farid Al-Tohamy allegedly not only covered up corruption by high Mubarak officials and his fellow officers (some engaged in fuel smuggling, and other misdeeds), but received millions of dollars in gifts from state companies. Morsi immediately fired General Tohamy. After Morsi's own ouster by the military in July 2013, General Abdul-Fattah Al-Sisi, the officer General Tohamy had mentored throughout his career, quickly returned General Tohamy to power.

Subsequently, he was instrumental in the crackdown on Morsi supporters following the July coup.[364] It is entirely possible, therefore, that the kind of off-the-books economic activity that General Tohamy epitomized is continuing, but the total lack of transparency over Egyptian military business makes assessment very difficult. As Marshall notes: "The military can continue to garner support from the mass of Egyptians because its delivery of collective goods such as infrastructure, basic commodities, and healthcare is much more visible to the public than the military's corruption, fraud, and waste."[365]

Turkey (BSPR)

Charges of military corruption also surfaced in Turkey, when retired Admiral Ilhami Erdil faced charges of procurement irregularities; ranging from steering military contracts to a firm headed by his daughter to siphoning military money to buy two luxury apartments for himself. The same court also charged retired General Tuncer Kilnic, former head of the National Security Council, with irregularities on property acquisition.[366] While some speculate about continuing Turkish military corruption, they cite no other proven cases.[367]

According to a 2012 Transparency International report on Turkey, the Turkish public views the military as very corrupt. According to the institution's Global Corruption Barometer (GCB), as they gave it a score of 3.2 on a 1–5 scale. Factors contributing to that perception include "urgent" military requirements for system that gets little monitoring due to a weak auditing system that makes oversight a challenge.[368]

Syria (BPR)

The military carved out a solid political role in Syria since the first days of independence. Thus, it is hardly surprising that military corruption has entrenched itself there; reaching from the military to other agents favored by the regime. Van Dam notes how corruption infested the military and its supporters, as the military personnel involved were very close to the ruling family.[369] The situation is typified by the actions of General Mahmud Al-Kurdi, Director General of the Military Construction Establishment, and Colonel Khalil Bahlul, manager of Syria's largest construction company. Each lived off corruption for years until 1987, when they finally were fired. Mustafa Tlas, former minister of defense (and an army general), is another example of a family becoming very wealthy through 'Asad-favored business interests.[370] General Tlas's son and daughter were both investigated for financial irregularities and for smuggling guns, drugs, and oil, and Tlas was forced out as defense minister in 2004.[371] The corrupt practices in the Syrian military continued after the Syrian civil war broke out in early 2011. Soldiers unwilling to fight against fellow Syrians could pay the sum of $400 US to avoid combat.[372] As the war progressed, Syrian soldiers joined the *Shahbiha* and Hezbollah in corrupt practices, aided by the breakdown in government distribution and the end of subsidies. Fuel oil and gas was routinely stolen and resold by corrupt army members.[373] Residents in several Syria cities reported that members of the armed forces remove bread from the parcels that they are supposed to deliver and sell it on the black market for more than double the price.[374]

CONCLUSIONS

This chapter considered and evaluated the civil-military implications of military spending, military rent-seeking, and military corruption. Middle Eastern countries top the list of military spenders, and while some of the funds go to military improvement and the professionalization of the armed forces, in other cases it pays military rents. It is likely that some countries, such as Yemen and Jordan among others, may be sacrificing alternative economic opportunities by spending large portions of their national economies on their militaries. Military participation in the national economies is also significant in other Middle East countries, Egypt in particular, and the threat to that role was a factor both in Egypt's armed forces working to help end both the Mubarak and Morsi regimes because both administrations threatened the military rent system.

Bully republics are more likely to use defense rents to stay in power, while conservative monarchies like Saudi Arabia also use such rents to buy loyalty. Bully republics are more likely to permit large portions of their defense industries to spread military resources among important constituents; while fragmented democracies like Israel and liberal monarchies like Jordan tend to use defense industries for military purposes, and to increase their regional and global influence through technology sharing and arms sales. Corruption is more likely in bully republics and conservative monarchs than in either liberal monarchies or fragmented democracies, as both transparency and a lack of need to hold power through side payments is a serious requirement in the latter two categories.

Defense economics is also the foundation of national military power. Though it is not a determinate factor, it does matter in assessing national military outcomes in wars, in war preparation, and in military status. It is one element to add to the material on the military dominion of civil-military relations, which shall be addressed in the next chapter.

Chapter Five

Middle East Civil-Military Relations
The Military Dimensions

On the road between downtown Cairo and the international airport is the Egyptian National Military Museum, with a diorama presenting the great victory of the 1973 war with Israel. The rotating display shows Egyptian pilots bombing Israeli targets, and brave Egyptian soldiers killing Israeli soldiers, as the stern voice narrates the combat. But hidden behind the displays of Egyptian military victories is the other story: that the 1973 Arab-Israeli war was also combat between Egypt's president, Anwar Sadat, and his generals. President Sadat first removed all the generals who opposed his war plans, and then continued to override his military leaders as he sought limited objectives. His leading general would later spend time in prison for opposing Sadat, whose strategic objectives in fighting Israel were unacceptable to his senior officers. Sadat would pay for those objectives, peace with Israel, with his life. His fight with his senior military is only one display of the tangled skein of wartime civil-military relations in the Middle East.

This chapter examines the civil-military relations of Middle East military policy. The intersection between military operations policy and the national strategy domain of civilian leadership is often a clash of interests between civilian officials and the armed forces. Civilian political leadership has the national strategy-making role, as war and military activities short of war are extensions of national politics. This chapter begins with a discussion on the politics of civil-military relations during militarized conflict, raising questions as to why and how the military and political leadership fight over military responsibilities. There are rarely clear lines between the strategic responsibilities of civilian leadership and the operations that the military use to implement strategy. This chapter discuss debates over the control of strategic assessment because the veracity of assessment is fundamental to decisions about war and peace. The civil-military relations of military effectiveness are considered because military effectiveness can be influenced by either the military (when they allow their innovators to challenge the normal realm of military bureaucratic politics), or by civilian reformers (who sometimes push the military out of its comfortable patterns reinforcing tradition). Finally, there is an examination of the often-controversial arena of military reform, which is sometimes associated with military effectiveness but is also used to exercise more civilian control of military space.

This chapter focuses upon the following questions:

- What roles do the military and national leadership take in the strategic decision arena of war, and why? (Political tradition)
- How much influence do professional soldiers have over operational phases of planning for and execution of military operations? (Political factors and military identity)
- How do military officers react to civilian oversight? Do they "shirk" civilian-imposed responsibilities, or do they generally accept civilian directions? A set of corollary question involves non-combat military policy.
- Do civilian leaders allow their military to prepare for wars and other militarized policy areas? Do they supply both resources and political support to equip and maintain viable militaries? Do civilians and the military share strategic assessments?
- Do civilians mandate military reform or does the impetus for reform come from within military ranks?

WAR, POLITICS, AND CIVIL-MILITARY RELATIONS

The most memorable passage from Karl von Clausewitz's treatise is that war is an extension of national politics—wars are political instrumentalities of state purpose.[1] Ideally, political leadership should provide the *political* objectives for war to the military, along with the political end-states they desire, the acceptable costs, and the limits on combat. The armed services ideally follow that guidance, creating military doctrine to maximize the chances of success while minimizing the costs of engagement and risks of failure. So, national political leadership writes and implements national military strategy, while the military drafts operational doctrine to tie military power and planning to national strategy. Thus, the application of civil-military studies to wartime is appropriate, as classic strategists Thucydides, Sun Tzu, and Clausewitz noted years ago.[2] Huntington captured the division in his discussion of the development of American military professionalism in the nineteenth century: "It was the function of the civilian policymaker to determine the ends of national policy and to allocate the resources the military might use to achieve those ends. It was then the job of the military to apply the resources to the achievement of that goal."[3] Feaver agrees, albeit for different theoretical reasons (agency theory), that even if they are wrong, civilian leaders must dictate war strategy to their generals, as noted in more detail below.[4] Two different sayings characterize that struggle: French Prime Minister Clemenceau's famous statement that "war is too important to be left to the generals"; and, in Stanley Kubrick's 1963 film *Dr. Strangelove*, General Jack Ripper's proclamation that "war is too important to be left to politicians. They have neither the time, the training, nor the inclination for strategic thought."

However, there is no clear line between "strategy" and "operations," because operational outcomes have strategic consequences, and strategy often shapes operational choices.[5] Consequently, national civilian leaders are tempted to oversee most phases of military operations, thus potentially challenging professional military competence. Moreover, military leaders are likely to question strategic choices, should they believe them to be too bold, or too cautious, because resolute strategy can demand more than the military believes it can support, whereas weak strategy may cause the military to believe that they cannot take advantage of their military prowess. This may be as true in the Middle East as it is elsewhere.

A related civil-military issue relative to authoritarian regimes is political intrusions on military policy that may prevent or at least challenge military professionalization. Some authoritarians gave strong support through robust budgets and the allowance of professional standards, while others supplied minimum military resources and staffed their armies with political appointees. The former situation is more likely when the regime does not fear its forces. The latter situation may occur because autocratic rent-seeking countries often attempt to "coup proof" their militaries by replacing competent officers with loyalists, as noted in chapter 3. Civilian politicians often staff militaries with favored family members, offer promotions for political loyalty, and side payments for favors (swank officer's clubs, military vacations, stakes in the economy, for example), thus disincentivizing and ultimately weakening military competency.[6] Belkin and Schofer put it starkly,

> When leaders stack the armed forces with loyalists rather than relying on merit-based standards for promotion; when they shuffle, arrest, and even execute officers on a frequent basis to prevent potential challengers from developing a stable base of followers; and when they divide their armies into numerous, mutually suspicious rival forces that check and balance one another, they may sacrifice organizational effectiveness to minimize the chances of a successful coup.[7]

Caitlin Talmadge, seeking explanations as to why some countries succeed on the battlefield, while other countries fail, examines the military conditions required for improving victory prospects. She finds that while elements like training, command arrangements, and information flow are critical to winning, armies that are run by distrustful dictators who coup-proof their militaries are usually going to lose wars that they fight.[8] More specifically, Talmadge finds that in, "Weakly institutionalized regimes with conflictual civil-military histories are much more likely to prioritize protection against coup threats, leading to the adoption of military organizational practices poorly suited to the demands of conventional warfighting."[9] This expectation ties in well with the distinction made in chapter 1 between *institutional* and *patrimonial* armies, as the former will more likely exist under a more institutionalized regime, and be more likely to perform well in wars, compared to a patrimonial regime. Biddle and Zirkle contrast two armies in autocratic countries; the Iraqi army under Saddam Hussein and the North Vietnamese army during the second Indochina war against the US and its South Vietnamese ally. They note that while Saddam turned his military into a praetorian force because of his constant fear of military coups, the North Vietnamese army had no history of coups against its leadership.[10] The difference was that while Saddam frequently rotated officers, appointed political toadies, broke units up to avoid collaboration, and frequently purged the military, the North Vietnamese leadership allowed competent officers to serve for long periods, and integrated forces (air and land, for example) for better combat efficiency. While Saddam frequently micromanaged his military, Iraqi senior civilians and military leaders shared strategic and operational decision-making. While the overwhelming success of the North Vietnamese military and the comparatively disastrous performance of Saddam's military are not explained by civil-military factors alone, it is hard to argue that they did not play a considerable role.[11] M. Taylor Fravel makes a similar argument about the Chinese military/Party relationship. Because senior military officers were also senior Communist Party members, the Party could delegate considerable responsibility to the military without fear that the military would pursue goals that were incompatible with Party policies.[12]

Military success in war is also influenced by the quality of military education. That is why most countries have war colleges: to not only educate senior officers not only in the arts and sciences of war, but also in civil-military relations. For democracies, this is especially important, as war colleges in democratic countries emphasize civilian democratic control of the military. As Steihm argues: "A US officer is taught to take direction from a civilian commander-in-chief whose authority comes solely from electoral victory."[13] But war colleges also teach *strategy*, the political-military nexus that allows military leaders a say in making and executing war policy. Therefore, autocratic leaders, who want to control strategy themselves, often fear war colleges and limit the curriculum to lessons on tactics and, possibly operations. They may be "war colleges" in name, but they hardly compare with the rigorous war college education in democracies. This lack of martial education can matter in wartime. Toronto finds that countries with a war college are 20 percent more likely to be successful in interstate wars than those countries without a war college.[14]

CIVIL-MILITARY RELATIONS AND THE CONDUCT OF WAR

If war is an extension of national politics, as Clausewitz and other strategists argue, then politicians should provide strategic guidance, if not direction, to the military for the preparation and conduct of war. The national military, as servants of the state and its politics, ideally receives state resources allotted by civilian politicians and uses those resources to bring the capabilities inherent to their profession to bear upon an adversary. Biddle and Long argue that successful grand strategy must combine military elements with the elements of national power—domestic politics, economics, and diplomacy—and that disagreement on these issues or even failure of civilian and military leadership to coordinate on them can doom military operations to failure.[15] Thus, civilian and military leaders share a collective responsibility for the successful pursuit of warfare, or, conversely, decisions to avoid war. Civilians need to supply strategic guidance, and soldiers need to provide their expertise on the operations and tactics of warfare. The decisional nexus that lies between these two pillars, operations, under ideal conditions is a shared responsibility. Because operations guide tactics, the military must advise and shape operational doctrine. Because operations also flow from strategy, civilians must also shape or at least consult on it. When either party does an inadequate job, war policy can fail. Civilians who meddle too much can deflect military expertise, yet excessive military influence on planning operations may fail to consider strategy. When military leaders attempt to design strategy, they interfere with the proper role of civilian political leaders. The soldiers' responsibility is to *understand* strategy in order to guide operations and tactics; it is not to *make* strategy. However, the lines of responsibility are almost never cleanly drawn, thus it is important to find a mechanism to explain the bargaining process over war–policymaking.

Agency theory may help to explain the patterns of relative military obedience to a civilian political authority. Peter Feaver argues that civilian leaders delegate certain authority to the military, the military accepts that authority, although with particular limits to that authority. While civilians want to the military to do its bidding, and expect military obedience, the military may favor its own interests. Feaver also argues: "The civilians cannot be sure that the military will do what they want; the military agents cannot be sure that the civilians will catch and punish them if they misbehave." Civilians expect the military to "work;" to obey their directives.[16] However, when the military finds those directives to be onerous because they contradict military preferences, they will "shirk;" finding ways to resist carrying out civilian directions. Thus, civilians attempt to maximize military compliance through intrusive monitoring. However, the military may demand considerable latitude in shaping operations,[17] sometimes evading, or disobeying civilian oversight.[18]

For Posen, "the tendency of soldiers to seek as much independence from civilian interference as possible, combine to make political-military integration an uncertain prospect."[19] Professional officers seek control over of as much of the military policy space as they can obtain. The German military prior to World War I preferred offensive strategies to defensive plans because such approaches made political oversight more complex: "Political considerations—and hence politicians—have to figure in operational decisions. The operational autonomy of the military is most likely to succeed when the operational goal is to disarm the adversary quickly and decisively by offensive means. For this reason, the military will seek to force doctrine and planning into this mold."[20] The generals may argue with civilians over strategic objectives, as did US Air Force generals during the cold war, or over operational matters.[21]

Cohen challenges what he calls the "normal theory of civil-military relations" in wartime, as noted above, where the military officer, as the expert in state-managed violence, runs a war with as little interference as possible from civilian heads of state. Following the Clauswitzian dictum that war is an extension of state politics, however, state leaders should be involved in the crafting and execution of war policy, and, for Cohen, some of the great twentieth-century wartime leaders—Lincoln, Churchill, Clemenceau, and Ben-Gurion—did just that. Their wars, and ultimately their countries, benefitted from their wisdom over often unimaginative or inexperienced field generals, or at least unclear end-states; while during the US Vietnam War, according to Cohen, General William Westmoreland, "straitlaced and, on the whole, unimaginative," according to Cohen, ran the war without much civilian oversight.[22]

Others argue that Cohen selected only the successful cases of civilian management of wartime generals; the counterexample is British Prime Minister Lloyd-George's inability to slow the slaughter of British soldiers in WWI, even though Lloyd-George was quite aware of the limitations of British generalship.[23] Adolf Hitler frequently interfered with his generals' planning and conduct during World War II and decisions, like the simultaneous campaigns against the Soviet Union and Britain and demanding that jet fighters be used for bombing, helped to bring defeat to the Third Reich. The US airpower role in Vietnam was complicated by civilian oversight in the targeting of bombing missions; primarily due to concerns that a strike that hit Soviet or Chinese advisors or equipment might result in dangerous escalation. This fear fueled claims by airpower advocates that excessive civilian control of targeting led to the US losing the war.[24] Yet in retrospect, the reasons for the failure of airpower in Vietnam went well beyond civilian control, which had a minimal impact on the failure of US airpower in Vietnam to do what its advocates promised.[25]

Thus, militaries sometimes keep civilian masters in the dark about their operations, to avoid agency oversight.[26] Referring to a 2007 Chinese military decision to destroy an obsolete Chinese satellite, Gill and Kleiber write: "The People's Liberation Army and its strategic rocket forces most likely proceeded with the ASAT (anti-satellite) testing program without consulting other key parts of the Chinese security and foreign policy bureaucracy." They note that the Chinese military had hidden other key issues from scrutiny, including the details of the April 2001 crash between a Chinese fighter plane and an American reconnaissance aircraft.[27] In other cases, civilian politicians have paid scant attention to military affairs, thus the militaries had a relatively free hand in war politics. As Pion-Berlin and Trinkunas have found: "Defense policy has not been and is not a priority item among Latin American politicians of the region. These states and their leaders do not face existential threats from foreign invasion, and the militarized disputes they do enter into are not serious enough to trigger genuine civilian interest in defense."[28] Thus, it is not surprising that Brazil has never had a minister of defense, and the coming of Brazilian democracy was not accompanied by civilianization of military control. Notes Stepan, "The successful retention of the military of their prerogatives in this area has directly sustained their comparative mastery vis-á-vis civilian over both strategic and technical defense issues. This makes the creation of an effective model of civilian control difficult."[29] Nevertheless, even in countries with recent wartime experience, civilians may lose interest in strategy making. Curiously, in Russia, former President Boris Yeltsin came to believe that he did not need to concern himself with military matters or the Russian military because the Cold War was over. Russian military leaders complained to Yeltsin that they were unprepared to launch an operation into Chechnya in 1995, but Yeltsin insisted that the operation go forward. More than five hundred officers resigned in protest, and the operation was a military disaster.[30]

The question as to the location of the line that separates military autonomy and civilian intrusion remains. The military should certainly have the right to choose military boot polish, or military music for its bands, for example, or the color of barracks paint. Yet tactics and operations also may have strategic consequences. It is the area in between the obvious where the contest for overall responsibility takes place, as shown in figure 5.1.

The axis at the bottom of figure 5.1 shows the type of civilian and military response: for the military it reflects efforts to hold or reclaim traditional areas of military policymaking, including weapons acquisition decisions and some part of operational control; and for civilians, the path involves assertive control over policy areas that might have strategic impacts, which leaves a broad swath of military policy that is subject to civilian oversight.

One of the most pernicious effects of civil-military relations is the practice of coup proofing, discussed in chapter 3. When civilian leaders fear a military takeover, or the growth of undue military interference in politics, they weaken the military by removing competent officers and by selecting replacements based on regime loyalty over military professionalism. Fearful civilian leaders also use the same criteria to control promotions inside the military. Other methods of coup proofing include the regime encouraging military officers to run sideline enterprises and by strengthening alternative security forces to monitor military loyalty. Such measures can and do have a considerable impact on war outcomes. Böhmelt and Pilster find that the relationship between coup-proofing and increases in military fractionalization, often a result of leaders staffing their militaries with fellow ethnic group members, is a potential indicator of combat performance.[31] Using measures of military effectiveness, Pilster and Böhmelt find a negative correlation between the degree of coup-proofing and combat performance.[32] The most convincing study of political interference in military affairs comes from Narang and Talmadge using a new data set, they find significant differences in war outcomes between independent militaries and those whose political masters interfere in military affairs. Note Narang and Talmadge,

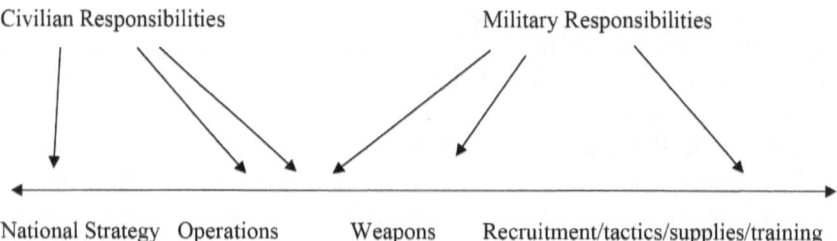

Figure 5.1. Span of Responsibility Between Civilian, Military Authorities

Officer exclusion, purges, and the other civil-military pathologies are all symptoms of the coup concerns we theorized should lead to poor military performance and a reduced likelihood of victory in war. Likewise, the military government variable and other variables related to the military's internal role also are negatively associated with victory, again consistent with our hypotheses.[33]

It is important to note multiple factors influence war outcomes, including state choices on force employment,[34] inequality in military ranks,[35] misestimation of intentions,[36] the state ability to effectively mobilize wartime resources,[37] and dozens of other variables. Civil-military relations in war only helps to build a more thorough understanding about victory or defeat in modern war.

WAR AND POLITICS IN THE MIDDLE EAST

Interstate war has been all-too-common in the Middle East, ranging from deadly Iran-Iraq war of 1981 to 1988 that may have cost a million lives, to small skirmishes that barely get international attention, like the "war of the dunes" between Morocco and Algeria in 1963, and the Saudi Arabia–Yemen war in the 1930s. In many of these wars, civilian and military leaders have competed for control of war-making decisions, and over the resources that the militaries require for success on the battlefield. As Florence Gaub states,

> The armed forces resent not only when civilians do not provide them with what they need, but also when they meddle in their key business: war. After all, fighting and winning wars is the military's *raison d'être* as an institution, and when the leadership does not provide the necessary leeway to do so, it will be held responsible in the eyes of the armed forces. Arab coups have consistently been preceded by operational defeats, either caused by civilian shortcomings (as the military sees it), or disagreement over how to react to a specific security challenge.[38]

Such civil-military disagreements were evidenced by Egyptian General Saad Shazli's angry resignation after the 1973 war[39] after learning of President Sadat's decision to terminate the conflict. The Israeli Defense Forces kept the civilian cabinet largely in the dark over its operations in Lebanon in the 1980s, as they feared that civilians would restrict their operations.[40] Sometimes the politicization of Arab militaries by a distrustful national leadership hampered their wartime capability, a problem faced by both the Syrian and Iraqi armed forces. As Pollack and Talmadge note, the Iraqi military performed poorly because Saddam Hussein did not trust his officer corps, and micromanaged his army, until repeated defeats finally forced him to rely more on officer performance instead of officer loyalty to him.[41] Many Arab militaries suffer from such political distrust and a corresponding lack of professionalization largely because Arab political leaders too often fear that professionalization will hamper their control over national defense forces. Often the consequence is a rent-seeking army that specializes in defending its regime but lacks the professionalization to defend its country. That is one reason why senior Syrian war college students push tanks around in sandboxes; for example, their leadership does not trust them with strategic thought, because with it, officers could challenge their leader's ability to call all the strategic shots.

Internal wars and military occupations in the Middle East also spawn civil-military conflict, for example, in Turkey over the fight with the Kurdish PKK, in Iraq after the US military withdrawal, and in Israel over the occupation of Palestinian territories seized in 1967. These quarrels are often deeper than are disagreements over external wars because internal wars and occupations are often central to national governance. Internal wars can produce even more contentious civil-miliary relations than external wars, partly because the armed forces themselves may divide, as they did in Lebanon and Yemen during civil wars, making it much more difficult for the state leadership to fight rebels with a divided military. In Syria, Yemen, and Iraq, civil war forced national political leaders to suddenly rely on militias, as their armies fragmented, thus Bashar ʿAsad turned to the Lebanese militia, Hezbollah, and elements of the Iranian-based Islamic Republican Guard, completely altering Syrian civil-military relations. In Yemen, former President Ali Abdullah Saleh tried to depend on his former enemy, the Houthi, in a fatal bid to return to power, after his army largely deserted him, and as he tried to return to his former allies, the Houthi killed him in December 2017. During the Lebanese civil war, the heads of state found that they had no military, as it fractured into rival religious-based militias. Moreover, states with politicized military forces are more likely to renew civil wars once they are terminated.[42] So the fate of Syria and Yemen, in particular, appears to be a continuation of their civil conflicts.

Wars have been fought in the Middle East for many reasons, including conquest, insecurity, or as an extension of outside power competition. Middle Eastern wars have also resulted from the peccadilloes of bold, careless, or foolish leadership, who either miscalculated the costs and benefits of warfare (Saddam Hussein famously misread Iranian weakness after the 1979 Islamic revolution), or preemption against a neighboring country that was preparing to invade. Sometimes wars were about status seeking, as when Arab leaders contested with one another to fight against Israel. Sometimes Middle Eastern leaders send their troops off to battle knowing the odds of success were long but believed that they had no other choice but to fight, as Sadat did in 1973. Outsiders also imported war into the Middle East, as empire builder followed empire builder into and out of the area, and in the twentieth century, the major wars usually had a Middle East theater. Other war causes included imposed borders, which Iraqi leaders used to invade Kuwait, and again against Iran in 1981, over a feud about the riverine border between the two countries.

Yet interstate wars are becoming less frequent globally, and specifically in the Middle East. Jordan, Syria, and Egypt have not gone to war with Israel for many decades, and all are signatories to either a peace accord, as is Egypt and Jordan, or at least a truce, which Syrian and Israeli signed in 1974. This is not to suggest that interstate wars might return, but at this point, the Middle East seems to have followed a larger global pattern, with fewer interstate wars and more internal conflict. The complicating factor is that external forces have joined "internal wars" in the Middle East. Thus, Russia, Turkey, the United States, and Iran have forces fighting in the Syrian civil war, and Egypt, Saudi Arabia, Iran, and the United Arab Emirates are both direct and indirect participants in the Yemeni civil war. The Libyan conflict after the 2011 Qadhafi overthrow has attracted Turkey, Russia, Saudi Arabia, the UAE, Egypt, and other players.

In many Middle Eastern countries, the civilian leadership does not fully trust their militaries, sometimes with good reason. Some militaries are too unprofessional to pay attention to even small military details like the proper maintenance of their equipment or proper battlefield communications, and thus civilians try to direct military performance in combat. In other cases, civilians have taken charge of military affairs in the wake of military withdrawal from politics.

Middle East Civil-Military Control over Military Affairs

This section develops the questions posed at the beginning of this chapter: How did the state of civil-military relations shape military policy? Did civilian or military leaders dominate the development and execution of war policies? Did civilians provide strategic direction and let the military carry forth the operations, or did civilians control most of the war-making decision chain? How prepared were Middle Eastern countries for war, and how much were preparedness levels a function of civil-military relations?

The next section considers some Middle East military-civilian war policy in greater depth through country cases.

Jordan (LM)

The Royal Jordanian armed forces, widely regarded as one of the most professional in the Middle East, have had mixed results in battle. In 1948, the Jordanian army fought Israeli forces to a draw, though preserving Jordanian control of East Jerusalem. King Abdullah had a very limited strategic objective, partly due to British orders that British advisors would depart if Jordan invaded Jewish territory,[43] and thus the king imposed limits on the Jordanian military. After the 1948 war, Jordanian forces struggled after an Israeli attack against the Jordanian town of Samu' in November 1966, and ultimately Jordan lost control of the West Bank and East Jerusalem after the 1967 war.[44] These losses do not reflect poor civil-military relations, however, as both the king and the military agreed on the 1948 war parameters, and on the 1967 war decision by King Hussein to withdraw forces from East Jerusalem, when it became apparent that the destruction of the sacred sites in the city would not be worth the value of defending it. Reflecting partly the considerable changes made to the Jordanian military after the coup crisis, Jordanian forces gave the Arab forces a rare victory over Israel in the 1960s at the battle of Karameh in March 1968, by forcing an Israeli withdrawal from southern Jordan after it attacked Palestinian forces there.[45] Hoping to increase the professionalization of Jordan's armed forces, King Hussein opened the Royal Jordanian National Defense College in 1986, entrusting it with a world-class military education curriculum.[46]

Iran (BPR)

Post-1979 Iran presents a confusing puzzle for civil-military relations, as two military forces, the IRGC and the Artesh contended for influence, with a divided civilian authority between the clerical regime and the executive, led by the president. Iran's clerics distrusted Artesh, the regular army, because it was one pillar of Pahlavi rule and thus a potential bastion of Western thinking.[47] The revolutionary leadership purged the Artesh, executing eighty-five senior officers in 1979, and imprisoned or retired more than twelve thousand senior officers.[48] The regime then created the forerunner of the IRGC, the Revolutionary Guard militia (*Pasdaran*), which they formed largely for regime protection rather than for military combat capability. But the combat requirements of the Iran-Iraq war transformed the IRGC into a conventional fighting armed force, with a command structure typical of Western-style militaries.[49] The IRCG reports directly to the supreme leader, bypassing the president.[50] The IRGC has its own air force and navy, in addition to its ground forces, and they operate Iranian ballistic missiles—an unusual responsibility for a militia, as conventional forces usually own the national missile systems.

That shift of the IRGC to a conventional military might have empowered the president at the expense of the supreme leader, as the president at the start of the Iran-Iraq war in 1980, President Abolhassan Bani-Sadr, tried to expand his political influence through his control of the Artesh, but Ayatollah

Khomeini sent his own representative to the Artesh, checking Bani-Sadr's influence while expanding his own.[51] The Artesh chief of staff threatened resignation if "unqualified people continue to meddle with the conduct of the war."[52] Pronounced differences grew, as the ruling clerics wanted mass offensives, while the military preferred a strategy of attrition against Iraqi forces, using Iraqi Kurds where possible. Ultimately, the clerical regime accepted the military position, but largely out of desperation; Iran was running out of troops because of the high casualties from previous offensives.[53]

Senior appointments demonstrate the confusion between the roles of the IRGC and Artesh in the making of war policy. The most significant was Rear Admiral Ali Shamkhani, appointed the representative of the supreme leader to the Supreme National Security Council, which also includes the president and the intelligence minister. The admiral, who had commanded both IRGC and Artesh naval units, was the lead figure in Iranian pressure to remove Iraqi Shi'a leader Nuri al-Maliki in August 2014, as the Islamic State forces closed in on the Iraq-Iran border.[54] Major General Qassim Suleimani, the former head of the Quds force, appeared in pictures on Iraqi battlefields as Iran battled the Islamic State group in that country.[55]

Iran's military performance in the Iran-Iraq war was spotty at best, with much more reliance on human wave attacks than on military proficiency. The divisions between the IRGC and the Artesh became stark, as the lack of coordination between the two forces hampered military performance.[56] The IRGC wanted to demonstrate its competence after the revolution, and there were rumors that the radical clerics wanted to dissolve the Artesh,[57] which hardly led to trust between the two militaries. Hashim puts it well, "Early in the war, Iran's response was haphazard and uncoordinated, causing much bad blood between the regular military and the IRGC," noting that Iranian President Abolhassan Bani-Sadr, favored the Artesh over the IRGC, causing tensions between those armies.[58]

Like Artesh, the IRGC in combat was hampered by contested civil-military relations, as the new Iranian leadership was still in transition when the Iraq-Iran war started. So as Tracy Samuel notes that the initial poor performance of the IRGC was partly a result of leadership turmoil, and, moreover, that Saddam Hussein had partly planned his invasion on the assumption of leadership disarray.[59] Iran's complicated civil-military relations carried over to Iranian national security policy. In 2015, The former IRGC commander, Major General Mohammad Ali Jaafari, opposed concessions offered by then-President Hassan Rouhani during the negotiations over the Joint Comprehensive Plan of Action that formed Iran's nuclear bargain with the US, France, Russia, China, Britain, and Germany.[60] That is not surprising, as the spillover of the Iran-Iraq war included an increase in the already high distrust of the

US, and since the IRGC bore much of the brunt of that war, opposition to the JCPOA by its commander was not surprising.[61]

Iraq (BPR)

Saddam Hussein micromanaged his military to two successive defeats, in 1991 and 2003, and one bloody draw, against Iran. Under Saddam, Iraq armed forces lagged severely in military professionalization, as Iraqi troops were simply unprepared for a conflict with Iran, and certainly not for the coalition that aligned against Iraq in 1990. A primary reason was that Saddam (and his predecessors) had coup-proofed the Iraqi military, replacing professional officers with Ba'th Party loyalists.[62] It is noteworthy, though, that after 1986, and years of poor Iraqi army performance, Saddam shifted to a greater emphasis on the Republican Guard forces, handpicked to partly watch for coup attempts in the regular army, and Iraq's military fortunes did improve.[63]

Talmadge finds that Iraqi forces performed poorly in the first phases of the war, noting a lack of clear military objectives, and a lack of ability to perform complex military operations.[64] Biddle and Zirkle document woeful Iraqi performance in the technological application of military force (air defense and air combat in particular) and the lack of combat imagination, maintenance, and other basic skills. They to conclude that, "The Iraqis' poor equipment maintenance, indifferent attention to formal operating procedures, and weak fire discipline are consistent with a model of politicized military promotion and frequent purge . . . in fact, superior military performance has a tendency to get the performers shot after the war."[65] Their lack of professionalism certainly hurt their performance as well. Biddle documents how inept operational practices by Iraqi armored units contributed to their crushing defeat at the hands of a numerically inferior American tank unit, because the Iraqi tankers did not practice even elemental tactics that might have given them a fighting chance.[66] It is worth noting again that dictators who do not trust their militaries do not normally allow them to professionalize, yet send them into battle only to lose, and then sometimes punish the surviving generals for their incompetence.

Saddam Hussein applied to military schools, but the school's leadership rejected him. Still, he fancied himself a military strategist and thus attempted to make even the smallest military decision from Baghdad. During the Iran war, for example, he sent orders to the front specifying the exact dimensions of trenches that soldiers were to dig,[67] and prohibited the withdrawal of Iraqi forces during an Iranian offensive in March 1982.[68] He micromanaged the air war, as all airstrikes required Baghdad's approval.[69] While the Iran-Iraq war ended on terms that probably favored Saddam, he paid a very high price for his small gains, which he quickly surrendered (control of parts of the Shatt al-Arab, for example) when he sent his troops into Kuwait in 1990.[70] In addition, while Saddam defined his strategic goals himself, he never passed them on to his military, for example, as he planned and ordered the 1980 invasion of Iran.[71] Since Saddam populated his military with Ba'th officers, it is doubtful that there would have been much military resistance, anyway, to his war policies.[72]

Prior to his 1979 invasion of Iran, it became clear that Saddam had no strategic objective for the campaign and got military concurrence for his undeveloped notions by picking his officers by loyalty rather than competence,[73] paying particular attention to his son-in-law Hussein Kamel, until Kamel defected to Jordan.[74] Fearing a military coup, Saddam discouraged cooperation between his land and air forces, believing that in doing so, they could not coordinate a coup.[75] While Saddam did have some professional officers in his military, he marginalized them unless they agreed with him, until the war became disastrous for Iraq. Despite achieving surprise at the outset of the war, Saddam's forces could capture only one major Iranian city, Khorramshahr, during the entire fall 1980 campaign.[76] The war dragged on without significant achievement by Saddam's better-equipped forces, but only when Iraq lost control of the Fao Peninsula in 1986, Saddam began to listen to his more competent commanders (the fortunate few that he had not executed).

In its other wars, Iraq's military suffered defeat after defeat, against its Kurdish population, against Israel in 1973. Of the four Arab armies whose forces saw the lion's share of combat during the October War, Iraq's almost certainly performed worst, notes Pollack, and against coalition forces in Kuwait in 1990–91.[77] As matters grew worse, one of Saddam's advisors says, "We will need bravery. We need to use methods other than those we were taught at military schools. We can overcome their overwhelming majority and technological superiority by the heroism of our troops." Saddam agrees: "When our people have the strength and can express their determination, other Arab and Muslim people will be motivated by the sense of honor and passion."[78] Actually, Iraq's military proved to be little more than thugs and thieves during their brief occupation of Kuwait, as large numbers of Iraqi troops engaged in looting, rape, and murder against Kuwaiti citizens. Iraqi authorities only punished them because they feared that they would continue their criminal behavior once they returned to Iraq.[79]

The United States attempted to modernize and professionalize Iraq's army after 2003, spending over $25 billion in the process. However, the Nuri Kamel al-Maliki regime continued Saddam's pattern of politicizing the armed forces. There were instances of disgraced generals receiving parliamentary appointments through tribal connections,[80] as well as others who served because they were Shi'a and were hired by al-Maliki because he feared that there were too many Sunni generals who might be closet Ba'thists. However, Pollack argues that not all the flaws in the 2014 Iraqi military were due to civil-military difficulties.[81] The Iraqi armed forces in 2014 also show the flaws documented in his *Arabs at War* book: lack of proper training in combined arms and tactics. Additionally, Prime Minister Nuri al-Maliki politicized the military by appointing political generals to replace professional officers and created structures that allowed him to subvert the chain of command,[82] often issuing orders from his mobile phone and arresting individual commanders.[83] Thus, the military had three problems: incompetent leadership, low skill levels, and prime ministerial interference. Corruption was also a major problem, as billions of dollars equivalent of military weapons and equipment were sold off by members of the Iraqi military, much of it new equipment provided by the United States after 2003.[84]

In the summer of 2014, the Jihadist group Islamic State of Iraq and al-Shams (ISIS) launched a series of surprise attacks across much of northern Iraq. The Iraqi army units in the area fled in disarray; abandoning their weapons, which ISIS members simply took for their own use. Investigations revealed deep corruption practices that had weakened the Iraq forces, including the practice of adding "ghost soldiers" to the military rolls so that officers could pocket the pay of nonexistent troops.[85] Under the Maliki regime, recruits reported that slots in officer training schools cost $3,000 in bribes, and the going rate for promotion to general was as high as $30,000.[86] However, the removal of al-Maliki allowed new Iraqi civilian leadership to lessen its influence over Iraq's armed forces, and the rise of ISIS galvanized its efforts to retrain and re-professionalize. The armed forces created new elite units, like the Special Operations Force, and used new tactics and operations to evict ISIS from Mosul and other Iraqi cities it had previously taken.[87] A 2020 Rand Corporation report noted that what improvements the Iraqi military made since 2014 are largely the result of American assistance.[88]

Algeria (BSPR)

Algeria's armed forces built their structure and doctrine on models borrowed from the former Soviet Union, and still retains its title, "The People's National Army" (PNA), as a reflection of those times. In trying to legitimize the PNA, President Houari Boumédiene both reduced its size and its professionalization. It became an economic power base within Algeria, as it controlled farms and other enterprises seized in 1962.[89] This set its paradigm as a political power base rather than an effective fighting force. Except for a brief fight with Morocco in 1963, the PNA has combat experience only in fighting insurgency inside the country. It was born a political military; though Korany argues that after poor performance against Morocco in the Western Sahara, President Chadli Bendjedid tried to professionalize the army by diminishing its political influence.[90] However, its political never disappeared, which likely hampers its military effectiveness. Cordesman comments on the Algerian military:

> The military "culture" of the army is ... an awkward mix of Algerian ideology and long-outdated and relatively slow-moving Soviet tactics and doctrine. The army has traditionally relied on mass and attrition, not maneuver and technology. Its leadership has never fully converted from an ideological focus on the army as a popular or revolutionary force to one that is fully capable of modern armored and maneuver combat. Algeria's internal security problems, and the high degree of politicization and bureaucratization of its forces, may well make it very difficult to change this situation during the next decade.[91]

Algeria's military rarely operates outside of its boundaries, but in a brief effort to expand its influence, it tried to form a regional pact with Mauritania, Mali, and Niger in order to address the threat of terrorism, the *Comite d'Etat-Major Operationnel Conjoint* (CEMOC). However, Algeria's refusal to support Mali in 2012 raised concerns about how competent the Algerian military was and led to the CEMOC's demise.[92]

The Algerian president is the minister of defense, exercising a firm hand over military matters large and small.[93] Spencer quotes Oliver Schlumberger, who positions the Algerian military thusly: "In Algeria, the president is actually a consensus figure for the military which stays behind the scenes. The president himself doesn't come from the military, but instead is a diplomat who was a minister during the 1970s. A group of 10 to 15 generals is the real power behind the scenes."[94] Moreover, the Algerian military, in contrast to most other Maghreb militaries, compounds its internal political power through control of the police.[95] How much the Algerian military power might aid or hamper its military performance, however, is hard to ascertain, as it has not sent its force into combat. Even during increased tensions between Morocco and Algeria in early 2021, Algeria limited its military response to a live-fire exercise on the Tindouf border area near the Western Sahara.

Libya (BPR)

Military officers led the coup of 1969 that toppled the Sanusi Monarchy, and one of their own, Muammar Qadhafi, became the national leader. However, Qadhafi mistrusted his army (as many coup leaders do) and micromanaged it. While the details are murky, his direction of the Libyan army in Chad resulted in coups against him (exactly how many is unknown), and his countermeasures crippled an already sclerotic military.[96] Qadhafi also tried to buy off his armed forces with a patronage system, but apparently rent payments alone failed to prevent the coup efforts.[97]

Under Qadhafi, Libya's armed forces suffered the defects of all other elements of Qadhafi's stateless society. The military became a rag-tag collection of units without cohesion or training, much less education (a fortunate few Libyan officers attended war college in Egypt, but the rest had little of any military education). Its army operated more than four thousand tanks, but most were inoperable, as were its aircraft. Yet Qadhafi sent his troops to fight on the Egyptian border (unsuccessfully), in Uganda in support of dictator Idi Amin against invading Tanzanian forces (unsuccessfully), and for ten years (1978–1987) in neighboring Chad—unsuccessfully.[98] The several coup efforts against Qadhafi and the divided performance of his military in defending his regime in 2011 suggests that many senior officers disagreed with Qadhafi on military policy. As DeVore argues: "As a result of this official animosity, Libya's dispirited military disintegrated in 2011 rather than either support the regime (as in Syria) or overthrow it (as in Egypt and Tunisia)."[99]

Libya's armed forces fractured after the end of the Qadhafi regime, with some joining the Government of National Accord, while others partnered with General Khalifa Hafter's rebel Libyan National Forces. Control of the Libyan army still affiliated with the GNA was shaky, as the regime clearly feared that its remaining units would either defect or join Hafter's forces. Thus, the GNA military commanders went so far as to prohibit any military movement in the country.[100] Moreover, given the loose control that the GNA had over the country in general, and the military in particular, there was the reality that foreign forces were using Libya's military for their own purposes. Turkey and Russia were major outside players in Libya's convoluted civil war and may have been directing Libyan military forces for their own purposes.[101] General Haftar, perhaps cognizant of his impossible military situation, announced in September 2021 that he was stepping down from his military role; possibly so he could run for Libya's president.[102]

Syria (BPR)

Syria's military is one of the more rent-seeking armies in the Middle East; born into politics and coup-plotting instead of military competency. It grew from the *Troupes Spéciales du Levant*, created by France, largely for internal security during the occupation. While its performance in the 1948 war was decidedly mixed; it fought well defensively, but usually avoided direct engagement with Israeli forces.[103] The spate of coups and attempted coups in 1949, 1954, 1961, 1963, and 1966 badly weakened the Syrian army and resulted in its disastrous performance in 1967. The late 1960s saw considerable coup-proofing, as promotions became based upon regime loyalty, Ba'th Party membership, and 'Alawi religions affiliation, instead of military competence. Additionally, there was the creation of a "People's Army" to guard the regime that had more soldiers than did the regular Syrian army.[104] While Syrian forces showed flashes of brilliance in the 1973 war, in the end Syria got back only a sliver of land in the 1974 peace agreement for its efforts.

Syria's military has spent more energy violently suppressing domestic insurgency (in Hama in 1964, 1981, and 2011 onward, for example) than preparing for external war; though it has experienced numerous wars against Israel. Syrian forces fought in the 1948, 1967, and 1973 wars, and joined the anti–Saddam Hussein coalition in 1990–91; though its forces almost never fired a shot against the Iraqis. While Syria could have professionalized its forces under Hafiz al-'Asad, 'Asad used tribal and religious loyalty instead of competence to construct his military's top leadership.[105] Thus training consists of its tank corps performing only the simplest maneuvers in exercises, helicopter training consisting only of lifting off and landing, fighter pilots flying thirty hours or less per year, and military vehicle maintenance consisting of enlisted troops fixing carburetors on ancient Peugeot sedans.[106] At the Syrian Higher Military Academy, its version of a war college, the curriculum involves teaching basic tactics. Additionally, lectures focus on successful Syrian battles, instead of on strategic and operational thinking. Sunni officers, in particular, complained about having to field old obsolete Russian aircraft and tanks; yet the 'Alawi officers in military units, primarily motivated by bribes paid from commanders who want their companies to look good on paper, write glowing reports about how good their units are.[107]

Syria's military found itself challenged severely by the outbreak of the Syrian civil war in March 2011. Some units disintegrated as the Sunni officers and enlisted either defected to the rebel side or just melted away, not wanting to get involved in a war to defend an 'Alawite regime. The army found itself having to turn its guns on its own citizens. While some units inflicted much death and destruction, the overall performance of the Syrian armed forces was so low that the 'Asad family ultimately had to rely on Russian and Iranian forces and state militias that they created from both loyalty and money. The 'Asads mobilized the *Shahbiha*, discussed in chapter 3, to suppress dissent, which the majority-'Alawi group did with much bloodshed. The remnants of the Syrian army, exhausted by the ongoing struggle and the inability of the regime to cover its costs, found itself losing members. With the exception of the majority-'Alawi units like the Special Forces and the Fourth Armored Division, the soldiers were forcibly conscripted and thus performed very poorly in fighting for the regime.[108] As a result of their poor performance,

Russian advisors took over much of the training, equipping, and leadership of remaining Syrian national army forces, and have taken on the task of rebuilding Syrian military forces. Iran's IRGC helped the ʿAsad regime establish the Syrian National Defense Force, modeled on the IRGC, and aided it by sending largely Shiʿa forces from other countries to join it.[109] Whether or not an independent Syrian military can emerge from the wreckage of the civil war, given its dependence on Russia and Iran, is quite doubtful.[110]

Egypt (BPR)

Robert Springborg puts it bluntly: "Republican Egypt, dominated by the military since its founding in 1952, has never won a war, all out or limited."[111] That pattern starts in 1952, when the leaders of the Egypt's Free Officer coup rid the Egyptian regime of the corruption that the Free Officers blamed for its 1948 defeat by Israel. But in doing so, they systematically replaced all the top military officers with politically loyal officers. The consequences have continued for decades.

Egyptian armies often went into battle poorly prepared, lacking combined arms experience, tactical proficiency, and communications effectiveness; yet soldiers mostly persisted on the battlefield, often taking disproportionate casualties, and fighting bravely against overwhelming odds, although a lack of internal cohesion hurt Egyptian military efforts.[112] Egypt's military lacks joint interoperability and suffers from inadequate training and maintenance. Training is especially poor, as an Egyptian pilot has, at most, a quarter of the flying hours of an American or even other regional air force F-16 pilots.[113] Leadership quarrels and civil-military relations also have harmed combat performance. After the disaster of the 1967 war, President Gamal Abdul Nasser cast the blame on Field Marshal Amir. Nasser was particularly watchful of General Amir during the 1960s; fearful that he represented a threat to Nasser's position.[114] Amir's performance during the Yemen war and as governor of Syria was disastrous, but when Nasser tried to remove him in 1961, his senior officers almost revolted.[115] Following Egypt's defeat in the 1967 war, Nasser had an opportunity to eliminate this threat when General Amir allegedly committed suicide after being detained for an alleged conspiracy against Nasser.[116] However, some officers loyal to Amir assigned the blamed the war's out come on Nasser as he placed incompetent leaders in charge of the military and for political miscalculations of the initial actions that contributed to the 1967 hostilities. Noted Karawan, the following trial of the officers revealed "the extent of corruption and incompetence in the inner circles of the junta; in the process it contributed further to the erosion of the entire defeated regime."[117]

The incompetence is partly attributable to Nasser's purge of the officer ranks after he seized power; replacing politically unreliable officers with political cronies who lacked competency for high military command.[118] Other sources indicate that it was General 'Amir and his chief, General Shams Badran, who emphasized loyalty over competence by awarding administrators and diplomats "honorary" commands, which did not work well when they suddenly had to put on uniforms and go to front lines in the 1967 war.[119]

There were significant civil-military quarrels over the 1973 war in particular. General Saad al-Shazli, who led Egyptian troops in that war, advocated for peace with Israel after the war turned sour, which was one of the reasons why President Sadat replaced him with the more pliant General 'abd al-Ghani Gamasy. Sadat made moves to get military support for a negotiated Israeli peace treaty,[120] though Sadat himself had such a treaty in mind when he planned his 1977 Jerusalem visit. Sadat knew that the military opposed his limited objectives, as the generals wanted to liberate the entire Sinai Peninsula, and to ensure that there would not be a military blowback to his willingness to sue for peace. Sadat later purged most of the army leaders of the 1973 war and in 1979 decreed that none could run for political office.[121]

More recently, the Egyptian armed forces have projected power into the Sinai region to combat Islamic militants, with little success. As Springborg notes, both Sadat and Mubarak feared giving the military power-projection capability (even though the Sinai is hardly distant from the rest of Egypt), because they feared failure, which could result in political disaster.[122] The consequences for that lack of preparation were clear, as in January 2014, the Egyptian armed forces lost helicopters, tanks, and suffered many casualties as the insurgents attacked towns at will. Violence continued to escalate in January 2015, with more than 880 attacks during 2015–16.[123] The reasons for the failure of the military are complex. In addition to the regime's failure to prepare the military for forward operations, the political leadership had failed to provide clear strategic guidance. Notes Ashour, the structural deficiencies in civil-military relations "is specifically related to the lack of oversight over national security policy formulation, its execution, in addition to the general lack of accountability when such policies fail or exacerbate a crisis."[124] Springborg also observes that the Egyptian military was stocked with weapons that they neither needed nor were able to maintain; yet the leadership kept it over-supplied with excess equipment because, "Preparing for a war that was not going to happen was, not coincidentally, an effective means of coup-proofing."[125]

Turkey (BSPR)

The Turkish armed forces had considerable independence prior to the 2002 election of the Islamist-oriented *Adalet ve Kalkınma Partisi*, or AKP. The general chief of staff had autonomy over most military matters, to include "defense policy, the military budget, future weapons systems, production and procurement of arms, intelligence gathering, internal security, and all promotions."[126] The AKP dramatically curbed Turkish military power primarily to restrict its appetite for internal political power and its desire for closer military ties with both Israel and the US.[127] In addition, with the overall diminishing of military power in Turkey, Turkish military decisions involved much more oversight by civilian authority.[128] After the failed July 2016 coup, the regime discharged 42 percent of Turkish senior officers from the military.[129] The military purge impacted the Turkish Air Force in particular, as it was a central coup participant. Thus, the AKP dismissed more than three hundred F-16 fighter pilots, resulting in shortages of not only trained combat pilots but also the trainers to train new pilots.[130] Promotion decisions also have been removed from the General Staff and shifted to the Defense Ministry. President Erdoğan sits on that promotion board and ensures that all who are promoted are loyal to him.[131] Erdoğan was able to reject earlier efforts to desecuritize the Turkish-Kurdish conflict,[132] partly because of his enhanced ability to commit Turkish forces to combat. And as Haugom has observed, the normal institutional checks in Turkish civil-military relations before July 2016 have been replaced with personal ties between Erdoğan and the minister of defense—a situation that could influence the combat employment of Turkish troops.[133] Noted Szarejko, "Despite the military's occasional discontent with the state of affairs, the AKP has rebuffed any pressure the military has brought to bear. That is, it has assumed control of the military. Civilians alone are now in charge of policy-making in Turkey."[134] Turkey's armed forces also detect a strong animosity toward them from AKP leadership, as then–Chief of Staff General Ilker Başbuğ openly criticized the AKP leadership; claiming that its purpose was to weaken and discredit the military, thus making it more vulnerable to civilian control.[135] The AKP had in fact transformed the military, demanding more professionalism while cashiering officers suspected of disloyalty.[136] In 2018, Erdoğan closed Turkey's war colleges, and a Turkish court sentenced 102 war college faculty and staff to life in prison, claiming that they were involved in the July 2016 failed coup.[137]

Additionally, while details remain unclear, President Erdoğan seems to be directing the military in its operations both inside and outside of Turkey. An early test of Turkish combat ability came with the 2011 incursion into Iraq in response to a PKK attack on Turkish border forces. The operation was limited; though it involved ten thousand troops and aircraft, the operation apparently killed only a handful of PKK fighters before the government terminated it.[138] Erdoğan then sent Turkish troops into Syria, initially in 2016, putting them into direct contact with Russian troops protecting the ʿAsad regime; resulting in possibly hundreds of casualties suffered by Turkish forces.[139] The second aim of the Syria mission, dubbed "Euphrates Shield," was also to eliminate the so-called Islamic State in Syria and to counter the Kurdish-dominated Yekîneyên Parastina Gel (YPG). The operation was a test as to whether Erdoğan's coup-proofing had weakened Turkey's military proficiency; the evidence suggests that it did. Sentek states that bombing was not accurate, equipment not up to the requirements, casualties were high, and objectives not obtained.[140] Eight Turkish soldiers died in an ambush and Turkish troops were accused of deliberately targeting civilians.[141] Part of the reason, argues Sentek, was that the regime had weakened Turkey's relatively strong military education system, and that instructor pilots were in short supply after the purge.[142] It is difficult to tell if the lack of F-16 pilots impacted Turkish combat capability in Kurdish areas; though overall there were concerns about how well Turkish forces were doing in combat. One former US defense official argued that during the offensive, President Erdoğan "may not understand how ill-prepared and hollowed out the Turkish military actually is."[143] Others argue that despite errors, casualties, and loss of equipment, "Euphrates Shield" did successfully achieve its mission in the end.[144] It was impossible to know if those issues occurred because of coup-proofing and tight civilian control or for other reasons. One could argue that even the most professional military (including the American military) makes mistakes, suffers equipment breakdowns, and ultimately loses wars, so caution must be exercised when attributing poor military performance to political factors such as coup-proofing.

Erdoğan also dispatched Turkish troops to Libya to defend the Government of National Unity (GNU) against General Khalifa Haftar's rebel forces, which had support from Russia, Egypt, and the United Arab Emirates. When Turkish forces first arrived in January 2020, the GNU was reeling from multiple defeats.[145] However, by May 2020, Turkish forces entered the fight, helping the GNU to gain the upper hand and Haftar was suing for peace. In the end, Turkish forces performed with determined professional skill against a coalition of actors in its deployment to Libya. Turkish military planners took over the military arm of the Government of National Accord and quickly turned it into a robust fighting force; ultimately leading it to defeat a coalition of the LNA and its supportive coalition, which included forces from the UAE and the Russian private military known as the Wagner Group.[146] Turkey also contributed military support to Azerbaijan; including its use of Bayraktar TB2 armed drones against Armenian forces in the struggle over

Nagorno-Karabakh. Again, Turkish forces out-performed both Armenia's military and its Russian-supported militia.[147]

There was no visible tension between civilian leadership and the military in both these theaters, most likely because the stronger presidential government under President Erdoğan has strengthened civilian control over the military, largely through his appointment of General Hulusi Akar to the post of Minister of National Defense.[148]

Israel (FD)

The IDF was born in a low-intensity conflict environment through participation in the Palestinian Mandate hostilities prior to the 1948 war. Then, as the 1948 war drew in Arab conventional forces, the IDF quickly adopted some of the tools and techniques of total war. Israeli forces bought and operated then–modern fighter and transport aircraft, and even sequestered four American-made B-17 heavy bombers, which they used to bomb Cairo. The outcome of the 1956 war against Egypt reinforced certain principles, primarily self-reliance (the British and French withdrawal from the fight doomed the Israelis to withdraw from a war they were winning). The 1967 and 1973 wars reinforced the necessity for total war preparation; including the drive for Israeli nuclear weapons should deterrence fail. At the same time, Israel waged low-intensity conflicts against the Palestinian *fedayyen* and their suspected supporters. These conflicts would spread into Jordan in 1956 and into Lebanon several times, most notably in 1982. Israeli troops were a constant presence in the Occupied Palestinian Territories, from 1967 on. While the civilian leadership had largely supported the IDF positions during total war times, controversy developed over IDF limited war strategy and operations.

Israel's status as a small, diverse, democratic state made it clear that Israel could not afford a long war of attrition, as a clever enemy would simply be able to outlast Israel in both costs and casualties. Thus, in 2000, the IDF started with a high attrition/early punishment type of campaign plan; accompanied by some effort to contain enemy actions.[149] However, this plan, developed in partial response to the second intifada, did not receive approval from incoming Prime Minister Ariel Sharon until March 2001, and only then was the level of discord within the IDF ranks over the policy revealed. Moreover, the short/intense war policy correctly understood that there were both military and political roads to success, however, they left considerable confusion about where the lines of control existed. Noted Peri,

> But who is in charge of military operations "of low level and limited scope"? Can the government, the prime minister, or the defense minister be responsible for such operations when every day dozens of them are conducted

simultaneously, many of them bearing political significance? On the other hand, can military commanders, even in the lower ranks, refrain from taking political considerations into account?[150]

This classic statement of the dilemma over boundaries between political and military policy would haunt the Israeli security policy decision-making community ever after 2006. Even a professional military is not always prepared for war. While it was apparent that the Israeli military failed to anticipate the 1973 war, its lack of preparedness became even more obvious after archival material revealed that not only were the intelligence assessments about the possibility of an attack poor, but the readiness of the IDF was also questionable. One soldier, ordered to prepare for combat, stated:

> Grenades were sealed and enclosed in plastic wrappers. Ammunition crates were sealed and no one was authorized to open them. Soldiers had no knowledge of the stronghold at night. Twenty-two officers went down for a drill on the workings of the stronghold system, but they wasted their time and didn't learn. A live-fire exercise for beefing up deployment when a stronghold is under attack was scheduled. The exercise did not take place, all because of indifference. When we practiced casualty evacuation procedure and getting a stretcher from a stronghold onto a tank, they didn't send a tank, only an armored personnel carrier, and over the field radio they were playing the pop-music chart. There was no operator for the generator, batteries weren't in use, they hadn't stocked up on water, hadn't greased all the places that should have been greased, and so the communications systems at the stronghold weren't in working order. From the battlefield rations that were supposed to take care of the soldiers' needs, the grapefruit wedges and plums had been pilfered. Soldiers arrived at the strongholds untrained, unprepared and incapable of proper operation of a stronghold.[151]

A similar situation existed before the 2006 Lebanon war, as Byman documents the impact of budget cuts on military preparations: "Tank crews did not train beyond their initial preparation. . . . Equipment for reserve units, which were necessary in a larger conflict, was often broken or obsolete. Reservists sometimes lacked bulletproof vests, radios, ammunition, and night-vision goggles."[152]

The lessons of these wars are important. Israel's democratic foundations mandated civilian control over military matters, which Ben Gurion recognized in 1949 in a letter to then–chief of staff Lieutenant General Yigael Yadin: "The Army determines neither the policies, administrations, or laws of the state. Nor does the army determine its structure, missions, or methods of operation, and it most certainly does not war or sign peace treaties."[153] This is partly due to the civilian origins of the IDF, as notes Yaniv, "the IDF was established by civilians, has remained largely dependent on the civilian sector . . . and has never lost the pervasively civilian ethos it was imbued with from the start."[154] This hardly means that the IDF fully consults with civilian political leadership on war matters, or fully informs it, as noted several times previously. However, in a democracy, military crossing of political red lines can result in both punishment and failure on the battlefield, as most recently shown in Lebanon 2006. The IDF has also clashed over policy with their defense minister; particularly when that defense minister was the mercurial Ariel Sharon, the only Likud member in an otherwise Labor Party–affiliated IDF military hierarchy.[155]

Yoram Peri argues senior officers have varied in their advocacy of war and peace propositions over time:

> Indeed, in 1981, Chief-of-Staff Haim Bar-Lev opposed Defense Minister Moshe Dayan's proposal for an interim settlement in the Suez Canal, and in 1977, Chief-of-Staff Motti Gur was skeptical and critical of the peace initiative of Egyptian president Anwar Sadat, as opposed to Prime Minister Menahem Begin and Defense Minister Ezer Weizman, who were partners in the initiative. On the other hand, it was Chief-of-Staff Moshe Levy who inspired a public and parliamentary lobby for Israel's withdrawal from Lebanon in 1994, in total contrast to the policy of Defense Minister Moshe Arens. In the summer of 1991, it was Chief-of-Staff Dan Shomron who expressed attitudes contradictory to those of Defense Minister Moshe Arens and strongly opposed Israel's involvement in the Gulf War. These examples, and there are many more, show that the military should not be seen as representing one unified position—always aggressive—vis-à-vis the civilian leadership.[156]

In 1963, senior IDF officers feared that Prime Minister Levi Eshkol would not permit them to exercise their option to expand Israeli territory, with both Deputy Chief of Staff Yitzhak Rabin and Air Force Chief Ezer Weizman lobbying for flexibility to "adjust" Israel's borders if war should come.[157] Michael states: "In the reality since 2003, the military echelon has been a restraining force, understanding that the military option alone cannot remain the only means, nor even the major means, of managing the conflict: These things require answers other than using force. Using force should be the last alternative."[158] This comment seemed to echo similar comments made in 1994 by then–IDF Chief of Staff Ehud Barak. Barak argued in favor of peace agreements with Arab neighbors and withdrawal from Golan (something he later unsuccessfully attempted as prime minister), and Major General Matan Vilnai, who publicly favored a withdrawal from Gaza prior to Prime Minister Sharon's decision to do so.[159] Such hesitancy is consistent with the dilemmas of war that democracies face; wars become unpopular as their length and cost grows, and Israel is no exception. The long occupation of south Lebanon soured the Israeli public mood, and ultimately Israel withdrew in the face of mounting protests and anti-war organizations (including the "Four Mothers" movement). This was probably part of a larger Israeli war weariness, as Sprecher and DeRouen find, "Protests increase as Israeli military actions increase, which suggests that there is a fatigue factor in the Israeli public for their government's uses of force."[160]

Maoz suggests that the Israeli national security apparatus generates and exaggerates threats for its own purposes: "The manipulation of threats to advance the bureaucratic and technological goals of this community and to deepen its control over foreign policy has not ceased."[161] Maoz examined the wars Israel fought since its founding and finds the military dominates the security decisional process, that IDF decisions precede almost unchallenged by the rest of the cabinet, and that military mistakes and over-steps rarely get challenged due to military bureaucratic skill: "These skills are not always in the areas of responsibility of the security community. Rather, they are demonstrated in the capacity of this community to disguise failures as successes, to cover up for mistakes, and—most importantly—to closely guard its imperialist capacity to affect policy and to prevent others from challenging it."[162] For Cohen, the IDF's almost absolute control of security contributed to the failure of the 1973 war as the IDF chief of staff failed to anticipate the pending Egyptian and Syrian offensive against Israeli positions.[163] Moreover, after 1967 Israeli planners neglected combined arms theory, relying more on armor and air rather than artillery and infantry; which cost dearly in the early days of the 1973 war.[164] In 2006, an IDF doctrinal shift to utilizing unconventional tactics to fight Palestinian insurgents led to a decline in conventional warfare capability. That decline revealed itself in the 2006 Lebanon war, where intelligence's focus on the Palestinian issue compounded the lack of military readiness against Hezbollah.[165] The IDF, according to its chief of staff, has been working to improve its performance, especially its ground forces, while "fighting off dangerous ideas from the political sector into the military arena."[166]

Saudi Arabia (CM)

Saudi Arabia has rarely dispatched forces internationally. Although Saudi Arabia and Qatar had a brief conflict on their border in 1992,[167] and Saudi Arabian troops fought in Oman's Green Mountain revolt in the late 1950s.[168] More recently, Saudi Air Force units participated in Yemen in the campaign against the Al-Huthi rebellion and reportedly have flown missions against the Islamic State in Iraq.

The al-Saud ruling family controls the Saudi Arabian armed forces, as they do all other ministries in the Kingdom. Hundreds of princes serve as both junior and senior officers and are in leadership positions in every unit down to the brigade level.[169] King Salman ibn Abdul Aziz al-Saud has control over the National Guard, while the current crown prince, Mohammed ibn Salman al-Saud, controls the Ministry of Defense and Aviation. There is a Saudi Arabia National Security Council, theoretically for security policy coordination, however, its membership is solely in the hands of the al-Saud family (the deputy is Khalid bin Salman, the crown prince's brother). The commander of the Royal Saudi Arabian Air Force is Lieutenant General Prince Turki bin Bandar bin Abdulaziz, whose brother, Lieutenant General Prince Khalid bin Bandar bin Abdulaziz, commands the land forces.[170]

Saudi Arabian military performance has been spotty in the few times the Kingdom has committed forces. For example, according to one report, Saudi Arabian pilots dispatched to intercept an Iranian fighter plane approaching Saudi territory in 1984 were told "shoot him down or don't come back," implying that Saudi Arabian pilots would otherwise be reluctant to engage in combat.[171] Saudi Arabian air force performance against Iraq in 1990–91 was uniformly poor (one Saudi pilot did shoot down two Iraqi fighters, largely because the Iraqi pilots had less skill than did the Saudi pilot), and in the end Saudi Arabian flight operations depended heavily upon US support.[172] Saudi Arabian ground forces also performed poorly, evacuating the border town of Khafji after Iraqi forces occupied it. As Barany reports: the Saudi Arabian commander requested that coalition commander General Norman Schwarzkopf order the evacuation of the town to cover up the Saudi commander's incompetence.[173]

More recently, officials report that Saudi Arabian aircrews performed poorly against targets in the Yemeni Al-Houthi rebellion in 2009; killing more Saudi ground troops than Yemeni rebels.[174] Part of the problem may have been the lack of recent combat experience for Saudi Arabian aircrews, who have rarely fired a shot in anger. There was a growing civil-military divide relative to the Royal Saudi Arabian Air Force, whose pilots have become reluctant to attack Islamic State targets in Iraq using Iranian-supplied intelligence data supplied by the Iraqi Defense Ministry. Consequently, rather than order the pilots to continue combat, the Saudi Arabian General Intelligence Directorate is seeking other partners to fly anti-IS missions and is seeking to develop ties to Israeli security services.[175] A large part of the problem for the Saudi Arabian Air Force is preparation; Barany notes that the Saudi Air Force does not require the rigorous training normally required to produce quality pilots, and there are high rates of absenteeism that contribute to the Saudi Arabian F-15s having the highest pilot-error rate in the world.[176] Oversight by the Royal Family in military affairs may also be a factor: said one senior Saudi Arabian officer about military input into operating no-fly zones near the Yemeni border: "We leave this to the politicians."[177]

Saudi Arabian intervention in Yemen has shown some of the weaknesses in the Saudi Arabian land forces. The country has bought an impressive arsenal of weapons, but Saudi Arabia has designed its forces more for large-scale conventional war than for a proxy war like that fought in Yemen.[178] Moreover, the Saudi Arabian ground forces suffer from both logistical and experience deficits; thus the Saudi Arabian campaign against the Houthi has relied almost exclusively on airpower, which has not been particularly effective against an elusive foe.[179] While Saudi Arabia bought sophisticated ground weapons, like American-designed M1A1 tanks, they did not use them effectively in Yemen, losing at least twenty tanks there.[180] Saudi Arabia announced optimistic results, claiming that their forces had devastated the Houthi ballistic missile and command centers, but satellite images revealed that the facilities remained intact.[181] Further illustrating the Saudi Arabian difficulties in Yemen was the announcement that a group of American Special Forces was assisting Saudi Arabia in defending its border.[182] It may be that the Saudi Arabian armed forces shortcomings in the Yemen campaign are a result of the death of Prince Sultan, who was the royal family member in charge of Yemen. His death in 2011 left unexperienced royal family members in charge, and thus no unified approach to Yemen.[183] As Crown Prince Muhammed ibn Salman tried to consolidate military control, he tried to bring in new senior blood to the officer ranks; though key positions remained in the hands of royal family members (Lieutenant General Fahd bin Turki bin Abdulaziz, became joint forces commander in February 2018). Despite these changes, Saudi Arabian performance in Yemen remained poor.[184] This was especially evident when comparing the Saudi Arabian promise of a "six-weeks war" in 2015, to their claimed objectives; none of which Saudi Arabian military forces achieved.[185] It is quite possible that the inconsistent Saudi Arabian military was due to the erratic nature of the policy crafted by the al-Saud family. To note just one instance, Saudi Arabia claimed that it was in the fight to combat Islamist militants, using that rationale to persuade the UAE to join the fight against Islamist groups like the Congregation for Reform. But only a few months into the fight, Saudi Arabia warmed up to the Congregation, while the UAE continued to back militias opposed to the Congregation.[186] Given the inconsistency of Prince Mohammed bin Salman, it is likely that his decision making thwarted the direction of the Saudi military in Yemen. The issue may rest partly on whether the crown prince will take the advice of the hundreds of foreign consultants and the reformed defense acquisition system that his father mandated after seeing the initial reports of poor Saudi Arabian combat performance in Yemen.[187]

The United Arab Emirates (CM)

This small, wealthy polity had not engaged in real combat until it dispatched its forced to join Saudi Arabian forces in Yemen in 2015. Given its lack of war experience, the UAE forces outperformed expectations. A year into the fight, UAE forces expelled Al-Qaeda from the Arabian Peninsula (AQAP), out of Mukalla, and helped to free Aden and Mokka from those forces.[188] UAE forces executed risky maneuvers like amphibious landings and close air support with considerable success. Roberts argues that the role of Crown Prince Mohammed bin Zayed al-Nahyan (son of the UAE founder), the UAE embrace of modern warfare doctrine, and years of UAE experience in previous deployments contributed to solid performance that belied the "normal" assessment of Arab military performance by scholars like Pollack.[189] The UAE also trains its aviators to high standards, often training in the United States with the best American air crews; though some argue that Emirates pilots perform well on fixed missions, yet do less well when required to use imaginative tactics.[190] The UAE has also developed a world-class military education system, though it is somewhat dependent on international faculty.[191]

As in the Saudi Arabian case, the ruling families of the UAE are the power brokers for that country's military. Mohammed bin Zayed Al Nahyan, the brother of the titular commander, Sheikh Khalifa bin Zayed Al Nahyan, is most responsible for military oversight, including its equipping, training, and funding.[192] But it can be argued that Mohammed bin Zayed al Nahyan has been more prudent in using his military force than has Crown Prince Mohammed bin Salman, and its recalibration of the objectives it originally set with Saudi Arabia in 2015 have allowed it to avoid long-term bleeding for its armed forces. As Juneau notes: "The UAE's ability to revise its assessment of the situation in Yemen and of its role in the war, and then to implement significant policy changes, testifies to the nimbleness of its foreign policy, at least as compared to Saudi Arabia's."[193] On the other hand, as Byman correctly points out: "the Saudi and Emirati intervention has failed to accomplish its primary objective—rolling back Iran—leaving its sponsors caught in a quagmire."[194]

The UAE is embarking on another trend that may challenge its civil-military control. Partly to make up for its small population and land size, the Emirates have turned to private contractors to provide a portion of their security. The regime contracted with Erik Prince, of the notorious Blackwater private security company, who then ran "Reflex, Ltd.," supplier of mercenaries from South Africa and Colombia (in Emirati uniforms), to perform "counter-terrorism" in defense of the UAE. But accountability and political control over foreign mercenaries working for a Western contractor was a challenge, as Krieg argues:

The essential issue with surrogate operations is patron control, which derives logically from the key benefit of surrogate operations: the dissociation between principal and agent. The greater the dissociation, the more surrogates are able to act autonomously and the less control the patron has over whether the agent delivers the objectives as intended. Therefore, in the longterm mercenaries rarely allow the client to seize, hold and build in an effort to bring about conflict resolution. For the UAE, mercenaries merely provide means to remain committed indefinitely in protracted conflicts at relatively low costs.[195]

It was very unclear how this bridge was to be implemented, with the risk that Reflex might be outside the bounds of control by the Emirate regime.

Yemen (BPR)

The Yemeni military has struggled with a lack of resources, given that nation's relative poverty, poorly maintained equipment, and its struggle to maintain a capable military with poorly educated soldiers. There is reportedly so much corruption in Yemen's armed forces that when the US wanted to improve Yemeni maritime capacities, officials established an entirely new coast guard rather than improve the Yemeni navy, as noted in earlier chapters.[196] The Yemeni military is an arm of the president, and that office uses it exclusively for domestic policing; despite the fact that it operates modern aircraft like the Russian MiG-29, designed for air superiority over other fighter aircraft.[197] It has fought Al-Qaeda forces in central and south Yemen, and against the al-Houthi Shi'a rebels in north Yemen, and during and after Yemen's turbulent "Arab Spring," some Yemeni armed forces battled other Yemeni military units as the military fragmented into camps based on loyalty to rival generals.

In unusual cases, circumstances may cause the existing chain of command to break, as it did in Yemen when President Saleh left the country for medical treatment during that country's 2011 popular uprising. Even in Saleh's absence, some Yemeni military units continued to strike Al-Qaeda targets, according to Yemeni press reports.[198] General Ali Mohsen al-Ahmar, a Yemeni army defector, appears to have led the operation, conducted in Zinzibar, capturing many weapons. Yet, in a battle of competing claims, General Mahdi Maqwalah, still in the Yemeni military, claimed that President Saleh actually provided the instructions to liberate Zinzibar, presumably from his exile in Saudi Arabia.[199] The same source also published allegations that General Mohsen had actually supplied Al-Qaeda with the very weapons that he claimed to have captured from them. Moreover, some Yemeni units chose looting over combat, specifically the Third Mountain Brigade, which raided local towns.[200]

THE CIVIL-MILITARY RELATIONS OF
STRATEGIC ASSESSMENT

Strategic assessment provides information and analysis on critical areas of national security: threats, vulnerabilities, and estimates of intentions, military and political capabilities, national and international organizations, individuals, and projections about ranges of outcomes. Strategic assessments are intended to identify issues, trends, challenges, and opportunities in regional and global military competition.[201] Yet strategic assessments must go beyond the military to analyze trends and capacities that support military capabilities. Good strategic assessment is vital to strategy making and implementation, as it provides both the raw material for strategic choice and the mechanisms to turn that material into strategic outcomes. Strategic assessment presents clear civil-military interaction, as Brooks argues: "the strategic, and pathological, quality of institutional outcomes is also evident in states where military and political leaders are both politically powerful and compete over rules and procedures."[202]

At one level, strategic assessment should be neutral and objective, based on best estimates of strategic capability and intensions, derived from careful analysis of data, and filtered through the expertise provided by both civilian and military experts. Under ideal conditions, strategic assessment produces rigorous debates among security professionals over how complete and accurate the available information is, and what it means. The product of such a process is a decision, or a series of decisions, about force commitment, ally choice, national resource commitment, and all the other factors that represent actionable policy. Under the best of conditions, though, strategic assessment can be fraught with incomplete or misleading information, misestimated threats and capabilities, and weak leadership decision-making. Leaders tend to select the strategic assessment indicators that confer winning,[203] and military organizations often select relatively clear *agency interests*, in contrast to the often vague and ideological *national* interests. Moreover, the information needed for strategic assessment can be particularly difficult during wartime; fighting produces "the fog of war" type information that becomes clearer as the war progresses,[204] so combatants may continue to fight partly to maximize information required for decent assessment.

Analysts have disaggregated strategic assessment into four component parts: information sharing, strategic coordination for considering alternative military choices, military structural competence in monitoring its internal activities, and the approval process for military decisions.[205] The specific nature of civil-military relations impacts each of these attributes. Divergence between civilian and military leaders on one can spill over to others, worsening the likely outcome of strategic assessment processes. For Brooks, the best strategic assessment occurs when leaders share information and political leadership dominates, while the worst occurs when leaders share power yet preferences for particular strategies diverge.[206] In World War I, Germany's strategic assessment suffered partly because the decisional locus between military and civilian was opaque at best.[207] Defense Secretary Donald Rumsfeld impeded strategic assessment before and during the 2003 US attack on the Saddam Hussein regime;[208] while the conflictual relationship between Pakistani Prime Minister Nawaz Sharif and the Pakistani military elite helped to weaken Pakistani strategic assessment in the Kargil crisis of 1999 and the earlier Sindh crisis. [209]

There are multiple reasons beyond preference discordance between civilians and soldiers that explains poor strategic assessment; including its opposite phenomena, close agreement on assessment that may stifle careful analysis and lead to "groupthink," poor intelligence, hubris, inexperience by both military and civilian leadership, among other factors. In some cases, it is because "great leaders" find themselves confronted by agency bureaucrats steeped in tradition and risk aversion; said Henry Kissinger in 1961: "It is no accident that most great statesmen were opposed by the experts in their foreign affairs, for the very greatness of the statesman's conception tend to make it inaccessible to those whose primary concern is with safety and minimum risk."[210] Still, preference divergence between military and civilian national elites may help to explain other strategic outcomes in the Middle East beyond those that Brooks evaluates.

STRATEGIC ASSESSMENT IN THE MIDDLE EAST

The modern history of warfare and other military operations in the Middle East is a story of a few brilliant successes and numerous failures. Analysts credit Israel with the bulk of those successes yet criticize Israeli mistakes and unnecessary wars, partly because of the conditions that Brooks observes in other contexts. A selection of case studies follows:

Egypt (BPR)

Egyptian military policy during the Yemeni civil war in the early 1960s reveals a lack of strategic planning and assessment. President Gamal Abdul Nasser committed political capital to north Yemen in his effort to spread Egyptian-dominated pan-Arabism. However, when rivals assassinated his chosen client, Imam Ahmad ibn Yahya, Egyptian troops invaded Yemen, supposedly to protect it from a "foreign attack." The real reason was to use Yemen to spread Nasserist Arab nationalism.[211] However, Egyptian "strategy" conflicted badly with Egypt's higher concerns with Israel. Therefore, when Israeli forces attacked in the 1967 war, they bloodied Egypt's forces in the first several days of the war. This was partly because Egypt had so many troops in far-off Yemen, and thus could not respond to the massive Israeli attack on Egyptian forces. Additionally, part of the failure was Nasser's reliance on General Abdel Hakim Amir's assessment.[212] However, Nasser added to the problems of the 1967 war by constantly interfering in military plans.[213]

Brooks finds high discordance between civilian leadership and military seniors in Egypt during the 1967 war but lessened during the 1973 conflict; partly because the status and thus independent power base of the military had declined between those wars.[214] Given the preponderance of retired military officers in the cabinet, it is natural that they turn to their uniformed colleagues for strategic assessment. The Egyptian military also learned bitter lessons about the consequences of civilian strategic neglect as they not only entered the 1948 war poorly prepared, but also strategically directed by the civilian Farouq regime that could not agree on a strategic purpose.[215] However, the Egyptian military improved its strategic assessment as civil-military relations changed; as President Sadat allowed for the promotion of more competent officers and demanded better training and intelligence. Those factors had a big impact on the difference between the disaster of 1967 and the (albeit temporary) triumph of 1973.[216]

Some critics argue that the Egyptian military gives little initiative to long-range planning or realistic training, preferring instead to emphasize the "for profit" nature of the Ministry of Defense.[217] During the post-Mubarak transition to new civilian leadership, Egyptian military commander Field Marshal Hussein Tantawi issued his own strategic assessment for Egypt in the absence of civilian guidance:

> I want you as well to watch out for what is being cooked underground against the army. We recognize why some would call to reduce the volume of the Egyptian army or to switch its mission from defending the country against hostile acts on the borders to fighting terrorism via claims that Egypt has no enemies after signing the peace treaty. This is the voice of defeat and loss. Look how things are going across the eastern borders and what can happen. You should cut the throat of anyone inside or outside who adopts such calls.[218]

Egypt's military was able to shape the constitution after its return to power in 2013, which suggests that Egypt's generals learned well from their confrontations with Egypt's previous autocratic leaders. The 2014 constitution requires that the defense minister must have served as a senior general, and thus, notes Goldberg: "legally and constitutionally it will be far more difficult for a president to limit the role of the army in high politics, and it will also be more difficult to use differences within the army to marginalize the generals." Thus, Egyptian strategic assessment may favor the military much more than it did previously, especially with the military-dominated cabinet that now surrounds President Sisi, as noted earlier.[219]

Israel (FD)

Civilian control of the Israeli military on security matters has usually been opaque. Technically the minister of defense serves as commander-in-chief of Israeli armed forces, yet the office does not confer the title, and the minister does not need to consult with other cabinet members or the Knesset before making military decisions.[220] In fact, the defense minister does not have to be a different person than the prime minister, because the prime minister can hold the defense portfolio, which Ben Gurion did for most of his prime ministerial term, as did his successor, Levi Eshkol. One consequence of Ben Gurion's role as defense minister was the weakening of the institutions and procedures responsible for defense decision-making.[221]

As defense minister, Ben Gurion ran the army with a heavy hand and did not coordinate or even inform other cabinet members of his decisions, a model of one-person decision-making that continued long after Ben Gurion left office in 1963. Eshkol inherited this weakness, and soon paid a price when the IDF, under Chief Yitzhak Rabin, launched a 1966 raid against the Jordanian town of Samu (noted above), inflicting heavy casualties against a country that Israel had no strategic reason to attack. Eshkol was furious with the IDF because the effort set back Jordan's own efforts to curb PLO operations against Israel. However, the damage was done.[222] Eshkol would later level his anger at Yitzhak Rabin (again) for his open statements in 1966 that Israel was plotting the overthrow of the Damascus regime.[223] In the end, Eshkol, who, like Ben Gurion, held the defense minister portfolio along with his prime ministerial job, ultimately had to hand the position to Moshe Dayan just before the 1967 war. Both Ben Gurion and Eshkol's single-handed management of military policy contrasted with that of Prime Minister Golda Meir, who consulted carefully with her entire cabinet and with senior IDF members on both the objectives and the methods in how to fight the 1973 war; though sharply departing from Defense Minister Dayan on the mechanisms for cease-fire.[224]

Some civil-military relations issues transcend prime ministers. Cohen observes: "In Israel, the army has a virtual monopoly on strategic thinking."[225] For Shlaim, the government had no strategy for the conduct of a war against the Arab states in 1967, even though Israel initiated the conflict—partly because it feared Arab military pre-emption, though there were other issues involved in the decision.[226] The military crafted a strategic assessment that the Arab armies were vulnerable, and once they initiated war, Prime Minister Eshkol failed to realize how little control he had over the pace and conduct of the war.[227]

Issues with strategic assessment also arose in the IDF's effort to stop a Turkish-based ship with supplies for Palestinians in Gaza in May 2010. The operation, which claimed nine lives when the crewmembers of the ship resisted IDF forces that boarded it, drew critical remarks globally. For Dror, the problem was the lack of political oversight of the IDF, as there was no cabinet-level discussion of the operation, nor any input from the Foreign Ministry.[228] Katz agreed, opining: "the questions need to be turned toward the top military-political level. One question that needs to be asked is why the government approved the IDF's plan to put troops on the ship via helicopter instead of perhaps sabotaging or diverting them."[229] Both critics suggest that the lack of political oversight contributed to a politically flawed military mission, as it damaged already frayed relations with Turkey, with which Israel had cooperated relative to security matters. They join the list of critics who argue that the Israeli cabinet would have provided better political guidance for the IDF by supplying both better oversight and insisting on improved strategic assessment.

The overall criticism about civil-military strategic assessment problems has counterarguments, however. Lahav argues that the Israeli cabinet engaged in substantial and probing debate prior to the 1956 war; noting that the cabinet was clearly aware of the ramifications of attacking with Britain and France on Egypt, and that skeptics raised pertinent questions about the possible justifications and outcomes of the war.[230] Moreover, the cabinet got almost all the necessary information from Ben Gurion, though he did exclude a French offer for a nuclear plant in the Negev and the consequences for Egypt's Jewish community.[231] Laron shows that while there was civilian-military debate before the 1956 Suez war, civilian and military agreement formed on the objective of expanding Israel's borders, if primarily to provide more security.[232] Adamsky indicates that such cabinet debates over strategy continued after Suez, noting the discussions within Knesset committees about offensive versus defensive doctrine, and the role of military technology as opposed to increasing the size of the IDF.[233] In fact, it is hardly surprising that in a democratic framework in a country facing threats from all quarters that debates on strategic assessment should spill out into the political sector. The alleged lack of strategic and operational thinking within the IDF professional ranks has likely contributed to the role of civilians in critical defense argumentation.[234]

It is also possible that overly optimistic assessments by IDF branches will empower civilians to challenge them. In April 2012, the air arm of the IDF assessed the damage resulting from a retaliation against an Israeli attack on Iran that came in the form of a three-week missile attack which killed around three hundred Israeli civilians. The IDF apparently based such low casualty estimates on "best guesses" that the air force could quickly find and destroy missile launchers in neighboring countries, and that civilians would not panic and instead follow instructions to minimize casualties.[235] Such "best case" assessments appeared to ignore the lessons of the 2006 Lebanon war, where both the IDF and the cabinet badly misread the threat from Hezbollah.

Senior IDF leaders, like their counterparts elsewhere, often come to believe that the application of military force can carry too high a cost. The IDF reportedly leaned toward compromise with the PLO during the 2011 Palestinian national recognition in the UN. According to Harel and Issacharoff, the IDF supported negotiation efforts because: "the IDF view is that it is best to return to talks instead of looking for ways to cut economic aid to the PA, which will bring about the breakdown of the security organizations there and revert to anarchy in the West Bank."[236] A similar situation opened between political and military leadership in a 2012 meeting between Prime Minister Benjamin Netanyahu and the Israeli military over the Iran nuclear threat, with Netanyahu and his defense minister, Ehud Barak, publicly suggesting Israeli preemptive strikes on suspected Iranian nuclear facilities. However, Lieutenant General Benny Gantz, IDF chief of staff, argued that he did not believe that Iran would build a nuclear weapon, suggesting that they were too rational to do so, while at the same time Netanyahu stated that he would not bet on Iranian rationality for the "security of the world."[237] Shortly after the message from the IDF chief, Netanyahu formed a national unity government with the Kadima party, then headed by Shaul Mofaz. Mofaz had argued that Netanyahu over-dramatized the Iranian threat. While there was no indication that the Likud-Kadima marriage came because of the IDF resistance to Netanyahu, it was certainly possible that Netanyahu formed the coalition to free his party of the small anti-Iranian parties and thus move closer to the IDF position. Mofaz, born in Iran, had stated that "the greatest threat to the state of Israel is not a nuclear Iran," a position closer to that of the IDF.[238] Over the years, that assessment had changed, but with nuance. In January 2018, the IDF released a threat assessment that ranked Iran as the "most serious" threat while arguing that the Palestinian front was the "most volatile," and Sunni jihadi groups coming in at third.[239] That position contrasted with the Netanyahu position that Iran was clearly the most threatening power that Israel faced.[240] While some have argued that Netanyahu (and earlier Likud Prime Ministers Yitzhak Shamir and Menahem Begin) grounded their strategic perspectives in the ideas of Vladimir Ze'ev Jabotinksy,[241] the replacement of Netanyahu by a coalition of less ideologically oriented civilians might reduce the cleavage between the prime minister's office and the IDF. While that coalition government did not necessarily speak with the authority that Netanyahu could, there did appear to be a consensus between the IDF and civilian leadership that an attack on Iran was becoming necessary to stop its nuclear program. Both parties also agreed that Iran's growing military capacity and the lack of Israeli capacity to counter it made the strike option less likely.[242]

Turkey (BRSP)

From Ottoman times onward, Turkish strategic assessment was the province of the military.[243] However, the rise of the Islamist-oriented AKP started challenging this prerogative after its cementing of power in the early 2000s. The military traditionally established Turkey's strategic contours, focusing initially on empire building and preservation, until the founding of the new Turkish Republic, which refocused its strategy to prevent unfavorable regional entanglements through relative neutrality. After World War II, Turkey ended neutrality, joining NATO in 1952 and purchased American weapons to equip its forces. Even under Atatürk, Turkish generals and admirals formed Turkish national security strategy and the corresponding operational art to implement it. However, the AKP altered the narrative of Turkish civil-military relations in many ways, though the AKP leadership and the military did not diverge as much on strategic assessment as they did on domestic issues.

Turkish strategic assessment initially tended to match the mantra "zero problems with the neighbors," focusing more on threats to internal security. The emphasis on "Turkishness" found threats to the ideation from both non-Turkish language populations and religious groups. There was once distance between Turkey's military and Turkish Islamist parties, such that when the mildly Islamist government headed by Necmettin Erbakan was briefly in power, the Turkish military compartmentalized its security policy, and thus providing Erbakan limited details of its operations in northern Iraq in the late 1990s.[244]

Yet the Turkish armed forces could not ignore the troublesome area around Turkey, and as threats from Iran, Syria, and Iraq grew, the assessment had to become more focused on regional threats. Particularly since Turkey's Kurdish situation became more complicated as non-Turkish Kurds were a source of supply and inspiration for Turkish Kurds. President Erdoğan and the Turkish military appeared to agree on the necessity to send Turkish forces into the Afrin region of Syria to combat PYD forces that the US had been supporting. "Operation Olive Branch," launched in early 2018, was intended to both show that there were no civil-military differences from the failed July 2016 military coup and to deter the US from supporting the PYD.[245]

Turkey's armed forces also viewed the countries Islamist political movements as a threat to their vision of "Turkishness," something learned in early reinforced throughout military life.[246] Thus, Turkey's soldiers view Turkey's political Islamists as not only dangerous themselves, but also as conduits to radical Islam elements outside Turkey. The Turkish military has used this assessment to strengthen ties to Israel, for example, partly because of its "anti-Islamic" symbolism, but also because Israel is a source of "strategic intimidation" for Turkey's more radical neighbors.[247] There may also be assessment differences between the AKP and the Turkish military on the Cyprus issue, though neither party is considering the type of military invasion of 1974. The issue was the possible downsizing of the thirty-thousand-strong Turkish military garrison in Cyprus, which Prime Minister Erdoğan wanted to reduce to a third of its size after his 2002 electoral majority. The Turkish General Staff believed that the current level was important to protect the minority Turkish Cypriot population from a possible Greek Cypriot attack.[248] There is less difference between civilians and the military on the issue of the PKK, as most Turkish political actors outside of the Kurdish community define PKK militancy as one of Turkey's leading security threats. Turkey's Islamist parties, including the AKP, have supported strong actions against the PKK,[249] though anti-PKK sentiment has been strongest in military-Turkish nationalist circles.[250]

After President Erdoğan's purges of the Turkish military in successive waves, concordance between the President and the military aligned. Turkish military assessment oriented more toward an offensive stance: projection of Turkish influence rather than to protect Turkish borders. As Erdoğan began a shift to offensive power, the military expanded their assessment and matched requirements to that calculation. They ordered new warships and focused on advanced technologies; so that when Turkish forces applied the president's vision to military operations, the Turkish military did quite well, defeating Russian-equipped forces in Azerbaijan, Libya, and northern Syria.[251]

Iraq (BPR)

After the Saddam ouster in 2003, the United States, with some assistance from other Arab countries, tried to rebuild the Iraqi military. Approximately $25 billion was spent on weapons, training, and other elements in order to allow the US to depart the country by turning the responsibility for its security over to Iraqi soldiers. If measured by the June 2014 reaction of Iraq's armed forces to the ISIS invasion from Syria, it failed dramatically due to operational failures as well as failures of strategic assessment. While Iraqi military leaders knew ISIS had entered the country and were recruiting Iraqis, they apparently failed to do careful strategic assessment, even after ISIS took Ramadi earlier in the year. One retired US general put it starkly: "I know no Iraqis saw this coming."[252] It was also possible that the Iraqi army, dominated by Shi'a officers as noted previously, framed their strategic assessment around religious identity through emphasizing more protection of Shi'a areas and relative indifference to threats against Sunni-dominant regions.[253] By 2016 US foreign assistance and training was bringing improvements to Iraqi military performance, but civilian distrust of senior leaders continued to bedevil Iraq's fight against ISIS as Prime Minister Haider al-Abadi's emphasis on religious loyalty over military skill gutted Iraq's military of its best commanders.[254] Anthony Cordesman states neither the Iraqi government nor its US military aid suppliers were willing to take the hard steps to professionalize Iraq's military leadership, and thus potentially imperiling an independent military assessment process.[255] The *Hashd al-Shaabi*, or "Popular Mobilization Units," gained strength after the 2014 collapse of regular Iraqi forces in the face of the Daesh attack that swept through much of the country north of Baghdad. The PMU also fought in Syria on behalf of Iran, but has also done domestic reconstruction work and, with a coalition, achieved second place in Iraq's parliamentary elections in May 2018.[256] Iraqi Prime Minister Hadi al-Abadi attempted to get the PMU to integrate with Iraq's military. However, it refused, and instead established a direct link to the Prime Minister's office and a $1.6 billion budget, all outside the purview of the Iraqi Ministry of Defense.[257] Other Iraqi Shi'a militias held loyalty to several Iraqi clerics, with the Mahdi Army bearing fealty to Ayatollah Ali Sistani, and the Saraya al-Salam with ties to another prominent Shi'a leader, Muqatada al-Sadr. The role of these militias indicates the complexity of Iraqi politics, as the groups all have important ties to Iran, but have also served as launching platforms for their leaders to reach political prominence. For example, Bader leader Hadi al-Amiri rose to become Iraq's Minister of Transportation in 2011, and then–Prime Minister Haider al-Abadi appointed the senior commander of Kitaib Hezbollah, Jamal Jaafar Ibrahimi, as deputy commander of the Popular Mobilization Forces.[258]

THE CIVIL-MILITARY ASPECTS OF SECURITY ASSISTANCE

Security assistance is the broad term used to identify military supplies, equipment, and training that some countries provide to friendly or allied military forces. While countries provide security assistance for many reasons (supporting allies, sharing weapon development costs and risks, support for domestic arms producers, and such), the impact is significant on recipient countries and sub-state groups. Security assistance also has civil-military relations implications. Writes Lenze, "the Algerian, Egyptian, Pakistani, and Turkish military establishment's behavior was directly affected by military aid received from the United States and/or the Soviet Union/Russia."[259] That impact was evidenced by the US's willingness to continue to provide the Egyptian military with weapons and training after they organized the movement that toppled the Mohammed Morsi regime in 2013.[260] Security assistance can also impact the relations between the national leadership and its military. When a national military can acquire security assistance, the flow of goods can enhance the armed force's position within the country and its political system. National leadership can be very reluctant to control the goose if the golden egg provides jobs and prestige. As Barany observes, "Gulf militaries maty be thought of a 'rentier armies.' In other words, Gulf armies do not quite function as conventional armies but as militaries that actually help buy the services of the regimes' protectors (the United States and the UK) through the purchase of vast quantities of often entirely unneeded, superfluous but expensive weapons."[261] Security assistance also provides employment for some countries like Egypt, which sops up unemployment by placing local workers in aircraft and maintenance shops to repair imported weapons.[262] Wealthier security assistance recipients usually add outside maintenance support to their arms purchasing contracts.

A serious byproduct of security assistance is corruption. Corruption can be especially pervasive in autocracies without independent parliamentary or judicial oversight, as Barany notes. [263] Vittori documents numerous cases of security assistance corruption, particularly with the UAE and Saudi Arabia, where contract awarding was marked with side-payments, lucrative offsets for powerful civilian and military elites, and a blind eye turned by the US to human rights abuses.[264]

US security assistance also helped to fuel Egyptian military corruption, which some Egyptian military officials siphoned for personal gain. In the 1990s, the US military contributed millions of dollars to build a 650-bed military hospital outside Cairo to care for Egyptian soldiers. Officials later discovered that its military operators had transformed it into a commercial venture, to include medical tourism with lavishly furnished "royal suites" for wealthy international patients and ex-presidents (President Hosni Mubarak was a "guest" there after his political removal). The investigation into the hospital situation revealed more questionable purchases by Egyptian military officials, including a fleet of Gulfstream jets for $333 million that were intended to be used for mapping but wound up as VIP transports.[265] Paradoxically, US financial assistance may also have contributed to privatization that challenged the Egyptian military economic sector. A $10 million endowment from the US Agency for International Development reportedly helped to create the Egyptian Center for Economic Studies, an impressive-sounding name for a group of wealthy Egyptians once led by Gamal Mubarak, the former president's son. This clique was accused of selling off public assets worth over $90 billion and pocketing the difference between what they returned to the treasury and the asset's worth.[266] At least some of these assets came from former and active military officers. In 2011, the Egyptian Supreme Military Council decided to remove almost all the Mubarak-era cabinet members, except for General Sayyid Meshaal as minister of military production,[267] fueling suspicions that the military-dominated interim government was protecting its own interests.

Security assistance can also have the effect of generating anti-military sentiment against the military, from both the elites and the mass publics. The lavish perks associated with security assistance often elevate the military who receive imported arms to exalted positions. Cronin documents the corrosive influence that arms sales (mostly American) had on the Iranian military under Shah Mohammed Reza Pahlavi, fostering corruption, vast military wealth, and an army of American military advisors who contributed to the Shah's unpopularity, thus helping the 1979 revolution.[268] Saudi Arabia also experienced corruption on aircraft sales and maintenance contracts in the 1970s.[269] In Yemen, more than $500 million in military aid from the US since 2007 provided weapons that corrupt officials often sent to the opposing Houthi forces, for a price.[270]

Security assistance can also prolong civil wars, generating obvious civil-military issues. The case of Yemen is again instructive, as outside forces contributed significantly to the intractability of the war, even as the remnants of civilian leadership wanted to terminate the bloody conflict. Observes Lawson, "the Hadi government suffered a substantial loss of power and prestige as a result of Saudi and UAE military intervention, which was compounded by General 'Ali Muhsin al-Ahmar's unwillingness to put elite regular army units under the president's command."[271] The al-Houthi coup following the start of the Yemeni "Arab Spring" allowed Saudi Arabia in particular to bolster its political influence in Yemen, while offering the titular president residence in Riyadh. This had the additional impact of weakening civil authority and thus increasing the power of the rump Yemeni armed forces that Saudi Arabia supported.[272] American security assistance empowered Saudi Arabian intervention in the Yemen civil war, as the US supplied equipment, logistics and intelligence to the Kingdom. While the US could argue that it was in line with Saudi Arabian goals of supporting the Hadi regime against the Houthi, the consequences of that assistance contributed to the mass civilian casualties in the Yemen crisis.²⁷³ Turkish foreign military sales to the GNA in Libya also helped to not only protract the conflict but tilted it to success over the rival Hafter Libyan National Army.²⁷⁴

Security assistance can have particularly pernicious effects in fragile states. Karlin notes that the US in particular has spent considerable efforts to build partner militaries in fragile states, defined as states that cannot establish effective security due to lack of capacity and weak governance.²⁷⁵ But the limited role in security assistance that the US attempts has not worked, as both external and non-state actors have undermined, limited US security assistance. As Karlin's 2018 study of Lebanon in particular showed, efforts in 1982 and in 2005 both failed to address the chronic military and political weaknesses that limited Lebanon's military.²⁷⁶ American refusal to support Lebanon's militias also impacted Lebanese civil-military relations, as Druze leader Walid Jumblatt, realizing that the US would not support his militia, turned gradually toward supporting the Shi'a militia Hezbollah.²⁷⁷

It is important to note that security assistance can also have positive effects if it is provided carefully. A good example is the security assistance provided to Tunisia by the US, which has resulted in a more proficient military force,²⁷⁸ and, it could be argued, for careful civilian control over the Tunisian armed forces. US security assistance is one reason why the Lebanese Armed Forces have not partnered with Hezbollah, which might simply turn them into an extension of the Shi'a-based militia.²⁷⁹ Another impact has been the termination or limitation of some US security assistance to Saudi Arabia in 2021 over concerns that the use by Saudi Arabia of offensive weapons was leading to large-scale civilian casualties.²⁸⁰

Despite positive impacts, security assistance, especially that provided by the US, has probably done more harm than good, and had a negative impact on the recipient country's civil-military relations. Note Wehrey and Dunne:

> with few exceptions, Arab rulers have been slow to make the changes needed to build productive, diversified economies let alone responsive, accountable governance. Their extraordinarily high levels of defense spending, often on high-end prestige items such as advanced fighter aircraft, underscore their continued conception of national security in narrow and outmoded terms, with an emphasis on ensuring regime survival and playing regional power games.²⁸¹

CONCLUSIONS

This chapter focuses attention on the military side of civil-military relations relative to the Middle East. Civil-military relations on military matters represent a symbiotic equation, with the mutual dependence of each party. Civilian political leadership jousts with military officers for degrees of control over the civilian political sphere, while officers try to preserve the relative autonomy of their military sphere. This chapter concludes, while the arrows of contestation still run in both directions, the military has become less able to influence national politics. Due in part to the velvet shove's replacement of the hard coup, and only "saving the country" currently justified the "velvet shove" scenario discussed in chapters 3 and 4. The rent-seeking Syrian military is fighting for its privileged position, although the minority officers also believe that they are protecting their communities from the majority Sunni Syrians. Yet while political influence of the military is waning, civilian influence over military spaces is increasing. In Turkey, the AKP has not only politically marginalized the military but also militarily, though it is still a professional force. Israeli political forces seem less willing to let the IDF have carte blanche over military affairs after the 2006 Lebanon conflict.

While the comparisons between regime types did not find stark differences, bully personalist republic militaries had the worst wartime civil-military relations, which certainly contributed to their poor battlefield performance. Bully single party republics did better, as Turkey has demonstrated with its recent campaigns in Syria and Libya, though those cases were both small and unique. Israel as a fragmented democracy illustrated that even a divided political system and argumentative civil-military relations did not appear to hamper Israeli wartime performance, though the 2006 Lebanon campaign did show effects of tense civil-military differences. But to underscore the obvious: Many factors determine war outcomes, and so civil-military relations conditions can only provide partial answers as to national wartime performance.

Chapter Six

Conclusions and Projections

The military plays a larger role in national politics in the Middle East than in almost any other region of the world. The military controls politics in Algeria and Egypt and is a significant political actor in Syria and many Arab Gulf states. It has a long history of shaping Turkey, from before the end of the Ottoman Empire until the election of the Justice and Development Party in 2002. While the Israeli Defense Forces officially remain neutral in Israeli politics, it still has supplied several Israeli prime ministers. The IDF also has social implications (the acceptance of Haredi into its ranks, for example), and its relative success on the field of battle can shape elections, as did the 2006 Lebanon war. The Lebanese military was one of the few agents in Lebanese politics to integrate its ranks with the broad swath of religious groups that represent the Lebanese national quilt.

The military is part of the elite in most Middle East countries, with active and retired officers playing a significant role in national society. This is not surprising, as the national militaries often were borne from the militia forces that helped to create modern Middle East nation-states. The Algerian armed forces trace their lineage to the revolutionary movements that won independence for that country after a protracted struggle with both French and European settler forces. The Israeli Defense Forces grew from the Yeshiva militias who fought in the 1948 war, and Egypt's military created the Arab Republic of Egypt in 1952 after ending the British-supported King Farooq monarchy. Oman's late Sultan Qaboos al-Said used Omani soldiers to help remove his father from power in July 1970. That military has played a quiet part on Omani life from that time on, though it does not govern. In other cases, the national military keeps minorities in power, as it does in Bahrain, suppressing the Shi'a majority that has challenged the minority Sunni Al-Khalifa family's dominance of Bahraini politics. Saddam Hussein's military also preserved his minority Sunni rule in Iraq until 2003. Both Hafiz and Bashar Al-Asad staffed the Syrian military with Alawi officers to keep the Alawi Asad family in power. Turkey's armed forces were the backbone of Turkish secular politics from 1923 until the election and rise to power of the Islamist AKP in 2002. In other cases, the military shaped national life because of what it did not do, as was the case in Tunisia. The Tunisian military refused to support President Zine al-Abidine Ben Ali, forcing him to flee the country, and triggering the Arab Awakening in late 2010. Egypt's military similarly refused to protect President Hosni Mubarak as the Arab Awakening moved to Cairo. Which opened the door for Mubarak's exit and the brief period of rule by political Islamist Mohammed Morsi, terminated by the military a year after his election.

The armed forces are significant agents of political change in the Middle East. Coups were once fairly common in the Middle East, especially in Iraq and Syria. One military clique would take power through the gun, only to be replaced by members of another military clique who envied their colleagues' access to state power. Iraqi coups were particularly violent, with the post-coup execution of Iraqi President abd al-Karim Qasim shown live on state television in 1963. Syria went through numerous coups until the 1970 takeover by Hafiz al-Asad, who gained some support among the public partly because he brought stability to Syrian politics.

While military coups have become uncommon in the region, the military has taken advantage of the political unrest that marked the Arab uprisings that started in Tunisia in late 2009. In Algeria, the military teamed with other security agencies to ensure that the regime was untouched by a brief display of public opposition. In Egypt, the military reluctantly sided with the massed demonstrators, stood by hesitantly when a political Islamist won the presidency in 2012, and then helped to orchestrate a return to autocracy a year later. Tunisia's military largely stepped aside and refused to aid the Ben Ali regime as it toppled due to massive anger over its performance. Syria's military, after suffering considerable defections from its Sunni ranks, largely made war on the participants in the Syrian uprising against the Asad regime, as that tragedy quickly became militarized. Unsurprisingly, the bully republics saw the most political instability, and their unprofessional armies often rushed in to fill a power vacuum left by public anger. In other cases, the militaries executed a pacted transition from one regime to the next, allowing them to build political influence as power brokers.

Militaries in many Middle East countries are important actors in the national economy, often running businesses that compete with non-military enterprises. Egypt's armed forces are most noteworthy, controlling a large business empire that employs many thousands of workers and constitutes perhaps 15 to 20 percent of the national income. Iran's quasi-military organizations under the Revolutionary Guard Corps also control a large share of Iran's national economy. National armies are also large spenders, with Middle East militaries filling the top positions of spending on national defense, with ten of the top twenty global military spenders coming from the Middle East (Oman, Saudi Arabia, Algeria, the UAE, Israel, Kuwait, Jordan, Yemen, Lebanon, and Iraq, for 2021).[1]

While civil-military relations studies have focused largely on the active armed forces, there are alternative military forces in the Middle East that have as much impact on civil-military relations as do the active forces. For example, in Iran, the Islamic Republican Guard Corps has larger shares of the military budget, political influence, and economic share than does the regular *Artesh* forces. The IRGC works directly under the supreme leader so it can claim that Shia jurisprudence guides its actions. It operates its own ground, sea, and air forces, and has control of internal security through its Basij forces, and international influence through its Quds forces. Those latter forces have fought in Syria and have assisted other Shia militias in the Middle East. Iraq has several Shia militias, including the Popular Mobilization Front (a coalition of several militias), the Badr Brigade, and the Mahdi Army; all of which have ties to the state and to prominent Shia leaders who used these groups to enhance their own political power in Iraq. Those militias, more than the regular Iraqi armed forces, worked to defeat the Daesh forces after they initially decimated northern Iraq in 2014. Their nexus in the mix of state and non-state actors in Iraq only makes Iraqi civil-military relations even more complex.

Military-society relations in the Middle East are significant as they influence both the political and economic spheres. The case of Turkey under Kemal Atatürk indicates how the armed forces can legitimize and protect not just a regime but also an identity. Atatürk's imagined Turkey was a secular polity emphasizing "Turkishness" over Islam, and the Turkish military protected and advanced that identity. Their military not only modernized along Western lines but additionally protected "Turkishness," by either removing or threatening to remove any post-Atatürk government that included political Islamists in its composition. As the Islamist-oriented Erdoğan regime entrenched itself more firmly into Turkish political space, it calculated that it had to curb Turkey's military domestic power to survive, which it did in a series of imagined military plots. A failed military coup in 2016 only accelerated the replacement of professional soldiers with regime loyalists. In a similar way, Iran's Shah Mohammed Reza Pahlavi relied on Iran's military to build his political power structure, often using the forces as symbols for modernity, an image the Pahlavi Dynasty needed as it strove to build an

Iranian equivalent of Atatürk's Turkey, a Western-oriented non-religious country. Mohammed Reza Pahlavi spent billions of dollar-equivalents of Iranian currency on the latest American weapons, increasing Iranian defense spending from $67 million in 1953 to $10.6 billion in 1977. Of that amount $5.7 billion alone went for purchases of US arms, exceeding the total of all other international purchases of US arms.[2] Mohammed Reza Pahlavi imported arms, not because he needed them to protect his country, but because they symbolized a modern Iran. Similar to the case of Turkey, the religious replacement for the Pahlavi Dynasty had to gut the Iranian military of its professional soldiers, executing many of them, while creating a parallel force with deep religious roots.

The Middle East's military relationship to the national economy has a significant impact on national civil-military relations. As noted earlier, the list of countries ranked by military spending (percent of GDP), the Middle East dominates the top of the list. While there is an ongoing debate among scholars as to the impact of defense spending on the national economy, research indicates that money spent on the military may either repress economic growth, or at least constrain spending on other public sectors like health care and education. It is especially difficult to map the so-called defense burden to economic conditions in the countries listed above. Part of the difficulty lies in the wealth disparity within the Middle East. Saudi Arabia, Kuwait, Israel, and the United Arab Emirates are prosperous countries while Yemen is the poorest Arab country. Though Oman is reasonably wealthy, its economy does not compare to the other GCC countries. Clearly, while other factors explain these relative wealth outcomes better than military spending, these spending levels do indicate the relative power of the military on the national political stage. As all funding is set in competition with other national requirements, the advantage goes to the entity with the most power. In addition, military spending is a measure of the security sector's ability to capture state resources. Soldiers create domestic power to get enough shares of the economy to create dependencies on them by the rest of the country. They spend their money in ways that create employment, infrastructure and more. The military portion of the national economy also allows them to expand their reach into civilian sectors, thus providing opportunities for expansion into domestic security roles. The armed forces can bring raw, uneducated recruits into their ranks and prepare them either for a career in the military (thus taking them off the unemployment ranks), or at least providing them with enough education and experience to improve their employment opportunities post-military service. As the military expands its economic reach into the country, it can become an "indispensable member" of the country, making its budgets not only more difficult to reduce, but easier to increase.

Military spending can go beyond budget shares to include investments in the national economy. No military has done as much as has the Egyptian armed forces, whose share of the total Egyptian economy is opaque but estimated at between 10 and 20 percent. The military engineered this involvement, as the armed forces overthrew the monarchy in 1952, and established for themselves a permanent position in Egypt's political life. Every president from 1952 to 2021 has been a retired Egyptian general, with the brief exception being the 2012–13 Morsi regime, and the military staffs the coterie surrounding the president. The Egyptian Parliament rarely challenges the executive on substantive policies, and while the judicial branch is nominally independent, it has not rendered a decision that fundamentally challenged the military-dominant national political system.

While the Egyptian case may illustrate the extensive mobilization of economic power by a national army, militaries have important economic influence at the political table in other Middle East countries. The Syrian Asad family surrounded itself with powerful officers from the Syrian armed forces, some of whom were Alawi, like the 'Asads, but others came from Syria's disparate religious groups, including both Sunni Muslims and Christians. Those officers got access to Syria's economy and, given the almost total collapse of Syria's economy, the soldiers are in a good position to take control of some economic sectors. With the Syrian regime unable to pay its military forces more than a few dollars' worth Syrian currency each month, the army, with its expertise and access to weapons, could take some sectors by force.

Why do countries differ on civilian control of the military, or the degree to which the military plays an economic role in the country? One factor is the nature of the political system, with countries that rank high on political accountability tending to have less military influence in the political and economic systems than do countries that rank lower on accountability. In the Middle East, two countries, Israel and Tunisia, rank as "free" as of 2022; while Freedom House designates Morocco, Lebanon, and Kuwait, as "partly free." In all these countries, the military is under civilian control, though the reasons for that control go beyond the relatively democratic state of the country. Both Morocco and Jordan experienced military coup attempts a long time ago; while they were unsuccessful, they led to tight scrutiny of the armed forces through civilian control. Kuwaiti armed forces may be under civilian control more due to the tradition of Gulf Arab countries. Royal families control the political arena in their countries, usually to the exclusion of the armed forces. Gulf royal families reward their militaries with ample resources, usually in exchange for their political neutrality. Therefore, while it is the case that democratically inclined countries have more civilian control over their militaries than do non-democratic one, the reasons go beyond democracy to include political tradition and coup-minimizing.

"Variables of interest" was listed earlier in the book to show what factors appear to be influential in both the general study of civil-military relations and Middle Eastern civil-military relations in particular. What did those variables tell us? *Political tradition and political factors* combine to set forces in place and provide a roadmap what their expected behavior has been and should be.

POLITICAL TRADITION

Political tradition often roots in the past, as it is easier for political societies to preserve established processes rather than to disrupt it. Militaries typically follow this paradigm as they are steeped in old traditions themselves, and often project those customs onto their countries. Thus, military coups or pacted transitions are often meant to preserve the past, as in the cases of Turkey and Egypt, where both British influence and the threat from Islamic religious conservatives sent troops out of their camps. Of course, the irony is that one could also argue that Islam was Turkey's real past, so why were the officers protecting the laïcité tradition? Militaries also follow tradition when they advocate for or protect autocratic regimes. As democracy can also reduce the military's ability to shape state power, militaries may act to preserve their status as an influential voice in state politics (Stephen Cook's "ruling but not governing"). Yet militaries have also ousted autocrats and helped to usher in democracy, as they did in Tunisia. However, a preference for democratic rule was rare among Middle East militaries. *Political factors* include not only regime type but also the degree to which nationalism impacts military behavior. One could argue that the armed forces have one of the strongest claims to nationalism in their countries. Who else is willing not only to wear the flags of their countries on their uniforms but also to be prepared to die to defend those flags. It follows that one of the more common reasons for military coups is that soldiers believe that national leadership has led the country astray from its national identity and argue only the military has the duty to take it back. That is consistent with *military identity*, which, in the Middle East, values tradition, order, obedience, and, often, isolation from society. Yet, again, there are differences, as the Free Officer's Movement in Egypt and the Kemalist Turkish military wanted radical change from the past. But were they arguing for real change, or that change would help preserve their traditions?

PROJECTIONS

Projections are always a hazard unless one is forecasting the obvious. Failed predictions litter the landscape in most fields; yet it is important to project research findings forward as long as the projector retains a sense of humility. Thus, a few forecasts are risked here:

Will the Middle East ultimately democratize and thus reduce military political power?

Democratic optimists sometimes think of democratization as wave-like, with at least three waves explained by Huntington, starting with the "long wave" beginning in the 1820s and continuing with the post–World War II wave.[3] De-democratization followed during 1960 to 1975, only to be reversed by the third wave. By 2018, the number of countries which declined in political rights and liberties was sixty-eight, compared with fifty that advanced on those measures.[4] However, if democracy comes in waves, then perhaps a re-democratization period may begin, or possibly has begun. The Freedom House measure sounds dire for the champions of democracy, but 2018 was better than was 2017, when seventy-one countries declined in measures of freedom, while only thirty-five improved. In 2014, only thirty-three countries improved. Perhaps renewed demonstrations in Russia, Algeria, Egypt, Hong Kong, Catalonia, Sudan, Haiti, and elsewhere may be one indicator of growing public dissatisfaction with undemocratic regimes. Massive crowds showed up in Istanbul after Turkish President Erdoğan called off a mayoral election after a member of the opposition party won the first round, and the opposition candidate won the post with 54 percent of the vote. Algeria, which had almost no "Arab Spring" in 2010–11, had massive crowds gather to protest the continuing rule of the military-business elite that had been running the country since independence. However, the Freedom House report for 2021 was especially bleak for the prospects of democracy: "The countries experiencing deterioration outnumbered those with improvements by the largest margin recorded since the negative trend began in 2006. The long democratic recession is deepening."[5] The Middle East has generally lagged behind other parts of the world on its democracy scores, so as the world becomes less democratic, the Middle East is probably not going to counter to the trend. Thus, in the bully republics that have been the source of coups, rent-seeking and sub-standard military performance are likely to continue.

ARE TRADITIONAL MILITARIES DISAPPEARING IN PARTS OF THE MIDDLE EAST?

As noted in chapter 1, this work defines "military" as an organization that has a monopoly on state-sanctioned violence. There is no clear definition of "military," as militaries may be located under a defense ministry or secretariat, but they may also be housed under a ministry of interior, or internal security, or "homeland security." Perhaps the loosest definition of "military" is that of an armed force responsible for protecting the state. However, even that definition is increasingly challenged in parts of the Middle East. The rise of Iranian militias probably started before the 1979 revolution, but quickly grew after the new regime ensconced itself in the capital. The new regime founded an alternative military force to counter the traditional Iranian Artesh that had largely kept the Pahlavi dynasty in power. The Islamic Republican Guard Corps developed a traditional military organization structure, with a land, sea, and air arm, along with a militia for internal policing. That model, once unique to Iran, is developing in Iraq and Lebanon, as Shia militias in those two countries model themselves after the IRGC. In Iraq, other forces developed as militias, including several Kurdish militias. In Lebanon, Hezbollah not only joined the government with members in the Parliament and the cabinet but also as a military force that rivaled the Lebanese armed forces. As these militias have less direct ties to the state, they have evolved into rent-seeking organizations that raise funds to pay for both their upkeep and their member's benefit. These militias continue to challenge the traditional study of civil-military relations, as they do not fit the standard understanding of a "military."

WILL WARS, AND THE NEED FOR A LARGE MILITARY, FADE FROM THE MIDDLE EAST?

In one sense, World War II was the last of the large global wars. There have certainly been large and costly wars since WWII, but the size and duration of wars has decreased, even though the frequency of wars remains as it was during World War I.[6] Gal sifts through the various explanations for the overall war decline and finds that war is no longer capable of enriching societies as it did for ancient Rome and Athens, and the horrifying consequences of "weapons of mass destruction" have contributed to make wars less likely.[7] Clauset finds that over a longer period, "long peace" periods have followed particularly violent wars, thus peace is in response to the consequences of the futility and cost of armed violence. This suggests that memory of war is the long-term preventative, but that as memory fades, wars become more likely.[8] Perhaps Vladimir Putin was hoping that memories of World War II had faded when he sent his armed forces into Ukraine in February 2022 (and probably guessed incorrectly). At the regional level, Straus finds that African wars have declined considerably in the twenty-first century from mid-1990s levels due to a combination of factors, including the end of the Cold War, the growth of regional democracy, and more effective peacekeeping.[9]

It is clearly too soon to tell if wars will become less frequent in the Middle East, and there are reasons for pessimism. The Middle East remains the world's least democratic region, with less democracy than sub-Saharan Africa and much less than in Latin America. In both Egypt and Libya, the military either returned to take control of much of the state or played a lead role in local politics. General Haider Khalifa has led a militia that battled for control of Libya, against the remnants of the government army, though his forces largely failed in the second half of 2020. While President Erdoğan has politically neutered the Turkish armed forces, his own policies smack of "neo-Ottomanism" as he has sent his troops into northern Syria to attack the Syrian Democratic Forces in October 2019. Turkish forces have also intervened against Kurds in Iraq on several occasions and, with support from the UAE and Egypt, on behalf of the Government of National Accord (GNA) in Libya against General Khalifa's forces. Turkey also sent natural gas exploration ships into the eastern Mediterranean with heavy military escort, threatening the fragile peace between Greece and Turkey. Lebanon's inherent political weaknesses were again on display in October 2019 as millions of Lebanese took to the streets to protest corruption, economic stagnation, and the failure of essential state services like electricity and garbage collection. Mass dissatisfaction with the regime can further disrupt a weak country and set in motion the forces of war in a country that has seen much war over its history.

Yet there are also regional signs that the major powers want to avoid war, which were particularly evident during the summer and fall of 2019, when a series of attacks occurred in the Arabian/Persian Gulf and its environs. Petroleum tankers came under attack, all from unspecified sources, with blame falling on Iran and the Yemeni-based al-Houthi. This lasted until missiles struck an Iranian tanker, for which Iran blamed Saudi Arabia. Yet despite the extreme tensions between Iran and Saudi Arabia, none of the tanker attacks escalated. In September 2019, cruise missiles struck a major Saudi Arabian petroleum processing plant at Abqaiq, taking much of Saudi Arabian production out of action. Where the attack came from stimulated considerable debate, but most studies concluded that it came either from Iran or from the Iranian-supported Houthis. Yet Saudi Arabia did not retaliate.

These non-retaliation events do not prove that war in the Gulf between these two rivals cannot happen. They do suggest that, beyond the bluster, all sides understand the need for extreme caution given the global consequences of a major Gulf war. The so-called Abraham Accords that established political ties between Israel and some Arab countries, including the UAE, Morocco, and Bahrain, might lessen war probabilities, though the Arab countries involved have not fought previous wars with Israel.

So, if war occurs again in the Middle East, it might be renewed civil war, or a warming of the already costly war in Libya. These are tragic and dangerous enough, but if interstate wars do decline, the role of civil-military relation on the military dimension may also change. Outside of the Gulf, countries may decide to reduce their armed forces. Lebanon's military, already small, might become smaller yet as that country really needs a national police force. Morocco and Tunisia could also pare back their armed forces, given that Tunisia has never really gone to war and Morocco's last war was in 1963. Morocco's military spending as a percent of its GDP was 1 percent in 2018, and Tunisia's was 2 percent. Yet the picture is decidedly mixed, as Algeria devotes 5.3 percent of its GDP to its military budget, making it fourth in the world. As they have been regional rivals for decades, this is a fact that Morocco in particular cannot ignore. It is also true that the top spenders are reducing their military budgets, as Saudi Arabia dropped from 13.3 percent in 2015 to 8.8 percent in 2018, and other Gulf Arab countries have recorded similar declines. Of course, it is easy to read too much into these tea leaves, and it would be foolish to argue that the chances of war are less solely because of drops in the military spending burden. But when coupled with the absence of major inter-state war in the Middle East, and an unwillingness to let armed crises rise to the level of war adds evidence to the likelihood of a more peaceful Middle East. Factoring in an apparent decline in large-scale terrorism, the possibilities for peace grow. The horrifying rise of the Daesh in 2014 was followed by its eradication as a "caliphate" by 2018. While the ideas behind Daesh remain, to a degree, among a small segment of Muslims, the extinction of the "Islamic State" convinced the vast majority of Muslims that it was a murderous and foolish notion. Moreover, smaller terror attacks that wracked many Middle East countries have declined sharply by 2021.

As a final word on Middle East civil-military relations, the number of interstate wars has decreased considerably since the end of World War II, globally and regionally. The Russian invasion of Ukraine remains an exception. Israel and its Arab neighbors last fought a true interstate war forty-eight years ago. The bloody Iran-Iraq war ended thirty-three years ago. War has certainly not disappeared, as the brutal Daesh fight indicated. Yet, the absence of interstate wars may be just a long-time lapse, like the long-time lapse after the Thirty Years War in Europe or the hundred-year peace period after the Napoleonic Wars. So perhaps one can hope that the periods of relative peace in the Middle East will become longer and lessen the necessity of a book like this.

Notes

CHAPTER ONE

1. Ronald R. Krebs, "A School for the Nation? How Military Service Does Not Build Nations, and How it Might," *International Security* 28, no. 4 (2004): 123.

2. In this book, I use "army," military," and "armed forces" interchangeably. I am fully aware that "army" specifically refers to the land component of a country's military, but it is also used more generally to refer to the armed forces. I also use "generals" when referring to military leaders but am quite aware, as a former US Navy sailor, that admirals are also senior officers. But there are far more generals than admirals in the Middle East, so I use "generals."

3. I do not cover some members of the League of Arab States, including Sudan, the Comoros Islands, or Mauritania, for example. I also do not cover Palestine, because it does not have a regular military.

4. James Burk, "Theories of Democratic Civil-Military Relations," *Armed Forces & Society* 29, no. 1 (2002): 7.

5. Mackubin Thomas Owens, *US Civil-Military Relations after 9/11: Renegotiating the Civil-Military Bargain* (New York: Continuum: 2011), 19.

6. Peter D. Feaver, "An Agency Theory Explanation of American Civil-Military Relations during the Cold War," Working Paper for the Program for the Study in Democracy, Institutions and Political Economy, Duke University, November 5, 1997, 1.

7. Florina Christiana Matei, "A New Conceptualization of Civil-Military Relations," in *The Routledge Handbook of Civil-Military Relations*, eds. Thomas C. Bruneau and Florina Christiana Matei (Oxfordshire: Routledge, 2013), 29.

8. Feaver, "An Agency Theory Explanation; Deborah D. Avant, *Political Institutions and Military Change: Lessons from Peripheral Wars* (Ithaca, NY: Cornell University Press, 1994); Rebecca L. Schiff, "The Indian Military and Nation-Building: Institutional and Cultural Concordance," in *To Sheathe the Sword: Civil-Military*

Relations in the Quest for Democracy, eds. John P. Lovell and David E. Albright (Westport, CT: Greenwood Press, 1997), 119–30; Gregory Winger, "Prospect Theory and Civil–Military Conflict: The Case of the 1976 Korean Axe Murder Incident," *Armed Forces & Society* 43, no. 4 (2017): 734–57.

9. Zoltan Barany, *The Soldier and the Changing State* (Princeton, NJ: Princeton University Press, 2012), 25.

10. Steven Ratuva, *Contested Terrain: Reconceptualizing Security in the Pacific* (Acton: Australian National University Press, 2019).

11. Dale Herspring, *Civil-Military Relations and Shared Responsibility: A Four-Nation Study* (Baltimore, MD: Johns Hopkins University Press, 2013).

12. Barany, *The Soldier and the Changing State*, 22–25; Samuel P. Huntington, *The Soldier and the State* (Cambridge, MA: Harvard University Press, 1957); Morris Janowitz, Morris, *The Professional Soldier: A Social and Political Portrait* (Glencoe, IL: The Free Press, 1960).

13. Barany, *The Soldier and the Changing State*.

14. Christopher W. Hughes, *Japan's Remilitarization* (London: International Institute for Strategic Studies, 2009), chap. 6.

15. "Ruled" is a slippery term for post-1949 China, as several senior officers have held high Communist Party positions, including Lin Biao, once named as Mao Zedong's successor until 1971, when Lin perished in a plane crash after allegedly trying to overthrow Mao. Lin held the rank of marshal and lieutenant general. John King Fairbank, 1974. *Chinese Ways in Warfare* (Cambridge, MA: Harvard University Press, 1974); Edward A. McCord, "Cries That Shake the Earth: Military Atrocities and Popular Protests in Warlord China," *Modern China* 31, no. 1 (2005): 3–34.

16. Richard H. Kohn, *Eagle and Sword: The Beginnings of the Military Establishment in America* (New York: The Free Press, 1975); Huntington, *The Soldier and the State*, chap. 6; Owens, *US Civil-Military Relations after 9/11*.

17. Brazil might be an exception, as President Jair Bolsonaro has romanticized the period when Brazil's military ran the country, yet there seems to be little public support for a return to military rule. Venezuela's President Nicolás Maduro Moros is not a military leader (he was a bus driver and trade union leader), so he rules the country with acquiescence of his military.

18. Edward D. Mansfield and Jack Snyder, *Electing to Fight: Why Emerging Democracies Go to War* (Cambridge, MA: MIT Press, 2005), 6–7.

19. Arbi Boumediene, "Algeria's Constitutional Amendments and Control of the Armed Forces," *Tawazun: Index of Arab Civil-Military Relations*, March 15, 2021, http://tawazun.net/english/blog1.php?id=586-tw.

20. More than 173,000 Algerian soldiers fought for France during World War I, with around 23,000 dying in battle. Ishaan Tharoor, "Bastille Day is a Reminder of What France owes its Colonial Soldiers," *Washington Post*, July 14, 2014, https://www.washingtonpost.com/news/worldviews/wp/2014/07/14/bastille-day-is-a-reminder-of-what-france-owes-its-colonial-soldiers/.

21. Jordan has moved back and forth from "partly free" to "not free." The Freedom House 2021 report moved Jordan to "not free," giving the country a 33 overall score

(top is 100). So, my decision to include Jordan as a "liberal monarchy" is a close one. But as restricted as Jordan is, it is not ranked close to Saudi Arabia with a score of 7, or Bahrain at 12. The UAE is scored at 17, so some of my placements are judgement calls.

22. Clement M. Henry and Robert Springborg, *Globalization and the Politics of Development in the Middle East* (Cambridge: Cambridge University Press, 2001), 20.
23. Henry and Springborg, *Globalization and the Politics of Development*, 66.
24. Barbara Geddes, "What Do We Know About Democratization after Twenty Years?" *Annual Review of Political Science* 2 (1999): 121–23.
25. Henry and Springborg, *Globalization and the Politics of Development*, 135.
26. Henry and Springborg, *Globalization and the Politics of Development*, 120–21.
27. Henry and Springborg, *Globalization and the Politics of Development*, 103.
28. Geddes, "What do We Know About Democratization," 122.
29. Anne Meng, *Constraining Dictatorship: From Personalized Rule to Institutionalized Regimes* (Cambridge: Cambridge University Press, 2020).
30. The Freedom House rankings are not without questions. For example, when Algeria held relatively free elections (by the accounts of outside observers) in 2004, its Freedom House ranking remained "not free, as was the case with Iraq, where several elections took place after 2003. Iliya Harik notes that relatively undemocratic Kuwait and relatively democratic Turkey hold the same score (partly free), and that some sub-Saharan African nations with severe democratic challenges rank higher than do most Arab countries. He argues, "The argument here is not that Arab countries have a stellar record of democratization, as indeed they do not. It is a matter of whether FH's quantitative measurement of democratization across the board is reliable at all." Iliya Harik, "Democracy, 'Arab Exceptionalism,' and Social Science," *Middle East Journal* 60, no. 4 (Autumn2006): 664. Freedom House ranks Turkey, classified as "Europe," as "not free" as of 2021.
31. Philippe Droz-Vincent, *Military Politics of the Contemporary World* (Cambridge University Press, 2021), 158.
32. Eleonora Ardemagni, "The Reshaping of Arab Civil-Military Relations," *Sada Journal*, Carnegie Endowment for International Peace, May 20, 2020, https://carnegieendowment.org/sada/81853.
33. I. William Zartman, "The Algerian Army in Politics," in *Soldier and State in Africa*, ed. Claude E. Welch Jr. (Evanston, IL: Northwestern University Press, 1970), 224–50. Two newspaper articles published on the fiftieth anniversary of Algerian independence both ignored the role of the military in achieving independence from France, and instead saluted "martyrs," Muslims, and other freedom fighters. شهداء
34. Huntington, *The Soldier and the State*, 8–10.
35. Florence Gaub, *Guardians of the Arab State: Why Militaries Intervene in Politics, from Iraq to Mauritania* (Oxford: Oxford University Press, 2017), 56.
36. Risa Brooks, "Militaries and Political Activity in Democracies," in *American Civil-Military Relations: The Soldier and the State in a New Era*, eds. Suzanne C. Nielsen and Don M. Snider (Baltimore, MD: Johns Hopkins University Press, 2009), 213–38.

37. Amos Perlmutter, "The Praetorian State and the Praetorian Army: Toward a Taxonomy of Civil-Military Relations in Developing Polities," *Comparative Politics* 1, no. 3 (1969): 382–404.

38. John Mukum Mbaku, "Military Coups as Rent-Seeking Behavior," *Journal of Political and Military Sociology* 22, (Winter 1994): 242; Gordon Tullock, "The Welfare Costs of Tariffs, Monopolies, and Theft," *Western Economic Journal* 5, no. 3 (1967): 224–32; A. O. Krueger, "The Political Economy of the Rent-Seeking Society," *American Economic Review* 64, no. 3 (1974): 291–303.

39. A. O. Krueger, "The Political Economy of the Rent-Seeking Society," *American Economic Review* 64, no. 3 (1974): 291.

40. Eva Bellin, "Reconsidering the Robustness of Authoritarianism in the Middle East: Lessons from the Arab Spring," *Comparative Politics* 44, no. 2 (2012): 132–33.

41. Fred H. Lawson, "Armed Forces, Internal Security Services, and Popular Contention," in *Armies and Insurgencies in the Arab Spring*, eds. Holger Albrecht, Aurel Croissant, and Fred H. Lawson (Philadelphia: University of Pennsylvania Press, 2016), 56.

42. Most militaries have both active and reserve branches, with active forces constituting the regular full-time professional military and reserve forces to supplement active forces in time of national emergency. Members of the active force have made the military their primary profession, while reservists normally have a full-time job outside of the military and serve their military function as a secondary profession. Reserves serve a twofold purpose: to supplement the regular forces in emergency times, and to inculcate values like national loyalty and devotion to regime in their neighborhoods, because, unlike regular soldiers, reserves normally live in civilian communities and thus are potential conduits for national values. Reservists also potentially save resources since they are normally paid only part-time wages.

43. There are always significant exceptions: the Chinese People's Liberation Army reports to the Central Military Commission, a Communist Party organ, and not to the Ministry of Defense, thus it does not report directly to the state.

44. As noted elsewhere in this book, this definition of military professionalism is problematic, because reserves in some countries sign on to the same code of professional ethics, often take the same training and education as to regular force members, read and write for the same professional journals, and, in times of emergencies, fight and die alongside regular forces. Huntington, *The Soldier and the State*.

45. Ardemagni, "The Reshaping of Arab Civil-Military Relations."

46. Sometimes the prime minister and the defense minister are the same, as in Jordan where Awn Shawkat Al-Khasawneh, with a background in diplomacy and law, rather than in military affairs, held both portfolios in 2012. In 2021, the pattern repeated with Bisher Al-Khasawneh serving as both prime minister and defence minister. Prince Salman ibn Abdulazziz served as Saudi Arabian minister of defence and aviation, maintaining a tradition of appointing a very senior prince to the post. After Salman became king in January 2015, the post went to his son, Crown Prince Mohammed ibn Salman al-Saud.

47. Interview 1O, 2010.

48. Zoltan Barany, "The Role of the Military," *Journal of Democracy* 22, no. 4 (2011): 31.

49. The Posse Comitatus Act, Section 1385 of Title 18, United States Code (USC), restricts US active-duty federal military personnel from engaging in direct domestic law enforcement, although there are exceptions, as under the Insurgency Act, Title 10 USC, Sections 331–35.

50. Robert Springborg, "Deep States in MENA," *Middle East Policy* 25, no. 1 (2007): 142.

51. J. C. Hurewitz, *Middle East Politics: The Military Dimension* (New York: Frederick A. Praeger, 1969), 341. That may have been a mistake on the king's part, as there was nobody to oversee the regular military, which attempted several coups against King Hassan II, as noted elsewhere in this book.

52. Hurewitz, *Middle East Politics*, 286.

53. Andrew McGregor, "Turkey's Gendarmerie: Reforming a Frontline Unit in the War on Terrorism," *Terrorism Monitor* 6, no. 22 (2008).

54. Corinna Jentzsch, Stathis N. Kalyvas and Livia Isabella Schubiger, "Militias in Civil Wars," *Journal of Conflict Resolution* 59, no. 5 (2015): 755–56.

55. Paul Staniland, "Militias, Ideology and the State," *Journal of Conflict Resolution* 59, no. 5 (2015): 775.

56. The Basij focus has moved away from military actions to take a more political pro-regime role after the 2009 unrest. Afshon Ostovar, "Iran's Basij: Membership in a Militant Islamist Organization," *Middle East Journal* 67, no. 3 (2013): 349.

57. In August 2014, the regular Lebanese Army fought ISIS militants who crossed over from Syria into the village of Arsal, marking the first time that the Lebanese military actually fought a foreign invader since 1948.

58. Imad Harb, "Why Would Hezbollah Never Integrate in the Lebanese Army?" *Tawazun Index of Arab Civil-Military Relations*, March 16, 2022, http://tawazun.net/english/blog1.php?id=634-ed.

59. Pierre Jumayyil formed the Phange Party in 1936, as a proto-fascist organization.

60. Ronald D. McLaurin, "From Professional to Political: The Redecline of the Lebanese Army," *Armed Forces & Society* 17, no. 4 (1991): 556.

61. Florence Gaub, *Military Integration after Civil Wars: Multiethnic Armies, Identity, and Post-Conflict Reconstruction* (London: Routledge, 2011), 3.

62. Barany, "The Role of the Military," 30.

63. Yagil Levy, "The Israeli Military: Imprisoned by the Religious Community," *Middle East Policy* 18, no. 2 (2011): 72.

64. Phillipe Droz-Vincent, "Fighting for a Monopoly on Governance: How the 'Asad State 'Won' the Syrian War and to What Extent," *The Middle East Journal* 75, no. 1 (2021): 38.

65. Ahmed S Hashim, "Military Power and State Formation in Modern Iraq," *Middle East Policy* 10, no. 4 (2003): 31. See also Zachary Lockman, *Contending Visions of the Middle East: The History and Politics of Orientalism* (Cambridge: Cambridge University Press, 2004).

CHAPTER TWO

1. Zoltan Barany, *The Soldier and the Changing State* (Princeton, NJ: Princeton University Press, 2012), 25.
2. Stephen Peter Rosen, "Military Effectiveness: Why Society Matters," *International Security* 19, no. 4 (1995): 5–31.
3. Humphrey A. Agyekum, "Complicating Entanglements: Societal Factors Intruding in the Ghana Armed Forces' Civil-Military Relations," *Armed Forces & Society* (2021), https://journals-sagepub-com.aufric.idm.oclc.org/doi/full/10.1177/0095327X2 11033010; Anthony Forster, "The Military Covenant and British Civil–Military Relations: Letting the Genie out of the Bottle," *Armed Forces & Society* 38, no. 2 (2012): 273–90.
4. Mackubin Thomas Owens, "What Military Officers Need to Know about Civil-Military Relations," *Naval War College Review* 65, no. 2 (2012): 67.
5. William E. Rapp, "Crisis in the Civil-Military Triangle?" in *Reconsidering American Civil-Military Relations: The Military, Society, and Modern War*, eds. Lionel Beehner, Risa Brooks, and Daniel Maurer (New York: Oxford University Press, 2021), 192.
6. Heidi Urben and James Golby "A Matter of Trust: Five Pitfalls That Could Squander the American Public's Confidence in the Military," in *Reconsidering American Civil-Military Relations: The Military, Society, Politics, and Modern War*, Eds. Lionel Beehner, Risa Brooks, and Daniel Maurer (New York: Oxford University Press, 2020), 137–48.
7. Cristina Jayme Montiel, "Social Representations of Democratic Transition: Was the Philippine People Power a Non-Violent Power Shift or a Military Coup?" *Asian Journal of Social Psychology* 13, no. 3 (2010): 173–84.
8. Steven Barracca, "Military Coups in the Post-Cold War Era: Pakistan, Ecuador, and Venezuela," *Third World Quarterly* 28, no. 1 (2007): 137–54.
9. J. Soedjati Djiwandono. "Civil-Military Relations in Indonesia: The Case of ARBI's Dual Function," in *Civil-Military Relations*, ed. David R. Mares (Boulder, CO: Westview Press), 45–58.
10. Stephen Philip Cohen, *The Idea of Pakistan* (Washington, DC: The Brookings Institution, 2004), chap. 3.
11. Nehginpao Kipgen, "The 2020 Myanmar Election and the 2021 Coup: Deepening Democracy or Widening Division?" *Asian Affairs* 52, no. 1 (2021): 1–17; Richard C. Paddock, "Myanmar's Army is Accused of Massacring Dozens of Civilians," *New York Times*, December 26, 2021, https://www.nytimes.com/2021/12/26/world/asiamyanmar-army-killings.html.
12. Risa Brooks, "An Autocracy at War: Explaining Egypt's Military Effectiveness, 1967 and 1973," *Security Studies* 15, no. 3 (2006): 403.
13. Zoltan Barany, *Democratic Breakdown and the Decline of the Russian Military* (Princeton, NJ: Princeton University Press, 2009).
14. Anton Troianovski, Ivan Nechepurenko, and Valerie Hopkins, "How the Kremlin is Militarizing Russian Society," *New York Times*, December 21, 2021, https://www.nytimes.com/2021 /12/21/world/europe/russia-military-putin-kremlin

.html. The Russian assault against Ukraine in March 2022 did not appear to draw much public support, unlike the 2014 Russian taking of Crimea, suggesting that Putin has not succeeded in trying to boost public support for Russia's military.

15. Claire Parker, "58 percent of Russians Support the Invasion of Ukraine, and 23 Percent Oppose it, New Poll Shows," *Washington Post*, March 8, 2022, https://www.washingtonpost.com/world/2022/03/08/russia-public-opinion-ukraine-invasion/.

16. Helen McCartney, "The Military Covenant and the Civil-Military Contract in Britain," *International Affairs* 86, no. 2 (2010): 421.

17. Richard J. Samuels, "New Fighting Power! Japan's Growing Maritime Capabilities and East Asian Security," *International Security* 32, no. 3 (2007–2008): 86.

18. Philippe Droz-Vincent, *Military Politics of the Contemporary World* (Cambridge: Cambridge University Press, 2021), 117.

19. Ghassan Salamé, "'Strong' and 'Weak' States: A Qualified Return to the *Muqaddimah*," in *The Foundations of the Arab State*, ed. Ghassan Salamé (London: Croom Helm, 1987), 205–40.

20. Yagil Levy, Edna Lomsky-Feder, and Noa Harel, "From 'Obligatory Militarism' to 'Contractual Militarism'—Competing Models of Citizenship," in *Militarism and Israeli Society*, eds. Gabriel Sheffer and Oren Barak (Bloomington: Indiana University Press, 2010), 147.

21. Mordechai Bar-On, "Remembering 1948," in *Making Israel*, ed. Benny Morris (Ann Arbor: University of Michigan Press, 2007), 29.

22. Ümit Cizre, "A New Politics of Engagement: The Turkish Military, Society, and the AKP," in *Democracy, Islam, and Secularism in Turkey*, eds. Ahmet T. Kuru and Alfred Stepan. (New York: Columbia University Press), 125; Jenny White, *Muslim Nationalism and the New Turks* (Princeton, NJ: Princeton University Press, 2013), 71–74.

23. In other cases, however, military service with a former occupier did not harm nationalist credentials; Emir Khaled, whom McDougall calls one of the "fathers of Algerian nationalism," graduated from the French military academy at St. Cyr and served as a decorated officer in the French military. James McDougall, *History and the Culture of Nationalism in Algeria* (Cambridge: Cambridge University Press, 2009), 46–47, 64.

24. Clement M. Henry and Robert Springborg, "Army Guys," *The American Interest* (May/June 2011), http://www.the-american-interest.com/article.cfm?piece=954.

25. Michael Herb, *All in the Family: Absolutism, Revolution, and Democracy in the Middle East Monarchies* (Albany: State University of New York Press, 1999), 213.

26. P. J. Vatikiotis, *The History of Modern Egypt: From Muhammad Ali to Mubarak* (Baltimore: Johns Hopkins University Press), 19.

27. Eric Chaney, "Democratic Change in the Arab World: Past and Present," Paper prepared for the Brookings Panel on Economic Activity, March 22–23, 2012, 9–13.

28. Chaney, "Democratic Change in the Arab World."

29. Interview 6TK, 2004.

30. Philippe Droz-Vincent, "Fighting for a Monopoly on Governance: How the 'Asad State 'Won' the Syrian War and to What Extent," *The Middle East Journal* 75, no. 12 (2021): 35–36.

31. Droz-Vincent, *Military Politics of the Contemporary World*, 186–87.

32. Ilkay Sunar and Sabri Sayari, "Democracy in Turkey: Problems and Prospects," in *Transitions from Authoritarian Rule: Prospects for Democracy*, eds. Guillermo O'Donnell, Philippe C. Schmitter, and Laurence Whitehead (Baltimore, MD: Johns Hopkins University Press, 1986), 168–69.

33. M. Şükrü Hanioğlu, *A Brief History of the Late Ottoman Empire* (Princeton, NJ: Princeton University Press, 2008), 200–201; Feroz Ahmad, *The Young Turks: The Committee of Union and Progress in Turkish Politics, 1908–1914* (New York: Columbia University Press, 2010), 136.

34. Zeki Sarigil, "Deconstructing the Turkish Military's Popularity," *Armed Forces & Society* 35, no. 4 (2009): 719.

35. Sarigil also notes that consolidation of democracy should take longer when certain civilian groups turn to the military when political deadlock happens ("Deconstructing the Turkish Military's Popularity," 720).

36. C. H. Dodd, "The Development of Turkish Democracy," *British Journal of Middle Eastern Studies* 19, no. 1 (1992): 22.

37. "*Türkiye Referanduma Evet diyor, AKP Binbaşı Triumph eller*" (Turkey Says Yes to Referendum, AKP Major Triumph), *Hürriyet*, September 13, 2010.

38. Yavuz Cilliler, "Popular Determinate on Civil-Military Relations in Turkey," *Arab Studies Quarterly* 38, no. 2 (2016): 510.

39. Ihsan Dagi, "Turkey's AKP in Power," *Journal of Democracy* 19, no. 3 (2008): 27, 29.

40. Soner Cağaptay, "In Long-Secular Turkey, Sharia Is Gradually Taking Over," *Washington Post*, February 16, 2018, https://www.washingtonpost.com/news/democracy-post/wp/2018/02/16/in-long-secular-turkey-sharia-is-gradually-taking-over/.

41. Sabrina Tavernise, "Election Results in Turkey a Snub to the Old Guard." *New York Times* July 23, 2007. https://www.nytimes.com/2007/07/23/world/europe/23iht-turkey.3.6787949.html.

42. Arzu Güler and Cemal Alpgiray Bölücek, "Motives for Reform on Civil-Military Relations in Turkey," *Turkish Studies* 17, no. 2 (2016): 251–71.

43. Steven A. Cook, *The Struggle for Egypt: From Nasser to Tahrir Square* (New York: Oxford University Press, 2012), 63.

44. Raymond William Baker, *Egypt's Uncertain Revolution under Nasser and Sadat* (Cambridge, MA: Harvard University Press, 1978), chap. 2.

45. Steven A. Cook, *The Unspoken Power: Civil-Military Relations and the Prospects for Reform*. Analysis Paper No. 7. The Saban Center for Middle East Policy at the Brookings Institution, September 2004, 8–9.

46. Galil Amin, *Egypt in the Era of Hosni Mubarak, 1981–2011* (Cairo: The American University in Cairo Press, 2011), 53–54; Peter Johnson, "Egypt under Nasser," *MERIP Reports* 10 (July 1972): 3–14.

47. John Waterbury, "The 'Soft State' and the Open Door: Egypt's Experience with Economic Liberalization, 1974–1984," *Comparative Politics* 18, no. 1 (1985): 65–83; Baker, *Egypt's Uncertain Revolution under Nasser and Sadat* (Cambridge, MA: Harvard University Press 1978), chap. 6.

48. Droz-Vincent, *Military Politics of the Contemporary World*, 227.

49. Florence Gaub, *Guardians of the Arab State: Why Militaries Intervene in Politics, from Iraq to Mauritania* (Oxford: Oxford University Press, 2017), 64.

50. Bahey Eldin Hassan, "New Political Struggles for Egypt's Military," *Sada: Middle East Analysis*, Carnegie Endowment for International Peace, May 9, 2019. https://carnegieendowment.org/sada/79096.

51. Droz-Vincent, (2021), *Military Politics of the Contemporary World.* Cambridge: Cambridge University Press, 2021:118; Shana Marshall, "The Egyptian Armed Forces and the Remaking of an Economic Empire," Carnegie Middle East Center, April 2015, 14, https://carnegieendowment.org/filesegyptian_armed_forces.pdf (carnegieendowment.org).

52. Ellen Lust-Okar, *Structuring Conflict in the Arab World: Incumbents, Opponents, and Institutions* (Cambridge: Cambridge University Press, 2005), 112–13; see also Steven A. Cook, *The Struggle for Egypt: From Nasser to Tahrir Square* (New York: Oxford University Press, 2012), 101; Ibrahim A. Karawan, "Egypt," in *The Political Role of the Military: An International Handbook*, eds. Constantine P. Danopoulos and Cynthia Watson (Westport, CT: Greenwood Press, 1996), 113; Ibrahim A. Karawan, "Politics and the Egyptian Army," *Survival* 53, no. 2 (2011): 44.

53. Droz-Vincent, *Military Politics of the Contemporary World*, 66.

54. Megan Brenan, "American Confidence in Major Institutions Dips," Gallup Organization, July 14, 2021, https://news.gallup.com/poll/352316/americans-confidence-major-institutions-dips.aspx.

55. Aleksandr Golts and Tonya L. Putnam "State Militarism and its Legacies: Why Military Reform Has Failed in Russia," *International Security* 29, no. 2 (2004): 148.

56. "Russian Trust in Military Grows While Political Parties Falter-Poll," *The Moscow Times*, October 12, 2017, https://www.themoscowtimes.com/2017/10/12/russians-trust-in-military-grows-while-political-parties-falter-poll-a59256.

57. Thomas Schaffner and Angelina Flood, "Poll: Majority of Young Russians Distrust NATO, Don't Consider Russia a European Country," *Russia Matters*, May 5, 2020, https://www.russiamatters.org/blog/poll-majority-young-russians-distrust-nato-dont-consider-russia-european-country. The impact of Russian military performance in Ukraine in 2022 could impact on Russian public approval of its armed forces, but it was difficult to determine, given the dominance of pro-Putin news in Russia.

58. Christopher W. Hughes, *Japan's Remilitarization* (London: International Institute for Strategic Studies, 2009), 99–100.

59. Thomas Fuller, "Floods Give Thai Military Chance to Launch Charm Offensive," *New York Times*, November 15, 2011, https://www.nytimes.com/2011/11/16/world/asia/floods-give-thai-military-a-chance-to-launch-charm-offensive.html/.

60. Courtney Johnson, "Trust in the Military Exceeds Trust in Other Institutions in Western Europe and US," Pew Research Center, September 4, 2018, https://www.pewresearch.org/fact-tank/2018/09/04/trust-in-the-military-exceeds-trust-in-other-institutions-in-western-europe-and-u-s/.

61. Manfred Halpern, *The Politics of Social Change in the Middle East and North Africa* (Princeton, NJ: Princeton University Press, 1963), 271.

62. Florence Gaub, *Guardians of the Arab State: Why Militaries Intervene in Politics, from Iraq to Mauritania* (Oxford: Oxford University Press, 2017), 78.

63. James N. Sater, "Parliamentary Elections and Authoritarian Rule in Morocco," *Middle East Journal* 63, no. 3 (2009): 397; Tim Llewellyn, *Spirit of the Phoenix: Beirut and the Story of Lebanon* (Chicago: Lawrence Hill Books, 2010), 174.

64. Gaub, *Guardians of the Arab State*, 80.

65. "Lebanon Country Report," Arab Barometer VI, https://www.arabbarometer.org/wp-content/uploads/Public-Opinion-Lebanon-Country-Report-2021-En-1.

66. Anne Marie Baylouny, "Building an Integrated Military in Post-Conflict Societies: Lebanon," in *The Routledge Handbook of Civil-Military Relations*, eds. Thomas C. Bruneas and Florina Christiana Matei (Oxfordshire: Routledge, 2015), 252.

67. Aya Majzoub, "Lebanon's Military Courts have no Business Trying Civilians," *Human Rights Watch*, February 5, 2020, https://www.hrw.org/news/2020/02/05/lebanons-military-courts-have-no-business-trying-civilians.

68. "Lebanon Army Deployed to Enforce Public Lockdown," *Al-Jazeera*, March 23, 2020, https://www.aljazeera.com/news/2020/03/lebanon-army-deployed-enforce-public-lockdown-200323134036485.html.

69. Jeff Martini and Julie Taylor, "Commanding Democracy in Egypt," *Foreign Affairs* 90, no. 5 (2011): 136.

70. "One Year after Morsi Ouster, Divides Persist on El-Sisi, Muslim Brotherhood," Pew Research Center, May 22, 2014 https://www.pewresearch.org/global/2014/05/22/one-year-after-morsis-ouster-divides-persist-on-el-sisi-muslim-brotherhood/.

71. Ann M. Lesch, "Egypt's Spring: Causes of the Revolution," *Middle East Policy* 18, no. 3 (2011): 35–48; Tarek Osman, *Egypt on the Brink: From Nasser to Mubarak*. New Haven, CT: Yale University Press, 2010), 115–43.

72. Interview 8E, 2012.

73. Samir Shehata, "Egyptians Embrace Revolt Leaders, Religious Parties and Military, As Well," Pew Research Center Global Attitudes Project, April 25, 2011, http://pewglobal.org/files/2011/04/Pew-Global-Attitudes-Egypt-Report-FINAL-April-25-2011.pdf.

74. "Survey Shows Declining Trust in Egyptian Army," *Al-Jazeera*, November 25, 2011.

75. Shibley Telhami, "2011 Annual Arab Public Opinion Survey." University of Maryland, October 2011, https://www.brookings.edu/wp-content/uploads/2016/06/1121_arab_public_opinion.

76. Gamal Essam El-Din, "Difficult Debut." *Al Ahram*, January 26–February 1, 2012.

77. Steven A. Cook, *The Unspoken Power: Civil-Military Relations and the Prospects for Reform*. Analysis Paper No. 7. The Saban Center for Middle East Policy at the Brookings Institution, September 2004, 4.

78. Gamal Abdel Nasser, "The Philosophy of the Revolution," reprinted in *The Political Influence of the Military: A Comparative Reader*, eds Amos Perlmutter and Valerie Plave Bennett (New Haven, CT: Yale University Press, 1980), 311.

79. Nanis Fahmy, "The Army, the Revolution, and the Youth," *Al-Ahram*, June 12, 2014.

80. Elizabeth Bumiller, "Egypt Stability Hinges on a Divided Military," *New York Times*, February 5, 2011.
81. Osman, *Egypt on the Brink*, 89–90.
82. Mona El-Ghobashy, *Bread and Freedom: Egypt's Revolutionary Situation* (Stanford, CA: Stanford University Press, 2021), 118.
83. Karabekir Akkoyunlu, *Military Reform and Democratisation: Turkish and Indonesian Experiences at the Turn of the Millennium* Adelphi Paper 392 (London: International Institute for Strategic Studies, 2007), 25.
84. Gareth Jenkins, *Context and Circumstance: The Turkish Military and Politics*. Adelphi Paper 337, London: The International Institute for Strategic Studies, 2001, 18; Nil S. Satana, "Transformation of the Turkish Military and the Path to Democracy," *Armed Forces & Society* 34, no. 3 (2008): 372.
85. Jacob Poushter, "Turks Divided on Erdogan and the Country's Direction," Pew Research Center, July 30, 2014, https://www.pewresearch.org/global/2014/07/30/turkey-survey-methods.
86. Tanel Demirel, "Soldiers and Civilians: The Dilemma of Turkish Democracy," *Middle Eastern Studies* 40, no. 1 (2004): 138; H. Birsen Örs, "The Perceptions of the Army by Armenian Minorities Living in Turkey," *Armed Forces & Society* 36, no. 4 (2010): 611; Mark Tessler and Ebru Altınoğlu "Political Culture in Turkey: Connections Among Attitudes Towards Democracy, the Military, and Islam," *Democratization* 11, no. 1 (2004): 25.
87. Ioannis N.Grigoriadis, "Friends no More? The Rise of Anti-American Nationalism in Turkey," *Middle East Journal* 64, no. 1 (2010): 58. A split emerged between rural and urban Turks on military approval; both populations showed decreasing approval of the Turkish military. Rural citizens saw their approval drop from 72 percent approval in 2008 to 66 percent in 2013, while urban Turks (defined as living in cities of at least one hundred thousand inhabitants) declined from 64 percent to 49 percent over the same time period. The split probably reflects the division between urban and rural support for the Islamist AKP, which gets much less approval in urban areas. "Urban Turks' Trust in Major Institutions Drops Sharply," *Gallup World*, August 15, 2013, http://www.gallup.com/poll/163979/urban-turks-trust-major-institutions-drops-sharply.aspx.
88. Ersel Aydinli, "Ergenekon, New Pacts, and the Decline of the Turkish 'Inner State,'" *Turkish Studies* 12, no. 2 (2011): 228.
89. Retired, and possibly active, members of the Turkish armed forces have been implicated in the so-called Ergenekon Affair, an alleged plot to thwart Turkish democracy by a coalition of retired military and police officials, lawyers, and members of far-right wing groups. According to some sources, the Ergenekon members planned assassinations of prominent Turkish intellectuals (including Nobel laureate Orhan Pamuk), and a military coup in 2009. Ioannis Grigoriadis and Irmak Özer, "Mutations of Turkish Nationalism," *Middle East Policy* 17, no. 4 (2010): 108; Aydinli, "Ergenekon," 227–39. In July 2008 security forces arrested two retired general officers along with twenty-two other suspects in the affair, and a police search uncovered diaries detailing two coup plans for 2004 against the AKP government planned by Admiral Ozden Ornek, head of the Turkish Navy, Turkish Army

commander Aytac Yalman, the commander of the Turkish army, and Air Force general Ibrahim Firtına. Ali Balci, "A Trajectory of Competing Narratives: The Turkish Media Debate Ergenekon," *Mediterranean Quarterly* 21, no. 1 (2010): 92. There is no evidence yet that the Ergenekon Affair has hurt the image of the Turkish military, but the ruling AKP leadership has used the reports to bolster its own narratives. The case also revealed schisms in the Turkish military that likely weaken its capacity to participate successfully in Turkish politics (Aydinli, "Ergenekon").

90. Interview 1O, 2010; Interview 2O, 2010.

91. Interview 3O, 2010.

92. Interview 1J, 2009.

93. Interview 6J, 2011. The rejoinder is that the demonstrators left because they fear military repression against them, or because they may confuse Jordanian military members with the internal security forces.

94. Kobi Michael, "Military Knowledge and Weak Civilian Control in the Reality of Low-Intensity Conflict: The Israeli Case," *Israel Studies* 12, no. 1 (2007): n9.

95. Roni Tiargan-Orr and Meytal Eran-Jona, "The Israeli Public's Perception of the IDF: Stability and Change," *Armed Forces & Society* 42, no. 2 (2015): 329.

96. Yehuda Ben Meir and Olena Bagno-Moldavsky, "Vox Populi: Trends in Israeli Public Opinion on National Security 2004–2009," Memorandum 106, Tel Aviv: The Institute for National Security Studies, November 2010.

97. David Lev, "Poll: Jews Trust IDF, President; Arabs Trust High Court, Media." *Arutz Shiva*, October 6, 2013, http://www.israelnationalnews.com/News/News.aspx/172563. Israeli Arabs gave decidedly different responses, with the IDF getting only a 35 percent "trust" response (Lev, 2013). The Israeli Democracy Institute conducted the survey.

98. Judah Ari Gross, "Poll: Almost Half of Jewish Israelis Support Making IDF a Professional Army," *The Times of Israel*, November 23, 2021, https://www.timesofisrael.com/poll-almost-half-of-jewish-israelis-support-making-idf-a-professional-army/.

99. Asher Arian, "*Vox Populi:* Public Opinion and National Security," in *National Security and Democracy in Israel*, ed. Avner Yaniv (Boulder, CO: Lynne Rienner Publishers, 1993), 137–38.

100. Zeev Rosenhek, Daniel Maman, and Eyal Ben-Ari, "The Study of War and the Military in Israel: An Empirical Investigation and a Reflective Critique," *International Journal of Middle East Studies* 35, no. 3 (2003): 468.

101. Zeev Maoz, *Defending the Holy Land: A Critical Analysis of Israel's Security & Foreign Policy* (Ann Arbor: University of Michigan Press, 2006), 525–27.

102. Zipi Israeli and Ruth Pines, "National Security Index: Public Opinion, 2020–2021," Institute for National Security Studies, Tel Aviv University (2021), https://www.inss.org.il/publication/strategic-survey-survey/.

103. Katherine Zoepf and Anthony Shadid, "Syrian Leader's Brother Seen as Enforcer of Crackdown," *New York Times*, June 7, 2011.

104. Nicholas J. Lotito, "Public Trust in Arab Armies," Carnegie Endowment for International Peace, October 30, 2018, https://carnegieendowment.org/sada/77610?lang=en.

105. Lotito, "Public Trust in Arab Armies," 2018.

106. Timothy Cocks, "Boko Haram Exploits Nigeria's Slow Military Decline," *Reuters*, May 5, 2011, http://uk.reuters.com/article/2014/05/09/uk-nigeria-military-insight-idUKKBN0DP0PV20140509; Fareed Zakaria, "The Radicalization of Pakistan's Military," *Washington Post*, June 22, 2011.

107. Author's visits over varying years to the Syrian Higher Military Academy, the Nasser Higher Military Academy in Cairo, the Tunisian War College, the Royal Moroccan War College, The Omani National Defence College, The Turkish War College, the Turkish Air War College, and the Royal Jordanian War College.

108. Sinem Gürbey, "Islam, the Nation-State, and the Military: A Discussion of Secularism in Turkey," *Comparative Studies of South Asia, Africa, and the Middle East* 29, no. 3 (2009): 371–80. Gürbey argues that far from secularizing Turkey, the Atatürk vision called for a transfer of authority for the study of and preservation of Islam into the state organs: studies on Turkish secularism suggest that secular reforms in Turkey never aimed at complete separation of religion and state, as Islam was put under state control through the establishment of the Diyanet. "What I would like to emphasize is not that the state *controls* religion but that through the Diyanet the state *produces* knowledge about a particular conception of Islam as a part of the project of nation making, hence exercising a theological function" (emphasis in original). Gürbey also challenges the notion that the Turkish state limits the practice of Islam to the private sphere, given its effort to define religious spheres relative to the Alevi. The question, then, is why is the state that claims to confine religion to the private sphere preoccupied with the transformation of Alevism into a religion or the alienation of Alevis from the "true" Islam? Gürbey, "Islam, the Nation-State, and the Military," 375.

109. Ümit Cizre Sakallioğlu, "The Anatomy of the Turkish Military's Political Autonomy," *Comparative Politics* 29, no. 2 (1996): 239.

110. Frank Tachau and Metin Heper, "The State, Politics, and the Military in Turkey," *Comparative Politics* 16, no. 1 (1983): 18.

111. Banu Eligür, *The Mobilization of Political Islam in Turkey* (Cambridge: Cambridge University Press, 2010), 108. General Evren led the 1980 coup and assumed the presidency of Turkey in 1982.

112. Ceren Lord, *Religious Politics in Turkey: From the Birth of the Republic to the AKP* (Cambridge: Cambridge University Press, 2018).

113. Nil S. Satana, "Transformation of the Turkish Military and the Path to Democracy," *Armed Forces & Society* 34, no. 3 (2008): 366–67; Eligür, *The Mobilization of Political Islam*, 93–95.

114. Amos Perlmutter, "The Praetorian State and the Praetorian Army: Toward a Taxonomy of Civil-Military Relations in Developing Polities," *Comparative Politics* 1, no. 3 (1969): 390.

115. John Calvert, *Sayyid Qutb and the Origins of Radical Islam* (New York: Columbia University Press, 2010), 182.

116. Steven A. Cook, *The Struggle for Egypt: From Nasser to Tahrir Square* (New York: Oxford University Press, 2012), 115.

117. P. J. Vatikiotis, *The Egyptian Army in Politics* (Bloomington: Indiana University Press, 1961), 191.

118. Eliezer Be'eri, *Army Officers in Arab Politics and Society* (London: Pall Mall, 1970), 113–15.

119. Interviews 2E, 2009; 3E, 2018.

120. Ahmed S. Hashim, "The Egyptian Military, Part Two: From Mubarak Onward," *Middle East Policy* 18, no. 4 (2011): 121, 123.

121. David D. Kirkpatrick and Mayy El Sheik, "Egyptian Military Enlists Religion to Quell Ranks," *New York Times*, August 25, 2013, https://www.nytimes.com/2013/08/26/world/middleeast/egypt.html?nl=afternoonupdate&emc=editau.

122. Noah Lewin-Epstein and Yinon Cohen, "Ethnic Origin and Identity in the Jewish Population of Israel," *Journal of Ethnic and Migration Studies*, July 2018, https://people.socsci.tau.ac.il/mu/noah/files/2018/07/Ethnic-origin-and-identity-in-Israel-JEMS-2018.pdf.

123. Navav G. Shelef, *Evolving Nationalism: Homeland, Identity, and Religion in Israel, 1925–2005* (Ithaca, NY: Cornell University Press, 2010); Idith Zertal, *Israel's Holocaust and the Politics of Nationhood* (Cambridge: Cambridge University Press, 2005); David Novak, *Zionism and Judaism: A New Theory* (Cambridge: Cambridge University Press, 2015).

124. Stuart Cohen, *The Scroll or the Sword? Dilemmas of Religion and Military Service in Israel* (Amsterdam: Harwood Academic Publishers, 1997), 44–45.

125. Amos Perlmutter, "The Israeli Army in Politics: The Persistence of the Civilian Over the Military," *World Politics* 20, no. 4 (1968): 620.

126. Alon Peled, *A Question of Loyalty: Military Manpower Policy in Multiethnic States* (Ithaca, NY: Cornell University Press, 1998), 133.

127. Paul Rivlin, *The Israeli Economy from the Foundation of the State through the 21st Century* (Cambridge: Cambridge University Press, 2011), 123; Hanne Røislien, "Religion and Military Conscription," *Armed Forces & Society* 39, no. 2 (2013): 218. The Druze are a subgroup of Shi'a Islam, though their status within Islam is disputed; the Circassians are Sunni Muslims with ethnic origins in the Caucasus Mountains.

128. Amichai Cohen and Stuart Alan Cohen, "Beyond the Conventional Civil–Military "Gap": Cleavages and Convergences in Israel," *Armed Forces & Society* 48, no. 1 (2022): 171–72.

129. Some military leaders did not oppose the religious exemption as they argued that yeshiva students who only studied religious texts had little competency in subjects like math or science that would allow the IDF to train them in desirable technical fields.

130. Jeremy Sharon, "Israeli bill gives ultra-Orthodox Choice between IDF Service, Work," *Al Monitor*, August 30, 2021, https://www.al-monitor.com/originals/2021/08/israeli-bill-gives-ultra-orthodox-choice-between-idf-service-work#ixzz7FbyqdpIt.

131. Itamar Rickover, Ofra Ben Ishai, and Ayala Keissar-Sugarman, "Hi-Tech-Oriented National Service: The Free Choice of Religious Women Recruits and the De-Monopolization of the Israeli Military," *Religions* 12, no. 11 (2021): 4–20.

132. Zertal, *Israel's Holocaust*, 183.

133. Shelef, *Evolving Nationalism*, 88.

134. Cohen, *The Scroll or the Sword?* 46–47.

135. Yagil Levy, "The Israeli Military: Imprisoned by the Religious Community," *Middle East Policy* 18, no. 2 (2011): 67–83.

136. Elisheva Rosman-Stollman, "Mediating Structures and the Military: The Case of Religious Soldiers," *Armed Forces & Society* 34, no. 4 (2008): 622.

137. Stuart Cohen, "The Re-Discovery of Orthodox Jewish Laws Relating to the Military and War (*Hilkhot Tzavah U-Milchamah*) in Contemporary Israel: Trends and Implications," *Israel Studies* 12, no. 2 (2007): 22–23.

138. Yagil Levy, "The Clash between Feminism and Religion in the Israeli Military: A Multilayered Analysis," *Social Politics: International Studies in Gender, State, and Society* 17, no. 2 (2010): 185–209.

139. Interview 5IS, 2019.

140. "More Muslims Joining the Israeli Army," *Israel Today*, June 25, 2021, https://www.israeltoday.co.il/read/more-muslims-joining-israeli-army/.

141. Rosman-Stollman, "Mediating Structures and the Military," 620; Steven R. Ward, *Immortal: A Military History of Iran and its Armed Forces* (Washington, DC: Georgetown University Press, 2009), 305.

142. Ray Takeyh, *Guardians of the Revolution: Iran in the World in the Age of the Ayatollahs* (New York: Oxford University Press, 2006), 80; Vali Nasr, *The Shia Revival* (New York: W.W. Norton, 2006), 132–33.

143. Mohammad Ayatollahi Tabaar, *Religious Statecraft: The Politics of Islam in Iran. New* (York: Columbia University Press, 2018), 157–58; Ariane M. Tabatabai, *No Conquest, No Defeat: Iran's National Security Strategy* (New York: Oxford University Press, 2020), 145.

144. Ken Dilanian, Ken, Paul Richter and Brian Bennett, "Iranian Leader Thought to Have OK'd Plot," *Los Angeles Times*, October 13, 2011. The killing of Quds force commander General Qasem Soleimani in January 2020 by a US military drone revealed more information about his activities, including his likely ordering of the assassination attempts on the Saudi Arabian Ambassador to the United States in 2011 (which was badly bungled).

145. Elizabeth Coles, and Marcus George, "Iran Commander Criticizes Government Over Influence from West," *Reuters*, December 11, 2013.

146. Amin Saikal, *Iran Rising: The Survival and Future of the Islamic Republic* (Princeton, NJ: Princeton University Press, 2019), 137.

147. Ronald R. Krebs, "A School for the Nation? How Military Service Does Not Build Nations, and How it Might," *International Security* 28, no. 4 (2004): 85–124.

148. The vast majority of the world's soldiers will not experience war, but preparation for war remains the primary reason for a military, in almost all states.

149. Albert O. Hirschman, *Exit, Voice, and Loyalty: Response to Decline in firms, Organizations, and States* (Cambridge, MA: Harvard University Press, 1970), 78.

150. Hirschman, *Exit, Voice, and Loyalty*, 92–105.

151. Theodore McLauchlin, "Loyalty Strategies and Military Defection in Rebellion," *Comparative Politics* 42, no. 3 (2010): 340.

152. Service identity may also help form military political and economic preferences, based partly on the class origins noted above. Some analysts argue that while the army prefers nationalist-driven authoritarian rule and corporatist economies, naval

officers tend toward liberalism in both the political and economic spheres. There are a variety of explanations for such differences; for example, army officers are more likely to originate from rural conservative milieus while naval officers tend to come from more aristocratic or at least middle-class backgrounds. Heginbotham writes that, "navies tend to favor liberal economic and social policies even if they do not always support democracy," and "In this preference ordering, navies are similar to their societies' middle classes (and especially upper-middle classes), with which they are almost invariably allied in domestic political disputes." Armies, by contrast, rely on recruiting from rural areas because of the frequent poverty there and thus the desperation of rural poor to gain entry into the army, and thus a job. So liberal welfare policies that improve rural conditions may worsen army recruiting. Eric Heginbotham, "The Fall and Rise of Navies in East Asia: Military Organizations, Domestic Politics, and Grand Strategy, *International Security* 27, no. 2 (2002): 97–99.

153. Marion J. Levy, "Some Implications of Japanese Social Structure," *The American Sociologist* 31, no. 2 (2000): 21.

154. P. E. Razzell, "Social Origins of Officers in the Indian and British Home Army: 1758–1962," *The British Journal of Sociology* 14, no. 3 (1963): 248–60.

155. Sven Gunnar Simonsen, "Leaving Security in Safe Hands: Identity, Legitimacy, and Cohesion in the New Afghan and Iraqi Armies," *Third World Quarterly* 30, no. 8 (2009): 1489.

156. Stephen Peter. Rosen, "Military Effectiveness: Why Society Matters," *International Security* 19, no. 4 (1995): 20–21.

157. Jason Lyall, *Divided Armies: Inequality and Battlefield Performance in Modern War* (Princeton, NJ: Princeton University Press, 2020), 404.

158. Kenneth M. Pollack, *Arabs at War: Military Effectiveness, 1948–1991* (Lincoln: University of Nebraska Press, 2002), 552–55.

159. McLauchlin, "Loyalty Strategies and Military Defection," 342–44.

160. Yara Bayoumi, "Military Defections Expose Cracks in Syrian Army," *Reuters*, June 29, 2011; Hanna Batatu, "Some Observations on the Social Roots of Syrian Ruling Military Groups and the Causes for its Dominance," *The Middle East Journal* 35, no. 3 (1981): 331–44; Raymond A. Hinnebusch, *Authoritarian Power and State Formation in Ba'athist Syria: Army, Party, and Peasant* (Boulder, CO: Westview Press, 1990); Stefan Winter, *A History of the 'Alawis: From Medieval Aleppo to the Turkish Republic* (Princeton, NJ: Princeton University Press, 2016).

161. The "Black September" incident involved a Palestinian Liberation Organization (PLO) revolt against the Jordanian monarchy, which the Jordanian military suppressed, ousting the PLO, which relocated to Beirut. Such efforts may succeed, as in Jordan, where the Bedouin armies favored initially by John Glubb proved loyal to King Hussein though in other cases it backfired, as when the Berber officers recruited by King Hassan II of Morocco twice attempted a coup against the king in 1971 and 1972. Michael Herb, *All in the Family: Absolutism, Revolution, and Democracy in the Middle East Monarchies* (Albany: State University of New York Press, 1999), 244–45.

162. Ruth Linn, "When the Individual Soldier Says 'No' to War: A Look at Selective Refusal during the Intifada," *Journal of Peace Research* 33, no. 4 (1996): 421–31.

163. McLauchin, "Loyalty Strategies," 344.

164. Feroz Ahmad, *The Young Turks: The Committee of Union and Progress in Turkish Politics, 1908–1914* (New York: Columbia University Press, 2010), 42–43.

165. Ahmad, *The Young Turks*, 94; Hazem Kandil, *The Power Triangle: Military, Security, and Politics in Regime Change* (New York: Oxford University Press, 2016), 143–44. The term "Young Turk" has become common parlance for a military coup, but as Ahmad argues, the Committee for Union and Progress (the "Young Turks") was primarily a political operation with only marginal military involvement. When the armed forces did intervene, it was members of the junior officer ranks, who had been educated in a politicized curriculum, and who gained influence only because the senior officers in the Ottoman military had performed so badly in the previous Balkan wars (Ahmad, *The Young Turks*, 154).

166. Elizabeth Bumiller, "Egypt Stability Hinges on a Divided Military," *New York Times*, February 5, 2011, https://www.nytimes.com/2011/02/06/world/middleeast/06military.html.

167. Kenneth M. Pollack, *Armies of Sand: The Past, Present, and Future of Arab Military Effectiveness* (New York: Oxford University Press, 2019), 32–33.

168. Simonsen, "Leaving Security in Safe Hands," 1495.

169. Alon Peled, *A Question of Loyalty: Military Manpower Policy in Multiethnic States* (Ithaca, NY: Cornell University Press, 1998).

170. Alejandro Panchon, "Loyalty and Defection: Misunderstanding Civil-Military Relations in Tunisia during the 'Arab Spring.'" *Journal of Strategic Studies* 37, no. 4 (2014): 527.

171. Interview 1TN, March 2011.

172. "Yemeni Air Force Commander Reportedly Distributes Weapons to Pro-Govt 'Thugs,'" Sanaa *Al-Salwah* (in Arabic), OpenSource Center, June 11, 2011.

173. Droz-Vincent, *Military Politics of the Contemporary World*, 194–95.

174. Zoltan Barany, "The Role of the Military," *Journal of Democracy* 22, no. 4 (2011): 31–32; Charles Tripp, *The Power and the People: Paths of Resistance in the Middle East* (Cambridge: Cambridge University Press, 2013), 108.

175. Michael S. Schmidt and Eric Schmidt, "Weapons Sales to Iraq Move Ahead Despite US Worries," *New York Times*, December 28, 2011.

176. Oren Barak, *The Lebanese Army: A National Institution in a Divided Society* (Albany: State University of New York Press, 2009), 93–110; David S. Sorenson, *Global Security Watch: Lebanon* (Santa Barbara, CA: Praeger Security International, 2010), 137–39.

177. Ronald D. McLaurin, "From Professional to Political: The Redecline of the Lebanese Army. *Armed Forces & Society* 17, no. 4 (1991): 545–68.

178. Ali Reza Eshraghi and Amir Hossein Mahdavi, "The Revolutionary Guards are Posed to Take Over Iran," *Foreign Affairs*, August 27, 2020, https://www.foreignaffairs.com/articles/middle-east/2020-08-27/revolutionary-guards-are-poised-take-over-iran.

CHAPTER THREE

1. A senior Tunisian official chastised those who referred to the Tunisian changes as the "Jasmine Revolution," claiming that this usage was a European invention, and arguing that it should be called the "Tunisian Revolution," because to him the Tunisian Revolution would become as important as the French Revolution. Hindsight suggests that he was incorrect (author's discussion, Tunisian Foreign Ministry, March 2011).
2. Clement Henry and Robert Springborg, *Globalization and the Politics of Development in the Middle East* (New York: Cambridge University Press, 2010).
3. Oren Barak and Dan Miodownik, "Military Autonomy and Balancing in Political Crises: Lessons from the Middle East," *Armed Forces & Society* 47, no. 1 (2021): 129.
4. Barak and Miodownik, "Military Autonomy," 129.
5. Jonathan Powell, and Clayton L. Thyne, "Global Instances of Coups from 1950 to 2010: A New Data Set," *Journal of Peace Research* 48, no. 2 (2011): 252.
6. Naunihal Singh, *Seizing Power: The Strategic Logic of Military Coups* (Baltimore: Johns Hopkins University Press, 2014), 5.
7. Abdullah Aydogan, "Constitutional Foundations of Military Coups," *Political Science Quarterly* 134, no. 1 (2019): 96.
8. Coup d'état Project, January 2021, https://clinecenter.illinois.edu/project/research-themes/democracy-and-development/coup-detat-project.
9. Erica De Bruin, *How to Prevent Coups d'État: Counterbalancing and Regime Survival* (Ithaca, NY: Cornell University Press, 2020), 15.
10. James T. Quinlivan, "Coup Proofing: Its Practices and Consequences in the Middle East," *International Security* 24, no. 2 (1999): 134.
11. Singh, *Seizing Power*, 3–4.
12. Narcis Serra, *The Military Transition: Democratic Reform of the Armed Forces* (Cambridge: Cambridge University Press, 2010).
13. Habiba Ben Barka, and Mthuli Ncube, "Political Fragility in Africa: Are Military Coups d'État a Never-Ending Phenomena?" African Development Bank, September 2012, 5. http://www.afdb.org/fileadmin/uploads/afdb/Documents/Publications/Economic%20Brief%20-%20Political%20Fragility%20in%20Africa%20Are%20Military%20Coups%20d%E2%80%99Etat%20a%20Never%20Ending%20Phenomenon.pdf.
14. Claude E. Welch, "Soldier and State in Africa," *The Journal of Modern African Studies* 5, no. 3 (1967): 305–22; Herbert Howe, *Ambiguous Order: Military Forces in African States* (Boulder, CO: Lynne Rienner Publishers, 2001), 46.
15. Joshua Kurlantzick and Shelby Leighton, "Military Rule 2.0," *Boston Globe*, July 11, 2010, http://archive.boston.com/bostonglobe/ideas/articles/2010/07/11/military_rule_ 20/.
16. Dave Lawler, "Coups are Making a Comeback," *Axios*, January 30, 2022, https://www.axios.com/coup-attemps-countries-around-world-e14f76d2-16b1- 43da-8411- 6f8fc07cec84.html. Lawler cites an earlier study by Jonathan Powell and Clayton L. Thyne, "Global Instances of Coups from 1950 to 2010: A New Data Set," *Journal of Peace Research* 48, no. 2 (2011): 249–59.

17. Naunihal Singh updated this list for me.
18. Singh, *Seizing Power*, 3.
19. Florina Christiana Matei, "A New Conceptualization of Civil-Military Relations," in *The Routledge Handbook of Civil-Military Relations*, eds. Thomas C. Bruneau and Florina Christiana Mate. (Oxfordshire: Routledge, 2010), 30–31.
20. Seva Gunitsky, "Democracy's Future: Riding the Hegemonic Wave," *The Washington Quarterly* 41, no. 2 (2018): 115–35; "Democracy Under Siege," Freedom House Democracy in the World, 2021, https://freedomhouse.org/report/freedom-world/2021/democracy-under-siege.
21. There have been very few coups for naked military self-interest. The Pakistani army's 1977 coup against Ali Bhutto allowed the winning officers to enrich themselves with higher pay, and land tracts, bank loans, and other perks that they could supply for themselves. Anthony Bell, "Military Disengagement from Politics: The Case of Pakistan's Revolving Barracks Door," *Georgetown Security Studies Review*, June 10, 2014, http://georgetownsecuritystudiesreview.org/2014/06/10/military-disengagement-from-politics-the-case-of-pakistans-revolving-barracks-door/. However, few military officers would admit to such crass motives and there are very few cases where self-interest was a primary motive. It becomes more of a motive to remain in power after launching a coup for another reason.
22. Samuel P. Huntington, *Political Order in Changing Societies* (New Haven, CT: Yale University Press, 1968), 200–201.
23. Robert C. Harding, *Military Foundations of Panamanian Politics* (New Brunswick, NJ: Transaction Publishers, 2001), 59–67.
24. Jimmy Kandeh, *Coups from Below: Armed Subalterns and State Power in West Africa* (New York: Palgrave, 2004); Singh, *Seizing Power*, 157–60.
25. Samuel Decalo, *Coups & Army Rule in Africa: Motivations and Constraints*, second edition (New Haven, CT: Yale University Press, 1990), 33–132.
26. Definitions of "ethnicity" are challenging, as the category often contains overlapping identities of religion, race, and language. This book thus adopts Fearon's use of ethnicity as the self-identification of members of a particular group. James D. Fearon, "Ethnic and Cultural Diversity by Country," *Journal of Economic Growth* 8, no. 2 (2003): 195–222. Thus, members of a particular ethnic group are conscious of their identity and its distinguishing factors, such as language, religion, a sense of a "homeland," and a sense of shared history.
27. Eric A. Nordlinger, *Soldiers in Politics: Military Coups and Governments* (Englewood Cliffs, NJ: Prentice-Hall, 1977), 40.
28. Brian Martin, *Social Defence, Social Change* (London: Freedom Press, 1993); Robert Norton, "Reconciling Ethnicity and Nation: Contending Discourses in Fiji's Constitutional Reform," *The Contemporary Pacific* 12, no. 1 (2000): 83–122; Andrew Scobell, "Politics, Professionalism, and Peacekeeping: An Analysis of the 1987 Military Coup in Fiji," *Comparative Politics* 26, no. 2 (1994): 187–201.
29. J. Craig Jenkins and Augustine J. Kposowa, "Explaining Military Coups d'état: Black Africa, 1957–1984," *American Sociological Review* 55, no. 6 (1992): 861–75; Philip Roessler, "The Enemy Within: Personal Rule, Coups, and Civil War in Africa," *World Politics* 63, no. 2 (2011): 300–346.

30. Kristen A. Harkness, "The Ethnic Stacking in Africa Dataset: When Leaders Use Ascriptive Identity to Build Military Loyalty," *Conflict Management and Peace Science*, 1–24. https://journals.sagepub.com/doi/pdf/10.1177/0738894221 1044 999.

31. Fuad Khuri and Gerald Obermeyer, "The Social Bases for Military Intervention in the Middle East," in *Political-Military Systems: Comparative Perspectives*, ed. Catherine M. Kelleher (Beverly Hills, CA: Sage Publications, 1974), 55–86.

32. Barbara Geddes, "What do We Know About Democratization after Twenty Years?" *Annual Review of Political Science* 2 (1999): 115–44.

33. Efforts at economic reform, or a change in the operation of the national economy can also impact on the economic sources of military power, as senior military officers also benefitted from conservative economic systems. In some countries, military preservation of the economic status quo for the economic elite would result in compensation for the military.

34. Nordlinger, *Soldiers in Politics*, 51.

35. Dale Krane, "Opposition Strategy and Survival in Praetorian Brazil, 1964–1979," *Journal of Politics* 45, no. 1 (1983): 28–63; Wendy Hunter, *Eroding Military Influence in Brazil: Politicians Against Soldiers* (Chapel Hill: University of North Carolina Press, 1997).

36. Paul Chambers, "Thailand on the Brink: Resurgent Military, Eroded Democracy," *Asian Survey* 50, no. 5 (2010): 835–58.

37. Aqil Shah, "Getting the Military Out of Pakistani Politics," *Foreign Affairs* 90, no. 3 (2011): 70.

38. Paul Staniland, "Explaining Civil-Military Relations in Complex Political Environments: India and Pakistan in Comparative Perspective," *Security Studies* 17, no. 2 (2008): 322–62.

39. Babar Sattar, "Pakistan: Return to Praetorianism," in *Coercion and Governance: The Declining Political Role of the Military in Asia*, ed. Muthiah Alagappa (Sanford, CA: Stanford University Press, 2001): 385–412; Steven Barracca, "Military Coups in the Post–Cold War Era: Pakistan, Ecuador, and Venezuela," *Third World Quarterly* 28, no. 1 (2007): 137–54.

40. Decalo, *Coups & Army Rule in Africa*, 134–98.

41. Nordlinger, *Soldiers in Politics*, 76. Some coups "for the nation" are sometimes more "for the military" to protect its own resource base; in Ghana, despite efforts by civilian leadership to keep the armed forces apolitical, the impact of world cocoa prices alone helped to promote military coups in 1966, 1972, and 1981, when cocoa, which supplies Ghana with much of its livelihood, dropped in price, stimulating the initial military budget cuts which led to coups. Claude E. Welch, *No Farewell to Arms? Military Disengagement from Politics in Africa and Latin America* (Boulder, CO: Westview Press, 1987): 72–73. The Bolivian army launched a series of coups after the new National Revolutionary Movement slashed the military and its budget dramatically in the early 1950s, suggesting a coup for Bolivia, but in reality, the military took over the country and ran it largely to suit their own interests. Bruce W. Farcau, *The Transition to Democracy in Latin America: The Role of the Military* (Westport, CT: Praeger Publishers, 1996), 111–38.

42. Syed Badrul Ahsan, "Bangladesh at 50: Coups, Assassinations, and Democratic Struggle," *Asian Affairs*, 52, no. 3 (2021), 554–62.

43. George A. Kelly, "Algeria, the Army, and the Fifth Republic (1959–1961): A Scenario of Civil-Military Conflict," *Political Science Quarterly* 79, no. 3 (1964): 337.

44. Jack Snyder, *The Ideology of the Offensive: Military Decision Making and the Disasters of 1914* (Ithaca, NY: Cornell University Press, 1984), 52–55.

45. Paul C. Sondrol, "The Emerging New Politics of Liberalizing Paraguay: Sustained Civil-Military Control without Democracy," *Journal of Interamerican Studies and World Affairs* 34, no. 2 (1992): 127–63.

46. It is important to note, however, that in some cases, defeat, or stalemate at best, does not always foster coup efforts, as Perlmutter notes, "In Israel, a highly professionalized army dependent on a reserve system, with an unusually high turnover of officers and men, was harnessed to civilian control . . . there was never, therefore, a chance for military coups." This after the disappointing performance of the IDF in the 1973 war and the 2006 Lebanon war. But, as noted above, Israel is a functioning democracy, and thus the military could wait for the electoral process to do what "coups for the nation" usually do; remove those who failed it. Amos Perlmutter, *The Military and Politics in Modern Times: On Professionals, Praetorians, and Revolutionary Soldiers* (New Haven, CT: Yale University Press, 1977), 275.

47. Michael Poznansky, "The Psychology of Overt and Covert Intervention," *Security Studies* 30, no. 3 (2021): 335.

48. Richard H. Immerman, *The CIA in Guatemala: The Foreign Policy of Intervention* (Austin: University of Texas Press, 1982).

49. Kristian Gustafson, *Hostile Intent: US Covert Operations in Chile, 1964–1974* (Washington, DC: Potomac Books, 2007).

50. Francis X. Winters, *The Year of the Hare: America in Vietnam, January 25, 1963–February 15, 1964* (Athens: University of Georgia Press, 1997); David E. Kaiser, *American Tragedy: Kennedy, Johnson, and the Origins of the Vietnam War* (Cambridge, MA: Harvard University Press, 2000).

51. Miles D. Wolpin, "Egalitarian Reformism in the Third World vs the Military: A Profile of Failure," *Journal of Peace Research* 15, no. 2 (1978): 95.

52. Alfred Stepan, *The Military in Politics: Changing Patterns in Brazil* (Princeton, NJ: Princeton University Press, 1971), 125–26.

53. Cynthia J. Arnson et al., *Argentina-United States Bilateral Relations* (Washington, DC: Woodrow Wilson International Center for Scholars, 2003).

54. Thomas Taylor Hammond, *Red Flag over Afghanistan: The Communist Coup, The Soviet Invasion, And the Consequences* (Boulder, CO: Westview Press, 1984).

55. Gary D. Payton, "The Somali Coup of 1969: The Case for Soviet Complicity," *The Journal of Modern Africa Studies* 18, no. 3 (1980): 493–508.

56. Steven R. David, "Soviet Involvement in Third World Coups," *International Security* 11, no. 1 (1986): 14.

57. Jesse Dillon Savage, and Jonathan D. Caverley, "When Human Capital Threatens the Capitol: Foreign Aid in the Form of Military Training and Coups," *Journal of Peace Research* 54, no. 4 (2017): 542–57.

58. Will Fowler, *Independent Mexico: The Pronunciamiento in the Age of Santa Anna, 1821–1858* (Lincoln: University of Nebraska Press, 2016).
59. John Doxey, "A 'Soft' Coup in Turkey," *New Leader* 80, no. 4 (1997): 1–12.
60. J. C. Hurewitz, *Middle East Politics: The Military Dimension* (New York: Frederick A. Praeger, 1969), 108–9.
61. Risa Brooks, *Political-Military Relations and the Stability of Arab Regimes*, Adelphi Paper 324 (London: International Institute for Strategic Studies, 1998), 13; Eliezer Be'eri "The Waning of the Military Coup in Arab Politics," *Middle East Studies* 18, no. 1 (1982): 69.
62. Quinlivan, "Coup Proofing," 133.
63. Philippe Droz-Vincent, *Military Politics of the Contemporary World* (Cambridge: Cambridge University Press, 2021), 13.
64. Michael Herb, *All in the Family: Absolutism, Revolution, and Democracy in the Middle East Monarchies* (Albany: State University of New York Press, 1999), 244–45.
65. Manfred Halpern, *The Politics of Social Change in the Middle East and North Africa* (Princeton, NJ: Princeton University Press, 1963), 256; Joel Gordon, *Nasser's Blessed Movement: Egypt's Free Officers and the July Revolution* (New York: Oxford University Press, 1992), 14–57; Hazem Kandil, *The Power Triangle: Military, Security, and Politics in Regime Change* (New York: Oxford University Press, 2016), chap. 12.
66. Robert L. Tignor, *Egypt: A Short History* (Princeton, NJ: Princeton University Press, 2010), 256–57; Afaf Lutfi Al–Sayyid Marsot, *A History of Egypt: From the Arab Conquest to the Present* (Cambridge: Cambridge University Press, 2007), 128–29; Steven A. Cook, *The Struggle for Egypt: From Nasser to Tahrir Square* (New York: Oxford University Press, 2010), 35–46.
67. Lutfi Al–Sayyid Marsot, *A Short History of Egypt*, 98–126; Interview 7E, 2007; Interview 12E, 2019.
68. Kandil, *The Power Triangle*, 234.
69. Anouar Abdel–Malik, *Egypt: The Military Society, The Army Regime, the Left, and Social Change Under Nasser* (New York: Random House, 1968), chaps. 2–4; Gordon, *Nasser's Blessed Movement*, chap. 2; Baker, *Egypt's Uncertain Revolution*, 60–69.
70. Derek Lutterbeck, "Arab Uprisings, Armed Forces, and Civil–Military Relations," *Armed Forces & Society*, April 2012, http://afs.sagepub.com/content/early/20 12/04/11/0095327X12442768.full.pdf+html; Cook, *The Struggle for Egypt*, 272–307; Kandil, *Soldiers, Spies, and Statesmen*, 175–98.
71. Barany, *How Armies Respond to Revolutions*, 138–39.
72. Lisa Blaydes and James Lo, "One Man, One Vote, One Time? A Model of Democratization in the Middle East," *Journal of Theoretical Politics* (2011), 24, http://web.stanford.edu/~blaydes/Democracy.pdf.
73. Neil Ketchley, *Egypt in a Time of Revolution: Contentious Politics and the Arab Spring* (Cambridge: Cambridge University Press, 2017), 117–29.
74. The US was faced with a quandary, as it faced the prospect of having to cut off Egyptian military assistance as required for any military that launches a coup,

according to the Foreign Assistance Act of 1961. The way around this problem, for the Obama administration, and for the subsequent Trump and Biden administrations, was to ignore the Egyptian coup. Another solution is to call it something else, like an "off-sequence, military-assisted temporary readjustment to the state balance of central political authority." Or something like that.

75. "Egypt's Interim President Defends Military Coup," *Al-Jazeera*, September 4, 2013, https://www.aljazeera.com/news/2013/9/4/egypt–interim–president–defends –military–coup.

76. Amy Austin Holmes, *Coups and Revolutions: Mass Mobilizations, the Egyptian Military, and the United States from Mubarak to Sisi* (New York: Oxford University Press, 2019), 178. It is interesting that as an Army officer, then–Colonel Sisi attended the US Army War College, perhaps supporting Savage and Caverley's finding that foreign military training graduates are more likely to launch successful coups than their non FMT counterparts. Jesse Dillon Savag and Jonathan D Caverley, "When Human Capital Threatens the Capitol: Foreign Aid in the Form of Military Training and Coups," *Journal of Peace Research* 54, no. 4 (2017): 542–57.

77. Fatma Khaled, "Egyptian Referendum Expands Presidential and Military Powers," *Washington Report on Middle East Affairs* 38. no. 4 (2019), https://go–gale –com.aufric.idm.oclc.org/ps/i.do?p=AONE&u=maxw30823&id=GALE|A59335216 3&v=2.1&it=.

78. Gordon H. Torrey, *Syrian Politics and the Military* (Columbus: Ohio State University Press, 1964), 121–23; Patrick Seale, *The Struggle for Syria: A Study of Post–War Arab Politics, 1945–1958* (New Haven, CT: Yale University Press, 1986), 37–45.

79. Nabil M. Kaylani, "The Rise of the Syrian Ba'th, 1940–1958: Political Success, Party Failure," *International Journal of Middle Eastern Studies* 3, no. 1 (1972): 11.

80. For an interesting account of Zaʻim's brief rule, see Elizabeth Whitman, *The Awakening of the Syrian Army: General Husni al–Za'im's Coup and Reign, 1949*, Senior Thesis, Columbia University, 2011.

81. Torrey, *Syrian Politics and the Military*, 143–46.

82. Kevin W. Martin, "Speaking with the 'Voice of Syria': Producing the Arab World's First Personality Cult," *The Middle East Journal* 72, no. 4 (2018): 631–53; Lisa Wedeen, *Ambiguities of Domination: Politics, Rhetoric, and Symbols in Contemporary Syria* (Chicago: University of Chicago Press, 1999).

83. The Ba'ath Party ideology dates to the 1930s, with an emphasis on Arab nationalism, socialism, and a single Arab state. See John F. Devlin, "The Baath Party: Rise and Metamorphosis," *The American Historical Review* 96, no. 5 (1991): 1396–407; Albert Hourani, *Arabic Thought in the Liberal Age, 1798–1939* (Cambridge: Cambridge University Press, 1962).

84. The differences between the Ba'athist and Nasserist officers were largely nationalistic, as the Ba'ath preferred a stronger Syrian identity in the military, while the Nasserist officers largely favored unity with Egypt. After the collapse of the "United Arab Republic," the Ba'athist officers whom the Egyptian–controlled

government purged got their revenge by purging the Nasserists. See John Galvani, "The Baathi Revolution in Iraq," *MERIP Reports* 12 (September–October 1972), 6–7.

85. Cynthia H. Enloe, *Ethnic Soldiers: State Security in Divided Societies* (Athens: University of Georgia Press, 1980), 144–45. The 'Alawites are related to the Twelver schools of Shi'a Islam. For their role in Syrian politics, see Leon T. Goldsmith, *Cycle of Fear: Syria's 'Alawites in War and Peace* (London: Hurst, 2015). The Druze have roots in the Shi'a Fatimid Caliphate in Cairo during the tenth and eleventh centuries, see Robert Brenton Betts, *The Druze* (New Haven, CT: Yale University Press, 1988).

86. David W. Lesch, "Syria: Playing with Fire," in *The 1967 War: Causes and Consequences*, eds. William Roger Louis and Avi Shlaim (Cambridge: Cambridge University Press, 2012), 87.

87. The consequences of the 1967 war were not the only reason why Asad took power, but he used the outcome to justify his seizure of power. It was a paradoxical reason, as Asad, as chief of the Syrian air force, had lost almost his entire force to the Israelis during the 1967 war.

88. Kaylani, "The Rise of the Syrian Ba'th," 23.

89. James L. Gelvin, *Divided Loyalties: Nationalism and Mass Politics in Syria at the Close of Empire* (Berkeley: University of California Press, 1998), 41–48; Seale, *The Struggle for Syria* (1986), 37; Hanna Batatu, "Some Observations on the Social Roots of Syrian Ruling Military Groups and the Causes for its Dominance," *The Middle East Journal* 35, no. 3 (1981): 331–44.

90. Raphaël Lefèvre, *Ashes of Hama: The Muslim Brotherhood in Syria* (Oxford: Oxford University Press, 2013), 51.

91. John Mukum Mbaku, "Military Coups as Rent–Seeking Behavior," *Journal of Political and Military Sociology* 22 (Winter 1994): 241.

92. Hicham Bou Nassif, "Turbulent from the Start: Revisiting Military Politics in Pre–Ba'th Syria," *International Journal of Middle East Studies* 52, no. 3 (2020): 482.

93. Dirk Vandewalle, *A History of Modern Libya* (Cambridge: Cambridge University Press, 2006), 51.

94. Florence Gaub, "The Libyan Armed Forces between Coup proofing and Repression," *Journal of Strategic Studies* 36, no. 2 (2013): 225; Vandewalle, *A History of Modern Libya* (2006), 72–73.

95. The Air Force officer who commanded Wheelus AFB when Qadhafi tried to enter was Daniel "Chappie" James Jr., who became the first Black four-star Air Force general.

96. Vandewalle, *A History of Modern Libya* 2006, chap. 4; Raymond A. Hinnebusch, "Charisma, Revolution, and State Formation: Qaddafi and Libya," *Third World Quarterly* 6, no. 1 (1984): 59.

97. Gaub, "The Libyan Armed Forces," 226.

98. Kenneth M. Pollack, *Arabs at War: Military Effectiveness, 1948–1991* (Lincoln: University of Nebraska Press, 2002), 358–424; Vandewalle, *A History of Modern Libya*, 100–101; Gaub, "The Libyan Armed Forces," 229; Ronald Bruce St John, *Libya: From Colony to Revolution* (Oxford: Oneworld), 223.

99. Mary Jane Deeb, "Political and Economic Developments in Libya in the 1990s," in *North Africa in Transition: State, Society, and Economic Transformations*

in the 1990s, ed. Yahia Zoubir (Gainesville: University of Florida Press, 1999), 77–89; Meghan O'Sullivan, *Shrewd Sanctions: Statecraft and State Sponsors of Terrorism* (Washington, DC: Brookings Institution Press, 2003), 204; Randall Newnham, "Carrots, Sticks, and Bombs: The End of Libya's WMD Program," *Mediterranean Quarterly* 20, no. 3 (2009): 86.

100. Steven R. David, "Soviet Involvement in Third World Coups," *International Security* 11, no. 1 (1986): 12–13.

101. Gaub, "The Libyan Armed Forces," 235.

102. "Too Early to Cry 'Coup' in Libya," *Al Jazeera*, May 20, 2014, http://america.aljazeera.com/articles/2014/5/20/libya–heftar–offensive.html; Marc R. DeVore, "Exploiting Anarchy: Violent Entrepreneurs and the Collapse of Libya's Post–Qadhafi Settlement," *Mediterranean Politics* 19, no. 3 (2014): 468. General Hafter (who name can also be spelled "Hifter) was once a senior officer under Qadhafi but defected to the US over twenty years ago after Chadian forces captured him in 1987. Thus, his return sparked rumors that the US was somehow involved, though it was unlikely that the US would want a military coup to further destabilize Libya. David D. Kirkpatrick, "In Libya, a Coup, or Perhaps Not," *New York Times*, February 14, 2014, https://www.nytimes.com/2014/02/15/world/middleeast/in–libya–a–coup–or–perhaps–not.

103. "Libya Foreign Minister Names Khalifa Haftar Army Chief," *Al Jazeera*, May 9, 2017, https://www.aljazeera.com/news/2017/5/9/libya–foreign–minister–names–khalifa–haftar–army–.

104. "'Big Loss': Libya's UN–Recognized Government Retakes Key Town," *Al Jazeera*, June 27, 2019, https://www.aljazeera.com/news/2019/06/libya–gna–allied–forces–claim–retake–key–town–haftar–190626204224514.html.

105. Tim Eaton, "The Libyan Arab Armed Forces," Chatham House, June 2, 2021, https://www.chathamhouse.org/2021/06/libyan–arab–armed–forces/04–utilizing–networks–state.

106. Majid Khadduri, "Coup and Counter–Coup in the Yaman 1948," *International Affairs* 28, no. 1 (1952): 59–68; Manfred W. Wenner, *Modern Yemen, 1918–1966* (Baltimore: Johns Hopkins University Press, 1967), 82–106.

107. Paul Dresch, *Tribes, Governments, and History in Yemen* (Oxford: Clarendon Press, 1989), 243–46; Robert W. Stookey, *Yemen: The Politics of the Yemen Arab Republic* (Boulder, CO: Westview Press, 1978), 229–31; Asher Orkaby, "The North Yemen Civil War and the Failure of the Federation of South Arabia," *Middle Eastern Studies* 53, no. 1 (2017): 72. The Zaydi Shiʻa follow the fifth Imam, Zayd ibn ʻAli, rather than the twelfth Iman, born as Abuʼl al–Hadi, followed by a majority of Shiʻa.

108. Erica De Bruin, *How to Prevent Coups d'État: Counterbalancing and Regime Survival* (Ithaca, NY: Cornell University Press), 128–29.

109. Victoria Clarke, *Yemen: Dancing on the Heads of Snakes* (New Haven, CT: Yale University Press, 2010), 63.

110. William B. Quandt, *Revolution and Political Leadership: Algeria, 1954–1968* (Cambridge, MA: The MIT Press, 1969).

111. Bahgat Korany, "The Foreign Policy of Algeria," in *The Foreign Policies of Arab States: The Challenge of Change*, eds. Bahgat Korany and Ali E. Hillal

Dessouki (Boulder, CO: Westview Press, 1991), 109; Paul E. Lenze Jr. *Civil–Military Relations in the Islamic World* (Lanham, MD: Lexington Books, 2016), 15.

112. David and Marina Ottoway, *Algeria: The Politics of a Socialist Revolution* (Berkeley: University of California Press, 1970), 106.

113. Ottoway, *Algeria: The Politics of a Socialist Revolution* 1970, 196–271; Quandt, *Revolution and Political Leadership*, 236–76.

114. Quandt, *Revolution and Political Leadership*, 17.

115. Martin Evans and John Phillips, *Algeria: Anger of the Dispossessed* (New Haven, CT: Yale University Press, 2007), 143–214; Bradford L. Dilman, "Globalization, Modernization, and the Islamic Salvation Front in Algeria," in *God, Guns, and Globalization: Religious Radicalism and International Political Economy*, eds. Mary Ann Tétreault and Robert A. Denemark (Boulder, CO: Lynne Rienner Publisher, 2004), 153–90; Michael J. Willis, *Politics and Power in the Maghreb: Algeria, Tunisia, and Morocco from Independence to the Arab Spring* (New York: Columbia University Press, 2012), 97–103.

116. Robert A. Mortimer, "Algeria: The Clash between Islam, Democracy, and the Military," *Current History* 92, no. 570 (1993): 39. Chadli Benjedid preferred to use his first name as a title, as did many Algerians. One reason for the preference was the French Civil Status Law of 1882 that allowed French authorities to rename Algerians, often with demeaning names.

117. Lenze, *Civil–Military Relations in the Islamic World*, 30

118. "*L'Anp–n'a–pas de Candidat etn'est Contre Aucun Autre Candidat*" (The PNA does not have a Candidate and is Against any Candidate) *El–Djeigh*, March 2004, http://www.algerie–dz.com/article76.html.

119. Larbi Sadiki, *Rethinking Arab Democratization: Elections without Democracy* (Oxford: Oxford University Press, 2009), 29.

120. Sadiki, *Rethinking Arab Democratization*, 120.

121. Quintan Wiktorowicz, "The new global threat: Transnational Salafis and Jihad," *Middle East Policy* 8, no. 4 (2001): 27–28.

122. Evans and Phillips, *Algeria: Anger of the Dispossessed*, 288–89.

123. Willis, *Politics and Power in the Maghreb*, 109; Evans, *Algeria: Anger of the Dispossessed*.

124. A. Asmae, "Chiefs of Staff of Air Force, Territorial Air Defense Forces Dismissed," *Ennahar el–Djadid*, September 6, 2018.

125. Mohammed Moslem, "Dismissals Terrorize Officials," *Echourouk El–Youmi*, September 5, 2018.

126. Sudarsan Raghavan, "Algeria's Powerful Army Chief Calls for President to be Declared Unfit for Office," *Washington Post*, March 26, 2019, https://www.washingtonpost.com/world/algerias–powerful–army–chief–calls–for–president–to–be–declared–unfit–for–office/2019/03/26/9aca9f04–4fd5–11e9–bdb7–44f948cc0605_story.html.

127. Ellen Lust-Okar, *Structuring Conflict in the Arab World: Incumbents, Opponents, and Institutions* (Cambridge: Cambridge University Press, 2005), 52–54.

128. Uriel Dann, *King Hussein and the Challenge of Arab Radicalism: Jordan, 1955–1967* (New York: Oxford University Press, 1989), 55–57; J. C. Hurewitz,

Middle East Politics: The Military Dimension (New York: Frederick A. Praeger, 1969), 308–9; Florence Gaub, *Guardians of the Arab State: Why Militaries Intervene in Politics, from Iraq to Mauritania.* Oxford: Oxford University Press, 2017), 139–41; Lawrence Tal, *Politics, the Military, and National Security in Jordan, 1955–1967* (New York: Palgrave MacMillan, 2002), 44–49.

129. Philip Robins, *A History of Jordan* (Cambridge: Cambridge University Press, 2004), 99.

130. Patrick Kingsley, Rana F. Sweis, and Eric Schmitt, "Royal Rivalry Bares Social Tensions Behind Jordan's Stable Veneer," *New York Times*, April 10, 2021, https://www.nytimes.com/2021/04/10/world/middleeast/jordan-king-crown-prince.html. General Huneiti was the author's student as a member of the Air War College student body, as a colonel, and has met with the author on the author's visits to Jordan.

131. Oren Barak and Dan Miodownik, "Military Autonomy and Balancing in Political Crises: Lessons from the Middle East," *Armed Forces & Society* 47, no. 1 (2021): 126–47.

132. Kandil, *The Power Triangle*, 155.

133. William Hale, *Turkish Politics and the Military* (London: Routledge, 1992), 93–94.

134. Berk Esen, "Praetorian Army in Action: A Critical Assessment of Civil–Military Relations in Turkey," *Armed Forces & Society* 47, no. 1 (2021): 205.

135. Hurewitz, *Middle East Politics*, 214; Nordlinger, *Soldiers in Politics*, 91.

136. Özbuden argues that the Democratic Party engaged in only a modest revival of some Islamic public practices, the military partly feared that the DP opened religious spaces for purely political purposes, thus one possible reason for the coup was the rise of the DP as an alternative political power center to the military. Ergun Özbudun, "The Role of the Military in Turkish Politics," *Occasional Papers in International Affairs*, no. 14 (November 1966): 16.

137. Daniel Lerner and Richard D. Robinson, "Swords and Ploughshares: The Turkish Army as a Modernizing Force," *World Politics* 13, no. 1 (1960): 40–41.

138. Ergun Özbudun, "The Role of the Military in Turkish Politics," *Occasional Papers in International Affairs*, no. 14 (November 1966): 21; Carter Vaughn Findley, *Turkey, Islam, Nationalism, and Modernity: A History* (New Haven, CT: Yale University Press, 2010), 305–10; Kandil, *The Power Triangle* (2016), 163–68; Yavuz Cilliler, "Popular Determinate on Civil–Military Relations in Turkey," *Arab Studies Quarterly* 38, no. 2 (2016): 500–520.

139. Hurewitz, *Middle East Politics*, 111.

140. Kemal H. Karpat, "The Military and Politics in Turkey, 1960–1964: A Socio–Cultural Analysis of a Revolution," *The American Historical Review* 75, no. 6 (1970): 1663.

141. George S. Harris, "Military Coups and Turkish Democracy, 1960–1980," *Turkish Studies* 12, no. 2 (2011): 203; Banu Eligür, *The Mobilization of Political Islam in Turkey* (Cambridge: Cambridge University Press, 2010), 59.

142. Kandil, *The Power Triangle*, 164.

143. Menderes and the two ministers are buried together in a cemetery in Istanbul's old city. Prime Minister Erdoğan has evoked Menderes's memory, as Turkish journalist Mustafa Akyol stated, "His narrative is Menderes was toppled by nefarious conspiratorial powers against the nation, by these putschists who want to defy most of the people. The Gülenists are just the new element in the same old tradition of Turkish coup plotters." Ishaan Tharoor, "The Execution of a Former Turkish Leader that still Haunts Erdogan," *Washington Post*, July 30, 2016, https://www.washingtonpost.com/world/the–execution–of–a–former–turkish–leader–that–still–haunts–erdogan/2016/07/29/4772c256–54b4–11e6–994c–4e3140414f34_story.html. According to Seal, the Committee of National Unity deadlocked on whether to execute Menderes, but outside military pressure forced the decision. Then the military executioners bungled the execution, and Menderes died an agonizing death by asphyxiation. Jeremy Seal, *A Coup in Turkey* (London: Chatto and Windus, 2021), 254–75.

144. Özbudun, "The Role of the Military in Turkish Politics," 34; Esen, "Praetorian Army in Action," 210.

145. Ilkay Sunar and Sabri Sayari, "Democracy in Turkey: Problems and Prospects," in *Transitions from Authoritarian Rule: Prospects for Democracy*, eds., Guillermo O'Donnell, Philippe C. Schmitter, and Laurence Whitehead (Baltimore: Johns Hopkins University Press, 1986), 175–76.

146. Ümit Cizre Sakallioğlu, "The Anatomy of the Turkish Military's Political Autonomy," *Comparative Politics* 29, no. 2 (1997): 155.

147. Sakallioğlu, "The Anatomy of the Turkish Military's Political Autonomy" (1997), 157; Karabekir Akkoyunlu, *Military Reform and Democratisation: Turkish and Indonesian Experiences at the Turn of the Millennium*, Adelphi Paper 392 (2007), London: International Institute for Strategic Studies, 36.

148. Sakallioğlu, "The Anatomy of the Turkish Military's Political Autonomy," 153.

149. Talukder Maniruzzaman, *Military Withdrawal from Politics: A Comparative Study* (Cambridge, MA: Ballinger, 1987), 76–77; Nilüfer Narlı, "Civil–Military Relations in Turkey," *Turkish Studies* 1, no. 1 (2000): 113; Kandil, *The Power Triangle* (2016), 169–71.

150. Mehran Kamrava, "Military Professionalization and Civil–Military Relations in the Middle East," *Political Science Quarterly* 115, no. 1 (2000): 72.

151. Kandil, *The Power Triangle*, 170–71.

152. Sunar and Sayari, "Democracy in Turkey (1986), 179–82; Hale, *Turkish Politics and the Military*," 216–46; Findley, *Turkey, Islam, Nationalism, and Modernity*, 316–22.

153. Jim Paul, "Turkey: The Generals Take Over," *MERIP Reports* 93 (January: 3–4, 1981).

154. Tanel Demirel, "Lessons of Military Regimes and Democracy: The Turkish Case in a Comparative Perspective," *Armed Forces & Society* 31, no. 2 (2005): 251. Paradoxically the military drafted a constitution that empowered a strong president, which initially went to a general (Sunar and Sayari, "Democracy in Turkey," 184). Now Erdoğan is president, much to the disappointment of the Turkish military.

155. Malcolm Cooper, "The Legacy of Atatürk: Turkish Political Structures and Policy–Making," *International Affairs* 78, no. 1 (2002): 115–28.

156. Frank Tachau and Metin Heper, "The State, Politics, and the Military in Turkey," *Comparative Politics* 16, no. 1 (1983): 25.

157. Eligür, *The Mobilization of Political Islam in Turkey*, 76.

158. The Welfare Party won around 21 percent of the total vote, slightly more than the Motherland Party, which got close to 20 percent, and the True Path Party with around 19 percent. Even that slight margin gave Erbakan the first chance to form a coalition, and the leadership of both losing parties ruled out joining his government.

159. Demirel, "Lessons of Military Regimes and Democracy 2004, 140–41; Begüm Burak, "The Role of the Turkish Military in Politics: To Guard Whom and From What?" *European Journal of Economic and Political Studies* 4, no. 1 (2011): 153–54; Kandil, *The Power Triangle*, 180–91.

160. Tanel Demirel, "Lessons of Military Regimes and Democracy: The Turkish Case in a Comparative Perspective," *Armed Forces & Society* 31, no. 2 (2005): 253.

161. Ersel Aydinli, "Ergenekon, New Pacts, and the Decline of the Turkish 'Inner State.'" *Turkish Studies* 12, no. 2 (2011): 228.

162. Ayşegül Kars Kaynar, "Political Activism in the National Security Council in Turkey after the Reforms," *Armed Forces & Society* 43, no. 3 (2017): 523–44.

163. George S. Harris, "Military Coups and Turkish Democracy, 1960–1980. *Turkish Studies* 12, no. 2 (2011): 212.

164. Paul E. Lenze Jr., *Civil–Military Relations in the Islamic World* (Lanham, MD: Lexington Books, 2016), 142–43.

165. Kavakci claims that a number of unsolved murders, including that of the journalist Hrant Dink, blamed on a militant teenager, was actually the work of Ergenekon, the criminal organization accused of having ties to both retired and active Turkish military members, but does not offer evidence to support the assertion. The name stems from a mythic valley in the Altay Mountains in Asia where Turkic speaking tribes rallied from defeat in the sixth century to found a Turkish empire. Merve Kavakci, "Turkey's Test with its Deep State," *Mediterranean Quarterly* 20, no. 4 (2009): 89.

166. Ali Balci, "A Trajectory of Competing Narratives: The Turkish Media Debate Ergenekon," *Mediterranean Quarterly* 21, no. 1 (2010): 76–100.

167. Gareth Jenkins, "Between Fact and Fantasy: The Ergenekon Investigation," *Silk Road Paper* (Washington, DC: Central Asia–Caucasus Institute & Silk Road Studies Program, Johns Hopkins University, August 2009). Gülen is a shadowy proto–Islamist movement inspired by Fethullah Gülen, a Turkish religious leader with Sufi origins who currently lives in the US. The movement is reported to have infiltrated the police and numerous Islamist political leaders, and reportedly is supporting the arrests of Ergenekon figures in retaliation for the repression of Islamist groups in Turkey prior to 2002. See Jenkins, "Between Fact and Fantasy"; Joshua D. Hendrick, *Gülen: The Ambiguous Politics of Market Islam in Turkey and the World* (New York: New York University Press, 2013); Dan Bilefsky and Sebnem Arsu, "Turks Feel Sway of Reclusive Cleric in the US," *New York Times*, April 24, 2012; M. Hakan Yavuz and Rasim Koç, "The Turkish Coup Attempt: The Gülenist Movement vs. the State," *Middle East Policy* 23, no. 4 (2016): 136–48.

168. Jenkins, "Between Fact and Fantasy"; Joost Lagendijk, "Turkey's Accession to the European Union and the Role of the Justice and Development Party," in *Democracy, Islam, and Secularism in Turkey*, eds. Ahmet T. Kuru and Alfred Stepan (New York: Columbia University Press, 2012), 178–81. The Turkish Hezbollah has no connection to the better–known Lebanese militia.

169. Jenkins, "Between Fact and Fantasy," 66–67; Kaynar, "Political Activism in the National Security Council."

170. Gareth Jenkins, "The Changing Objects of Fear: The Arrest of İlker Başbuğ," *Turkey Analyst* 5, no. 1 (2012).

171. The judges who sentenced General Başbuğ were themselves arrested in July 2016, accused of being Gülen supporters.

172. "Generals trying to Distance themselves from Belyoz Plot," *Today's Zaman*, March 2, 2012; Dexter Filkins, "The 'Deep State:' Behind Istanbul's Conspiracy Trials," *The New Yorker*, March 12, 2012, 45; Sertif Demir and Oktay Bingöl, "From Military Tutelage to Civilian Control: An Analysis of the Evolution of Turkish Civil–Military Relations," *British Journal of Middle Eastern Studies* 47, no. 2 (2020): 184–85.

173. Jenkins, "The Changing Objects of Fear."

174. Gul Tuysuz and Sabrina Tavernise, "Turkey's Top Military Leaders Resign," *New York Times*, July 29, 2011. Membership in international bodies may be another way to forestall military coups. The presumption is that some international organizations may demand through their membership charters certain membership features such as democracy. As Reiter observes, Turkish membership in NATO did not prevent the Turkish military from either taking power directly, as they did in 1960, 1971, and 1980, or the "velvet memorandum" of 1997 where the military threatened a coup if the Islamist–oriented government did not resign. Dan Reiter, "Why NATO Enlargement does not Spread Democracy," *International Security*, 25, no. 4 (2001): 57. NATO members did not criticize the military nor threaten to suspend Turkey, even after the military executed the prime minister and other key civilians after the 1960 coup. NATO excluded Spain until the end of the Franco dictatorship but included autocratic Portugal.

175. Interview 13TK, 2012.

176. Berna Turam, *Between Islam and the State: The Politics of Engagement* (Stanford, CA: Stanford University Press, 2007), 148.

177. Gülen was acting through agents, as he had fled Turkey in 1999, and was in exile in rural Pennsylvania.

178. Berk Esen and Sebnem Gumuscu, "Turkey: How the Coup Failed," *Journal of Democracy*, 28, no. 1 (2017): 60–66.

179. Timothy Arango and Ceylan Yeginsu. "With Army in Disarray, a Pillar of Modern Turkey Lies Broken," *New York Times*, July 28, 2016, https://www.nytimes.com/2016/07/29/world/europe/turkey–military–coup.

180. Aaron Stein, "Turkey's Fighter Pilot Problems," Atlantic Council, September 8, 2017, http://www.atlanticcouncil.org/blogs/menasource/turkey–s–fighter–pilot–problems.

181. Charlotte Gall, "Turkey Jails 151 for Life for Roles in Failed 2016 Coup," *New York Times*, June 20, 2019, https://www.nytimes.com/2019/06/20/world/europe/turkey–coup–2016–trial–life–sentences.html.

182. Ceren Lord, *Religious Politics in Turkey: From the Birth of the Republic to the AKP* (Cambridge: Cambridge University Press), 269.

183. Sertif Demir and Oktay Bingöl, "From Military Tutelage to Civilian Control: An Analysis of the Evolution of Turkish Civil–Military Relations," *British Journal of Middle Eastern Studies* 47, no. 2 (2020): 191.

184. Aram Nerguizian, "The Lebanese Armed Forces: Challenges and Opportunities in Post–Syria Lebanon," Working Draft (Center for International and Strategic Studies, February 10, 2009), 8, http://csis.org/files/media/csis/pubs/090210_laf security.pdf; Oren Barak, *The Lebanese Army: A National Institution in a Divided Society* (Albany: State University of New York Press, 2009), 68–70.

185. Adel Beshara, *Lebanon: The Politics of Frustration—the Failed Coup of 1961* (London: Routledge Curzon, 2005). The US embassy in Beirut regarded the coup as a minor incident, involving a Lebanese captain and a few of his soldiers, trying to rescue a fellow officer who had been detained for alleged improper political activity, with the report noting "three army dead," Action Department 630, Information Amman NIACT 121, Baghdad AD NIACT December 31, 1961, Folder 013151 –005–0812, US Department of State, https://hv–proquest–com.aufric.idm.oclc.org/historyvault/docview.jsp?folderId=013151–005–0812&q=&position=.

186. Barak, *The Lebanese Army*, 102–3.

187. Ronald D. McLaurin, "From Professional to Political: The Redecline of the Lebanese Army. *Armed Forces & Society* 17, no. 4 (1991): 545–68; "Lebanon: The Lebanese Forces Militia," Directorate of Intelligence, Central Intelligence Agency, November 17, 1982.

188. Eugene Rogan, *The Arabs: A History* (New York: Basic Books, 2009), 458.

189. Mohammed Tarbush, *The Role of the Military in Politics: A Case Study of Iraq to 1941* (London: Routledge, 1982), chap. 6; Martin Walker, "The Making of Modern Iraq," *The Wilson Quarterly* 27, no. 2 (2003): 34; Michael Provence, *The Last Ottoman Generation and the Making of the Modern Middle East* (Cambridge: Cambridge University Press, 2017), 243–45.

190. Eliezer Be'eri, *Army Officers in Arab Politics and Society* (London: Pall Mall, 1970), 15–40; Ahmed S. Hashim, "Saddam Husayn and Civil–Military Relations in Iraq: The Quest for Legitimacy and Power," *Middle East Journal* 57, no. 1 (2003): 15; Charles Tripp, *A History of Iraq* (Cambridge: Cambridge University Press, 2000), 88–97.

191. Be'eri, *Army Officers in Arab Politics and Society*, 37–40; Majid Khadduri, "General Nuri's Flirtation with the Axis Powers," *Middle East Journal* 16, no. 3 (1962): 328–36.

192. "Unrest in Iraq Seen by Former Leaders," *New York Times*, April 11, 1941.

193. Tripp, *A History of Iraq*, 146–48; John Galvani, "The Baathi Revolution in Iraq," *MERIP Reports* 12 (September–October 1972), 7; Herb, *All in the Family*, 244–45.

194. They may have feared Jordanian efforts to reconstruct a neo–Hashemite regime based on Hashemi solidarity, though there was very little chance of that happening after July 1958.

195. Joseph Sassoon, *Saddam Hussein's Ba'th Party: Inside an Authoritarian Regime* (Cambridge: Cambridge University Press, 2012), 23–24.

196. Pollock, *Arabs at War*, 161.

197. Amazia Baram, "The Ruling Political Elite in Bathi Iraq, 1968–1986: The Changing Features of a Collective Profile," *International Journal of Middle East Studies* 21, no. 4 (1989): 447–93.

198. Kiyani "Coup–Proofing and Political Violence."

199. Patrick E. Tyler, "US and Iraqis Tell of Coup Attempt against Baghdad," *New York Times*, July 3, 1992.

200. Juan Cole, "Iraq: Is Al–Maliki Preparing to Make a Coup?" *Informed Comment: Thoughts on the Middle East, History, and Religion*, August 11, 2014, http://www.juancole.com/2014/08/maliki–preparing–coup.html; Florence Gaub, *Guardians of the Arab State: Why Militaries Intervene in Politics, from Iraq to Mauritania* (Oxford University Press, 2017), 22.

201. Timothy Arango, "Maliki Seems to Back Away from Using Military Force to Retain Power," *New York Times*, August 12, 2014, https://www.nytimes.com/2014/08/13/world/middleeast/maliki–seems–to–back–away–from–using–military–force–to–retain–power.html.

202. Hurewitz, *Middle East Politics*, 339.

203. Interviews 1M, 1997; 2M, 1997; 3M, 2008; 4M, 2014; 5M, 2018.

204. Interview 3M, 2014; 5M, 2018.

205. The Moroccan military maintain their aircraft, including engine maintenance, at a modern facility at Sidi Slamine Air Base, and Kenitra Air Base.

206. Lust-Okar, *Structuring Conflict in the Arab World*, 56–57; Marvine Howe, *Morocco: The Islamist Awakening and Other Challenges* (New York: Oxford University Press, 2005), 109–13.

207. There are several stories about how both coups transpired; Lust-Okar states that the King asked the coup agents to pray with him at his palace at Skhirat, disrupting the effort, while other stories claim that the King fled out a back door and escaped them. Lust-Okar, *Structuring Conflict in the Arab World*, 57. During the second attempt, claims that the king came on the Royal aircraft's radio to call off the second attack, while others state that the pilot of the king's plane, himself a fellow Moroccan air force officer, told the plotter pilots that the king was killed by their gunfire, and to stop the attack, but the coup leaders ordered the attack anew as the crippled plane, operating on only one of its three engines, was landing, but the plane landed safely. Another story holds that the head of the air force was shot dead as he played golf with the American air attaché (author's personal communication).

208. Omar Bendourou, "Power and Opposition in Morocco," *Journal of Democracy* 7, no. 3 (1996): 108–22; Susan Gilson Miller, *A History of Modern Morocco* (Cambridge: Cambridge University Press, 2013), 174–79; Abdeslam Maghraoui, "Monarchy and Political Reform in Morocco," *Journal of Democracy* 12, no. 1 (2001): 78.

209. Howe, *Morocco: The Islamist Awakening*, 109–12.

210. Michael J. Willis, *Politics and Power in the Maghreb: Algeria, Tunisia, and Morocco from Independence to the Arab Spring* (New York: Columbia University Press, 2013), 91; John Damis, "The Moroccan Political Scene," *Middle East Journal* 26, no. 1 (1972): 31.

211. Willis, *Politics and Power in the Maghreb*, 92.

212. Douglas Little, "Cold War and Covert Action: The United States and Syria, 1945–1958," *The Middle East Journal* 44, no. 1 (1990): 51–75.

213. Hugh Wilford, *America's Great Game: The CIA's Secret Arabists and the Shaping of the Modern Middle East* (New York: Basic Books, 2013), chap. 8.

214. Wilford, *America's Great Game*, chap. 18; Jacob Abadi, "US–Syria Relations in the Shadow of Cold War and Détente," *Middle Eastern Studies*, 57, no. 4 (2021): 535.

215. Michael Poznansky, "The Psychology of Overt and Covert Intervention," *Security Studies* 30, no. 3 (2021): 325–53.

216. Stephen Blackwell, *British Military Intervention and the Struggle for Jordan* (New York: Routledge, 2009), 70–88; Poznansky, "The Psychology of Overt and Covert Intervention."

217. Robert W. Stookey, *Yemen: The Politics of the Yemen Arab Republic* (Boulder, CO: Westview Press, 1978), 231–32.

218. Steven R. David, *Third World Coups d'état and International Security* (Baltimore: Johns Hopkins University Press, 1987), 90–91; Victoria Clarke, *Yemen: Dancing on the Heads of Snakes* (New Haven, CT: Yale University Press, 2010), 110–11.

219. David, *Third World Coups d'État*, 91.

220. Jean Gueyras, "North Yemen Faces Embryonic Civil War," *MERIP Reports* 18 (October 1979), 22.

221. "Yemen Removes Sana'a Artillery Over Coup Fears," *Gulf News*, June 14, 2014; Maria–Louise Clausen, "Justifying Military Intervention: Yemen as a Failed State," *Third World Quarterly* 40, no. 3 (2019): 492.

222. Eleonora Ardemagni, "Patchwork Security: The New Face of Yemen's Hybridity," Carnegie Center for Middle East Studies, October 2018, https://carnegie–mec.org/2018/10/30/patchwork–security–new–face–of–yemen–s–hybridity–pub–77603.

223. Gregory D. Johnsen, "The End of Yemen," The Brookings Institution, March 25, 2021, https://www.brookings.edu/blog/order–from–chaos/2021/03/25/the–end–of–yemen/.

224. Shaher Abdulhak Saleh, "President Abdurabu Hadi was Recently Interviewed by the London–based Arabic Newspaper Al–Hayat," *Yemen Post*, April 9, 2014.

225. Kandil, *The Power Triangle*, 35–36.

226. Hurewitz, *Middle East Politics*, 286.

227. Kenneth M. Pollack, *The Persian Puzzle: The Conflict between Iran and America*. (New York: Random House, 2005), 52–71; Stephen Kinzer, *All the Shah's Men: An American Coup and the Roots of Middle East Terror* (New York: John Wiley & Son); Amin Saikal, *The Rise and Fall of the Shah: Iran from Autocracy to Religious Rule* (Princeton, NJ: Princeton University Press, 1980), 35–45; Malcolm Byrne, "The Road to Intervention," in *Mohammad Mosaddeq and the 1953 Coup in*

Iran, eds. Mark J. Gasiorowski and Malcolm Byrne (Syracuse: Syracuse University Press, 2004), 201; Mark J. Gasiorowski, "The 1953 Coup d'État Against Mosaddeq," in *Mohammad Mosaddeq and the 1953 Coup in Iran*, eds. Mark J. Gasiorowski and Malcolm Byrne (Syracuse: Syracuse University Press, 2004), 227–60.

228. James Risen, "Secrets of History: The CIA in Iran," *New York Times*, April 16, 2000; John Ghazvinian, *American and Iran: A History, 1720 to the Present* (New York: Alfred A. Knopf, 2021), chaps. 12–14; Abbas Amanat, *Iran: A Modern History* (New Haven, CT: Yale University Press, 2017), chaps. 9–11; Ariane M. Tabatabai, *No Conquest, No Defeat: Iran's National Security Strategy* (New York: Oxford University Press, 2020), 113–14.

229. Risen, "Secrets of History."

230. Steven R. Ward. *Immortal: A Military History of Iran and its Armed Forces.* (Washington, DC: Georgetown University Press, 2009), 186–90. Ray Takeyh suggests that the role of outside forces in the 1953 coup has been exaggerated, and that Mosaddeq's actions were the real root of his demise. Ray Takeyh, "What Really Happened in Iran: The CIA, The Ouster of Mosaddeq, and the Restoration of the Shah," *Foreign Affairs* 93, no. 4 (2014): 2–13. While there is no question that Mosaddeq did endanger his hold on the prime ministership, it is also hard to argue that had the CIA and MI–5 not had agents in key positions and had not worked diligently to provide Shah Reza Pahlavi with a backbone (partly through the mediation of his sister), that that Mosaddeq's prime ministership would have survived, though not without deep scars.

231. David, *Third World Coups d'État*, 54–57.

232. Zoltan Barany, "Who Will Shield the Imams? Regime Protection in Iran and the Middle East," *Middle East Policy* 26, no. 1 (2019): 52; Stephanie Cronin, *Armies and State–Building in the Modern Middle East: Politics, Nationalism, and Military Reform* (London: I. B. Tauris, 2014), 193–200.

233. Both monarchs are Sunni, the branch of Islam which devalues kinship to the Prophet Muhammad's family.

234. "One Earth Future," *Annual Risk of Coup Report*, April 2019, https://oef research.org/sites/default/files/documents/publications/Risk_of_Coup_Report_2019.pdf.

235. Quinlivan "Coup Proofing," 138–39.

236. Droz-Vincent, *Military Politics of the Contemporary World*, 78; Risa Brooks, *Political–Military Relations and the Stability of Arab Regimes*, Adelphi Paper 324, London: International Institute for Strategic Studies, 1998; Steffen Hertog, "Rentier Militaries in the Gulf States: The Price of Coup–Proofing," *International Journal of Middle East Studies* 43 (August 2011), 400–402.

237. Talmadge, *The Dictator's Army*, 171.

238. Droz-Vincent, *Military Politics of the Contemporary World*, 97.

239. Florence Gaub, "Libya in Limbo: How to Fill the Security Vacuum," NATO/OTAN Research Report, Rome: NATO Defense College, September 1, 2011.

240. Zoltan Barany, "The Role of the Military," *Journal of Democracy* 22, no. 4 (2011): 30.

241. Roberts and Mueller, "Does Charisma Affect Survival," 492–93.

242. Hertog, "Rentier Militaries in the Gulf States," 400–402.
243. Kandil, *The Power Triangle*, 68.
244. Abel Escribà–Folch, Tobias Böhmelt, and Ulrich Pilster, "Authoritarian Regimes and Civil–Military Relations: Explaining Counterbalancing in Autocracies," *Conflict Management and Peace Science* 37, no. 5 (2020): 563–65.
245. Holger Albrecht, "Military Uprisings in Popular Mass Uprisings," *Political Science Quarterly* 134, no. 2 (2019): 303–28.
246. Holger Albrecht and Ferdinand Eibl, "How to Keep Officers in the Barracks: Causes, Agents, and Types of Military Coups," *International Studies Quarterly* 62, no. 2 (2018): 315–28.
247. Holger Albrecht, "The Myth of Coup Proofing: Risk and Instances of Military Coups d'État in the Middle East and North Africa, 1950–2013," *Armed Forces & Society* 41, no. 4 (2015): 659–87.
248. Michael D. Driessen, "Public Religion, Democracy, and Islam: Examining the Moderation Thesis in Algeria," *Comparative Politics* 44, no. 2 (2012): 171–90.
249. "1980 Military Coup Leaders Sentenced to Life in Prison," *Hurriyet Daily News*, June 18, 2014, https://www.com/1980–military–coup–leaders–sentenced–to–life–in–prison–67954.
250. The "deep state" (*derin devlet*) is partly mythic, and partly real, allegedly comprised of military (active and retired), gangsters, business elite, and others who Filkins portrays as a shadow government that uses assassinations, propaganda, and other covert means to eliminate governments not to its liking. Filkins, "The 'Deep State," For Kavakci, the deep state "espoused a culture of resistance to change. Every time Turkey strived to open itself up to diversity, multiculturalism, and more transparency, or attempted to introduce change that would democratize the country, it faced the resistance of the deep state." Merve Kavakci, "Turkey's Test with its Deep State," *Mediterranean Quarterly* 20, no. 4 (2009): 86. For others, the term "deep state" started with the mysterious 1996 car crash in Susurluk that killed a member of Parliament, a mob boss, his girlfriend, and a senior police official, all of whom had ties to the interior minister. The passengers were reportedly on their way to conduct an assassination. Others focus the term as it was used to describe the activities of Şah İsmail in Izmir at the end of the Ottoman Empire. See Ryan Gingeras, "Last Rites for a 'Pure Bandit': Clandestine Service, Historiography, and the Origins of the Turkish 'Deep State,'" *Past & Present* 206 (February 2010), 151–74. The term may also have been used to describe the connections between criminal mobs and the state over Turkey's heroin marketing, see Ryan Gingeras, "In the Hunt for the 'Sultans of Smack:' Dope, Gangsters, and the Construction of the Turkish Deep State," *Middle East Journal* 65, no. 3 (2011): 426–41.
251. "Turkish Prosecutors Launch New Crackdown against Military, Order Arrests of 4 ex–Generals," *Washington Post*, April 12, 2012.
252. Kandil, *The Power Triangle*, 368.
253. Ayşegül Kars Kaynar, "Post-2016 Military Restructuring in Turkey from the Perspective of Coup–Proofing," *Turkish Studies* (2021) (ahead of print), 1–24. https://doi–org.aufric.idm.oclc.org/10.1080/14683849.2021.1977631.

254. Charlotte Gall, "Erdogan, Flush with Victory, Seizes New Powers in Turkey," *New York Times*, July 19, 2018, https://www.nytimes.com/2018/07/19/world/asia/turkey–erdogan.html?hp&action=click&pgtype=Homepage&clickSource=story–heading&module=first–column–region&region=top–news&WT.nav=top–news.

255. Varun Piplani, and Caitlin Talmadge. "When War Helps Civil–Military Relations: Prolonged Interstate Conflict and the Reduced Risk of Coups," *The Journal of Conflict Resolution* 60, no. 8 (2016): 1368–94.

256. Jeremy Bowen, "1967 War: Six Days that Changed the Middle East," BBC News, June 5, 2017, https://www.bbc.com/news/world–middle–east–39960461.

257. Moshe Gat, "Nasser and the Six Day War, 5 June 1967: A Premeditated Strategy or An Inexorable Drift to War?" *Israel Affairs* 11, no. 4 (2005): 609–10.

258. Adam E. Casey, "The Durability of Client Regimes: Foreign Sponsorship and Military Loyalty, 1946–2020," *World Politics* 73, no. 3 (2020): 412.

259. Casey, "The Durability of Client Regimes," 413.

260. Andrea Kendall–Taylor and Erica Frantz, "How Autocracies Fall," *The Washington Quarterly* 37, no. 1 (2014): 35–47.

261. Kandil, *The Power Triangle*, 234.

262. Kandil, *Soldiers, Spies, and Statesmen*, 21.

263. Bahey Eldin Hassan, "New Political Struggles for Egypt's Military." *Sada: Middle East Analysis*, Carnegie Endowment for International Peace, May 9, 2019. https://carnegieendowment.org/sada/79096.

264. Abubakr Al–Shamahi, "Egypt's Military Dominates 10 Years After Revolution," *Al Jazeera*, January 26, 2021. https://www.aljazeera.com/news/2021/1/26/egypt–revolution–anniversary.

265. Interview 8E, 2012.

266. "Power Games in Yemen," *Al–Jazeera*, April 10, 2012, https://www.aljazeera.com/program/inside–story/2012/4/10/power–games–in–yemen.

267. مصادر عسكرية : هادي يتسلّم خطة هيكلة الجيش قبل منتصف الشهر المقبل ("Hadi Received the Restructuring Plan of the Army"); مصادر عسكرية : هادي يتسلّم خطة هيكلة الجيش قبل منتصف الشهر المقبل "Hadi Received the Restructuring Plan the Army Hadi Received the Restructuring Plan the Army," *Al–Tagheer*, July 19, 2012; Gaub, *Guardians of the Arab State*, 117–11.

268. Fromherz suggests that Qatari military support to the rebel forces who fought against Muamar Qadhafi in 2011 came partly because of long memories of Libyan involvement in the 1983 episode. Allan J. Fromherz, *Qatar: A Modern History* (Washington, DC: Georgetown University Press, 2012), 80.

269. Fromherz, *Qatar*, 80, 143–44.

270. Berk Esen, "Praetorian Army in Action: A Critical Assessment of Civil–Military Relations in Turkey," *Armed Forces & Society* 47, no. 1 (2021): 203.

271. Caitlin Talmadge, "Different Threats, Different Militaries: Explaining Organizational Practices in Authoritarian Armies," *Security Studies* 25, no. 1 (2016): 119–20.

272. Al–Rasheed argues that most of Abdul Aziz's marriages were to tribal members whose tribe had already been pacified or defeated, and, moreover, polygamous marriage patterns produce conflict between contending family members, and, finally,

most of the unity in Saudi Arabia under Abdul Aziz had come from a combination of alliances and tribal defeats. Madawi Al-Rasheed, *A History of Saudi Arabia* (Cambridge: Cambridge University Press, 2002), 75–80. Notes Al-Rasheed, "Marital strategies sealed what had already achieved politically and militarily" (80).

273. Pollack, *Arabs at War*, 429.

274. Steffen Hertog, *Princes, Brokers, and Bureaucrats: Oil and the State in Saudi Arabia* (Ithaca, NY: Cornell University Press, 2010), 82.

275. Cronin, *Armies and State–Building*, 230–31.

276. Hurewitz, *Middle East Politics*, 25–251.

277. Quinlivan, "Coup Proofing," 153–55.

278. Interview 3SA, 2011.

279. Zoltan Barany, *Armies of Arabia: Military Politics and Effectiveness in the Gulf* (New York: Oxford University Press, 2021), 88.

280. "Saudi Arabia Boosts Troop Levels in South Yemen as Tensions Rise," *Reuters*, September 3, 2019, https://www.reuters.com/article/us–yemen–security/saudi–arabia–boosts–troop–levels–in–south–yemen–as–tensions–rise–idUSKCN1VO1FA.

281. Quinlivan, "Coup Proofing," 139–41; Hanna Batatu, "Some Observations on the Social Roots of Syrian Ruling Military Groups and the Causes for its Dominance," *The Middle East Journal* 35, no. 3 (1981): 331–44; Philippe Droz-Vincent, *Military Politics of the Contemporary World* (Cambridge: Cambridge University Press, 2021), 88.

282. Gordon H. Torrey, *Syrian Politics and the Military* (Columbus: Ohio State University Press, 1964), 248.

283. Talukder Maniruzzaman, *Military Withdrawal from Politics: A Comparative Study* (Cambridge, MA: Ballinger, 1987), 46.

284. Patrick Seale, *Asad: The Struggle for the Middle East* (Berkeley: University of California Press, 1988), 421–40.

285. Hicham Bou Nassif, "'Second Class': The Grievances of Sunni Officers in the Syrian Armed Forces," *Journal of Strategic Studies* 38 (July 2015): 626–49.

286. Tyson Roberts and Lisa Mueller, "Does Charisma Affect Survival in Office for Leaders Who Take Power via Military Coup?" *Studies in Comparative International Development* 56, no. 4: (2021): 485–510.

287. Reinoud Leenders and Antonio Giustozzi, "Outsourcing State Violence: The National Defence Force, 'Stateness' and Regime Resilience in the Syrian War," *Mediterranean Politics* 24, no. 2 (2019): 157–80.

288. The name *Shahbiha* comes from the Arab word for "ghost" (*sabh*) but it also may refer to the black Mercedes S-600 sedans that the group favors. The author had an opportunity to ride with a group of Shahbiha in Damascus and noted that passersby gave the car a wide berth, as did the police, watching passively as the car broke traffic rules with impunity, with a Shahbiha member assaulting an unlucky police officer who unwisely tried to stop the car. The Shahbiha commonly used deadly force after the start of the Syrian civil war, often against the Sunni protestors, as most of the Shahbiha come from the ranks of the Syrian 'Alawi.

289. De Bruin, *How to Prevent Coups d'État*.

290. Caitlin Talmadge, *The Dictator's Army: Battlefield Effectiveness in Authoritarian Regimes* (Ithaca, NY: Cornell University Press, 2018), 52–55.

291. Ghashia Kiyani, "Coup–Proofing and Political Violence: The Case of Iraq," *Middle Eastern Studies* 57, no. 6 (2021): 4.

292. Guillermo O'Donnell and Philippe C. Schmitter. "Part IV: Tentative Conclusions about Uncertain Democracies," in *Transitions from Authoritarian Rule: Prospects for Democracy*, eds. Guillermo and Schmitter (Baltimore: Johns Hopkins University Press, 1986), 40.

293. Alfred Stepan, *The Military in Politics: Changing Patterns in Brazil* (Princeton, NJ: Princeton University Press, 1971), 62–66.

294. Stepan, *The Military in Politics*, 63; J. Samuel Fitch, *The Armed Forces and Democracy in Latin America* (Baltimore: Johns Hopkins University Press, 1998), 17.

295. Amati Etzioni, *A Comparative Analysis of complex Organizations: On Power, Involvement, and their Correlates* (Glencoe, IL: The Free Press, 1961); Dan Slater, *Ordering Power: Contentious Politics and Authoritarian Leviathans in Southeast Asia* (Cambridge: Cambridge University Press, 2010).

296. David C. Williams, "Cracks in the Firmament of Burma's Military Government: From Unity through Coercion to Buying Support," *Third World Quarterly* 32, no. 7 (2011): 1201.

297. Zayar Lay Swe, "Why the NLD Fails to Consolidate Democratic Transition in Myanmar," *Asian Journal of Comparative Politics* 6, no. 4 (2021): 442.

298. T. J. Pemple, *A Region of Regimes: Prosperity and Plunder in the Asia–Pacific* (Ithaca, NY: Cornell University Press, 2021), 51.

299. Siddarth Chandra and Douglas Anton Kammen, "Generating Reforms and Reforming Generations Military Politics in Indonesia's Democratic Transition and Consolidation," *World Politics* 55, October (2002): 96–136, esp. 116.

300. David E. Sanger, "When Armies Decide," *New York Times*, February 19, 2011. https://www.nytimes.com/2011/02/20/weekinreview/20military.html; Terence Lee, "The Armed Forces and Transitions from Authoritarian Rule: Explaining the Role of the Military in 1986 Philippines and 1998 Indonesia," *Comparative Political Studies* 42, no. 5 (2009): 654–60.

301. Lee, "The Armed Forces and Transitions," 649–54.

302. Eva–Lotta E. Hedman, "The Philippines: Not So Military, Not So Civil," in *Coercion and Governance: The Declining Political Role of the Military in Asia*, ed. Muthiah Alagappa (Stanford, CA: Stanford University Press, 2001), 165–87. Joseph Estrada served as Philippine president from 1998 to 2001, when a Filipino court convicted him of graft. He was a former movie actor who espoused populism but reportedly spent most of his time gorging himself with food, drink, and extramarital affairs.

303. David Pion-Berlin, "Military Autonomy and Emerging Democracies in South America," *Comparative Politics* 25, no. 1 (1992): 86.

304. Adam Przeworski, *Democracy and the Market: Political and Economic Reforms in Eastern Europe and Latin America* (Cambridge: Cambridge University Press, 1991) 78; Ursula E. Daxecker, "Opposition Movements, Liberalization, and Civil War: Evidence from Algeria and Chile," *Civil Wars* 11, no. 3 (2009): 234–54.

305. Catherine E. Walsh, "The Ecuadorian Political Irruption: Uprisings, Coups, Rebellions, and Democracy," *Nepantla: Views from South* 2, no. 1 (2001): 177.

306. "Indonesia's Tentative Democracy," *New York Times*, June 12, 1999.

307. Celestine Bohlen, "How the Ceausescu's Fell: Harnessing Popular Rage," *New York Times*, January 6, 1990.

308. Noureddine Jebnoun, "Tunisia: Patterns and Implications of Civilian Control," in *Civil–Military Relations: Control and Effectiveness Across Regimes*, eds. Thomas C. Bruneau and Aurel Croissant (Boulder, CO: Lynne Rienner Publishers, 2019), 120.

309. Hurewitz, *Middle East Politics*, 409; David S. Sorenson, "Civil–Military Relations in North Africa," *Middle East Policy* 14, no. 4 (2007): 106–7; Derek Lutterbeck, "Arab Uprisings, Armed Forces, and Civil–Military Relations," *Armed Forces & Society* (April 2012): 7, http://afs.sagepub.com/content/early/2012/04/11/0095327X12442768.full.pdf+html; Zoltan Barany, "Military Influence in Foreign Policy-Making: Changing Dynamics in North African Regimes," *The Journal of North African Studies* 24 (July 2019): 586.

310. Droz-Vincent, *Military Politics of the Contemporary World*, 58.

311. Louis B. Ware, "The Role of the Tunisian Military in the Post–Bourguiba Era," *Middle East Journal* 39, no. 1 (1985): 27–47.

312. Noureddine Jebnoun, "In the Shadow of Power: Civil–Military Relations and the Tunisian Popular Uprising," *Journal of North African Studies* 19, no. 3 (2014): 300.

313. Christopher Alexander, *Tunisia: Stability and Reform in the Modern Maghreb* (London: Routledge, 2010), 51.

314. Jebnoun, "In the Shadow of Power," 302.

315. David D. Kirkpatrick, "Power Again Changes Hands in Tunisia as Chaos Remains," *New York Times*, January 15, 2011; Michele Penner Angrist, "Understanding the Success of Mass Civic Protest in Tunisia," *Middle East Journal* 67, no. 4 (2013): 550–51.

316. David D. Kirkpatrick, "Chief of Tunisian Army Pledges His Support for the 'Revolution'" *New York Times*, January 24, 2011; Barany, "Military Influence in Foreign Policy-Making," 52.

317. Risa Brooks, "Abandoned at the Palace: Why the Tunisian Military Defected from the Ben Ali Regime in January 2011," *Journal of Strategic Studies* 36, no. 2 (2013): 216.

318. Interview 2TN, 2011; Angrist, "Understanding the Success," 551.

319. Brooks, "Abandoned at the Palace," 216.

320. Brooks, "Abandoned at the Palace," 219; Jebnoun, "Tunisia: Patterns and Implications of Civilian Control," 123.

321. Alejandro Panchon, "Loyalty and Defection: Misunderstanding Civil–Military Relations in Tunisia during the 'Arab Spring,'" *Journal of Strategic Studies* 37, no 4 (2014): 508–31.

322. Safwan M. Masri, *Tunisia: An Arab Anomaly* (New York: Columbia University Press, 2017), 48–49.

323. Aurel Croissant and Tobias Selge, "Should I Stay or Should I Go? Comparing Military (Non–) Cooperation during Authoritarian Regime Crises in the Arab World and Asia," in *Armies and Insurgencies in the Arab Spring*, eds. Holger Albrecht, Aurel Croissant, and Fred H. Lawson (Philadelphia: University of Pennsylvania Press, 2016), 106.

324. Barany, "Military Influence in Foreign Policy–Making," 52.

325. Ali Sarihan, "A New Theory of Military Behavior in the Arab Uprisings: 'Pro–State' and 'Pro–Regime,'" *Journal of International Studies* 14, no. 1 (2021): 18.

326. Jebnoun, "Tunisia: Patterns and Implications of Civilian Control."

327. Ahmed A. Attala, "A New Role for the Tunisian Armed Forces?" *Tawazun Index of Arab Civil–Military Relations.*, September 6, 2021, http://tawazun.net/english/blog1.php?id=625–.

328. Neil Ketchley, *Egypt in a Time of Revolution: Contentious Politics and the Arab Spring* (Cambridge: Cambridge University Press, 2017).

329. Ahmed S. Hashim, "The Egyptian Military, Part Two: From Mubarak Onward," *Middle East Policy* 18, no. 4 (2011): 106–28; Sharon Erickson Nepstad, "Mutiny and Nonviolence in the Arab Spring: Military Defections and Loyalty in Egypt, Bahrain, and Syria," *Journal of Peace Research* 50, no. 3 (2013): 342.

330. Hillel Frisch, "The Egyptian Army and Egypt's 'Spring,'" *Journal of Strategic Studies*, 36, no. 2 (2013): 182–83.

331. Zeinab Abul–Magd, *Militarizing the Nation: The Army, Business, and Revolution in Egypt* (New York: Columbia University Press, 2017), 188–98.

332. "Egypt Military Mulls its Options," *Al–Jazeera*, February 5, 2011.

333. Zoltan Barany, "The Role of the Military," *Journal of Democracy* 22, no. 4 (2011): 28; Khaled Elgindy, "Egypt's Troubled Transition: Elections without Democracy," *The Washington Quarterly* 35, no. 2 (2012): 94.

334. Jeff Martini and Julie Taylor, "Commanding Democracy in Egypt," *Foreign Affairs* 90, no. 5 (2011): 129.

335. Steven A. Cook, "The Promise of Pacts," *Journal of Democracy* 17, no. 1 (2006): 72.

336. Michael Slackman, "Choice of Suleiman Likely to Please Military, Not Crowds," *New York Times*, January 29, 2011.

337. Hazem Kandil, *Soldiers, Spies, and Statesmen: Egypt's Road to Revolution* (London: Verso, 2012), 231.

338. Tarek Osman, *Egypt on the Brink: From Nasser to Mubarak* (New Haven, CT: Yale University Press, 2010), 228.

339. Elizabeth Bumiller, "Egypt Stability Hinges on a Divided Military," *New York Times*, February 5, 2011.

340. Mona El–Naggar and Michael Slackman, "Hero of Egypt's Revolution, Military Now Faces Critics," *New York Times*, April 8, 2011.

341. Khaled Elgindy, "Egypt's Troubled Transition: Elections without Democracy," *The Washington Quarterly* 35, no. 2 (2012): 92–93.

342. Elgindy, "Egypt's Troubled Transition," 96–97.

343. David D. Kirkpatrick, "Egyptian Military Aims to Cement Muscular Role in Government," *New York Times*, July 16, 2011; Barany, "The Role of the Military," 28.

344. Neil MacFarquhar, "Ahead of Vote, Egypt's Parties and Skepticism are Growing," *New York Times*, November 9, 2011.

345. David D. Kirkpatrick and Stephen Lee Myers, "US Hones Warnings to Egypt as Military Stalls Transition," *New York Times*, November 17, 2011.

346. David D. Kirkpatrick, "Military Flexes Muscles as Islamists Gain in Egypt," *New York Times*, December 7, 2011. When a reporter asked General Mullah if the Egyptian military would submit its budget to Parliament for oversight, he said that the idea was ridiculous, saying that he knew of no military that made its budget public. Actually, most European and North American military budgets must be approved by the legislation and are thus public.

347. David D. Kirkpatrick, "Blow to Transition as Court Dissolves Egypt's Parliament," *New York Times*, June 14, 2012.

348. "Egypt's Military Pledges Support to Mursi," *Arab News*, July 2, 2012, https://www.arabnews.com/egypts–military–pledges–support–mursi.

349. David D. Kirkpatrick, "Judge Helped Egypt's Military to Cement Power," *New York Times*, July 3, 2012.

350. "Egypt's Judges Reject Mursi's Plea Reinstating Dissolved Parliament," Cairo MENA, July 10, 2012.

351. Ziad Akl, "Commentary: The Bipolarity of Politics," *Al–Ahram*, July 5–11, 2012.

352. Michael Slackman, "Islamist Group is Rising Force in a New Egypt," *New York Times*, March 24, 2011.

353. Amirah Ibrahim, "A Salute to Competence," *Al Ahram*, December 7, 2011.

354. Ibrahim A. Karawan, "Politics and the Egyptian Army," *Survival* 53, no. 2 (2011): 45.

355. "Egypt's Morsi Calls for Unity After Poll Win," *Al–Jazeera* June 25, 2012.

356. Albarraa Abdullah, "Sisi Surrounds Himself in Latest Cabinet Shuffle," *Al–Monitor*, June 22, 2018, https://www.al–monitor.com/pulse/originals/2018/06/egypt–cabinet–reshuffle–new–ministers–military–background.html.

357. Bruce K. Rutherford, "Egypt's New Authoritarianism under Sisi," *Middle East Journal* 72, no. 2 (2018): 197–98.

358. Interview 12E, 2018.

359. Rutherford, "Egypt's New Authoritarianism under Sisi," 204–5.

360. Risa Brooks, "Civil–Military Relations in Sisi's Egypt," in Yezid Sayigh, *Politics of Military Authoritarianism in North Africa*, Malcomb Kerr Carnegie Middle East Center, March 17, 2021, https://carnegie–mec.org/2021/03/17/civil–military–relations–in–sisi–s–egypt–pub–84074.

361. Ed Blanche, "Algeria: The Battle Within," *Middle East*, May 1, 2006, 25–26.

362. Robert A. Mortimer, "Algeria: The Clash between Islam, Democracy, and the Military," *Current History* 92, no. 570 (1993): 40.

363. Steven A. Cook, *Ruling but Not Governing: The Military and Political Development in Egypt, Algeria, and Turkey* (Baltimore, MD: The Johns Hopkins University Press, 2007), 61.

364. Hugh Roberts, *Demilitarizing Algeria*, Carnegie Papers no. 86 (Washington, DC: Carnegie Endowment for International Peace, May 8, 2007), 14, https://

carnegieendowment.org/2007/05/08/demilitarizing–algeria–pub–19153. It is probably doubtful that Boutiflika's successor can build on his power base, as Roberts notes, "There is little reason to expect Bouteflika to be able to bequeath to his successor the authority he has built up, and cause to fear that the succession would be the occasion for a fresh intensification of factional conflict within the political–military elite, which only the army commanders would be able to arbitrate. Roberts, *Demilitarizing Algeria* (2007), 17.

365. Francis Ghilès and Akram Kharief, "Updating Algeria's Military Doctrine," Middle East Institute, June 6, 2017, http://www.mei.edu/content/map/updating–algerias–military–doctrine.

366. Abdallah Brahimi, "Algeria's Military Makeover," Carnegie Endowment for International Peace," April 19, 2016, http://carnegieendowment.org/sada/63373.

367. Ramy Allahoun, "Algeria" President Bouteflika and the Army's Political End Game," *Al–Jazeera*, April 25, 2018, https://www.aljazeera.com/indepth/features/algeria–president–bouteflika–army–political–game–180423114018685.html.

368. Sharan Grewal, M. Tahir Kilavuz, and Robert Kinibec, "Algeria's Uprising: A Survey of Protesters and the Military," Washington, DC: The Brookings Institution, July 2019: https://www.brookings.edu/wp–content/uploads/2019/07/FP_20190711_algeria.pdf.

369. Bouteflika was so incapacitated that many believed he was actually dead. His handlers stopped rolling him out in a wheelchair, and instead rolled out a wheelchair with a cutout of the president. Some Algerians began to refer to him as "Cutout."

370. "What's Next for Algeria," *Al Jazeera*, April 4, 2019, https://www.aljazeera.com/news/2019/4/4/whats–next–for–algeria–2.

371. Ghada Hamrouche, "Algeria's Army Moves from Arbiter to Central Player in Politics," *Al–Monitor*, April 30, 2019, https://www.al–monitor.com/originals/2019/04/algeria–protests–bouteflika–army–arbiter–central–player.html.

372. Adam Nossiter, "In an Epic Standoff, Unarmed Algerians get the Army to Blink," *New York Times*, July 29, 2019, https://www.nytimes.com/2019/07/29/world/africa/algeria–revolution–standoff.html.

373. Furkan Halit Yolcu, "The Democratizer Army Paradox: The Role of the Algerian Army in Impeded Democratization," *Journal of Asian and African Studies* 54, no. 7 (2019): 1033–47.

374. Dahlia Ghanem, "Civil–Military Relations in the MENA Region: Past and Future," *Med Dialogue Series*, no. 24, Konrad Adenhaur Siftung. March 2020, https://www.kas.de/documents/282499/282548/CMR.pdf/06d6667a–fbbc–cf41–817d–41cd35727366?version=1.0&t=1590148987472.

375. Eva Bellin, "Reconsidering the Robustness of Authoritarianism in the Middle East: Lessons from the Arab Spring," *Comparative Politics* 44, no. 2 (2012): 129.

376. Bellin, "Reconsidering the Robustness of Authoritarianism," 131–34.

377. Eva Bellin, "The Robustness of Authoritarianism in the Middle East: Exceptionalism in Comparative Perspective," *Comparative Politics* 36, no. 2 (2004): 144.

378. Bellin, "The Robustness of Authoritarianism," 149. An example occurred in the case where Hafiz al-Asad appointed a friend as head of the Syrian Air Force even though he was not a pilot.

379. Joseph Sassoon, *Saddam Hussein's Ba'th Party: Inside an Authoritarian Regime*. (Cambridge: Cambridge University Press), 139.

380. Philippe Droz-Vincent, "'State of Barbary' (Take Two): From the Arab Spring to the Return of Violence to Syria," *Middle East Journal* 68, no. 1 (2014): 39. Maher al–Asad, Bashir al-Asad's brother, commanded both The Fourth Armored Division and the Republican Guard.

381. Droz-Vincent "The Syrian Military and the 2011 Uprising," 176.

382. Yezid Sayigh, "Syrian Politics Trumps Russian Reform," Carnegie Middle East Center, March 26, 2020, https://carnegie-mec.org/2020/03/26/syrian–politics–trump–russian–military–reforms–pub–81149.

383. Barany, "The Role of the Military," 31.

384. Tahiyya Lulu, "The Real Story of Bahrain's Divided Society," *The Guardian*, March 3, 2011, https://www.theguardian.com/commentisfree/2011/mar/03/bahrain–sunnis–shia–divided–society.

385. Sharon Erickson Nepstad, "Mutiny and Nonviolence in the Arab Spring: Military Defections and Loyalty in Egypt, Bahrain, and Syria," *Journal of Peace Research* 50, no. 3 (2021): 337–49; Abdulhadi Khalaf, "Bahrain's Military is Closely Tied to the Monarch," *New York Times*, August 28, 2012, https://www.nytimes.com/roomfordebate/2012/08/28/the–staying–power–of–arab–monarchies/bahrains–military–is–closely–tied–to–the–monarch.

386. "Dissident Troops 'Protect anti–Saleh Protest," *Al–Jazeera* September 16, 2011, https://www.aljazeera.com/news/2011/9/16/dissident–troops–protect–anti–saleh–protest.

387. "Yemen's Saleh makes Eid plea for peace; dissident general says Eid bombing foiled," *Al–Arabiya* November 6, 2011. https://english.alarabiya.net/articles/2011/11/06/175701.

388. Ali Saeed, "General Mohamed Mohsen Talks to Yemen Times," *Yemen Times*, May 10, 2012.

389. April Longley Alley, "Assessing (In)security after the Arab Spring: The Case of Yemen," *PS: Political Science & Politics* 46, no. 4 (2013): 725.

390. "Yemeni Forces Retake Strategic Stronghold of Jaar," *New York Times*, June 12, 2012.

391. "The Army is Gaining the Upper Hand in Yemen's Civil War," *The Economist*, January 4, 2018, https://www.economist.com/middle–east–and–africa/2018/01/04/the–army–is–gaining–the–upper–hand–in–yemens–civil–war.

392. Hassanein Ali, "War Without End? Why are Peace Efforts Faltering in Yemen?" *Asian Affairs* (2021), https://www.tandfonline.com/doi/full/10.1080/03068374.2021.1993665.

393. Clement M. Henry and Robert Springborg, *Globalization and the Politics of Development in the Middle East* (Cambridge: Cambridge University Press, 2001), 223.

CHAPTER FOUR

1. Samuel E. Finer, *The Man on Horseback: The Role of the Military in Politics* (New York: Frederick A. Praeger, 1962): 16.
2. Morris Janowitz, *Military Institutions and Coercion in Developing Nations*, expanded edition (Chicago: University of Chicago Press, 1977), 153.
3. Bruce M. Russett, *What Price Vigilance? The Burdens of National Defense* (New Haven, CT: Yale University Press, 1970); Robert W. DeGrasse Jr., *Military Expansion, Economic Decline* (Armonk, NY: M. E. Sharpe, 1983).
4. Vernon W. Ruttan, *Is War Necessary for Economic Growth?* (Oxford: Oxford University Press, 2006).
5. Harold D. Lasswell, "The Garrison State," *The American Journal of Sociology* 46, no. 1 (1941): 455–68.
6. Lasswell, "The Garrison State," 465.
7. Richard H. Kohn, "How Democracies Control the Military," *Journal of Democracy* 8, no. 4 (1997): 140–53; J. Mark Ruhl, "Curbing Central America's Militaries," *Journal of Democracy* 15, no. 3 (2004): 137–51; Claudia Heiss and Particio Navia, "You Win Some, You Lose Some: Constitutional Reforms in Chile's Transition to Democracy," *Latin American Politics & Society* 49, no. 3 (2007): 179; Zoltan Barany, *The Soldier and the Changing State* (Princeton, NJ: Princeton University Press, 2012), 153; Elias Huzar, *The Purse and the Sword: Control of the Army by Congress through Military Appropriations, 1933–1950* (Ithaca, NY: Cornell University Press, 1950), 1–25.
8. Richard C. Eichenberg and Richard Stoll, "Representing Defense: Democratic Control of the Defense Budget in the United States and Western Europe," *The Journal of Conflict Resolution* 47, no. 4 (2003): 399–422; Mike M. Mochiguchi, "Japan's Search for Strategy," *International Security* 8, no. 3 (1984–84): 152–79.
9. Quoted in Samuel P. Huntington, *The Soldier and the State* (Cambridge, MA: Harvard University Press, 1957), 440.
10. These and similar reports on military spending must be understood as estimates with often unknown error terms because, as Cordesman notes relative to Saudi Arabian defense spending, "It is impossible to assess how Saudi military and security expenditures are spent in any detail using unclassified data." This is because such budget amounts do not often specify whether the funds are going to the regular armed forces, the state security forces that are often under a different ministry, or both. These amounts do not necessarily include spending on paramilitary forces, whose budgets sometimes exceed the funds spent on conventional military forces. Many other Middle Eastern countries devote considerable portions of their overall security spending to paramilitary forces, which often field equipment comparable to regular militaries, and Iran's Islamic Revolutionary Guard Corps maintains an air force and navy in addition to its considerable ground forces. Anthony H. Cordesman, *Saudi Arabia: National Security in a Troubled Region* (Santa Barbara, CA: Praeger Security International, 2009), 134.

11. "Transparency and Accountability in Military Spending and Procurement," Stockholm International Peace Research Institute, 2014, http://www.sipri.org/research/armaments/milex/transparency.

12. Jeanne Kinney Giraldo, "Defense Budgets, Democratic Civilian Control, and Effective Governance," in *Who Guards the Guardians and How: Democratic Civil-Military Relations*, eds. Thomas C. Bruneau and Scott D. Tollefson (Austin: University of Texas Press, 2006), 178–207.

13. James H. Lebovic and Ashfaq Ishaq, "Military Burden, Security Needs, and Economic Growth in the Middle East," *The Journal of Conflict Resolution* 31, no. 1 (1987): 107.

14. J. C. Hurewitz, *Middle East Politics: The Military Dimension* (New York: Frederick A. Praeger, 1969), 105–6.

15. Paul Rivlin, *The Israeli Economy from the Foundation of the State through the 21st Century* (Cambridge: Cambridge University Press, 2011), 120.

16. John Waterbury, *The Egypt of Nasser and Sadat: The Political Economy of Two Regimes* (Princeton, NJ: Princeton University Press, 1983), 112.

17. Yonha Jeremy Bob, "2018 Global Defense Spending to Hit Post-Cold War High of $1.67 Trillion," *Jerusalem Post*, December 19, 2017, https://www.jpost.com/Middle-East/2018-Global-defense-spending-to-hit-post-Cold-War-high-of-167-trillion-518440.

18. Tova C. Norlén, "Middle East Pre-Existing Conditions: Regional Security after COVID-19 MIDDLE EAST POLICY," *Middle East Policy* 29 (2022): 118, https://onlinelibrary-wiley-com.aufric.idm.oclc.org/doi/pdf/10.1111/mepo.

19. Even in the US, Congress rarely cuts the military budget, and Congress routinely approves major weapons programs. In Morocco, memories of the 1970s coup efforts have given professional soldiers the privilege of not having their budget shares questioned in Parliament, which is why the 2006 questioning of that budget item (around 15 percent of the state budget) was highly unusual. James N. Sater, "Parliamentary Elections and Authoritarian Rule in Morocco," *Middle East Journal* 63, no. 3 (2009): 381–400.

20. Ertugrul Kurkeu, "The Crisis of the Turkish State," *Middle East Report* 199, April–June 2–7, 1997.

21. Elliot Hen-Tov, "The Political Economy of Turkish Military Modernization," *Middle East Review of International Affairs* 8, no. 4 (2004): 50.

22. Fırat Demir, "A Political Economy Analysis of the Turkish Military's Split Personality: The Patriarchal Master or Crony Capitalist?" in *Understanding the Process of Economic Change in Turkey: An Institutional Approach*, eds. T. Cetin and F. Yilmaz (Nova Science Publishers, 2010), 3, http://faculty-staff.ou.edu/D/Firat.Demir_Turkish_Military_Patriarchal_Master_or_Crony_Capitalist.pdf.

23. Ertugrul Tekeoglu, *Defense Expenditure and Economic Growth: Empirical Study on Case of Turkey* (Monterey, CA: Naval Postgraduate School), 46–49.

24. "Turkish Military Spending Jumps 86% Over Last Decade," *Daily Sabah*, April 29, 2020.

25. "Turkey Spent $20.4 Billion on its Military in 2019: Report," *Nordic Monitor*, April 29, 2020, https://www.nordicmonitor.com/2020/04/turkey-spent-a-20-4-billion-on-its-military-in-2019/.

26. Zülfikar Doğan, "The Unspoken Cost of Turkey's Ever-Escalating Military Spending," *Ahval*, September 2, 2020, https://ahvalnews.com/greece-turkey/unspoken-cost-turkeys-ever-escalating-military-spending.

27. "Turkey's 2021 Budget to Include a Substantial Increase in Defense, Security Spending," *Turkish Minute*, October 22, 2020, https://www.turkishminute.com/2020/10/22/turkeys-2021-budget-to-include-substantial-increase-in-defense-security-spending/.

28. Şeyma Sarıca, "Turkey's Defence and Security Budget for 2022 is 181 Billion Liras," *Defence Turk*, October 19, 2021, https://en.defenceturk.net/turkeys-defence-and-security-budget-for-2022-is-181-billion-liras/.

29. Yehuda Ben Meir, *Civil-Military Relations in Israel* (New York: Columbia University Press, 1995), 47.

30. Zalman F. Shiffer, "The Debate over the Defense Budget in Israel," in *Militarism and Israeli Society*, eds. Gabriel Sheffer and Oren Barak (Bloomington: Indiana University Press, 2010), 221. There may be much more budget inspection within the IDF. In September 2010, the government announced that it would participate in buying the American-designed F-35 fighter aircraft. The deal, agreed to by a civilian panel headed by Prime Minister Netanyahu and Defense Minister Ehud Barak and expected to cost around $2.75 billion US, drew unnamed opposition from some general staff members who argued that it would deprive Israeli land and sea forces of necessary funds for their own programs. Barak Ravid, "Israel Decides to buy F-35 Fighter Jets, Despite Row over Cost of Deal," *Ha'aretz*, September 17, 2010.

31. Ben Meir, *Civil-Military Relations in Israel*, 92.

32. Asher Arian, *The Second Republic: Politics in Israel* (Chatham, NJ: Chatham House, 1998), 239.

33. For example, see Elad Benari, "Knesset Committee Approves 2014 Defense Budget," *Arutz Shiva*, February 5, 2014. This is not to suggest that there are no fireworks during Knesset debates over defense; in 2014 Labor Party MP Stav Shaffir was physically ejected from the committee room when she accused the committee chair of lying about the addition of funds from the transportation budget to the military budget. After she returned, she questioned the chair's Zionist credentials and he in turn suggested that she "had gone totally mad." Zvi Zrahiya, "Knesset Panel Approves NIS 3.8b in Military Spending in Stormy Session," *Ha'aretz*, August 13, 2014.

34. "Israel Grapples with Slashing Military Budget," *Al Jazeera*, June 1, 2014.

35. "Locker Hurt," *The Economist*, August 15–21, 2015.

36. Judah Ari Gross, "Netanyahu calls for a NIS 3.3 Billion Increase for the Defense Budget," *The Times of Israel*, July 20, 2020, https://www.timesofisrael.com/netanyahu-calls-for-nis-3-3-billion-increase-to-the-defense-budget.

37. Shmuel Even and Sasson Haddad, "The Defense Budget for 2021," INSS, March 3, 2021, https://www.inss.org.il/publication/2021-defense-budget/.

38. "Israel Approves Supplemental Defense Budget to Confront Iran's Threat," *Asharq al-Awsat*, December 25, 2021, https://english.aawsat.com/home/article/3378106/israel-approves-supplemental-defense-budget-confront-iran's-threat.

39. Lilach Shoval, Government Agrees on Increased Defense Budget for 2022," *Israel Hayom*, July 28, 2021, https://www.israelhayom.com/2021/07/28/government-agrees-on-increased-defense-budget-for-2022/.

40. Gordon H. Torrey, *Syrian Politics and the Military* (Columbus: Ohio State University Press, 1964), 188–89.

41. Volker Perthes, "The Syrian Economy in the 1980s," *Middle East Journal* 46, no. 1 (1992): 44.

42. Volker Perthes, "*Si Vis Stabilitatem, Para Bellum*: State Building, National Security, and War Preparations in Syria," in *War, Institutions, and Social Change in the Middle East*, ed. Steven Heydemann (Berkeley, University of California Press, 2000), 158–59.

43. "Syria Update, 27 November–3 December," Center for Operational Analysis and Research, 2019, https://coar-global.org/2019/12/04/syria-update-27-november-03-december-2019/.

44. Ben Hubbard, "Syria's Economy Collapses Even as the Civil War Winds to a Close," *New York Times*, June 15, 2020, https://www.nytimes.com/2020/06/15/world/middleeast/syria-economy-assad-makhlouf.html.

45. "Syria Approves $5b Budget for 2022," *Jordan Times*, December 15, 2021, https://www.jordantimes.com/news/business/syria-approves-5b-budget-2022.

46. Bassem Abo Alabass, "Egypt Military Budget Allocations to Reach LE31 bn in 2013/14," *Al Ahram*, May 29, 2013.

47. Sherine Tadros, "Egypt's Military Economic Empire," *Al Jazeera*, February 15, 2012.

48. Abigale Hauslohner, "Egypt's Military Expands its Control over the Country's Economy," *Washington Post*, March 16, 2014, https://www.washingtonpost.com/world/middle_east/egyptian-military-expands-its-economic-control/.

49. Zeinab Abul-Magd, İsmet Akça, and Shana Marshall, "Two Paths to Dominance: Military Businesses in Turkey and Egypt," Working Paper, Carnegie Middle East Center, June 2020, 2.

50. Amin Saikal, *The Rise and Fall of the Shah: Iran from Autocracy to Religious Rule* (Princeton, NJ: Princeton University Press, 1980), 157.

51. Theodore H. Moran, "Iran's Defense Expenditures and the Social Crisis," *International Security* 3, no. 3 (1978–1979): 179.

52. Ben Piven, "Iran and Israel: Comparing Military Machines," *Al Jazeera*, April 24, 2012.

53. Henry Rome, "Iran's Defense Spending," *The Iran Primer*. United States Institute for Peace, June 17, 2020, https://iranprimer.usip.org/blog/2020/jun/17/iran%E2%80%99s-defense-spending.

54. Saeed Ghasseminejad and Tzvi Kahn, "New Iranian Draft Budget Slashes Military Spending," Foundation for the Defense of Democracies, January 8, 2019, https://www.fdd.org/analysis/2019/01/08/new-iranian-draft-budget-slashes-military-spending/.

55. Rome, "Iran's Defense Spending."

56. "Profile: Iran's Revolutionary Guard," BBC, January 3, 2020, https://www.bbc.com/news/world-middle-east-47852262.

57. "Government Proposes to Boost IRGC Budget More than Twofold," *Iran International*, December 14, 2021, https://www.iranintl.com/en/20211214314346.

58. Emile Benoit, *Defense and Economic Growth in Developing Countries* (Lanham, MD: Lexington Books, 1973), 2.

59. Lisa M. Grobar and Richard C. Porter, "Benoit Revisited: Defense Spending and Economic Growth in LDSs," *The Journal of Conflict Resolution* 33, no. 2 (1989): 318–45.

60. E. Desli and A. Gkoulgkoutsika, "Military Spending and Economic Growth: A Panel Data Investigation," *Economic Change and Restructuring* 54, no. 3 (2021): 781–806.

61. Sefa Anaworyi Churchill and Siew Ling Yew, "The Effect of Military Expenditure on Growth: An Empirical Synthesis," *Empirical Economics* 55 (2018): 1357–87.

62. Karl DeRouen Jr. and Uk Heo, "Modernization and the Military in Latin America," *British Journal of Political Science* 31, no. 3 (2001): 475–96.

63. Benjamin E. Goldsmith, "Bearing the Defense Burden, 1886–1989: Why Spend More?" *Journal of Conflict Resolution* 47, no. 5 (2003): 562.

64. J. Paul Dunne and Nadir A. L. Mohammed, "Military Spending in Sub-Saharan Africa: Some Evidence for 1967–85," *Journal of Peace Research* 32, no. 3 (1995): 341.

65. T. Paul Dunne and Nan Tian, "Military Expenditure and Economic Growth, 1960–2014," *The Economics of Peace and Security Journal* 11, no. 2 (2016): 50–56.

66. Ådne Cappelen, Nils Petter Gleditsch, and Olav Bjerkholt, "Military Spending and Economic Growth in OECD Countries," *Journal of Peace Research* 21, no. 4 (1984): 372.

67. Wassily Leontief and Faye Duchin, *Military Spending: Facts and Figures, Worldwide Implications, and Future Outlook* (New York: Oxford University Press, 1983), 66.

68. Malcolm Knight, Norman Loayza, and Delano Villanueva, "Military Spending Cuts and Economic Growth," Policy Research Working Paper 1577 (19660), The World Bank, Policy Research Department, Macroeconomics and Growth Division, and International Monetary Fund, February.

69. Jasen Castillo, Julia Lowell, Ashley Tellis, Jorge Muñoz, and Benjamin Zycher, *Military Expenditures and Economic Growth*. Santa Monica, CA: The Rand Corporation, 2001.

70. Chiwei Su, Yingying Xu, Hsu Ling Chang, Oana-Ramona Lobont, and Zhixin Liu, "Dynamic Causalities between Defense Expenditure and Economic Growth in China: Evidence from Rolling Granger Causality Test," *Defence and Peace Economics* 31, no. 5 (2020): 565–82, DOI: 10.1080/10242694.2018.1505583.

71. David Brady, "The Welfare State and Relative Poverty in Rich Western Democracies, 1967–1997," *Social Forces* 83, no. 4 (2005): 1329–64. "State-mediated" poverty is poverty after taxes and transfer spending.

72. Muhammed Luqman and Nikolaos Antonakakis, "Guns Better than Butter in Pakistan? The Dilemma of Military Expenditure, Human Development, and Economic Growth," *Technological Forecasting and Social Change* 173, no. 12 (2021): 121–43.

73. David S. Sorenson, "Democracy, Financial Crises, and National Defense Spending: The Cases of United States, Taiwan, and Israel," Paper presented at the 2010 Meeting of the American Political Science Association, Washington, DC, September 2020, 32. Military service itself may contribute to national economic growth because some militaries take raw poorly educated recruits and provide for them training that may enable them to become viable civilian employees following their stint in uniform. The US military has faced pressure to provide such opportunities, as have other militaries. Yet the counter argument is that military service sometimes deprives society of its best and brightest, who might otherwise be in college or technical school or writing plays or otherwise contributing to national economic and cultural development. But instead, military services send them off to guard a border fence or wash dishes or shine boots in the name of national military service.

74. Dunne and Mohammad, "Military Spending in Sub-Saharan Africa," 335.

75. Zuk and Thompson note, however, that while military regimes spend more military money than do either civilian or "mixed" (civilian and military) regimes, they also decreased military spending at a proportionately higher rate than do other regimes. Gary Zuk and William R. Thompson, "The Post-Coup Military Spending Question: A Pooled Cross-Sectional Time Series Analysis," *The American Political Science Review* 76, no. 1 (1982): 60–74.

76. James H. Lebovic, "Spending Priorities and Democratic Rule in Latin America," *Journal of Conflict Resolution* 45 (August 2001): 450. Hunter finds that some of this reduction was purposeful punishment of the Brazilian military by the civilian regimes that replaced military dictators after 1985. Wendy Hunter, *Eroding Military Influence in Brazil: Politicians Against Soldiers* (Chapel Hill: University of North Carolina Press, 1997), 95–96.

77. Johannes Blum, "Democracy's Third Wave and National Defense Spending," *Ifo Working Papers*, No. 339 (October 2020): 1–48.

78. Justin Clardie, "The Impact of Military Spending on the Likelihood of Democratic Transition Failure: Testing Two Competing Theories," *Armed Forces & Society* 37, no. 1 (2011): 163–79.

79. Benjamin O. Fordham and Thomas C. Walker, "Kantian Liberalism, Regime Type, and Military Resource Allocation: Do Democracies Spend Less?" *International Studies Quarterly* 49, no. 1 (2005): 141–57.

80. "S. Korea's Defense Rises by 7.4% to over 50 Trillion Wan," *The Korea Herald*, December 11, 2019, http://www.koreaherald.com/view.php?ud=20191211000099. Yet there may be limits; In Albania, the first post-communist government drastically cut military expenditures without military consultation, and one consequence was that when rioting followed the collapse of a government-condoned financial pyramid scheme, the military refused to comply with government demands to quell the disorder. Instead, the army collapsed as soldiers joined in looting and rioting, and the government subsequently collapsed. Constantine P. Danopoulos and Konstantinos

Skandalis. "The Military and Its Role in Albania's Democratization," *Armed Forces & Society* 37, no. 3 (2001): 412.

81. Richard C. Eichenberg and Richard Stoll, "Representing Defense: Democratic Control of the Defense Budget in the United States and Western Europe," *The Journal of Conflict Resolution* 47, no. 4 (2003): 399–422.

82. Daniel Chudnovsky and Andrés López, *The Elusive Quest for Growth in Argentina*. (New York: Palgrave, 2007), 48. Military support was obviously not the only or even the primary reason for the popularity of ISI, which received theoretical support during the often-chaotic wave of developmental economics. See Joseph LeRoy Love, "The Rise and Decline of Economic Structuralism in Latin America: New Dimensions," *Latin American Research Review* 40, no. 3 (2005): 100–125.

83. Stepan, *The Military in Politics*, 84.

84. Lebovic and Ishaq, "Military Burden."

85. Florence Gaub, "Arab Military Spending: Behind the Figures," European Institute for Security Studies, May 2014, https://www.iss.europa.eu/sites/default/files/EUISSFiles/Alert_27_Arab_military_spending.pdf.

86. Suleiman Abu-Bader and Aamer S. Abu-Qarn "Government Expenditures, Military Spending, and Economic Growth: Causality Evidence from Egypt, Israel, and Syria," *Journal of Policy Modeling* 25, nos. 6–7 (2003): 567–83; Suleiman Abu-Bader and Aamer S. Abu-Qarn, "Trade Liberalization or Oil Shocks: Which Better Explains Structural Breaks in International Trade Ratios?" Review of International Economics 18, no. 2 (2010): 250–64.

87. Chia-I Pan, Tsangyao Chang, and Yemane Wolde-Rufael, "Military Spending and Economic Growth in the Middle East Countries: Bootstrap Panel Causality Test," *Defence and Peace Economics* 26, no. 4 (2015): 443–56.

88. Charles Shaaba Saba, and Nicholas Ngepah, "Nexus Between Defence Spending, Economic Growth and Development: Evidence from a Disaggregated Panel Data Analysis. *Economic Change and Restructuring* 55, no. 1 (2022): 109–15.

89. Jülide Yildirim and Nadir Öcal, "Military Expenditures, Economic Growth and Spatial Spillovers," *Defence and Peace Economics* 27, no. 1 (2016): 87–104.

90. Adam Coutts, Adel Daoud, Ali Fakih, Walid Marrouch, and Bernhard Reinsberg, "Guns and Butter? Military Expenditure and Health Spending on the Eve of the Arab Spring," *Defence and Peace Economics* 30, no. 2 (2018): 227–37, https://doi.org/10.1080/10242694.2018.1497372.

91. Hamad E. Ali, "Military Expenditures and Human Development: Guns and Butter Arguments Revisited: A Case Study from Egypt," *Peace Economics, Peace Science and Public Policy* 17, no. 1 (2011): 1–19.

92. Paul C. Noble, "The Arab System," in *The Foreign Policies of Arab States: The Challenge of Change*, eds. Bahgat Korany and Ali E. Hillal Dessouki, *The Foreign Policies of Arab States: The Challenge of Change* (Boulder, CO: Westview Press, 1991), 62.

93. Ourani Dimitraki and Sandar Win, "Military Expenditure Economic Growth Nexus in Jordan: An Application of ARDL Bound Test Analysis in the Presence of Breaks," *Defence and Peace Economics* 32, no. 7 (2021): 864–81, DOI: 10.1080/10242694.2020.1730113.

94. Donald L. Losman, "The Rentier State and National Oil Companies: An Economic and Political Perspective," *Middle East Journal* 64, no. 3 (2010): 427–45.

95. Nader Kabbani and Negia Ben Mimoune, "Economic Diversification in the Gulf: Time to Redouble Efforts," The Brookings Institution, January 31, 2021, https://www.brookings.edu/research/economic-diversification-in-the-gulf-time-to-redouble-efforts/.

96. Eva Bellin, "The Robustness of Authoritarianism in the Middle East: Exceptionalism in Comparative Perspective," *Comparative Politics* 36, no. 2 (2004): 148.

97. Camilla Sandbakken, "The Limits to Democracy Posed by Oil Rentier States: The Cases of Algeria, Nigeria and Libya," *Democratization* 13, no. 1 (2006): 141.

98. Michael J. Willis, *Politics and Power in the Maghreb: Algeria, Tunisia, and Morocco from Independence to the Arab Spring* (New York: Columbia University Press, 2012), 109.

99. William B. Quandt, *Between Ballots and Bullets: Algeria's Transition from Authoritarianism.* (Washington, DC: The Brookings Institution Press, 1998), 135.

100. Philippe Droz-Vincent, *Military Politics of the Contemporary World* (Cambridge: Cambridge University Press, 2021), 139.

101. "Draft Report: 'Defence Procurement, Corruption and Illicit Financial Flows," The TANA High-Level Forum on Security in Africa (London: Justice Africa, February 2014), https://sites.tufts.edu/wpf/files/2017/05/Defence-Procurement-IFFs.pdf.

102. Fenella McGerty and Tom Waldwyn, "Middle East Defence Spending Showing Signs of Stabilising," Military Balance Blog, International Institute for Strategic Studies, November 18, 2021, https://www.iiss.org/blogs/military-balance/2021/11/middle-east-defence-spending-showing-signs-of-stabilising.

103. McGerty and Waldwyn, "Middle East Defence Spending."

104. Fred H. Lawson, "Armed Forces, Internal Security Services, and Popular Contention," in *Armed Forces and Insurgencies in the Arab Spring*, eds. Holger Albrecht, Aurel Croissant, and Fred H. Lawson (Philadelphia: University of Pennsylvania Press, 2016), 61.

105. Lawson, "Armed Forces," 63.

106. I am grateful to James Lebovic for this point.

107. Zalman F. Shiffer, "The Debate over the Defense Budget in Israel," in *Militarism and Israeli Society*, eds. Gabriel Sheffer and Oren Barak (Bloomington: Indiana University Press, 2010), 221.

108. Paul Rivlin, *The Israeli Economy from the Foundation of the State through the 21st Century* (Cambridge: Cambridge University Press, 2011), 122.

109. Interview IIS, 1986.

110. Jordin S. Cohen, Randolph Stevenson, Alex Mintz, and Michael D. Ward, "Defense Expenditures and Economic Growth in Israel: The Indirect Link," *Journal of Peace Research*, 33, no. 3 (1996): 351.

111. Alex Mintz and Michael D. Ward, "The Political Economy of Military Spending in Israel," *The American Political Science Review* 83, no. 2 (1989): 521–33. A middle-ground argument is that while high levels of defense spending are harmful to the Israeli economy, lower levels are apparently neutral. "In contrast to the 1970s

and 1980s, the defense budget at its current level does not jeopardize economic stability," said Shmuel Even, "Israel's Defense Expenditure," *Strategic Assessment* 12, no. 4 (2010): 38.

112. Ofira Seliktar, "The Cost of Vigilance in Israel: Linking the Economic and Social Costs of Defense," *Journal of Peace Research* 17, no. 4 (1980): 339–55. During the late 1970s, Israeli chief of staff General Rafael "Raful" Eitan adopted a program known as "Raful's Kids" to recruit some of Israel's disenfranchised youth, high school dropouts, adolescents with criminal records, for example, into the Israeli military. Unlike American efforts, which were abandoned after they failed to accomplish their goals, the Raful's Kids program survives with considerable public support, because it not only takes these recruits off Israeli streets but allows them the benefit of IDF training. Guy Seidman, "From Nationalization to Privatization: The Case of the IDF," *Armed Forces & Society* 36, no. 4 (2010): 727.

113. Baruch Kimmerling, "Making Conflict Routine: Cumulative Effects of the Arab-Jewish Conflict Upon Israeli Society," in *Israeli Society and its Defense Establishment: The Social and Political Impact of a Protracted Violent Conflict*, ed. Moshe Lissak (London: Frank Cass, 1984), 13–45.

114. Jeremy M. Sharp, "US Foreign Aid to Israel," Congressional Research Service, August 2019, 7.

115. Joel Beinin, "Israel: The Political Economy of a Garrison State and its Future," in *The Next Arab Decade: Alternative Futures*, ed. Hisham Sharabi (Boulder, CO: Westview Press, 1988), 242–43.

116. Yoram Peri, *Generals in the Cabinet Room* (Washington, DC: United States Institute for Peace Press, 2006), 149–50.

117. Hagai Amit, "Reversing Policy, Netanyahu Seeks Long-term Rise in Defense Spending," *Ha'aretz*, August 16, 2018, https://www.haaretz.com/israel-news/reversing-policy-netanyahu-seeks-long-term-rise-in-defense-spending-1.6386942.

118. Lilach Shoval and Ariel Kahana, ""Netanyahu Backs Bid to Increase Defense Spending by Almost $1 Billion," *Israel Hayom*, July 23, 2020, https://www.israelhayom.com/2020/07/23/netanyahu-backs-bid-to-increase-defense-spending-by-nearly-1b/.

119. Ertugrul Tekeoglu, *Defense Expenditure and Economic Growth: Empirical Study on Case of Turkey* (Monterey, CA: Naval Postgraduate School, 2008). Yet in 2011, Turkish Aircraft Industries alone sold over $1 billion in defense goods along abroad, and sale of its military drones to Qatar should earn around $120 million a year. "Turkey Sells Mini-Drones to Qatar," *TR Defence*. May 3, 2012, http://www.tr defence.com/?p=128133.

120. Onur Ozsoy, "Budgetary Trade-Offs Between Defense, Education, and Health Expenditures: The Case of Turkey," *Defence and Peace Economics* 13, no. 2 (2002): 129–36. Other analysis has produced mixed results; Yildirim and Sezgin find a negative relationship between defense and health expenditures in Turkey (1924–1996) but a positive relationship between defense and education spending. Selami Sezgin, and Jülide Yildirim, "The Demand for Turkish Defence Expenditure," *Defence and Peace Economics* 12, no. 2 (2002): 121–28. The long span of years of this study also diminishes its accuracy, as there were some real political and economic shifts during these years.

121. Adem Y. Elveren, Military Spending and Profit Rate: A Circuit of Capital Model with a Military Sector, *Defence and Peace Economics* 33, no. 1 (2022): 59–76. DOI: 10.1080/10242694.2020.1832394. The author urged caution in interpreting the results, for several methodological reasons. The long timespan of the study also limits its applicability.

122. Usman Khalid and Olivier Habimana, "Military Spending and Economic Growth in Turkey: A Wavelet Approach," *Defence and Peace Economics* 32, no. 3 (2019). DOI: 10.1080/10242694.2019.1664865.

123. Yildirim and Sezgin, "The Demand for Turkish Defence Expenditure."

124. Duyğu Yolcu Karadam, Jülide Yildrim, and Nadir Öcal, "Military Expenditure and Economic Growth in Middle Eastern Countries and Turkey: Non-Linear Panel Data Approach," *Defence and Peace Economics* 28, no. 6 (2017): 719–30.

125. Ünal Töngür and Adem Yavuz Elveren, "The Impact of Military Spending and Income Inequality on Economic Growth in Turkey," *Defence and Peace Economics* 27, no. 3 (2016): 433–52.

126. Interview 4T, 2010.

127. Michael Robert Hickok," Peace Onyx: A Story of Turkish F-16 Co-Production," in *International Military Aerospace Collaboration*, eds. Pia Christina Wood and David S. Sorenson (Aldershot, VT: Ashgate, 2000), 153–82.

128. Interview 14TK, 2012. Turkey planned to operate one hundred F-35 aircraft, but claimed that it could pay for only two, and thus the US tentatively agreed to pay for the other ninety-eight.

129. Interview 17TK, March 2018.

130. The US Department of Defense initially allowed the contracts with Turkish F-35 producers to continue into 2022, though bipartisan Senate opposition to the plan quickly developed. Joe Gould, "Stop Buying Turkey's F-35 Parts, Lawmakers tell DoD," *Defense News*, July 7, 2020, https://www.defensenews.com/congress/2020/07/07/stop-buying-turkeys-f-35-parts-already-lawmakers-tell-dod/.

131. Interview 3TK, March 2010.

132. Interview 3TK, March 2010.

133. Ceyda Caglayan and Nevsat Devanoğlu, "Turkish Budget Deficit Leapt 70% in 2019 on Government Spending," *Reuters*, January 15, 2020, https://www.reuters.com/article/us-turkey-economy-homesales/turkish-budget-deficit-leapt-70-in-2019-on-government-spending-idUSKBN1ZE1PL.

134. "Turkish Military Spending Jumps 86% Over Last Decade," *Daily Sabah*, April 29, 2020.

135. Interview 10TK, 2007.

136. Gülay Günlük-Şenesen, "Measuring the Extent of Defence Expenditures: The Turkish Case with Turkish Data," *Defence and Peace Economics* 12, no. 1 (2001): 37.

137. David K. Whynes, *The Economics of Third World Military Expenditure* (Austin: University of Texas Press, 1979), 152. However, Whynes does not demonstrate that these unfortunate 250,000 Egyptians would not have died if Egypt's defense burden had been lower, a common problem in trying to estimate the effect of spending priorities in general.

138. David Makovsky, "Reviewing Egypt's Gains from Its Peace Treaty with Israel," *Policywatch 1772*, The Washington Institute for Near East Policy, March 7, 2011.

139. Mohamed Maher and Yanji Zhao, "Do Political Instability and Military Expenditure Undermine Economic Growth in Egypt? Evidence from the ARDL Approach," *Defence and Peace Economics* (2021): 1–14, https://www-tandfonline-com.aufric.idm.oclc.org/doi/full/10.1080/10242694.2021.1943625.

140. "Pharaonic Frailties," *The Economist*, July 19, 2014.

141. Maher and Zhao, "Do Political Instability."

142. Robert Springborg and F. C. "Pink" Williams, "The Egyptian Military: A Sleeping Giant Awakens," Carnegie Middle East Center, February 2019.

143. "Necessary Spending," *The Jordan Times*, January 29, 2012.

144. Philippe Droz-Vincent, "From Political to Economic Actors: The Changing Role of Middle Eastern Armies," in *Debating Arab Authoritarianism: Dynamics and Durability in Nondemocratic Regimes*, ed. Oliver Schlumberger (Stanford, CA: Stanford University Press, 2006), 199.

145. Rex Brynen, "Economic Crisis and Post-Rentier Democratization in the Arab World: The Case of Jordan," *Canadian Journal of Political Science / Revue Canadienne de Science Politique* 25, no. 1 (1992): 80–81.

146. Anne Marie Baylouny, "Militarizing Welfare: Neo-Liberalism and Jordanian Policy," *The Middle East Journal* 62, no. 2 (2008): 301.

147. Jeremy M. Sharp, "Jordan: US Background and Relations," Congressional Research Service, June 18, 2020.

148. "Lower House Passes 2021 State Budget Draft Law," *Jordan Times*, February 21, 2021, https://www.jordantimes.com/news/local/lower-house-passes-2021-state-budget-draft-law.

149. Anthony H. Cordesman, *Saudi Arabia: National Security in a Troubled Region*. (Santa Barbara, CA: Praeger Security International, 2009), 136. Arms sales have returned to record levels, with Saudi Arabia signing long-term contracts in 2011 for close to $75 billion US over a decade. Between 2015 and 2020, actual deliveries averaged around $10.7 per year.

150. Graeme Baker, "Saudis Lead Middle East Military Spending," *Al Jazeera*, April 15, 2014.

151. Charles Forrester, "Saudi Arabia Cuts Defence Spending," *Janes*, December 18, 2020, https://www.janes.com/defence-news/news-detail/saudi-arabia-cuts-defence-spending#:~:text=Saudi%20Arab%2.

152. David S. Sorenson, "Why the Saudi Arabian Defense Binge?" *Contemporary Security Policy* 35, no. 1 (2014): 116–37.

153. Choe Sang-Hun, "Rivalries within North Korean Elite Led to Purge, South's Spy Chief Says," *New York Times*, December 23, 2013.

154. Babar Sattar, "Pakistan: Return to Praetorianism," in *Coercion and Governance: The Declining Political Role of the Military in Asia*, ed. Muthiah Alagappa (Sanford, CA: Stanford University Press, 2001), 398–99; Aqil Shah, *The Army and Democracy: Military Politics in Pakistan* (Cambridge, MA: Harvard University Press, 2014), 154–55.

155. Hoo Tiang Boon and Glenn K. H. Ong, "Military Dominance in Pakistan, and Pakistan-China Relations. *Australian Journal of International Affairs* 75, no. 1 (2021): 86.

156. Mary P. Callahan, "Burma: Soldiers as State-Builders," in *Coercion and Governance: The Declining Political Role of the Military in Asia*, ed. Muthiah Alagappa (Stanford, CA: Stanford University Press, 2001), 426.

157. K. Ohan Ha, Khine Lin Kyaw, and Jin Wu, "Myanmar's Generals Run a Nearly Sanction-Proof Business Empire," *Bloomberg*, May 10, 2021, https://www.bloomberg.com/graphics/2021-myanmar-military-business/.

158. "The Road up from Mandalay, *The Economist*, April 21, 2012, https://www.economist.com/asia/2012/04/21/the-road-up-from-mandalay.

159. "In Bigger Barracks," *The Economist*, June 4, 2011, 52.

160. Moshe Lissak, "Modernization and Role-Expansion of the Military in Developing Countries: A Comparative Analysis," *Comparative Studies in Society and History* 9, no. 3 (1967): 241.

161. Elizabeth D. Gibbons, *Sanctions in Haiti: Human Rights and Democracy under Assault* (New York: Praeger Publishers, 1999), 64.

162. "Sergeant López Obrador," *The Economist*, May 1, 2021; "The Puritan from Tepetitán," *The Economist*, May 29, 2021.

163. Mary Beth Sheridan, "As Mexico's Security Deteriorates, the Power of the Military Grows," *Washington Post*, December 17, 2020, https://www.washingtonpost.com/graphics/2020/world/mexico-losing-control/mexico-military-security-drug-war/.

164. Thomas J. Bickford, "The Chinese Military and its Business Operations," *Asian Survey* 34, no. 5 (1994): 460–74; David Shambaugh, *Modernizing China's Military: Progress, Problems, and Prospects* (Berkeley: University of California Press, 2002), 196–204.

165. "Khaki Capitalism," *The Economist*, December 3, 2011; Alexis Rieffel and Jaleswari Pramodhawardani, *Out of Business and on Budget: The Challenge of Military Financing in Indonesia* (Washington, DC: The Brookings Institution, 2007).

166. Benjamin S. Lambeth, "Russia's Wounded Military," *Foreign Affairs* 74, no. 2 (1995): 91, 93.

167. David Pion-Berlin, "Civil-Military Circumvention: How Argentine State Institutions Compensate for a Weakened Chain of Command," in *Civil-Military Relations in Latin America: New Analytical Perspectives*, ed. David Pion-Berlin (Chapel Hill: University of North Carolina Press, 2001), 135–60.

168. Maiah Jaskowski, *Military and Politics in the Andes* (Baltimore, MD: Johns Hopkins University Press, 2013).

169. Alfred Vagts, *A History of Militarism*, revised edition (New York: The Free Press, 1959), 360–70.

170. Julian Cooper, "The Defense Industry," in *Soldiers and the Soviet State: Civil-Military Relations from Brezhnev to Gorbachev*, eds. Timothy J. Colton and Thane Gustafson (Princeton, NJ: Princeton University Press, 1990), 189–90.

171. Collin Grimes, "Defense Sector Politics: The Political Economy of Transferring the Military's Industries," *Studies in Comparative International Development* 56 (December 2021): 463–84.

172. Thomas J. Bickford, "The People's Liberation Army and its Changing Economic Roles: Implications for Civil-Military Relations," in *Chinese Civil-Military Relations: The Transformation of the People's Liberation Army*, ed. Nan Li (London: Routledge, 2006), 161–77; Andrew Scobell, "China's Evolving Civil-Military Relations: Creeping *Quojiajhua*," in *Chinese Civil-Military Relations: The Transformation of the People's Liberation Army*, ed. Nan Li (London: Routledge, 2006), 25–40.

173. Tai Ming Cheung, *Fortifying China: The Struggle to Build a Modern Defense Economy* (Ithaca, NY: Cornell University Press, 2008), 1–21.

174. Tony Badran, "Lebanon's Militia Wars," chap. 3 in *Lebanon: Liberation, Conflict, and Crisis*, ed. Barry Rubin (New York: Palgrave Macmillan, 2009), 48–49.

175. Omar Bendourou, "Power and Opposition in Morocco," *Journal of Democracy* 7, no. 3 (1996): 108–22.

176. Abdeslam Maghraoui, "Monarchy and Political Reform in Morocco," *Journal of Democracy* 12, no. 1 (2001): 78; John Damis, "The Moroccan Political Scene," *Middle East Journal* 26, no. 1 (1972): 31.

177. Eva Bellin, "The Robustness of Authoritarianism in the Middle East: Exceptionalism in Comparative Perspective," *Comparative Politics* 36, no. 2 (2004): 144–45.

178. Anthony Shadid, "Syria's Ailing Economy Poses a Threat to Assad," *New York Times*, June 23, 2011, https://www.nytimes.com/2011/06/24/world/middleeast/24damascus.html.

179. Charles Lister, *Dynamic Stalemate: Surveying Syria's Military Landscape* (Doha: Brookings Doha Center, 2014), 10–12.

180. Michael Eisenstadt, "Has the Assad Regime 'Won' Syria's Civil War?" The Washington Institute for Near East Policy, May 15, 2018, https://www.washingtoninstitute.org/policy-analysis/view/has-the-assad-regime-won-syrias-civil-war.

181. "The Syrian Economy at War," *COAR*, September 30, 2020, https://coar-global.org/2020/09/30/the-economy-of-war-in-syria-armed-group-mobilization-as-livelihood-and-protection-strategy/.

182. Stephen Lee Myers, "Maliki Given 30 Days to Form Government in Iraq," *New York Times*, November 25, 2021.

183. Andrew Parasiliti and Sinan Antoon, "Friends in Need, Foes to Heed: The Iraqi Military in Politics," *Middle East Policy* 7, no. 4 (2000): 131.

184. Kirk Semple, "Iraq Army Woos Deserters Back to War on ISIS," *New York Times*, September 28, 2014, https://www.nytimes.com/2014/09/29/world/middleeast/iraq-army-woos-deserters-back-to-war-on-isis.html. To be sure, rent-seeking was only one of the reasons why the Iraqi military failed in the ISIS assault; other reasons included: the politization of the army by Nouri al-Malaki, who used its units for clear sectarian purposes; turning army units on Kurdish and Sunna groups; and adding "political commissars" to military groups to assure loyalty to Malaki, rather than to the state. These factors are discussed further in chapter 4.

185. Anthony H. Cordesman, "America's Failed Strategy in the Middle East: Losing Iraq and the Gulf," Center for Strategic and International Studies, January 2, 2020, https://www.csis.org/analysis/americas-failed-strategy-middle-east-losing-iraq-and-gulf.

186. Clement M. Henry and Robert Springborg, "Army Guys," *The American Interest* (May/June 2011): 397–99, http://www.the-american-interest.com/article.cfm?piece=954.

187. Yezid Sayigh, "Egypt's Military Now Controls Much of its Economy. Is that Wise?" Carnegie Middle East Center, November 25, 2019, https://carnegie-mec.org/2019/11/25/egypt-s-military-now-controls-much-of-its-economy.-is-this-wise-pub-80281.

188. Hicham Nassif, "'Second Class': The Grievances of Sunni Officers in the Syrian Armed Forces," *Journal of Strategic Studies* 38 (July 2015): 514.

189. Ahmed S. Hashim, "The Egyptian Military, Part One," *Middle East Policy* 18, no. 3 (2011): 71; Andrew McGregor, *A Military History of Modern Egypt: From the Ottoman Conquest to the Ramadan War* (Westport, CT: Praeger International Security International, 2006), 261.

190. J. C. Hurewitz, *Middle East Politics: The Military Dimension* (New York: Frederick A. Praeger, 1969), 135.

191. "Khaki Capitalism"; Zeinab Abul-Magd, "Egypt's Adaptable Officers: Business, Nationalism, and Discontent," in *Businessmen in Arms: How the Military and Other Armed Groups Profit in the MENA Region*, eds. Elke Grawert and Zeinab Abdul-Magd (Lanham, MD: Rowman & Littlefield, 2016), 27.

192. Hazem Kandil, "Back on Horse? The Military Between Two Revolutions," in *Arab Spring in Egypt: Revolution and Beyond*, eds. Bahgat Korany and Rabab El-Hahdi (Cairo: The American University in Cairo Press, 2012), 181.

193. Yezid Sayigh, *Owners of the Republic: An Anatomy of Egypt's Military Economy.* (Washington, DC: Carnegie Middle East Center, 2019), 20.

194. Samir Shehata, "Egyptians Embrace Revolt Leaders, Religious Parties and Military, As Well," Pew Research Center Global Attitudes Project, April 25, 2011, http://pewglobal.org/files/2011/04/Pew-Global-Attitudes-Egypt-Report-FINAL-April-25-2011.pdf. See also "Egyptian Generals Running Child Care Means Transition Profit Motive," 2011) "Egyptian Generals Running Child Care Means Transition Profit Motive," *San Francisco Chronicle*, February 15, 2011.

195. P. J. Vatikiotis, *The Egyptian Army in Politics* (Bloomington: Indiana University Press, 1961), 126–27.

196. In one of the more curious cases of potential rent-seeking behavior, the fabled Cairo Opera, a centerpiece of Cairo culture since at least 1869, found itself with an Egyptian general as its director. The consequences were predictable, outlined by Ati Metwaly,

> The early 2000s brought General Samir Farag as the head of the Cairo Opera House. During his directorship, the whole Opera House underwent a reshuffling of artistic priorities. A military person is not expected to understand musical dynamics or the requirements of an artistic institution; but this remains inexcusable. The slow decay of artistic values, which infiltrated the opera every year, started affecting all the companies working under its umbrella. During Farag's management, internal quarrels started escalating that eventually led to the removal of El Saeedy. Subsequent directors of the Opera may not have been strong enough to bring it back to its grand years, as when the grand voice of Umm

Khulsum, one of the world's greatest singers, projected from the Cairo Opera House to most of the Arab world via radio.

Ati Metwali, "Seasonal Concerns," *Al-Ahram*, September 8–14, 2011.

197. Interview 5E, 2006.

198. Officials cautioned the author not to drive near Egyptian military bases in the late afternoon due to fears that soldiers may commandeer the vehicle and use it to take them to their afternoon jobs.

199. Bruce K. Rutherford, "Egypt's New Authoritarianism under Sisi," *Middle East Journal* 72, no. 2 (2018): 190; Yezid Sayigh, *Owners of the Republic*, 2019.

200. Personal communication, February 2012.

201. Florence Gaub, *Guardians of the Arab State: Why Militaries Intervene in Politics, from Iraq to Mauritania* (Oxford: Oxford University Press, 2017), 170.

202. Hillel Frisch, "The Egyptian Army and Egypt's 'Spring,'" *Journal of Strategic Studies* 36, no. 2 (2013): 184.

203. Robert Springborg, *Mubarak's Egypt: Fragmentation of the Political Order* (Boulder, CO: Westview Press, 1989), 115.

204. Robert Springborg, "Learning from Failure: Egypt," in *The Routledge Handbook of Civil-Military Relations*, eds. Thomas C. Bruneau and Florina Christiana Matei (London: Routledge, 2013), 95.

205. Shana Marshall, "Why the US Won't Cut Military Aid to Egypt. *Foreign Policy: The Middle East Channel*, February 29, 2012, https://foreignpolicy.com/2012/02/29/why-the-u-s-wont-cut-military-aid-to-egypt.

206. Philippe Droz-Vincent, "From Political to Economic Actors: The Changing Role of Middle Eastern Armies," in *Debating Arab Authoritarianism: Dynamics and Durability in Nondemocratic Regimes*, ed. Oliver Schlumberger (Stanford, CA: Stanford University Press, 2006), 200.

207. Interview 9E, 2012.

208. Interview 6E, 2007.

209. Droz-Vincent, "From Political to Economic Actors," 201; Nassif, "'Second Class.'"

210. Droz-Vincent, *Military Politics of the Contemporary World*, 260.

211. Sarah Childers, "The Deep State: How Egypt's Shadow State Won Out," PBS Frontline, September 17, 2013, https://www.pbs.org/wgbh/frontline/article/the-deep-state-how-egypts-shadow-state-won-out/; Paul E. Lenze Jr., *Civil-Military Relations in the Islamic World* (Lanham, MD: Lexington Books, 2016), 62.

212. Springborg, *Mubarak's Egypt*, 110–11.

213. Elizabeth Bumiller, "Egypt Stability Hinges on a Divided Military," *New York Times*, February 5, 2011, https://www.nytimes.com/2011/02/06/world/middleeast/06military.html.

214. "Egyptian Generals Running Child Care." The power of the military managers became more apparent when the Supreme Military Council dismissed almost all of the Mubarak-era ministers from the cabinet, but retained General Sayyid Meshaal as Minister of Military Production, leaving the impression that the military was protecting its own economic niche Neil MacFarquhar and Mona Al-Naggar, "Answering the

Public, Egypt Names a new Cabinet," *New York Times*, March 6, 2011, https://www.nytimes.com/2011/03/07/world/middleeast/07egypt.html.

215. Adel Al-Toraifi, "Egypt's Army: Too Big to Fail?" *Asharq Al-Awsat*, February 9, 2012.

216. Scott Shane and David D. Kirkpatrick, "Military Caught Between Mubarak and Protesters," *New York Times*, February 10, 2011, https://www.nytimes.com/2011/02/11/world/middleeast/11military.html.

217. Interview 9E, 8E, 2012; Khaled Elgindy, "Egypt's Troubled Transition: Elections without Democracy," *The Washington Quarterly* 35, no. 2 (2012): 94.

218. Yezid Sayigh, "Egypt's Military Now Controls Much of its Economy. Is that Wise?" Carnegie Middle East Center, November 25, 2019, https://carnegie-mec.org/2019/11/25/egypt-s-military-now-controls-much-of-its-economy.-is-this-wise-pub-80281.

219. "Egypt, China Discuss Green Modes of Transport, Gas Cylinders," *Al Ahram*, December 27, 2021, https://english.ahram.org.eg/NewsContent/1/1235/452203/Egypt/Urban—Transport/Egypt,-China-discuss-production-of-green-modes-of-.aspx.

220. "AM, Egyptian Ministry of Military Production to Form Automotive Partnership," *Al Defaiya*, June 25, 2021, https://defaiya.com/news/Joint%20Ventures/Joint%20Ventures/2021/06/25/am-general-egyptian-ministry-of-military-production-to-establish-automotive-partnership.

221. "Egypt's Sisi Opens New Factories Under Ministry of Military Production," *Egyptian Independent*, February 18, 2020, https://www.egyptindependent.com/egypts-sisi-opens-new-factories-under-ministry-of-military-production/.

222. Ahmed S. Hashim, "The Egyptian Military, Part Two: From Mubarak Onward," *Middle East Policy* 18, no. 4 (2011): 109; "From War Room to Boardroom: Military Firms Flourish Under Sisi's Egypt," *Reuters*, May 16, 2018, https://www.reuters.com/investigates/special-report/egypt-economy-military/; Yezid Sayigh, "Egypt's Military Now Controls Much of its Economy"; Yezid Sayigh, *Owners of the Republic: An Anatomy of Egypt's Military Economy* (Washington, DC: Carnegie Middle East Center, 2019), 27–28.

223. "From War Room to Boardroom."

224. Interview 6E, 2007.

225. Sayigh, *"Owners of the Republic,"* 29.

226. "From War Room to Board Room."

227. "Sour Milky Way," *The Economist*, April 23, 2022.

228. Bessma Momani, "Egypt's IMF Program: Assessing the Political Economy Challenges," Brookings Institute, January 30, 2018, https://www.brookings.edu/research/egypts-imf-program-assessing-the-political-economy-challenges/.

229. Zeinab Abul-Magd, İsmet Akça, and Shana Marshall, "Two Paths to Dominance: Military Businesses in Turkey and Egypt," Working Paper, Carnegie Middle East Center, June 2020, 15.

230. Ishac Diwan, "Armed Forces in Power and Business," Carnegie Middle East Center, October 26, 2020, https://carnegie-mec.org/2020/10/26/armed-forces-in-power-and-in-business-pub-83030.

231. Sayigh, *Owners of the Republic* (2019), 61–62; Sarah Chayes, "The Egyptian Restoration," Carnegie Endowment for International Peace, August 1, 2013, https://bit.ly/2BKNwFL.

232. Cook, *Ruling but Not Governing*, 81.

233. Imad Harb, "The Egyptian Military in Politics: Disengagement or Accommodation?" *The Middle East Journal* 57, no. 2 (2003): 269–90.

234. Mira Maged, "Egypt's Military is 9th Strongest in the World, Jumping Three Places in 2019," *Egypt Independent*, February 4, 2020, https://egyptindependent.com/egypts-military-is-the-9th-strongest-in-the-world-jumping-three-places-in-2019/.

235. Timothy Kaldus, "Egypt's Military Companies Aren't Going Anywhere," *Bloomberg*, December 24, 2020, https://www.bloomberg.com/opinion/articles/2020-12-24/egypt-s-military-companies-aren-t-going-anywhere.

236. Dina Ezzat, "Mega-Projects Make a Comeback," *Al-Ahram*, August 7, 2014.

237. Frisch, "The Egyptian Army," 184–86; Rutherford, "Egypt's New Authoritarianism," 191.

238. "Showdown on the Nile," *The Economist* July 4–10, 2020, 38.

239. Kenneth M. Pollack, *Arabs at War: Military Effectiveness, 1948–1991* (Lincoln: University of Nebraska Press, 2002), chap. 6; Kenneth M. Pollack, *Armies of Sand: The Past, Present, and Future of Arab Military Effectiveness* (New York: Oxford University Press, 2019), chap. 1.

240. Interview 8J, 2011.

241. Anne Marie Baylouny, "Militarizing Welfare: Neo-Liberalism and Jordanian Policy," *The Middle East Journal* 62, no. 2 (2008): 302.

242. Shana Marshall, "Jordan's Military-Industrial Complex and the Middle East's New Model Army," *Middle East Report*, no. 267 (Summer 2014): 42–45; Shana Marshall "Jordan's Military-Industrial Sector: Maintaining Institutional Prestige in the Era of Neoliberalism," in *Businessmen in Arms: How the Military and other Armed Groups Profit in the MENA Region*, eds. Elke Grawert and Zeinab Abul-Magd (Lanham, MD: Rowman & Littlefield, 2016), 120–28.

243. Florence Gaub and Zoe Stanley-Lockman, "Defense Industries in Arab States," Paris: Chaillot Papers, No. 141 (March 2016): 64–65.

244. Marshall, "Jordan's Military-Industrial Sector," 130.

245. "Global: Military Corruption in Middle East and North African States, Jordan," October 29, 2015, Transparency International, 2020, https://corruption.net/global-military-corruption-in-middle-eastern-and-north-african-states/.

246. Theodore Karasik, "Saudi Arabia's Defense Posture is Robust," *Al Arabiya*, September 23, 2013.

247. "SAMI Aims to Make Saudi Arabia a Defense Industry Powerhouse by 2030," *Defense News*, September 17, 2018, https://www.defensenews.com/native/sami/2018/09/14/sami-aims-to-make-saudi-arabia-a-defense-industry-powerhouse-by-2030/.

248. Zoltan Barany, *Armies of Arabia: Military Politics and Effectiveness in the Gulf.* (New York: Oxford University Press, 2021), 189.

249. Agnes Al- Helou, "Oshkosh Defense in Talks with Saudi Manufacturer to Produce Armored Vehicles," *Defense News*, November 13, 2017, https://

www.defensenews.com/digital-show-dailies/dubai-air-show/2017/11/13/oshkosh-defense-in-talks-with-saudi-manufacturer-to-produce-armored-vehicles/.

250. Agnes Al-Helou, "Amid Western Arms Embargoes on Saudi Arabia, SAMI has a Backup Plan," *Defense News*, January 14, 2020, https://defence.pk/pdf/threads/amid-western-arms-embargoes-on-saudi-arabia-sami-has-a-backup-plan.650015/.

251. "First Military Industries Agreement between Saudi and Emirati Companies in the Kingdom," SAMI, February 22, 2021, https://www.sami.com.sa/en/media-center/news/first-military-industries-agreement-between-saudi-and-emirati-companies-kingdom.

252. "Saudi Military Industry Booms Fueled by Local Companies: GAMI," *Arab News* July 13, 2021, https://www.arabnews.com/node/1893276/business-economy.

253. Zoltan Barany, "Indigenous Defense Industries in the Gulf," Center for Strategic and International Studies, April 24, 2020, https://www.csis.org/analysis/indigenous-defense-industries-gulf.

254. Vali Nasr, "Politics within the Late Pahlavi State: The Ministry of Economy and Industrial Policy, 1963–1969," *International Journal of Middle East Studies* 32, no. 1 (2000): 103.

255. Mark J. Gasiorowski, "The Qarani Affair and Iranian Politics," *International Journal of Middle East Studies* 25, no. 4 (1993): 627.

256. Theda Skocpol, "Rentier State and Shi'a Islam in the Iranian Revolution," *Theory and Society* 11, no. 3 (1982): 270.

257. Skocpol "Rentier State and Shia Islam," 280.

258. Mohammad Reza Farzanegan, "Military Spending and Economic Growth: The Case of Iran," *Defence and Peace Economics* 25, no. 4 (2014): 4, f1–23.

259. Bijan Khajehpour, "The Real Footprint of the IRGC in Iran's Economy," *Al-Monitor*, August 9, 2017, https://www.al-monitor.com/originals/2017/08/iran-irgc-economy-footprint-khatam-olanbia.html.

260. Hadi Sohrabi, "Clerics and Generals: Assessing the Stability of the Iranian Regime," *Middle East Policy* 25, no. 3 (2018): 37.

261. Miroslav Nincic, "Getting What You Want: Positive Inducements in International Relations," *International Security*, 35, no. 1 (2010): 170; Akbar Ganji, "The Latter-Day Sultan," *Foreign Affairs* 87, no. 6 (2008): 57–59.

262. Farzanegan, "Military Spending and Economic Growth," 4.

263. David Pion-Berlin, "Military Relations in Comparative Perspective," in *Armies and Insurgencies in the Arab Spring*, eds. Holger Albrecht, Aurel Croissant, and Fred H. Lawson. (Philadelphia: University of Pennsylvania Press, 2016), 22.

264. Greg Bruno, Jayshree Bajoria, and Jonathan Masters, "Iran's Revolutionary Guards," *Backgrounders*, Council on Foreign Relations, June 14, 2013, http://www.cfr.org/iran/irans-revolutionary-guards/p14324.

265. "Khaki Capitalism."

266. Munqith Dagher, "The Iranian Islamic Revolutionary Guard Corps (IRGC) from an Iraqi View—A Lost Role or a Bright Future?" Center for Strategic and International Studies, July 30, 2020, https://www.csis.org/analysis/iranian-islamic-revolutionary-guard-corps-irgc-iraqi-view-%E2%80%93-lost-role-or-bright-future.

267. Ali Reza Eshraghi and Amir Hossein Mahdavi. "The Revolutionary Guards are Posed to Take Over Iran," *Foreign Affairs*, August 27, 2020, https://www.foreignaffairs.com/articles/middle-east/2020-08-27/revolutionary-guards-are-poised-take-over-Iran.

268. Shamsi Saadati, "Is there a Solution to Iran's Economic Crisis?" NCRI, October 4, 2021, https://www.ncr-iran.org/en/news/economy/is-there-a-solution-to-irans-economic-crisis/.

269. Nincic, "Getting What You Want," 171.

270. Suzanne Maloney, "Islamism and Iran's Postrevolutionary Economy: The Case of the *Bonyads*," in *Gods, Guns, and Globalization: Religious Radicalism and International Political Economy*, eds. Mary Ann Tétreault and Robert A. Denemark (Boulder, CO: Lynne Rienner Publishers, 2004), 205; Erin Cunningham and Emily Tamkin, "What is the Revolutionary Guard? A look at the Iranian Military Unit Trump has Deemed Terrorists," *Washington Post*, April 8, 2019, https://www.washingtonpost.com/world/2019/04/08/who-are-revolutionary-guards-look-iranian-military-unit-trump-has-deemed-terrorists/.

271. Babak Taghvaee, "Deception and Corruption in Iran's Defense Industries," *Kayhan*, January 23, 2017, https://kayhanlife.com/business/deception-corruption-in-irans-defense-industries/. A display version of the plane was apparently made up of old aircraft parts.

272. Elliot Hen-Tov and Nathan Gonzales, "The Militarization of Post-Khomeini Iran: Praetorianism 2.0," *Washington Quarterly* 34, no. 1 (2011): 52–53.

273. Bijan Khajehpour, "The Real Footprint of the IRGC in Iran's Economy," *Al-Monitor*, August 9, 2017, https://www.al-monitor.com/originals/2017/08/iran-irgc-economy-footprint-khatam-olanbia.html.

274. Khajehpour, "The Real Footprint."

275. Kevan Harris, "All the Sepah's Men: Iran's Revolutionary Guards in Theory and Practice," in *Businessmen in Arms: How the Military and other Armed Groups Profit in the MENA Region*, eds. Elke Grawert and Zeinab Abul-Magd (Lanham, MD: Rowman & Littlefield, 2016), 108–9.

276. "Yemen's Security Sector: Seeds of New Conflict," 2013. Middle East Report No. 139, International Crisis Group, April 4, 2013, http://www.crisisgroup.org/en/regions/middle-east-north-africa/iraq-iran-gulf/yemen/139-yemens-military-security-reform-seeds-of-new-conflict.aspx.

277. Interview 2Y, 2005.

278. Clark, *Dancing on the Heads of Snakes*, 122–23.

279. Sam Kimball, "Yemeni Army: The Regime's Cash Cow," *Al Akhbar*, July 13, 2012.

280. "Despite New Era, Anti-Corruption Agenda Struggles in Yemen," IRIN News, April 29, 2014, http://www.irinnews.org/report/100005/despite-new-era-anti-corruption-agenda-struggles-in-yemen.

281. *Yemen Corruption Assessment* United States Agency for International Development, September 25, 2006, https://yemen.usembassy.gov//yemen-corruption-assessment.pdf.

282. Philippe Droz-Vincent, *Military Politics of the Contemporary World* (Cambridge: Cambridge University Press, 2021), 141.

283. David Ignatius, "To Calm Yemen, Curb Corruption and Spread National Wealth," *Al-Arabiya*, March 2, 2012.

284. Adam C. Seitz, "Patronage Politics in Transition: Political and Economic Interests of the Yemeni Armed Forces," in *Businessmen in Arms: How the Military and Other Armed Groups Profit in the MENA Region*, eds. Elke Grawert and Zeinab Abul-Magd (Lanham, MD: Rowman & Littlefield, 2016), 169–70.

285. "Corruption in Yemen's War Economy," Sanaʿa Center for Strategic Studies, November 5, 2018, https://sanaacenter.org/files/Rethinking_Yemens_Economy_policy_brief_9.pdf.

286. Tanel Demirel, "Soldiers and Civilians: The Dilemma of Turkish Democracy, *Middle Eastern Studies* 40, no. 1 (2004): 130; İsmet Akça, "The Conglomerate of the Turkish Military (OYAK) and the Dynamics of Turkish Capitalism," in *Businessmen in Arms: How the Military and Other Armed Groups Profit in the MENA Region*, eds. Elke Grawert and Zainab Abdul-Magd (Lanham, MD: Rowman & Littlefield, 2016), 69–96.

287. Dorian Jones, "Turkey: Will AKP Government Crack Down on Military's Business Interests?" Eurasianet.org, July 23, 2012, http://www.eurasianet.org/node/65696.

288. Akça, "The Conglomerate of the Turkish Military," 71.

289. *Oyak: Above and Beyond, Annual Report 2019*, OYAK_FR_2019_EN-603.pdf.

290. Zeinab Abul-Magd, İsmet Akça, and Shana Marshall, "Two Paths to Dominance: Military Businesses in Turkey and Egypt," Working Paper, Carnegie Middle East Center, June 2020.

291. Abul-Magd, Akça, and Marshall, "Two Paths to Dominance," 8.

292. "Beyond the Horizon: OYAK Annual Report, 2020, 21. https://www.oyak.com.tr/sites/1/upload/files/OYAK_Annual_Report_2020_WEB-664.pdf.

293. Cook, *Ruling but Not Governing*, 21.

294. Cook, *Ruling but Not Governing*, 111.

295. Banu Eligür, *The Mobilization of Political Islam in Turkey* (Cambridge: Cambridge University Press, 2010), 200.

296. That perception goes back to the removal of US intermediate-range ballistic missiles in 1963 following the Cuban missile crisis, and the 1974 US arms embargo crisis over Cyprus.

297. Ridvan Bari Urcosta, "The Revolution in Drone Warfare: The Lessons from the Idlib De-Escalation Zone," *European, Middle Eastern, and African Affairs* (Fall 2020): 50–65. https://media.defense.gov/2020/Aug/31/2002487583/-1/-1/1/URCOSTA.PDF. In 2016, Turkish Defense Minister İsmail Demir, stated, "I don't want to be sarcastic, but I would like to thank [the US government] for any of the projects that were not approved of by the US because this forced us to develop our own systems," Urcosta, "The Revolution in Drone Warfare," 54. The designer and producer of the Bayraktar drone is Selçuk Bayraktar, who is married to Sümeyee

Erdoğan, the youngest daughter of President Erdoğan. See Stephen Witt, "Weapon of Influence," *The New Yorker*, May 16, 2022, 22–26.

298. "Turkiye's Top 10 Major Defense Breakthroughs in 2021, Explained," *TRT World*, December 28, 2021, https://www.trtworld.com/magazine/turkiye-s-top-7-major-defence-industry-breakthroughs-in-2021-explained-53086.

299. Dave Philipps and Eric Schmitt, "Over Ukraine, Lumbering Turkish-Made Drones are an Ominous Sign for Russia," *New York Times*, March 11, 2022, https://www.nytimes.com/2022/03/11/us/politics/ukraine-military-drones-russia.html.

300. Steven A. Cook, "Closing the Channels of the Military's Economic Influence in Turkey," Middle East Institute, April 20, 2014, https://www.mei.edu/publications/closing-channels-militarys-economic-influence-turkey.

301. Burak Bekdil, "Turkish Industry Prospers, but Foreign Relations are Limiting its Potential," *Defense News*, August 17, 2020, https://www.defensenews.com/top-100/2020/08/17/turkish-industry-prospers-but-foreign-relations-are-limiting-its-potential/.

302. Asher Tishler and Gil Pinchas, "Challenges of the Israeli Defense Industry in the Global Security Market," in *Israel's Defense Industry and US Security Aid*, eds. Sassan Haddad, Tomer Fadlon, and Shmuel Even (Tel Aviv: Institute for National Security Studies, July 2020), 38.

303. Alex Mintz, "The Military-Industrial Complex: The Israeli Case," in *Israeli Society and Its Defense Establishment: The Social and Political Impact of a Protracted Violent Conflict*, ed. Moshe Lissak (London: Frank Cass, 1984), 113.

304. David A. Lewis, "Diversification and Niche Market Exporting: The Restructuring of Israel's Defense Industry in the Post-Cold War Era," in *From Defense to Development: International Perspectives on Realizing the Peace Dividend*, eds. Ann Markusen, Sean DiGiovanna, and Michael C. Leary (New York: Routledge, 2003), 126.

305. Paul Rivlin, *The Israeli Economy from the Foundation of the State through the 21st Century* (Cambridge: Cambridge University Press, 2011), 136–37.

306. IMI was acquired by Elbit Industries in 2019, an interesting example of a state-owned company being absorbed by a private industry.

307. "IAI Takes Wing," *The Economist*, March 3, 2011. IAI's relationship with the Defense Ministry has been difficult; apparently the Defense Ministry was delinquent in its payments to IAI, owing it $250 million US. Oren Cohen, "Israel Aerospace Industries in Talks to Sell $1.2 Billion of Electronic Systems," *Ha'aretz*, July 14, 2014, https://www.haaretz.com/israel-news/business/2014-07-14/ty-article/iai-in-talks-to-sell-1-2b-of-electronic-systems/0000017f-dc13-df9c-a.

308. Interview 6IS, March 2019.

309. Seth J. Frantzman, "Israel's Revolutionary Defense Industry," *Jerusalem Post*, May 23, 2019, https://www.jpost.com/israel-news/israels-revolutionary-defense-industry-590370.b

310. Interview 6IS, March 2019.

311. Arie Egozi, "Israel Industry Pushing Jerusalem to Drop MCTR Drone Export Restrictions," *Breaking Defense*, September 27, 2021, https://breakingdefense.com/2021/09/israeli-industry-pushing-jerusalem-to-drop-mtcr-drone-export-restrictions/.

312. Frank Mora and Quinton Wiktoriwicz, "Economic Reform and the Military: China, Cuba, and Syria in Comparative Perspective," *International Journal of Comparative Sociology* 44, no. 2 (2002): 103.

313. Rivlin, *Arab Economies in the Twentieth Century*, 251.

314. Hicham Bou Nassif, "'Second Class': The Grievances of Sunni Officers in the Syrian Armed Forces," *Journal of Strategic Studies* 38 (July 2015): 633–34.

315. Ben Hubbard and Hwaida Saad, "On Syria's Ruins, a Drug Empire Flourishes," *New York Times*, December 5, 2021, https://www.nytimes.com/2021/12/05/world/middleeast/syria-drugs-captagon-assad.html.

316. Alexy Khlebnikov, "Russia and Syrian Military Reform: Challenges and Opportunities," Carnegie Middle East Center, March 26, 2020, https://carnegie-mec.org/2020/03/26/russia-and-syrian-military-reform-challenges-and-opportunities-pub-81154.

317. Zindane Zeraoui, "Algeria: Army, Revolution, and Political Power," *Language and Intercultural Communication* 12, no. 2 (2012): 138.

318. Tom Kington, "Algeria Prepares to Receive LPD amid Defense Spending Boost," *Defense News*, January 31, 2014.

319. "SAFAV MB Delivers 708 Mercedes Vehicles Public Institutions, Private Companies," 2021, Algeria Press Service, February 10, 2021, https://www.aps.dz/en/economy/37986-safav-mb-delivers-708-mercedes-benz-vehicles-public-institutions-private-companies.

320. Interview 2A, 2005.

321. Susan Slyomovics, "Algeria's Military Capabilities," *Jadaliyya*, February 27, 2011, http://www.jadaliyya.com/pages/index/751/algerias-military-capabilities.

322. Bradford L. Dilman, *State and Private Sector in Algeria: The Politics of Rent-Seeking and Failed Development* (Boulder, CO: Westview Press, 2000), 95.

323. Dilman *State and Private Sector in Algeria*, 95–96.

324. Belkacem Elguettaa, "The Military's Political Role in the New Algeria," in Yezid Sayigh (ed.), *The Politics of Military Authoritarianism in North Africa*, Malcolm H. Kerr Carnegie Middle East Center, March 17, 2021, https://carnegie-mec.org/2021/03/17/military-s-political-role-in-new-algeria-pub-84076.

325. Steffen Hertog, *Princes, Brokers, and Bureaucrats: Oil and the State in Saudi Arabia* (Ithaca, NY: Cornell University Press, 2010), 23.

326. Christopher M. Davidson, *Dubai: The Vulnerability of Success* (New York: Columbia University Press, 2008), 266–68.

327. Interview 3U, March 2019.

328. Barany. *Armies of Arabia*, 44.

329. "Egyptian Defense Analyst," "Egypt's Military Limitations: Cairo's Options to Defend Eastern Libya," Foreign Policy Research Institute, July 13, 2020, https://www.fpri.org/article/2020/07/egypts-military-limitations-cairos-options-to-defend-eastern-libya/. "Egyptian Defense Analyst" is a pseudonym for an Egyptian defense analyst.

330. David D. Kirkpatrick, "Egyptians Say Military Discourages an Open Economy," *New York Times*, February 17, 2011, https://www.nytimes.com/2011/02/18/world/middleeast/18military.html.

331. Marcus Mietzner, "Successful and Failed Democratic Transitions from Military Rule in Majority Muslim Societies: The Cases of Indonesia and Egypt," *Contemporary Politics* 20, no. 4 (2014): 442–43.

332. John Gillespie, Thang Van Nguyen, Hung Vu Nguyen, and Canh Quang Le, "Exploring a Public Interest Definition of Corruption: Public Private Partnerships in Socialist Asia," *Journal of Business Ethics* 165 (2020): 579.

333. Habib Zafarullah, and Muhammad Yeahia Akhter, Military Rule, "Civilianisation and Electoral Corruption: Pakistan and Bangladesh in Perspective," *Asian Studies in Review* 25, no. 1 (2001): 73–94; Larry Jay Diamond, "Nigeria's Perennial Struggle," *Journal of Democracy* 2 no. 4 (1991): 73–85; Kimberley Thachuk, "Corruption and International Security," *SAIS Review* 25, no.1 (2005): 143–52.

334. Herbert Howe, *Ambiguous Order: Military Forces in African States* (Boulder, CO: Lynne Rienner Publishers, 2001), 41–42; William Ehwarieme, "The Military Factor in Nigeria's Democratic Stability, 1999–2009," *Armed Forces & Society* 37, no. 3 (2011): 499.

335. Daniel Kofi Banani, "Security Sector Corruption and Military Effectiveness: The Influence of Corruption on Countermeasures Against Boko Haram in Nigeria," *Small Wars & Insurgencies* 31, no. 1 (2020): 131–58.

336. Marybeth Peterson Ulrich, *Democratizing Communist Militaries: The Cases of the Czech and Russian Armed Forces* (Ann Arbor: University of Michigan Press, 1999), 88.

337. Tor Bukkvoll, "Their Hands in the Till: Scale and Causes of Russian Military Corruption," *Armed Forces & Society* 34, no. 2 (2008): 259–75.

338. Teylour Ring, "Rank and File Corrupted: Uncertain Attribution and Corruption in Russia's Military Cyber Units," Center for Strategic and International Studies, September 22, 2020, https://www.csis.org/blogs/post-soviet-post/rank-and-file-corrupted-uncertain-attribution-and-corruption-russias-military.

339. Xiaoting Li, Cronyism and Military Corruption in the Post-Deng Xiaoping Era: Rethinking the Party-Commands-the-Gun Model," *Journal of Contemporary China* 26, no. 107 (2017): 696–710.

340. Ayesha Siddiqa, *Military Inc.: Inside Pakistan's Military Economy* (London: Pluto Press, 2007).

341. Ned Parker, "The Iraq We Left Behind," *Foreign Affairs* 91, no. 2 (2012): 103.

342. Michael J. Willis, *Politics and Power in the Maghreb: Algeria, Tunisia, and Morocco from Independence to the Arab Spring* (New York: Columbia University Press), 113.

343. Joshua Lipson, "Israel among Most Corrupt of OECD Countries," *Jerusalem Post*, July 9, 2013, https://www.jpost.com/National-News/Israel-among-most-corrupt-of-OECD-countries-319315.

344. Ora Coren, "India Blacklists Israeli Defense Firm Amid Corruption Charges," *Ha'aretz*, March 12, 2012.

345. *Yemen Corruption Assessment*, v.

346. Committee on Foreign Relations, United States Senate, *Following the Money in Yemen and Lebanon: Maximizing the Effectiveness of US Security Assistance and*

International Financial Institution Lending. One Hundred Eleventh Congress, First Session January 5 (Washington, DC: Government Printing Office, 2010).

347. "In New Face of Yemen's Opposition, Reflections of an Old Regime," *Yemen Post*, March 25, 2011.

348. Clarke, *Dancing on the Heads of Snakes*, 265–66.

349. *Yemen Corruption Assessment*, 4.

350. "Saudi Arabia Probes Corruption, Mismanagement in Yemen War," *The Arab Weekly*, September 2, 2020, https://thearabweekly.com/saudi-arabia-probes-corruption-mismanagement-yemen-war.

351. "Combating Corruption in Yemen," Sanaʻa Center for Strategic Studies, November 2018, 29–30.

352. Interview 2Y, 2005.

353. Barany, *Armies of Arabia*, 167.

354. Clayton Swisher, Ewen McAskill, and Rob Evans, "US Investigation into BAE Saudi Arms Deal Watered Down, Leaked Memo Suggests," *The Guardian*, March 6, 2018. https://www.theguardian.com/world/2018/mar/06/us-investigation-into-bae-saudi-arms-deal-watered-down-leaked-memo-suggests.

355. "BAE Says US is Investigating Deals with Saudi Arabia," *International Herald Tribune*, June 26, 2007; Barany, *Armies of Arabia*, 167.

356. "Saudi Arabia: New Mass Corruption Arrests," Human Rights Watch. March 17, 2020, https://www.hrw.org/news/2020/03/17/saudi-arabia-new-mass-corruption-arrests.

357. "Saudi King Sacks Commander of Yemen Forces over Corruption Claims," *Al Jazeera*, September 1, 2020, https://www.aljazeera.com/news/2020/09/saudi-king-sacks-commander-yemen-forces-corruption-claims-200901025956712.html. Crown Prince Mohammed bin-Salman has dismissed many senior ranking officials and princes, often charging them with corruption. However, some speculate that the charges are a mechanism to remove opponents to Prince Mohammed's reform policies, rather than on corruption.

358. John Waterbury, *The Egypt of Nasser and Sadat: The Political Economy of Two Regimes* (Princeton, NJ: Princeton University Press, 1983), 337.

359. " القائد الأسطوري " (The Legendary Commander)," 2008. *Al-Ahram*, September 11–17, 2008.

360. Adam Roston and David Rohde, "Egyptian Army's Business Side Blurs Lines of US Military Aid," *New York Times*, March 5, 2011, https://www.nytimes.com/2011/03/06/world/middleeast/06military.html.

361. David D. Kilpatrick, "Egyptian Official Vexes Generals and US by Pressing Investigation," *New York Times*, February 14, 2012, https://www.nytimes.com/2012/02/15/world/middleeast/fayza-abul-naga-presses-inquiry-against-us-in-egypt.html.

362. Robert Springborg, *Mubarak's Egypt: Fragmentation of the Political Order* (Boulder, CO: Westview Press, 1989), 106.

363. Hicham Bou Nassif, "Wedded to Mubarak: The Second Careers and Financial Rewards of Egypt's Military Elite, 1981–2011," *Middle East Journal* 67, no. 4 (2013): 528.

364. David D. Kirkpatrick, "Ousted General in Egypt is Back, as Islamist Foe," *New York Times*, October 30, 2013. In 2019, Egyptian officials ordered Kirkpatrick deported, apparently unhappy with his reporting.

365. Shana Marshall, "Egypt's Emerging Ruling Class," Malcolm H. Kerr Carnegie Middle East Center, October 26, 2020, https://carnegie-mec.org/2020/10/26/egypt-s-emerging-ruling-class-pub-83025.

366. Jon Gorvett, "Anti-Corruption Drives Uncovering Something Rotten in Turkey," *Washington Report on Middle Eastern Affairs* 24, no. 3 (2005): 38.

367. Bekdil, "Defense Procurement Reform in Turkey."

368. Marie Chêne, "Overview of Corruption and Anti-Corruption in Turkey," Transparency International, January 17, 2012, https://www.transparency.org/files/content/corruptionqas/313_Overview_of_corruption_and_anti-corruption_in_Turkey.pdf.

369. Nikolaos Van Dam, *The Struggle for Power in Syria* (London: I. B. Tauris, 1996), 142.

370. Perthes Volker, "A Look at Syria's Upper Class: The Bourgeoisie and the Ba'th," *Middle East Report* 170 (May–June 1991), 34–35.

371. Howard Joffe, "Mustafa Tlass Obituary," *The Guardian*, July 20, 2017, https://www.theguardian.com/world/2017/jul/20/mustafa-tlass-obituary. The author met with Mustafa Tlas in a session recorded on Syrian TV. During the protracted discussion, Tlas explained the real meaning of the President Clinton sex scandal. "She was under Clinton's desk tapping his phones, as she was a Mossad agent," Of course.

372. Haifa Bitar, "Some of the Corruption in Syria," *Al-Araby Al- Jadeed*, February 10, 2017.

373. Abdul Razzaq al-Hawassali, "Syria's Fuel Crisis Reveals a Corrupt Assad Regime," *Al-Araby al-Jadeed*, May 14, 2019.

374. "Syria: Bread Crisis Exposes Government Failure," Human Rights Watch, March 21, 2021, https://www.hrw.org/news/2021/03/21/syria-bread-crisis-exposes-government-failure.

CHAPTER FIVE

1. Carl Von Clausewitz, *On War*, edited and translated by Michael Howard and Peter Paret (Princeton, NJ: Princeton University Press, 1976), 606.

2. Vipin Narang and Caitlin Talmadge. "Civil-Military Pathologies and Defeat in War: Tests Using New Data," *Journal of Conflict Resolution* 62, no. 7 (2018): 1381–82.

3. Samuel P. Huntington, *The Soldier and the State* (Cambridge, MA: Harvard University Press, 1957), 262.

4. Peter D. Feaver, *Armed Servants: Agency, Oversight, and Civil-Military Relations* (Cambridge, MA: Harvard University Press, 2003).

5. Eliot A. Cohen, *Supreme Command: Soldiers, Statesman, and Leadership in Wartime* (New York: The Free Press, 2002); Feaver, *Armed Servants*, 2003.

6. R. Blake McMahon, "Shooting Yourself in the Foot" Strategic Selection and Coup Proofing," Paper presented at the annual International Studies Association conference, San Diego, CA, March 21, 2012; Dan Reiter and Allan C. Stam III, "Democracy and Battlefield Military Effectiveness," *The Journal of Conflict Resolution* 42, no. 3 (1998): 259–77; Ulrich H. Pilster and Tobias Böhmelt, "Coup Proofing and Military Effectiveness in Interstate Wars, 1967–1999," *Conflict Management and Peace Science* 28, no. 4 (2011): 1–20; Jonathan Powell, "Determinants of the Attempting and Outcomes of Coups d'état," *Journal of Conflict Resolution* 56, no. 6 (2012): 1024; Emizet Kisangani, "Explaining the Rise and Fall of Military Regimes: Civil-Military Relations in the Congo," *Armed Forces & Society* 26, no. 2 (2000): 215.

7. Aaron Belkin and Evan Schofer, "Toward a Structural Understanding of Coup Risk," *The Journal of Conflict Resolution* 47, no. 5 (2003): 596.

8. Caitlin Talmadge, *The Dictator's Army: Battlefield Effectiveness in Authoritarian Regimes* (Ithaca, NY: Cornell University Press, 2018).

9. Talmadge, *The Dictator's Army*, 233.

10. Stephen Biddle and Robert Zirkle, "Technology, Civil-Military Relations, and Warfare in the Developing World," *The Journal of Strategic Studies* 19, no. 2 (1996): 171–212.

11. When war outcomes became disastrous for Iraq, Saddam did sometimes reward military competence, as he did after the loss of the Faw Peninsula to Iraq in 1986. Some of the difference between Iraqi and North Vietnamese performance could also been a result of different war types; while North Vietnam concentrated more on unconventional war, Iraqi forces fought conventionally. Kenneth M. Pollack, *Arabs at War: Military Effectiveness, 1948–1991* (Lincoln: University of Nebraska Press, 2002), 208; Kevin B Woods, Williamson Murray, Elizabeth A. Nathan, Laila Sabara, and Ana M. Venegas, *Saddam's General: Perspectives of the Iran-Iraq War* (Washington, DC: Institute for Defense Analysis, 2011), 15. I thank W. Andrew Terrill for this point.

12. M. Taylor Fravel, *Active Defense: China's Military Strategy since 1949* (Princeton: Princeton University Press, 2019), 271.

13. Judith Hicks Stiehm, *The US Army War College: Military Education in a Democracy* (Philadelphia: Temple University Press, 2002), 2.

14. Nathan W. Toronto, *How Militaries Learn: Human Capital, Military Education, and Battlefield Effectiveness* (Lanham, MD: Lexington Books, 2018), 7.

15. Stephen Biddle and Stephen Long, "Democracy and Military Effectiveness: A Deeper Look," *The Journal of Conflict Resolution* 48, no. 4 (2004): 532.

16. Feaver, *Armed Servants*, 58.

17. Jeffrey W. Legro, "Military Culture and Inadvertent Escalation in World War II," *International Security* 18, no. 4 (1994): 114; B. R. Posen, *The Sources of Military Doctrine: France, Britain, and Germany Between the World Wars* (Ithaca: Cornell University Press, 1984); Andrew F. Krepinevich Jr., *The Army and Vietnam* (Baltimore: Johns Hopkins University Press, 1986).

18. Richard H. Kohn, "How Democracies Control the Military," *Journal of Democracy* 8, no. 4 (1997): 146–47.

19. Posen, *The Sources of Military Doctrine*, 52–53.

20. Jack Snyder, "Civil-Military Relations and the Cult of the Offensive, 1914 and 1984," *International Security* 9, no. 1 (1984): 121.

21. Richard K. Betts, *Soldiers, Statesmen, and Cold War Crises* (Cambridge, MA: Harvard University Press), 104–14; David Alan Rosenberg, "A Smoking, Radiating Ruin at the End of Two Hours: Documents on American Plans for Nuclear War with the Soviet Union, 1954–1955," *International Security* 6, no. 3 (1981–1982): 3–38; David Alan Rosenberg, "The Origins of Overkill: Nuclear Weapons and American Strategy, 1945–1960. "*International Security* 7, no. 4 (1983): 3–71. Civilian policy intrusions may get to the barracks level, as when Russian Defense Minister Anatolii Serdyukov, a former tax official with almost no military experience, entered the back door of the Nakhimov Naval College in March 2007 and sacked its admiral commander on the spot when he found deplorable conditions there. Dale Herspring, *Civil-Military Relations and Shared Responsibility: A Four-Nation Study* (Baltimore: Johns Hopkins University Press, 2013), 262–63.

22. Cohen, *Supreme Command*, 182. The author recalls a story circulating in Vietnam, that an officer asked President Johnson, on a rare visit to Vietnam, what he expected the troops to do. Johnson responded, "I want you to nail the coonskin to the wall!" Whether or not the story is true, I do not know, but among the Americans in Vietnam, it made the rounds.

23. Ian Roxborough, "Review: Thinking About War," *Sociological Forum*, 19, no. 3 (2004): 516.

24. Jeffrey W. Donnithorne, *Four Guardians: A Principled Agent View of American Civil-Military Relations* (Baltimore: The Johns Hopkins University Press, 2018), 112–13; Benjamin S. Lambeth, *The Transformation of American Airpower* (Ithaca, NY: Cornell University Press, 2000), 48–51.

25. Brian D. Laslie, *Airpower's Lost Cause: The American Air Wars of Vietnam* (Lanham, MD: Rowman & Littlefield, 2021); Lambeth, *The Transformation of American Airpower* (2000), chap. 2.

26. One way to ensure civilian dominance in strategic matters is by civilian insertion into those strategic decision areas; another is to remove senior military leaders from those taskings. In 1958, an Act of Congress removed the US Joint Chiefs of Staff from the chain of command, thus also removing them from direct control of military operations. The French military chiefs also do not have operational control of forces In Japan, civilians control both defense and public security operations for the Self-Defense Force. Pakistani president Zulfikar Ali Bhutto revised army command structure in order to curb its power after a disastrous defeat by India, and the Russian military inherited the Soviet military tradition of dual control, with party commissars at every level. Though the erosion of civil authority in Russia probably leaves the military in a much more independent position.

27. Bates Gill and Martin Kleiber, "China's Space Odyssey," *Foreign Affairs* 86, no. 3 (2007): 2–6. In 2011, China tested a new "stealth" combat aircraft right before a visit from US defense secretary Robert Gates, who had previously stated that Chinese development of such technology was far off, and thus was embarrassed by the appearance of the plane. Apparently, when Gates inquired about the aircraft to President Hu

Jintao, the president appeared to have no knowledge of the test, which occurred just hours before Gates arrived. "China Is Said to Test Stealth Fighter as Gates Visits," *New York Times*, January 11, 2011, https://www.nytimes.com/2011/01/12/world/asia/12fighter.html.

28. David Pion-Berlin and Harold Trinkunas, "Attention Deficit: Why Politicians Ignore Defense Policy in Latin America," *Latin America Research Review* 42, no. 3 (2007): 95.

29. Alfred Stepan, *Rethinking Military Politics: Brazil and the Southern Cone* (Princeton, NJ: Princeton University Press, 1988), 106.

30. Dale Herspring, "Civil-Military Relations in the United States and Russia: Al Alternative Approach," *Armed Forces & Society* 35, no. 4 (2009): 674. The parallels to Vladimir Putin's invasion of Ukraine in February 2022 are interesting, but the definitive study must await further civil-military analysis.

31. Tobias Böhmelt and Ulrich Pilster, "The Impact on Institutional Coup-Proofing on Coup Attempts and Coup Outcomes," *International Interactions* 41, no. 1 (2015): 158–82.

32. Ulrich H. Pilster, and Tobias Böhmelt, "Coup proofing and Military Effectiveness in Interstate Wars, 1967–99," *Conflict Management and Peace Science* 28, no. 4 (2011): 1–20.

33. Vipin Narang and Caitlin Talmadge, "Civil-Military Pathologies and Defeat in War: Tests Using New Data," *Journal of Conflict Resolution* 62, no. 7 (2008): 1394–95.

34. Stephen Biddle and Stephen Long, "Democracy and Military Effectiveness: A Deeper Look," *The Journal of Conflict Resolution* 48, no. 4 (2004): 525–46; Snyder, "Civil-Military Relations and the Cult of the Offensive."

35. Jason Lyall, *Divided Armies: Inequality and Battlefield Performance in Modern War* (Princeton, NJ: Princeton University Press, 2020).

36. Sebastian Rosato, *Intentions in Great Power Politics: Uncertainty and the Roots of Conflict* (New Haven, CT: Yale University Press, 2021).

37. Sarah E. Kreps, *Taxing Wars: The American War of War and the Decline of Democracy* (Oxford: Oxford University Press, 2018); Mark R Wilson, *Creative Destruction: American Business and the Winning of World War II* (Philadelphia: University of Pennsylvania Press, 2016).

38. Florence Gaub, *Guardians of the Arab State: Why Militaries Intervene in Politics, from Iraq to Mauritania* (Oxford: Oxford University Press, 2017), 41.

39. The 1973 war is often called the Yom Kippur War, particularly by Israeli supporters, or the Ramadan War, by Arab supporters. I call it the 1973 war.

40. Charles D. Freilich, *Zion's Dilemmas: How Israel Makes National Security Policy* (Ithaca, NY: Cornell University Press, 2012), 127–32; Zeev Moaz, *Defending the Holy Land: A Critical Analysis of Israel's Security & Foreign Policy* (Ann Arbor: University of Michigan Press, 2006), 171–230.

41. Kenneth M. Pollack, *Arabs at War: Military Effectiveness, 1948–1991* (Lincoln: University of Nebraska Press, 2002), chap. 2; Talmadge, *The Dictator's Army*, chaps. 4 and 5.

42. Louis-Alexandre Berg, "Civil–Military Relations and Civil War Recurrence: Security Forces in Postwar Politics," *Journal of Conflict Resolution* 64, nos. 7–8 (2020): 1307–34.

43. Pollack, *Arabs at War*, 271

44. Pollack, *Arabs at War*, 267–357.

45. Philip Robins, *A History of Jordan* (Cambridge: Cambridge University Press, 2004), 127; Daniel Byman, *A High Price: The Triumphs and Failures of Israeli Counterterrorism* (Oxford: Oxford University Press, 2011), 38–39; Pollack, *Arabs at War*, 330–35; W. Andrew Terrill, "The Political Mythology of the Battle of Karameh," *Middle East Journal* 55, no. 1 (2001): 91–111.

46. The author has lectured at the Royal Jordanian National Defense College on several occasions.

47. It is likely that coup-proofing by the former Shah Mohammed Reza Pahlavi, which removed the most competent Artesh officers, also led to Iran's wartime shortfalls. Rebecca Carr and Constantine Danopolis, "The Military and Politics in a Theocratic State: Iran as a Case Study," *Armed Forces & Society* 24, no. 2 (1997): 273–74.

48. Efraim Karsh, *The Iran-Iraq War: A Military Analysis*. Adelphi Papers No. 220. (London: International Institute for Strategic Studies, 1987), 14; Shahram Chubin and Charles Tripp *Iran and Iraq at War* (Boulder, CO: Westview Press, 1988), 35.

49. "Iran's Revolutionary Guards," Council on Foreign Relations, May 6, 2019, https://www.cfr.org/backgrounder/irans-revolutionary-guard; Ariane M.Tabatabai, *No Conquest, No Defeat: Iran's National Security Strategy* (New York: Oxford University Press, 2020), chap. 5; Hazem Kandil, *The Power Triangle: Military, Security, and Politics in Regime Change* (New York: Oxford University Press, 2016), 118–26.

50. Greg Bruno, Jayshree Bajoria, and Jonathan Masters, "Iran's Revolutionary Guards," *Backgrounders*, Council on Foreign Relations, June 14, 2013, http://www.cfr.org/iran/irans-revolutionary-guards/p14324.

51. Annie Tracy Samuel, "Attacking Iran: Lessons from the Iran-Iraq War," The Dubai Initiative, the Belfer Center for Science and International Security (2011): 4, http://belfercenter.ksg.harvard.edu/files/samuel-policy-brief-12-11.pdf.

52. Karsh, *The Iran-Iraq War*, 26.

53. Stephen C. Pelletiere, *The Iran-Iraq War: Chaos in a Vacuum* (New York: Praeger, 1992), 75; Annie Tracy Samuel, *The Unfinished History of the Iran-Iraq War: Faith, Firepower, and Iran's Revolutionary Guards* (Cambridge: Cambridge University Press, 2022), 197–99; Afshon Ostovar, *Vanguard of the Imam: Religion, Politics, and Iran's Revolutionary Guards* (Oxford: Oxford University Press, 2016), 98–99.

54. Soraya Lenny, "Analysis: Iran's Double Game in Iraq," *Al-Jazeera*, June 27, 2014, https://www.aljazeera.com/news/2014/6/27/analysis-irans-double-game-in-iraq; Ali Hashem, "How Haider al-Abadi Became Iraq's Next Prime Minister," *Al-Monitor*, August 14, 2014, https://www.al-monitor.com/originals/2014/08/iraq-iran-prime-minister-alabadi-maliki.html.

55. Timothy Arango and Thomas Erdbrink, "US and Iran both Attack ISIS, but Try Not to Look like Allies," *New York Times*, December 3, 2014, https://www.nytimes.com/2014/12/04/world/middleeast/iran-airstrikes-hit-islamic-state-in-iraq.html.

56. Talmadge, *The Dictator's Army*, 204–5.
57. Mohammad Ayatollahi Tabaar, *Religious Statecraft: The Politics of Islam in Iran* (New York: Columbia University Press, 2018), 158.
58. Ahmed S. Hashim, "Civil-Military Relations in Iran: Internal and External Pressures," *Middle East Policy* 25, no. 3 (2018): 50.
59. Tracy Samuel, *The Unfinished History*, 81–83.
60. "Profile: Iran's Revolutionary Guard," BBC, January 3, 2020, https://www.bbc.com/news/world-middle-east-47852262.
61. Ariane M. Tabatabai and Annie Tracy Samuel. "What the Iran-Iraq War Tells Us about the Future of the Iran Nuclear Deal," *International Security* 42, no. 1 (2017): 152–85. Politically, the IRGC was a primary beneficiary of the 2021 election of conservative president Ebrahim Raisi in 2021, as its budget almost doubled from 2020, from 403 trillion rials to 930 trillion rials (US $22 billion), a much larger increase that the conventional Artesh received. Agnes Al-Helou, "Iran More than Doubles Revolutionary Guard's Budget in FY22 Bill," *Defense News*, December 16, 2021, https://www.defensenews.com/global/mideast-africa2021/12/16/iran-more-than-doubles-revolutionary-guards-budget-in-fy22-bill/.
62. Talmadge, *The Dictator's Army*, 153–57; Gaub, *Guardians of the Arab State*, 24–25.
63. Talmadge, *The Dictator's Army*, 232.
64. Caitlin Talmadge, "The Puzzle of Personalist Performance: Iraqi Battlefield Effectiveness in the Iran-Iraq War," *Security Studies* 22, no. 2 (2013): 180–221.
65. Stephen Biddle and Robert Zirkle, "Technology, Civil-Military Relations, and Warfare in the Developing World," *The Journal of Strategic Studies* 19, no. 2 (1996): 171–212.
66. Stephen Biddle, "Victory Misunderstood: What the Gulf War Tells Us about the future of Conflict," *International Security* 21, no. 2 (1996): 139–79.
67. Joseph Sassoon, *Saddam Hussein's Ba'th Party: Inside an Authoritarian Regime* (Cambridge: Cambridge University Press, 2012), 138.
68. Biddle and Zirkle, "Technology, Civil-Military Relations, and Warfare," 182.
69. Pollack, *Arabs at War*, 191.
70. Lawrence Freedman and Efraim Karsh, *The Gulf Conflict 1990–1991: Diplomacy and War in the New World Order* (Princeton, NJ: Princeton University Press, 1993), 107–9.
71. Kevin B. Woods, Williamson Murray, Elizabeth A. Nathan, Laila Sabara, and Ana M. Venegas, *Saddam's General: Perspectives of the Iran-Iraq War* (Washington, DC: Institute for Defense Analysis, 2011), 10; Freidman and Karsh, *The Gulf Conflict*, 20–21.
72. Sassoon, *Saddam Hussein's Ba'th Party*, 129–61.
73. Hashim, *Military Power and State Formation*, 35.
74. Woods et al., *Saddam's General: Perspectives of the Iran-Iraq War*, 9–15, 63–65. Inexplicitly, Kamel returned to Iraq, and Saddam quickly had him killed.
75. Caitlin Talmadge, "The Puzzle of Personalist Performance: Iraqi Battlefield Effectiveness in the Iran-Iraq War," *Security Studies* 22, no. 2 (2013): 180–221.
76. Talmadge, "The Puzzle of Personalist Performance," 192.

77. Pollack, *Arabs at War*, 173.
78. "Saddam Hussein Collection," Conflict Records Research Center, National Defense University, http://www.ndu.edu/inss/index.cfm?secID=101&pageID=4&type=section.
79. Joseph Sassoon and Alissa Walter, "The Iraqi Occupation of Kuwait: New Historical Perspectives," *Middle East Journal* 71, no. 4 (2017): 619–22; Interview 1K Kuwait City, March 1994.
80. C. J. Chivers, "After Retreat, Iraqi Soldiers Fault Officers," *New York Times*, July 2, 2014, https://www.nytimes.com/2014/07/02/world/middleeast/after-retreat-iraqi-soldiers-fault-officers.html.
81. Kenneth M. Pollack, "Iraq Military Situation Report," Washington, DC: The Brookings Institution, June 14, 2014.
82. Toby Dodge, "Can Iraq be Saved?" *Survival* 56, no. 5 (2014): 12–13.
83. Gaub, *Guardians of the Arab State*, 107.
84. Abbas Kadhim, "Rebuilding the Military Under Democratic Control: Iraq," in *The Routledge Handbook of Civil-Military Relations*, eds. Thomas C. Bruneau and Florina Christiana Matei (Oxfordshire: Routledge, 2015), 141.
85. Loveday Morris, "Investigation Finds 50,000 'Ghost' Soldiers in Iraqi Army, Prime Minister Says," *Washington Post*, November 30, 2014, https://www.washingtonpost.com/world/middle_east/investigation-finds-50000-ghost-soldiers-in-iraqi-army-prime-minister-says/2014/11/30/d8864d6c/html; Dominic Evans, "50,000 'Ghost' Soldiers Found on Iraq Payroll," *Arab News*, December 1, 2014.
86. Dodge, "Can Iraq be Saved?" 12.
87. Seth J. Frantzman, "On the Ground in Mosul: The Face of a New Iraqi Military, Forged in War," *Jerusalem Post*, April 5, 2017, https://www.jpost.com/Middle-East/On-the-ground-in-Mosul-The-face-of-a-new-Iraqi-military-forged-in-war-486112.
88. Ben Connable, *An Enduring American Commitment to Iraq*, Santa Monica: Rand Corporation (March 2020), 27.
89. David and Marina Ottoway, *Algeria: The Politics of a Socialist Revolution* (Berkeley: University of California Press, 1970), 198–99.
90. Bahgat Korany, "The Foreign Policy of Algeria," in *The Foreign Policies of Arab States: The Challenge of Change*, eds. Bahgat Korany and Ali E. Hillal Dessouki (Boulder, CO: Westview Press), 118–19.
91. Anthony H. Cordesman, *The North African Military Balance: Force Developments and Regional Challenges* (Washington, DC: Center for Strategic and International Studies, December 7, 2010), 54.
92. Anouar Boukhars, "Reassessing the Power of Regional Security Providers: The Case of Algeria and Morocco," *Middle Eastern Studies* 55, no. 2 (2019): 245–46.
93. Interview 2A, 2005.
94. Kimball Spencer, "Powerful Military Makes Regime Change in Algeria Unlikely," *DW Akademie*, February 14, 2014, http://www.dw.de/dw/0,,9519,00.html.
95. Zindane Zeraoui, "Algeria: Army, Revolution, and Political Power," *Language and Intercultural Communication* 12, no. 2 (2012): 137.

96. Pollack, *Arabs at War*, 385–87; Florence Gaub, "The Libyan Armed Forces between Coup Proofing and Repression," *Journal of Strategic Studies* 36, no. 2 (2013): 232–33.

97. Dirk Vandewalle, *A History of Modern Libya* (Cambridge: Cambridge University Press, 2006), 136. Reports hold that Islamist groups had infiltrated Libya's armed forces, though the extent is not known. Hussein Solomon and Gerrie Swart, "Libya's Foreign Policy in Flux," *African Affairs* 104, no. 416 (2005): 484.

98. Pollack, *Arabs at War*, 358–412.

99. Marc R. DeVore, "Exploiting Anarchy: Violent Entrepreneurs and the Collapse of Libya's Post-Qadhafi Settlement," *Mediterranean Politics* 19, no. 3 (2014): 464.

100. "Libya: Military Movements Banned after Hafter's Border Takeover," *Al Jazeera*, June 20, 2021, https://www.aljazeera.com/news/2021/6/20/libya-haftars-lna-says-it-seized-control-of-border-with-algeria.

101. "Crisis Group Libya Update #2," International Crisis Group, December 24, 2020, https://www.crisisgroup.org/middle-east-north-africa/north-africa/libya/crisis-group-libya-update-2.

102. "Libya: Haftar Stands Down from Military Role before Polls," *Al Jazzera*, September 22, 2021, https://www.aljazeera.com/news/2021/9/22/libya-haftar-suspends-military-role-ahead-of-polls.

103. Pollack, *Arabs at War*, 455–57.

104. Pilster and Bömelt, "Coup Proofing and Military Effectiveness," 15.

105. Hanna Batatu, "Some Observations on the Social Roots of Syrian Ruling Military Groups and the Causes for its Dominance," *The Middle East Journal* 35, no. 3 (1981): 331–44; Patrick Seale, *Asad: The Struggle for the Middle East* (Berkeley: University of California Press, 1988), 106–7; Raymond A. Hinnebusch, *Authoritarian Power and State Formation in Ba'athist Syria: Army, Party, and Peasant* (Boulder, CO: Westview Press, 1990), 158.

106. Author's observations, Syria, 1994, 1996, 1998, 2000.

107. Nassif, "'Second Class," 638.

108. Elizabeth Tsurkov, "Assad's New Syria: A Police State with Rampant Poverty and a Playground for Superpowers," *Ha'aretz*, March 31, 2019, https://www.haaretz.com/israel-news/.premium-assad-s-new-syria-a-police-state-more-aggressive-than-ever-1.7048642.

109. Emile Hokayem, "Iran, the Gulf States and the Syrian Civil War," *Adelphi Papers*, 54, nos. 447–48 (2014): 56.

110. Anton Lavron, "The Efficiency of the Syrian Armed Forces: An Analysis of Russian Assistance," Malcolm H. Kerr Carnegie Middle East Center, March 26, 2020, https://carnegie-mec.org/2020/03/26/efficiency-of-syrian-armed-forces-analysis-of-russian-assistance-pub-81150.

111. Robert Springborg, 2019. "Egypt: An Ineffective Military Beyond Control," in *Civil-Military Relations: Control and Effectiveness Across Regimes*, eds. Thomas C. Bruneau and Aurel Croissant (Boulder, CO: Lynne Reinner Publishers, 2019), 194.

112. Pollock, *Arabs at War*, chap. 1; Allan R. Millett, Williamson Murray, and Kenneth N. Watman, "The Effectiveness of Military Organizations," *International Security* 11, no. 1 (1986): 65–66.

113. Springborg. "Egypt: An Ineffective Military" (2013), 101–3. The author visited Beni Suef Air Base and found that of the thirty-two F-16's based there, only eight were airworthy. The Egyptian pilots were scheduled to fly that day, yet the author was told that the weather was too bad. There was a bit of haze in the air, thus it seemed that even a small loss of visibility meant that the pilots training was so inadequate that they refused to fly in anything but ideal flying conditions. In a similar visit to al-Farad Air Base near the Suez Canal, the author was shown the barracks and the recreation room but was not invited to meet the pilots or see the F-16s stationed there.

114. Afaf Lutfi Al-Sayyid Marsot, *A History of Egypt: From the Arab Conquest to the Present* (Cambridge: Cambridge University Press, 2007), 145, 147–48. Nasser had reason to be suspicious of his fellow Free Officers, as they came from diverse backgrounds. Major Khalid al-Din was a Communist, Major Salah Salim was a Circassian, then–Lieutenant Colonel Anwar Sadat had been imprisoned several times and had ties to the Muslim Brotherhood, and then-Major Amir was an active member of the Muslim Brotherhood (Steven A. Cook, *The Struggle for Egypt: From Nasser to Tahrir Square* [New York: Oxford University Press, 2012], 40); Andrew McGregor, *A Military History of Modern Egypt: From the Ottoman Conquest to the Ramadan War* (Westport, CT: Praeger International Security International, 2006), 249;

115. Ahmed S. Hashim 2011. "The Egyptian Military, Part One," *Middle East Policy* 18, no. 3 (2011): 63–78; Kandil, *The Power Triangle*.

116. Eliezer Be'eri, *Army Officers in Arab Politics and Society* (London: Pall Mall, 1970), 124–25; Cook, *The Struggle for Egypt* (2012), 100. Stories vary on Amir's "suicide." According to one account, from then–minister of state Amin Hewedy, security forces arrested Amir and took him to Nasser's house, and when Nasser left the room, Amir allegedly went into an adjoining bathroom and emerged later stating that he had drank poison. When Nasser was informed, he said, "Amer is a coward, and if he had the courage to commit suicide, we would have not been in this mess in the first place." But Hewedy added, "The doctor was called, however, and Amer was saved. I drove him home." "The End of Amir," *Al-Ahram*, June 11, 1997.

117. Ibrahim A. Karawan, "Egypt," in *The Political Role of the Military: An International Handbook*, eds. Constantine P. Danopoulos and Cynthia Watson (Westport, CT: Greenwood Press, 1996), 113.

118. Talukder Maniruzzaman, *Military Withdrawal from Politics: A Comparative Study* (Cambridge, MA: Ballinger, 1987), 8–9; Hurewitz, *Middle East Politics* (1969), 134; Avi Shlaim, "Jordan: Walking the Tightrope," in *The 1967 Arab-Israeli War: Origins and Consequences*, eds. William Roger Louis and Avi Shlaim (Cambridge: Cambridge University Press, 2012), 113; Toronto, *How Militaries Learn*, 53.

119. Waterbury, *The Egypt of Nasser and Sadat*, 337.

120. Hashim, "The Egyptian Military, Part One," 73; Saad al Shazly, 1980. *The Crossing of the Suez* (San Francisco: American Mideast Research, 1980), 189–93; Kandil, *Soldiers, Spies, and Statesmen*, 124–47.

121. Droz-Vincent, *Military Politics of the Contemporary World*, 71.

122. Springborg, "Egypt: An Ineffective Military," 196–97.
123. Omar Ashour, "Sinai's Insurgency: Implications of Enhanced Guerilla Warfare," *Studies in Conflict and Terrorism* 42, no. 6 (2019): 546.
124. Ashour "Sinai's Insurgency," 554.
125. Springborg "Egypt: An Ineffective Military," 199.
126. Ümit Cizre Sakallioğlu, "The Anatomy of the Turkish Military's Political Autonomy," *Comparative Politics* 29, no. 2 (1997): 159.
127. Graham E. Fuller, *The New Turkish Republic: Turkey as a Pivotal State in the Muslim World* (Washington, DC: United States Institute for Peace, 2008), 116–19.
128. Metin Heper, "Civil-Military Relations in Turkey: Toward a Liberal Model?" *Turkish Studies* 12, no. 2 (2011): 241–52.
129. Aaron Stein, "The Fallout from the Failed Coup," *The American Interest*, August 16, 2018, https://www.the-american-interest.com/2016/08/16/the-fallout-of-the-failed-coup/.
130. Stein, "The Fallout from the Failed Coup,"
131. Interview 18TK, March 2021.
132. Özlem Kayhan Pusane, The Role of Context in Desecuritization: Turkish Foreign Policy Towards Northern Iraq (2008–2017)," *Turkish Studies* 21, no. 3 (2020): 392–413.
133. Lars Haugom, "The Turkish Armed Forces and Civil-military Relations in Turkey after the 15 July 2016 Coup Attempt," *Scandinavian Journal of Military Studies* 2, no. 1 (2019): 1–8.
134. Andrew A. Szarejko, "The Soldier and the Turkish State: Toward a General Theory of Civil-Military Relations," *Perceptions* 19, no. 2 (2014): 139–58.
135. Zeki Sarigil, "The Turkish Military: Principal or Agent?" *Armed Forces & Society* 40, no. 1 (2014): 186–87.
136. Interview 16TK, March 2015.
137. "Turkish Court Sentences 102 War Colleges Staff Members to Life in Prison over Coup Attempt," Stockholm Center for Freedom, August 17, 2018, https://stockholmcf.org/turkish-court-sentences-102-war-colleges-staff-members-to-life-in-prison-over-coup-attempt/. The author visited all the Turkish war colleges numerous times. Before they were closed, they had very high military education standards. A number of the officers that the author spoke to are now serving those sentences.
138. Sebnem Arsu and Dan Bilefsky, "Turkish Reforms Pass by Wide Margins," *New York Times*, September 12, 2010.
139. Simon Tisdal, "Erdoğan is Reaping What He Sowed: Turkey is on the Brink of Disaster in Syria," *The Guardian*, March 2, 2020, https://www.theguardian.com/commentisfree/2020/mar/02/erdogan-turkey-syria-assad.
140. Zeynep Sentek, "Turkey: Strengthening Personalized Political Control," in *Civil-Military Relations: Control and Effectiveness Across Regimes*, eds. Thomas C. Bruneau and Aurel Croissant (Boulder, CO: Lynne Rienner Publishers,2019), 175–90.
141. "Afrin Offensive: Eight Turkish Soldiers Killed in Syria Clashes," BBC News, March 8, 2018, https://www.bbc.com/news/world-middle-east-43251652.
142. Sentek "Turkey: Strengthening Personalized Political Control," 186–87.

143. Jeff Daniels, "Turkey's Afrin Offensive against US-Backed Kurdish Forces 'A Big Mistake,' Says ex-DOD Official," CNBC, January 22, 2018, https://www.cnbc.com/2018/01/22/turkey-could-lose-in-its-attack-on-us-backed-syrian-kurds-says-expert.html.

144. Tahir Ganiev and Vladimir Karyakin, "Military Power of the Republic of Turkey in Regional Projections of Transborder Military Operations," *Central Asia and the Caucasus* 22, no. 3 (2021): 55.

145. Charlotte Gall, "Turkey, Flexing its Muscles, will send Troops to Libya," *New York Times*, January 2, 2020, https://www.nytimes.com/2020/01/02/world/europe/erdogan-turkey-libya.html.

146. Jason Pack and Wolfgang Pusztai, "Turning the Tide: How Turkey Won the War for Tripoli," Policy Paper, The Middle East Institute, November 2020, https://www.mei.edu/sites/default/files/2020-11/Turning%20tPahe%20Tide%20-%20How%20Turkey%20Won%20the%20War%20for%20Tripoli.pdf.

147. Patrick Keddie, "What's Turkey's Role in the Nagorno-Karabakh Conflict?" *Al Jazeera*, October 30, 2020, https://www.aljazeera.com/features/2020/10/30/whats-turkeys-role-in-the-nagorno-karabakh-conflict.

148. Haugom, "The Turkish Armed Forces."

149. Yoram Peri, *Generals in the Cabinet Room* (Washington, DC: United States Institute for Peace Press, 2006), 126.

150. Peri, *Generals in the Cabinet Room*, 127.

151. Amir Oren, "Newly Released Documents Shed Light on Fateful Exchange in The Wake of the Yom Kippur War," *Ha'aretz*, April 26, 2012, https://www.haaretz.com/2012-04-24/ty-article/newly-released-documents-shed-light-on-fateful-exchange-in-the-wake-of-the-yom-kippur-war/0000017f-def5-df9c-a17f-fefd39ea0000.

152. Daniel Byman, *A High Price: The Triumphs and Failures of Israeli Counterterrorism* (Oxford: Oxford University Press, 2011), 248–49.

153. Amir Bar-Or and Karl W. Haltiner, "Democratic Control of the Armed Forces in Israel and Switzerland in Times of Security Threats," in *Existential Threats and Civil-Security Relations*, eds. Oren Barak and Gabriel Sheffer (Lanham, MD: Lexington Books, 2009), 163.

154. Avner Yaniv, "An Imperfect Democracy?" in *National Security and Democracy in Israel*, ed. Avner Yaniv (Boulder, CO: Lynne Rienner Publishers,1993), 92.

155. Brian R. Parkinson, "Israel's Lebanon War: Ariel Sharon and 'Operation Peace for Galilee,'" *Journal of Third World Studies* 24, no. 2 (2007): 67.

156. Peri, *Generals in the Cabinet Room*, 248.

157. Ami Gluska, *The Israeli Military and the Origins of the 1967 War* (London: Routledge, 2007), 16–17.

158. Kobi Michael, "Military Knowledge and Weak Civilian Control in the Reality of Low-Intensity Conflict: The Israeli Case," *Israel Studies* 12, no. 1 (2007): 45.

159. Eva Etzioni-Halevy, "Civil-Military Relations and Democracy: The Case of the Military-Political Elites' Connection in Israel," in *Civil-Military Relations: A Collection of Essays*, ed. Peter Karsten (New York: Garland Publishing, 1998), 118–19.

160. Christopher Sprecher and Karl DeRouen Jr., "Israeli Military Actions and Internalization-Externalization Processes," *The Journal of Conflict Resolution* 46, no. 2 (2002): 255–56.

161. Zeev Maoz, "Threat Perception and Threat Manipulation: The Uses and Misuses of Threats in Israel's National Security, 1949–2008," in *Existential Threats and Civil-Security Relations*, eds. Oren Barak and Gabriel Sheffer (Lanham, MD: Lexington Books, 2009), 209.

162. Maoz, *Defending the Holy Land*, 536.

163. Sami Cohen, "Civilian Control over the Army in Israel and France," in *Militarism in Israel*, eds. Gabriel Sheffer and Oren Barak (Bloomington: Indiana University Press, 2010), 243.

164. Millett, Murray, and Watman, "The Effectiveness of Military Organizations," 53.

165. Byman, *A High Price*, 249.

166. Amos Harel and Yaniv Kubovich, "Despite Faults, Iran Nuclear Deal Works, Israeli Military Chief tells Haaretz," *Haaretz*, March 30, 2018, https://www.haaretz.com/israel-news/.premium-israeli-military-chief-despite-its-faults-iran-nuclear-deal-works-1.5962099.

167. Gawdat Bahgat, "Military Security and Political Stability in the Gulf," *Arab Studies Quarterly* 17, no. 3 (1995): 55–61.

168. Pollack, *Arabs at War*, 433.

169. David Rundell, *Vision or Mirage: Saudi Arabia at the Crossroads* (London: I. B. Tauris, 2021), 120.

170. Rundell, *Vision or Mirage*, 212.

171. Interview 2SA, 1989.

172. Pollack, *Arabs at War*, 435–36.

173. Zoltan Barany, *Armies of Arabia: Military Politics and Effectiveness in the Gulf* (New York: Oxford University Press, 2021), 47.

174. Interview 3SA, 2011.

175. "Washington's Sunni Allies Disgruntled," Paris Intelligence Online, December 10, 2014, OpenSource, https://www.opensource.gov/portal/server.pt/gateway/PTARGS_0_0_200_203_121123_43/content/Display/EUN2014121056233795#index=10&searchKey=17384351&rpp=10.

176. Barany, *Armies of Arabia*, 254.

177. Interview 4SA, 2011.

178. Ben Brimelow, "Saudi Arabia has the best Equipment Money Can Buy, but It's Still Not a Threat to Iran," *Business Insider*, December 16, 2017, http://www.businessinsider.com/saudi-arabia-iran-yemen-military-proxy-war-2017-12.

179. Brimelow, "Saudi Arabia Has the Best Equipment."

180. Barany, *Armies of Arabia*, 284.

181. Emile Hokayem and David B. Roberts, "The War in Yemen," *Survival* 58, no. 6 (2016): 166.

182. Helene Cooper, Thomas Gibbons-Neff, and Eric Schmitt, "Army Security Forces Secretly Help Saudis Combat Threat from Yemen Rebels," *New York Times*,

May 3, 2018, https://www.nytimes.com/2018/05/03/us/politics/green-berets-saudi-yemen-border-houthi.html.

183. Hokayem and Roberts, "The War in Yemen," 178.

184. Neal Partrick, "Saudi Arabia's Efforts at Reforming its Armed Forces may be more about Politics and PR than Substantive Change," Carnegie Endowment for International Peace, May 31, 2018, https://carnegieendowment.org/sada/76487.

185. Gregory D. Johnsen, "The End of Yemen," The Brookings Institution, March 25, 2021, https://www.brookings.edu/blog/order-from-chaos/2021/03/25/the-end-of-yemen/.

186. Fred H. Lawson, "Why Foreign Military Interventions Prolong Civil Wars: Lessons from Yemen," *International Politics* (2021), https://doi.org/10.1057/s41311-021-00357-6.

187. Rundell, *Vision or Mirage*, 121.

188. Ibrahim Jalal, "The UAE May Have Withdrawn from Yemen, but Its Influence Remains Strong," *Middle East Institute*, February 25, 2020, https://www.mei.edu/publications/uae-may-have-withdrawn-yemen-its-influence-remains-strong.

189. Roberts also notes the lessons that the UAE learned from the east to which Kuwait was overrun by Iraq in 1990. David B. Roberts, "Bucking the Trend: The UAE and the Development of Military Capabilities in the Arab World," *Security Studies* 29, no. 2 (2020): 301–34.

190. Barany, *Armies of Arabia*, 256.

191. Toronto, *How Militaries Learn*, chap. 4.

192. Melissa Dalton and Hijab Shah, "Evolving UAE Military and Foreign Security Cooperation: Path Toward Military Professionalism," Malcom H. Kerr Carnegie Middle East Center or the Carnegie Endowment for International Peace, January 2020, 9, https://carnegieendowment.org/files/DaltonShah_UAEMilitary.pdf#:~:text=After%20two%20decades%20of%20concerted%20investment%20and%20operational,while%20there%20may%20be%20variance%20across%20the%20force.4.

193. Thomas Juneau, "The UAE and the War in Yemen: From Surge to Recalibration," *Survival* 62, no. 4 (2020): 196.

194. Daniel Byman, "Yemen's Disastrous War," *Survival* 60, no. 5 (2018): 154.

195. Andreas Krieg, "The UAE's 'Dogs of War': Boosting a Small State's Regional Power Projection," *Small Wars & Insurgencies* 33, nos. 1–2 (2022): 165.

196. Interview 1Y, 2005.

197. Interview 1Y, March 2005.

198. "The Army Deals Heavy Blows to Al-Qa'ida in Abyan and Controls Parts of Al-Kud," *Al-Mu'tamar.net* (in Arabic), OpenSource Center, August 29, 2011.

199. Mohammed Al-Kibsi, "Yemen Government and Defected Army Exchange Accusations of Supporting Al-Qaeda," *Yemen Observer*, September 12, 2011.

200. غادر الغالبية العظمى من أفراد اللواء الثالث مشاة جبلي يومي الاثنين والثلاثاء من محافظة مأر. *Al'ezma Mn Afrad Allwa' Althalth Mshah Jbly Ywmy Alathnyn Walthlatha' Mn Mhafzh Marb*, "Soldiers from Third Mountain Brigade Leaving After Looting Weapons and Equipment, 2013).

201. Jeffrey S. McKitrick, "Analytical Tools and Techniques," in *Net Assessment and Military Strategy: Retrospective and Prospective Essays*, ed. Thomas Mahnken (Amherst, NY: Cambria Press, 2020), 195.

202. Risa Brooks, *Shaping Strategy: The Civil-Military Politics of Strategic Assessment* (Princeton, NJ: Princeton University Press, 2008), 21.

203. Scott Sigmund Gartner, *Strategic Assessment in War* (New Haven, CT: Yale University Press, 1997), 45–46.

204. Branislav Slantchev, "The Principle of Convergence in Wartime Negotiations," *The American Political Science Review* 97, no. 4 (2003): 622.

205. Brooks, *Shaping Strategy*, 4.

206. Brooks *Shaping Strategy*, 42–44

207. Brooks, *Shaping Strategy*, 177–91.

208. Matthew Moten, "A Broken Dialog: Rumsfeld, Shinseki, and Civil-Military Tension," in *American Civil-Military Relations: The Soldier and the State in a New Era*, eds. Suzanne C. Nielsen and Don M. Snider (Baltimore, MD: Johns Hopkins University Press, 2009), 42–71; Brooks, *Shaping Strategy*, 226–55); Mackubin Thomas Owens, *US Civil-Military Relations after 9/11: Renegotiating the Civil-Military Bargain* (New York: Continuum, 2011), 107–17.

209. Stephen Philip Cohen, *The Idea of Pakistan* (Washington, DC: The Brookings Institution, 2004), 293; Brooks, *Shaping Strategy* (2008), 196–207; Hasan Askari Rizvi, "Civil-Military Relations in Contemporary Pakistan," *Survival* 40, no. 2 (1998): 105.

210. Quoted in Campbell Craig and Fredrik Logevall, *America's Cold War: The Politics of Insecurity* (Cambridge: MA: Harvard University Press, 2009), 256.

211. McGregor, *A Military History of Modern Egypt*, 260; Clark, *Yemen: Dancing on the Heads of Snakes*, 94–95.

212. Kandil, *Soldiers, Spies, and Statesmen*, 70–72, 79.

213. Laura M. James, "Egypt: Dangerous Illusions," in *The 1967 Arab-Israeli War: Origins and Consequences*, eds William Roger Louis and Avi Shlaim (Cambridge: Cambridge University Press, 2012), 66.

214. Brooks, *Shaping Strategy*, 62–142.

215. Joel Gordon, *Nasser's Blessed Movement: Egypt's Free Officers and the July Revolution* (New York: Oxford University Press, 1992), 45.

216. Risa Brooks, "An Autocracy at War: Explaining Egypt's Military Effectiveness, 1967 and 1973," *Security Studies* 15, no. 3 (2006): 396–430.

217. Interview 6E, 2007; Interview 8E, 2012.

218. Amirah Ibrahim, "Messages of Warning," *Al-Ahram*, May 1, 2021.

219. Ellis Goldberg, "A New Political Dilemma for Egypt's Ruling Military," *Washington Post*, June 2, 2014, https://www.washingtonpost.com/news/monkey-cage/wp/2014/06/02/a-new-political-dilemma-for-egypts-ruling-military/.

220. Hurewitz, *Middle East Politics*, 373.

221. Amos Perlmutter, "The Israeli Army in Politics: The Persistence of the Civilian Over the Military," *World Politics* 20, no. 4 (1968): 624.

222. Avi Shlaim, "Jordan: Walking the Tightrope," in *The 1967 Arab-Israeli War: Origins and Consequences*, eds. William Roger Louis and Avi Shlaim (Cambridge:

Cambridge University Press, 2012), 101–2; Moshe Shemesh, "The IDF Raid on Samu': The Turning Point in Jordan's Relations with Israel and the West Bank Palestinians," *Israel Studies* 7, no. 1 (2002): 139–67.

223. Gluska, *The Israeli Military*, 80.

224. Hagai Tsoref, "Golda Meir's Leadership in the Yom Kippur War," *Israel Studies* 23, no. 1 (2018): 50–72.

225. Sami Cohen, "Civilian Control over the Army in Israel and France," in *Militarism in Israel*, eds. Gabriel Sheffer and Oren Barak (Bloomington: Indiana University Press, 2010), 243.

226. Shlaim "Jordan: Walking the Tightrope," 23; Richard B. Parker, *The Politics of Miscalculation in the Middle East* (Bloomington: Indiana University Press, 1993).

227. Patrick E. Tyler, *Fortress Israel: The Inside Story of the Military Elite who run the Country: and Why They Can't Make Peace* (New York: Farrar, Straus, and Giroux, 2012), 154.

228. Yehezkel Dror, "Our Primitive Policy-Making," *Ha'aretz*, February 6, 2010, https://www.haaretz.com/2010-06-02/ty-article/our-primitive-policy-making/0000017f-db3f-db5a-a57f-db7f03100000.

229. Yaakov Katz, "Questions Abound Over Planning of Sea Op," *Jerusalem Post*, June 1, 2010, https://www.jpost.com/Israel/Questions-abound-over-planning-of-sea-op.

230. Pnina Lahav, "A Small Nation Goes to War: Israel's Cabinet Authorization of the 1956 War," *Israel Studies* 15, no. 3 (2010): 61–86.

231. Lahav, "A Small Nation Goes to War," 79.

232. Guy Laron, "'Logic Dictates That They May Attack When They Feel They Can Win:' The 1955 Czech-Egyptian Arms Deal, the Egyptian Army, and Israeli Intelligence," *Middle East Journal* 63, no. 1 (2009): 69–84.

233. Dima Adamsky, *The Culture of Military Innovation: The Impact of Cultural Factors on the Revolution in Military Affairs in Russia, the US, and Israel* (Stanford, CA: Stanford University Press, 2010), 97–98.

234. Adamsky, *The Culture of Military Innovation*, 98–99.

235. Anshel Pfeffer, "Israeli Politicians are Playing Number Games With a War against Iran," *Ha'aretz*, April 3, 2012, https://www.haaretz.com/2012-04-03/ty-article/israeli-politicians-are-playing-number-games-with-a-war-against-iran/000017f-e108-d568-ad7f-f36bfdc50000.

236. Amos Harel and Avi Issacharoff, "Abbas Emerging as New Breed of Arab Leader," *Ha'aretz*, September 25, 2011, https://www.haaretz.com/2011-09-25/ty-article/abbas-emerging-as-new-breed-of-arab-leader/0000017f-dc32-d3ff-a7ff-fdb2faa20000.

237. Jodi Rudoren, "Israeli Army Chief Says He Believes Iran Won't Build Bomb," *New York Times*, April 26, 2012, https://www.nytimes.com/2012/04/26/world/middleeast/israeli-army-chief-says-he-believes-iran-wont-build-bomb.html.

238. Isabel Kershner, "New Israeli Partner Offers Moderate Voice on Iran," *New York Times*, May 8, 2012. Obviously, any distance between the IDF and the political leadership will also depend on the personality of the prime minister. Unlike Netanyahu, who has consistently appeared skeptical about the outcome and purpose

of Israeli-Palestinian negotiations, former Prime Minister Yitzhak Rabin, himself a former military commander, began to favor a political avenue along with a military response to Palestinian acts against Israel. Efraim Inbar, "Yitzhak Rabin and Israel's National Security," *The Journal of Strategic Studies* 20, no. 2 (1997): 32–33.

239. Amos Harel, "Of all the Threats Facing Israel, Army believes that Palestinian Front is 'Most Volatile," *Haaretz*, January 27, 2018, https://www.haaretz.com/israel-news/.premium-israeli-army-s-threat-map-focuses-on-iran-lebanon-and-syria-1.5766963.

240. Chaya Eisenberg, "'Iran, Iran, Iran:' in Fox Interview, Netanyahu Identifies Greatest Threat to Israel," *Jerusalem Post*, March 12, 2018, https://www.jpost.com/Israel-News/Benjamin-Netanyahu/Iran-Iran-Iran-In-Fox-interview-Netanyahu-identifies-greatest-threat-to-Israel-544837.

241. Philipp O. Amour, "Israel, the Arab Spring, and the Unfolding Regional Order in the Middle East: A Strategic Assessment," *British Journal of Middle East Studies* 44, no. 3 (2017): 301.

242. Ronen Bergman and Patrick Kingsley, "Israeli Officials Cast Doubt on Threat to Attack Iran," *New York Times*, December 18, 2021, https://www.nytimes.com/2021/12/18/world/middleeast/israel-iran-nuclear-attack.html.

243. Interview 7TR, 2004.

244. Brooks, *Shaping Strategy*, 209–18.

245. Jan Kasapoğlu and Sinan Ülgen, "Operation Olive Branch: a Political-Military Assessment," EDAM Centre for Economics and Foreign Policy Studies: (January 2018): 14. http://edam.org.tr/wp-content/uploads/2018/01/Operation-Olive Branch-01.pdf.

246. Jenny White, *Muslim Nationalism and the New Turks* (Princeton, NJ: Princeton University Press, 2013), 77–79; Ümit Cizre, "A New Politics of Engagement: The Turkish Military, Society, and the AKP," in *Democracy, Islam, and Secularism in Turkey*, eds. Ahmet T. Kuru and Alfred Stepan (New York: Columbia University Press, 2012), 122–48.

247. Graham E. Fuller, *The New Turkish Republic: Turkey as a Pivotal State in the Muslim World* (Washington, DC: United States Institute for Peace, 2008), 116–17.

248. Philip Robins, "Confusion at Home, Confusion Abroad: Turkey between Copenhagen and Iraq," *International Affairs* 79, no. 3 (2003): 557–59.

249. Banu Eligür, *The Mobilization of Political Islam in Turkey* (Cambridge: Cambridge University Press, 2010).

250. Fuller, *The New Turkish Republic*, 90.

251. Can Kasapoğlu, Turkey Prepares for Action in Northeast Syria: Military-Strategic Assessment. EDAM Defense Intelligence Sentinel, August 10, 2019, https://edam.org.tr/en/turkey-prepares-for-action-in-northeast-syria-military-strategic-assessment/; Jennifer Cafarella, "Turkey Commits to Idlib," Institute for the Study of War, March 18, 2020, http://www.understandingwar.org/backgrounder/turkey-commits-idlib.

252. Kevin Sullivan and Greg Jaffe, "Collapse of Iraqi Army a Failure for Nation's Premier and for US Military," *Washington Post*, June 12, 2014, https://www.washingtonpost.com/world/national-security/collapse-of-iraqi-army-a-failure-for-nations

-premier-and-for-us-military/2014/06/12/25191bc0-f24f-11e3-914c-1fbd0614e2d4_story.html.

253. "Iraq Army Advances Toward Rebel-Held Tikrit," *Al-Jazeera*, August 19, 2014.

254. Loveday Morris and Missy Ryan, "After More than $1.6 billion in US Aid, Iraq's Army Still Struggles," *Washington Post*, June 10, 2016, https://www.washingtonpost.com/world/middle_east/iraqs-army-is-still-a-mess-two-years-after-a-stunning-defeat/2016/06/09/0867f334-1868-11e6-971a-dadf9ab18869_story.html?utm_term=.f6d2b9cad514.

255. Anthony H. Cordesman, "Annex One: Creating Effective Iraqi Security Forces," in "Iraq: The Missing Keystone in US Policy in the Gulf," eds. Anthony Cordesman and Grace Hwang, Center for Strategic and International Studies, April 29, 2021, https://csis-website-prod.s3.amazonaws.com/s3fs-public/publication/210427_Burke_Iraq_Missing_Keystone_ANNEX_1.pdf?jrRqYd7.CWz99FayFnJYQEBF_tSiohwy.

256. Andrew England, "Iraq's Shia Militias: Capturing the State," *Financial Times*, July 30, 2018, https://www.ft.com/content/ba4f7bb2-6d4d-11e8-852d-d8b934ff5ffa.

257. England, "Iraq's Shia Militias."

258. Garrett Nada and Mattisan Rowan, "Part 2: Pro-Iran Militias in Iraq," The Wilson Center, April 27, 2018.

259. Paul E. Lenze Jr., *Civil-Military Relations in the Islamic World* (Lanham, MD: Lexington Books, 2016), 10.

260. One way to nuance the reasons for continued security assistance is to change the language. So instead of a "coup," the military exercised a "off-sequence, military-assisted temporary adjustment in the state balance of central political authority," as noted in an earlier chapter. Possibly the Chief of Staff of the Sudanese military could help. General Abdel Fattah al-Buran denied that his military had executed a coup in October 2021. Instead, said the general, it was a "correction of course, and a correction of the power transition." Or something like that.

261. Barany, *Armies of Arabia*, 149.

262. Author's visits to Beni Suef Airbase, Egypt, 1999, Royal Moroccan Air Force Base, Kenitra, 2014, 2018, Royal Moroccan Air Force Base, Sidi Slimane, 1999, 2001, Tunisian Air Force Bizerte-Sidi Ahmed Air Base, 2011, Royal Jordanian Air Force Muwaffaq Salti Air Base, 2016.

263. Barany *Armies of Arabia*, 165–71.

264. Jodi Vittori, "A Mutual Extortion Racket: The Military-Industrial Complex and US Foreign Policy—The Cases of Saudi Arabia and UAE," Transparency International Defense & Security Program, 2019, https://www.transparency.org.uk/publications/usa-defence-arms-industry-corruption-risk-exports saudi-uae-middle-east.

265. Interview 1E, 2009; Adam Roston, and David Rohde, "Egyptian Army's Business Side Blurs Lines of U.S. Military Aid," *New York Times*, March 5, 2011.

266. James V. Grimaldi, and Robert O'Harrow, "In Egypt, Corruption Cases had an American Root," *Washington Post*, October 20, 2011, https://www.washingtonpost.com/investigations/in-egypt-corruption-had-an-american-root/2011/10/07/gIQAApWoyL_story.html.

267. MacFarquhar and Al-Naggar, "Answering the Public."
268. Stephanie Cronin, *Armies and State-Building in the Modern Middle East: Politics, Nationalism, and Military Reform* (London: I. B. Tauris, 2014), 183–200.
269. Kate Gillespie, and Gwenn Okruhlik, "Cleaning up Corruption in the Middle East," *Middle East Journal* 42 (Winter 1988): 76.
270. "Global: Military Corruption in Middle East and North African States," Corruption.net, October 29, 2015, https://corruption.net/global-military-corruption-in-middle-eastern-and-north-african-states/; Droz-Vincent, *Military Politics of the Contemporary World*, 135.
271. Fred H. Lawson, "Why Foreign Military Interventions Prolong Civil Wars: Lessons from Yemen," *International Politics* (2021), https://doi.org/10.1057/s41311-021-00357-6. The distinction between "security assistance" and "foreign intervention" is a slight one, to be sure. Both are often related, as both Saudi Arabia and the UAE sent troops, but additionally transferred military equipment to the Yemeni military units that they supported.
272. May Darwich, "Escalation in Failed Military Interventions: Saudi and Emirati Quagmires in Yemen," *Global Policy* 11 (February 2020): 103–12.
273. Timothy Robbins, Hijab Shah, and Melissa Dalton, "US Support for Saudi Military Operations in Yemen," Center for Strategic and International Studies, March 23, 2018, https://www.csis.org/analysis/us-support-saudi-military-operations-yemen#:~:text=Since%202015%2C%20the%20United%20States%20has%20provided%20intelligence%2C,territorial%20integrity%20from%20incursion%20by%20Yemen-based%20Houthi%20rebels.
274. Levent Kenez, "Statistics Show Turkish Arms Sales to Africa Boomed in 2021," *Nordic Monitor*, December 10, 2021, https://nordicmonitor.com/2021/12/statistics-show-turkeys-arms-sales-to-africa-boomed-in-2021/.
275. Mara E. Karlin, *Building Militaries in Fragile States: Challenges for the United States* (Philadelphia: University of Pennsylvania Press, 2018), 4–19.
276. Karlin, *Building Militaries in Fragile States*, chaps. 4–5.
277. Karlin, *Building Militaries in Fragile States*, 183–84
278. Noureddine Jebnoun, "Tunisia: Patterns and Implications of Civilian Control," in *Civil-Military Relations: Control and Effectiveness Across Regimes*, eds. Thomas C. Bruneau and Aurel Croissant (Boulder, CO: Lynne Rienner Publishers, 2019), 132–36.
279. Imad Harb, "Why Would Hezbollah Never Integrate in the Lebanese Army?" *Tawazun Index of Arab Civil-Military Relations*, March 16, 2022, http://tawazun.net/english/blog1.php?id=634-ed.
280. "Congress and the War in Yemen: Oversight and Legislation, 2015–2021," Congressional Research Service, February 10, 2022, R45046.pdf (fas.org).
281. Fredric Wehrey and Michelle Dunne, "Rebalancing America's Security Engagement with Arab States," *Tawazun Index of Arab Civil-Military Relations*, June 29, 2021, http://tawazun.net/english/blog1.php?id=624-tw.

CHAPTER SIX

1. According to defense spending as a percent of GDP, the CIA World Factbook, accessed May 10, 2021.
2. Amin Saikal, *The Rise and Fall of the Shah: Iran from Autocracy to Religious Rule*
(Princeton, NJ: Princeton University Press, 1980): 157–58; Hazem Kandil, *The Power Triangle: Military, Security, and Politics in Regime Change* (New York: Oxford University Press, 2016): 64.
3. Samuel P. Huntington, *The Third Wave: Democratization in the Late Twentieth Century* (Norman: University of Oklahoma Press, 1991).
4. "Freedom in the World 2018 Scores," Freedom House, https://freedomhouse.org/report/freedom-world/2018/scores#:~:text=Freedom%20in%20the%20World%202018%20Scores%20%20,%20%2025%20%2069%20more%20rows%2.
5. "Freedom in the World 2021: Democracy Under Siege," Freedom House, 2021, https://freedomhouse.org/report/freedom-world/2021/democracy-under-siege.
6. Mark Harrison and Nikolaus Wolf, "The Frequency of Wars," *The Economic History Review* 65, no. 3 (2012): 1055–76.
7. Azar Gal, "Is War Declining—and Why?" *Journal of Peace Research* 50, no. 2 (2013): 149–57.
8. Aaron Clauset, "Trends and Fluctuations in the Severity of Interstate Wars," *Science and Advances* 4, no. 2 (2018): 1–9.
9. Scott Straus, "Wars do End! Changing Patterns of Political Violence in Sub-Saharan Africa." *African Affairs* 111, no. 443 (2012): 179–201.

Selected Bibliography

Abadi, Jacob. "US-Syria Relations in the Shadow of Cold War and Détente." *Middle Eastern Studies* 57, no. 4 (2021): 534–52.
Abdel-Malik, Anouar. *Egypt: The Military Society, The Army Regime, the Left, and Social Change Under Nasser.* New York: Random House, 1968.
Abu-Bader, S., and Aamer S. Abu-Qarn. "Government Expenditures, Military Spending, and Economic Growth: Causality Evidence from Egypt, Israel, and Syria." *Journal of Policy Modeling* 25, nos. 6–7 (2003): 567–83.
Abul-Magd, Zeinab. *Militarizing the Nation: The Army, Business, and Revolution in Egypt.* New York: Columbia University Press, 2016.
Abu-Qarn, Aamer S. "The Defence–Growth Nexus Revisited: Evidence from the Israeli–Arab Conflict *Defence and Peace Economics* 21, no. 4 (2010): 291–300.
Ahmad, Feroz. *The Young Turks: The Committee of Union and Progress in Turkish Politics, 1908–1914.* New York: Columbia University Press, 2010.
Albrecht, Holger. "Military Uprisings in Popular Mass Uprisings." *Political Science Quarterly* 134, no. 2 (2019): 303–28.
Albrecht, Holger, and Ferdinand Eibl. "How to Keep Officers in the Barracks: Causes, Agents, and Types of Military Coups." *International Studies Quarterly* 62, no. 2 (2018): 315–28.
Alexander, Christopher. *Tunisia: Stability and Reform in the Modern Maghreb.* London: Routledge, 2010.
Alley, April Longley. "Assessing (In)security after the Arab Spring: The Case of Yemen." *PS: Political Science & Politics* 46, no. 4 (2013): 721–26.
Amanat, Abbas. *Iran: A Modern History.* New Haven, CT: Yale University Press, 2017.
Amin, Galil. *Egypt in the Era of Hosni Mubarak, 1981–2011.* Cairo: The American University in Cairo Press, 2011.
Amour, Philipp O. "Israel, the Arab Spring, and the Unfolding Regional Order in the Middle East: A Strategic Assessment." *British Journal of Middle East Studies* 44, no. 3 (2017): 293–309.

Angrist, Michele Penner. "Understanding the Success of Mass Civic Protest in Tunisia." *Middle East Journal* 67, no. 4 (2013): 547–646.
Ashour, Omar. "Sinai's Insurgency: Implications of Enhanced Guerilla Warfare." *Studies in Conflict and Terrorism* 42, no. 6 (2019): 541–58.
Aydinli, Ersel. "Ergenekon, New Pacts, and the Decline of the Turkish 'Inner State.'" *Turkish Studies* 12, no. 2 (2011): 227–39.
Badran, Tony. "Lebanon's Militia Wars." chap. 3 in *Lebanon: Liberation, Conflict, and Crisis*, edited by Barry Rubin, 35–62. New York: Palgrave Macmillan, 2009.
Bahgat, Gawdat. "Military Security and Political Stability in the Gulf." *Arab Studies Quarterly* 17, no. 3 (1995): 55–61.
Baker, Raymond William. *Egypt's Uncertain Revolution under Nasser and Sadat*. Cambridge, MA: Harvard University Press, 1978.
Barak, Oren. *The Lebanese Army: A National Institution in a Divided Society*. Albany: State University of New York Press, 2009.
Barak, Oren, and Gabriel Sheffer. "The Study of Civil-Military Relations in Israel: A New Perspective." *Israel Studies* 12, no. 1 (2007): 1–27.
Baram, Amazia. "The Ruling Political Elite in Bathi Iraq, 1968–1986: The Changing Features of a Collective Profile." *International Journal of Middle East Studies* 21, no. 4 (1989): 447–93.
Barany, Zoltan. *The Soldier and the Changing State*. Princeton, NJ: Princeton University Press, 2012.
———. *How Armies Respond to Revolutions, and Why*. Princeton, NJ: Princeton University Press, 2016.
———. *Armies of Arabia: Military Politics and Effectiveness in the Gulf*. New York: Oxford University Press, 2021.
Batatu, Hanna, *The Old Social Classes and the Revolutionary Movements of Iraq*. Princeton, NJ: Princeton University Press, 1978.
Baylouny, Anne Marie. "Militarizing Welfare: Neo-Liberalism and Jordanian Policy." *The Middle East Journal* 62, no. 2 (2008): 277–303.
Be'eri, Eliezer. *Army Officers in Arab Politics and Society*. London: Pall Mall, 1970.
Bellin, Eva. "The Robustness of Authoritarianism in the Middle East: Exceptionalism in Comparative Perspective," *Comparative Politics* 36, no. 2 (2004): 139–57.
———. "Reconsidering the Robustness of Authoritarianism in the Middle East: Lessons from the Arab Spring." *Comparative Politics* 44, no. 2 (2012): 127–50.
Ben Meir, Yehuda. *Civil-Military Relations in Israel*. New York: Columbia University Press, 1995.
Beshara, Adel. *Lebanon: The Politics of Frustration—the Failed Coup of 1961*. London: Routledge Curzon, 2005.
Biddle, Stephen, and Stephen Long. "Democracy and Military Effectiveness: A Deeper Look." *The Journal of Conflict Resolution* 48, no. 4 (2004): 525–46.
Blackwell, Stephen. *British Military Intervention and the Struggle for Jordan*. New York: Routledge, 2009.
Blanche, Ed. "Algeria: The Battle Within: President Bouteflika Clips the Wings of Algeria's Long-Powerful Military." *The Middle East* 367 (2006): 24.

Boukhars, Anouar. "Reassessing the Power of Regional Security Providers: The Case of Algeria and Morocco." *Middle Eastern Studies* 55, no. 2 (2019): 242–60.
Brooks, Risa. "Making Military Might: Why do States Fail and Succeed: A Review Essay." *International Security* 28, no. 2 (2003): 149–91.
———. *Shaping Strategy: The Civil-Military Politics of Strategic Assessment*. Princeton, NJ: Princeton University Press, 2008.
———. "Abandoned at the Palace: Why the Tunisian Military Defected from the Ben Ali Regime in January 2011." *Journal of Strategic Studies* 36, no. 2 (2013): 205–20.
Burak, Begüm. "The Role of the Turkish Military in Politics: To Guard Whom and from What?" *European Journal of Economic and Political Studies* 4, no. 1 (2011): 143–69.
Byrne, Malcolm. "The Road to Intervention." In *Mohammad Mosaddeq and the 1953 Coup in Iran*, edited by Mark J. Gasiorowski and Malcolm Byrne, 201–26. Syracuse: Syracuse University Press, 2004.
Carleton, Alford. "The Syrian Coups d'état of 1949. *The Middle East Journal* 4, no. 1 (1950): 1–11.
Carr, Rebecca, and Constantine Danopolis. "The Military and Politics in a Theocratic State: Iran as a Case Study." *Armed Forces & Society* 24, no. 2 (1997): 269–88.
Chaney, Eric. "Democratic Change in the Arab World: Past and Present." Paper prepared for the Brookings Panel on Economic Activity, March 22–23, 2012.
Chubin, Shahram. *Iran's Nuclear Ambitions*. Washington, DC: Carnegie endowment for International Peace, 2006.
Chubin, Shahram, and Charles Tripp. *Iran and Iraq at War*. Boulder, CO: Westview Press, 1988)
Cilliler, Yavuz. "Popular Determinate on Civil-Military Relations in Turkey." *Arab Studies Quarterly* 38, no. 2 (2016): 500–20.
Cizre, Ümit. "Parameters and Strategies of Islam-State Interaction in Republican Turkey." *International Journal of Middle East Studies* 28, no. 2 (1996): 231–51.
———. "A New Politics of Engagement: The Turkish Military, Society, and the AKP." In *Democracy, Islam, and Secularism in Turkey*, edited by Ahmet T. Kuru and Alfred Stepan, 122–48. New York: Columbia University Press, 2012.
Clarke, Victoria. *Yemen: Dancing on the Heads of Snakes*. New Haven, CT: Yale University Press, 2010.
Clausen, Maria-Louise. "Justifying Military Intervention: Yemen as a Failed State." *Third World Quarterly* 40, no. 3 (2019): 488–502.
Cohen, Amichai, and Stuart Alan Cohen. "Beyond the Conventional Civil–Military "Gap": Cleavages and Convergences in Israel." *Armed Forces & Society* 48, no. 1 (2022): 164–84.
Cohen, Stuart. *The Scroll or the Sword? Dilemmas of Religion and Military Service in Israel*. Amsterdam: Harwood Academic Publishers, 1997.
Cook, Steven A. *Ruling but not Governing: The Military and Political Development in Egypt, Algeria, and Turkey*. Baltimore: Johns Hopkins University Press, 2007.
———. *The Struggle for Egypt: From Nasser to Tahrir Square*. New York: Oxford University Press, 2012.

Cooper, Malcolm. "The Legacy of Atatürk: Turkish Political Structures and Policy-Making." *International Affairs* 78, no. 1 (2002): 115–28.
Cooper, Mark N. "The Demilitarization of the Egyptian Cabinet." *International Journal of Middle East Studies* 14, no. 2 (1982): 203–25.
Cordesman, Anthony H. *"Saudi Arabia: National Security in a Troubled Region.* Santa Barbara, CA: Praeger Security International, 2009.
———. *The North African Military Balance: Force Developments and Regional Challenges*. Washington, DC: Center for Strategic and International Studies, December 7, 2010.
Cronin, Stephanie. *Armies and State-Building in the Modern Middle East: Politics, Nationalism, and Military Reform*. London: I. B. Tauris, 2014.
Dann, Uriel. *King Hussein and the Challenge of Arab Radicalism: Jordan, 1955–1967*. New York: Oxford University Press, 1989.
Darwich, May. Escalation in Failed Military Interventions: Saudi and Emirati Quagmires in Yemen." *Global Policy* 11, February (2020): 103–12.
Davidson, Christopher M. *Dubai: The Vulnerability of Success*. New York: Columbia University Press, 2008.
De Bruin, Erica. *How to Prevent Coups d'état: Counterbalancing and Regime Survival.* Ithaca, NY: Cornell University Press, 2020.
Demirel, Tanel. "Soldiers and Civilians: The Dilemma of Turkish Democracy." *Middle Eastern Studies*, 40, no. 1 (2004): 127–50.
Desli, E, and A. Gkoulgkoutsika. "Military Spending and Economic Growth: A Panel Data Investigation." *Economic Change and Restructuring* 54, no. 3 (2021): 781–806.
DeVore, Marc R. "Exploiting Anarchy: Violent Entrepreneurs and the Collapse of Libya's Post-Qadhafi Settlement." *Mediterranean Politics* 19, no. 3 (2014): 463–70.
Dilman, Bradford L. *State and Private Sector in Algeria: The Politics of Rent-Seeking and Failed Development*. Boulder, CO: Westview Press, 2000.
Dodge, Toby. "Can Iraq be Saved?" *Survival* 56, no. 5 (2014): 7–20.
Dresch, Paul. *Tribes, Governments, and History in Yemen*. Oxford: Clarendon Press, 1989.
Droz-Vincent, Philippe. "From Political to Economic Actors: The Changing Role of Middle Eastern Armies." In *Debating Arab Authoritarianism: Dynamics and Durability in Nondemocratic Regimes*, edited by Oliver Schlumberger, 195–214. Stanford, CA: Stanford University Press, 2006.
———. "The Syrian Military and the 2011 Uprising," in *Armies and Insurgencies in the Arab Spring*, edited by Holger Albrecht, Aurel Croissant, and Fred H. Lawson, 168–84. Philadelphia: University of Pennsylvania Press, 2016.
———. *Military Politics of the Contemporary World.* Cambridge: Cambridge University Press, 2021.
———. "Fighting for a Monopoly on Governance: How the 'Asad State 'Won' the Syrian War and to What Extent." *The Middle East Journal* 75, no. 1 (2021): 33–54.
Elguettaa, Belkacem, "The Military's Political Role in the New Algeria." In *The Politics of Military Authoritarianism in North Africa*, edited by Yezid Sayigh.

Malcolm H. Kerr Carnegie Middle East Center, March 17, 2021. https://carnegie-mec.org/2021/03/17/military-s-political-role-in-new-algeria-pub-84076.
El-Ghobashy, Mona. *Bread and Freedom: Egypt's Revolutionary Situation.* Stanford, CA: Stanford University Press, 2021.
Eligür, Banu. *The Mobilization of Political Islam in Turkey.* Cambridge: Cambridge University Press, 2010.
Esen, Berk. "Praetorian Army in Action: A Critical Assessment of Civil– Military Relations in Turkey." *Armed Forces & Society* 47, no. 1 (2021): 201–22.
Esen, Berk, and Sebnem Gumuscu. "Turkey: How the Coup Failed." *Journal of Democracy* 28, no. 1 (2017): 59–73.
Evans, Martin, and John Phillips. *Algeria: Anger of the Dispossessed.* New Haven, CT: Yale University Press, 2007.
Farzanegan, Mohammad Reza. "Military Spending and Economic Growth: The Case of Iran." *Defence and Peace Economics* 25 (No. 4) 2014: 1–23.
Feaver, Peter D. "The Civil-Military Relations Problematique: Huntington, Janowitz, and the Question of Civilian Control." *Armed Forces & Society* 23, no. 2 (1996): 149–78.
———. *Armed Servants: Agency, Oversight, and Civil-Military Relations.* Cambridge, MA: Harvard University Press, 2003.
Fildis, Ayse Tekdal "Troubles in Syria: Spawned by the French." *Middle East Policy* 18 no. 4 (2012): 129–38.
Findley, Carter Vaughn. *Turkey, Islam, Nationalism, and Modernity: A History.* New Haven, CT: Yale University Press, 2010.
Finer, S. E. *The Man on Horseback: The Role of the Military in Politics.* New York: Frederick A. Praeger, 1962.
Freedman, Lawrence, and Efraim Karsh. *The Gulf Conflict 1990–1991: Diplomacy and War in the New World Order.* Princeton, NJ: Princeton University Press, 1993.
Freilich, Charles D. *Zion's Dilemmas: How Israel Makes National Security Policy.* Ithaca, NY: Cornell University Press, 2012.
Gasiorowski, Mark J. "The 1953 Coup d'État in Iran." *International Journal of Middle East Studies* 19, no. 3 (1987): 261–86.
———. "The 1953 Coup d'État Against Mosaddeq." In *Mohammad Mosaddeq and the 1953 Coup in Iran,* edited by Mark J. Gasiorowski and Malcolm Byrne, 227–60. Syracuse: Syracuse University Press, 2004.
Gat, Moshe. "Nasser and the Six Day War, 5 June 1967: A Premeditated Strategy or An Inexorable Drift to War?" *Israel Affairs* 11, no.4 (2005): 608–35.
Gaub, Florence. *Military Integration after Civil Wars: Multiethnic Armies, Identity, and Post-Conflict Reconstruction.* London: Routledge, 2011.
———. "The Libyan Armed Forces between Coup proofing and Repression." *Journal of Strategic Studies* 36, no. 2 (2013): 221–44.
———. *Guardians of the Arab State: Why Militaries Intervene in Politics, from Iraq to Mauritania.* Oxford: Oxford University Press, 2017.
Gaub, Florence, and Zoe Stanley-Lockman. *Defense Industries in Arab States.* Paris: Chaillot Papers No. 141 (March 2016).

Gelvin, James L. *The Arab Uprisings: What Everyone Needs to Know*. New York: Oxford University Press, 2012.

Ghanem, Dahlia. "Civil-Military Relations in the MENA Region: Past and Future." *Med Dialogue Series*. no. 24 (March 2020): Konrad Adenhaur Siftung. https://www.kas.de/documents/282499/282548/CMR.pdf/06d6667a-fbbc-cf41-817d-.

El-Ghobashy, Mona. *Bread and Freedom: Egypt's Revolutionary Situation*. Stanford, CA: Stanford University Press, 2021.

Gillespie, Kate, and Gwenn Okruhlik. "Cleaning up Corruption in the Middle East." *Middle East Journal* 42, no. 1 (1988): 59–82.

Gingeras, Ryan. "In the Hunt for the 'Sultans of Smack': Dope, Gangsters and the Construction of the Turkish Deep State." *Middle East Journal* 65, no. 3 (2011): 426–41.

Gluska, Ami. *The Israeli Military and the Origins of the 1967 War*. London: Routledge, 2007.

Gordon, Joel. *Nasser's Blessed Movement: Egypt's Free Officers and the July Revolution*. New York: Oxford University Press, 1992.

Grewal, Sharan. "Tunisia's Foiled Coup of 1987: The November 8th Group." *Middle East Journal* 74, no. 1 (2020): 53–71.

Grigoriadis, Ioannis and Irmak Özer. "Mutations of Turkish Nationalism." *Middle East Policy*, 17, no. 4 (2010): 101–13.

Güler, Arzu, and Cemal Alpgiray Bölücek. "Motives for Reform on Civil-Military Relations in Turkey." *Turkish Studies* 17, no. 2 (2016): 251–71.

Gürbey, Sinem. "Islam, the Nation-State, and the Military: A Discussion of Secularism in Turkey," *Comparative Studies of South Asia, Africa, and the Middle East*. 29, no. 3 (2009): 371–80.

Hale, William. *Turkish Politics and the Military*. London: Routledge, 1994.

Halpern, Manfred. *The Politics of Social Change in the Middle East and North Africa*. Princeton, NJ: Princeton University Press, 1963.

Harb, Imad. "The Egyptian Military in Politics: Disengagement or Accommodation?" *The Middle East Journal* 57, no. 2 (2003): 269–90.

Harik, Iliya. "The Origins of the Arab State." In *The Foundations of the Arab State*, edited by Ghassan Salamé, 19–46. London: Croom Helm, 1987.

Harris, Kevan. "All the Sepah's Men: Iran's Revolutionary Guards in Theory and Practice." In *Businessmen in Arms: How the Military and other Armed Groups Profit in the MENA Region*, edited by Elke Grawert and Zeinab Abul-Magd, 97–118. Lanham, MD: Rowman & Littlefield.

Hashim, Ahmed S. "Saddam Husayn and Civil-Military Relations in Iraq: The Quest for Legitimacy and Power." *Middle East Journal* 57, no. 1 (2003): 9–41.

Hassan, Bahey Eldin. "New Political Struggles for Egypt's Military." *Sada: Middle East Analysis*, Carnegie Endowment for International Peace, May 9, 2019. https://carnegieendowment.org/sada/79096.

Haugom, Lars. "The Turkish Armed Forces and Civil-military Relations in Turkey after the 15 July 2016 Coup Attempt." *Scandinavian Journal of Military Studies* 2, no. 1 (2019): 1–8.

Henry, Clement M., and Robert Springborg. *Globalization and the Politics of Development in the Middle East*. Cambridge: Cambridge University Press, 2001.
Hen-Tov, Elliot. "The Political Economy of Turkish Military Modernization." *Middle East Review of International Affairs* 8, no. 4 (2004): 49–59.
Hen-Tov, Elliot and Nathan Gonzales. "The Militarization of Post-Khomeini Iran: Praetorianism 2.0." *Washington Quarterly* 34, no. 1 (2011): 45–59.
Heper, Metin. "Civil-Military Relations in Turkey: Toward a Liberal Model?" *Turkish Studies* 12, no. 2 (2011): 241–52.
Herb, Michael. *All in the Family: Absolutism, Revolution, and Democracy in the Middle East Monarchies*. Albany: State University of New York Press, 1999.
Hertog, Steffen. *Princes, Brokers, and Bureaucrats: Oil and the State in Saudi Arabia*. Ithaca, NY: Cornell University Press, 2010.
Heydemann, Steven. *Authoritarianism in Syria: Institutions and Social Conflict, 1946–1970*. Ithaca, NY: Cornell University Press, 1999.
———. "Social Pacts and the Persistence of Authoritarianism in the Middle East." In *Debating Arab Authoritarianism: Dynamics and Durability in Nondemocratic Regimes*, edited by Oliver Schlumberger, 21–38. Stanford, CA: Stanford University Press, 2006.
Hinnebusch, Raymond A. *Authoritarian Power and State Formation in Ba'athist Syria: Army, Party, and Peasant*. Boulder, CO: Westview Press, 1990.
Hokayem, Emile. "Iran, the Gulf States and the Syrian Civil War." *Adelphi Papers* 54 nos. 447–48 (2014): 39–70.
Hokayem, Emile, and David B. Roberts. "The War in Yemen." *Survival* 58, no. 6 (2016–2017): 157–86.
Holmes, Amy Austin, *Coups and Revolutions: Mass Mobilizations, the Egyptian Military, and the United States from Mubarak to Sisi*. New York: Oxford University Press, 2019.
Huntington, Samuel P. *"The Soldier and the State*. Cambridge, MA: Harvard University Press, 1957.
———. *Political Order in Changing Societies*. New Haven, CT: Yale University Press, 1968.
———. *The Third Wave: Democratization in the Late Twentieth Century*. Norman: University of Oklahoma Press, 1991.
Hurewitz, J. C. *Middle East Politics: The Military Dimension*. New York: Frederick A. Praeger, 1969.
Ibrahim, Saad Iddin. "Towards Muslim Democracies." *Journal of Democracy*, 18, no. 2 (2007): 5–13.
Inbar, Efraim. "Yitzhak Rabin and Israel's National Security." *The Journal of Strategic Studies* 20, no. 2 (1997): 25–40.
İrem, Nazim. "Turkish Conservative Modernism: Birth of a Nationalist Quest for Cultural Renewal." *International Journal of Middle East Studies* 34, no. 1 (2002): 87–112.
Jaoude, Tarek Abou. "Chehabism Revisited: The Consequences of Reform in Lebanon." *Middle Eastern Studies* 57, no. 5 (2021): 810–32.

Janowitz, Morris. *The Military in the Political Development of New Nations*. Chicago: University of Chicago Press, 1964.

———. *Military Institutions and Coercion in Developing Nations*. Chicago: University of Chicago Press, 1977.

Jebnoun, Noureddine. "Tunisia: Patterns and Implications of Civilian Control." In *Civil-Military Relations: Control and Effectiveness Across Regimes*, edited by Thomas C. Bruneau and Aurel Croissant, 103–18. Boulder, CO: Lynne Rienner Publishers, 2019.

Jenkins, Gareth. *Context and Circumstance: The Turkish Military and Politics*. Adelphi Paper 337. London: The International Institute for Strategic Studies, 2001.

Jenkins, J. Craig and Augustine J. Kposowa, "Explaining Military Coups d'État: Black Africa, 1957–1984," *American Sociological Review* 55, no. 6 (1992): 861–75

Johnsen, Gregory D. "The End of Yemen." The Brookings Institution, March 25, 2021. https://www.brookings.edu/blog/order-from-chaos/2021/03/25/the-end-of-yemen/.

Jones, Toby Craig. 2010. *Desert Kingdom: How Oil and Water Forged Modern Saudi Arabia*. Cambridge, MA: Harvard University Press, 2010.

Juneau, Thomas. "The UAE and the War in Yemen: From Surge to Recalibration." *Survival* 62, no. 4 (2020): 183–208.

Kamrava, Mehran. "Military Professionalization and Civil-Military Relations in the Middle East." *Political Science Quarterly* 115, no. 1 (2000): 67–92.

———. "The Politics of Weak Control: State Capacity and Economic Semi-Formality in the Middle East." *Comparative Studies of South Asia, Africa, and the Middle East* 22, nos. 1–2 (2002): 43–52.

Kandil, Hazem, *Soldiers, Spies, and Statesmen: Egypt's Road to Revolution*. London: Verso, 2012.

———. *The Power Triangle: Military, Security, and Politics in Regime Change*. New York: Oxford University Press, 2016.

Karsh, Efraim. *The Iran-Iraq War: A Military Analysis*. Adelphi Papers no. 220. London: International Institute for Strategic Studies, 1987.

Kavakci, Merve "Turkey's Test with its Deep State," *Mediterranean Quarterly* 20, no. 4 (2009): 83-97.

Kaylani, Nabil M. "The Rise of the Syrian Ba'th, 1940–1958: Political Success, Party Failure." *International Journal of Middle Eastern Studies* 3, no. 1 (1972): 3–23.

Ketchley, Neil. *Egypt in a Time of Revolution: Contentious Politics and the Arab Spring*. Cambridge: Cambridge University Press, 2017.

Khadduri, Majid. "The Role of the Military in Middle East Politics." *The American Political Science Review* 47, no. 2 (1953): 511–24.

Al-Khafaji, Isam. "War as a Vehicle for the Rise and Demise of a State-Controlled Society: The Case of Ba'thist Iraq." In *War, Institutions, and Social Change in the Middle East*, edited by Steven Heydemann, 258–91. Berkeley: University of California Press, 2000.

Khoury, Philip S. *Syria and the French Mandate: The Politics of Arab Nationalism, 1920–1945*. Princeton, NJ: Princeton University Press, 1987.

Khuri, Fuad I. "Modernizing Societies in the Middle East," in *Civil-Military Relations: Regional Perspectives*, edited by Morris Janowitz, 160–88. Beverly Hills, CA: Sage Publications, 1981.
Kimmerling, Baruch. "Making Conflict Routine: Cumulative Effects of the Arab-Jewish Conflict Upon Israeli Society," in *Israeli Society and its Defense Establishment: The Social and Political Impact of a Protracted Violent Conflict*, edited by Moshe Lissak, 13–45. London: Frank Cass, 1984.
Kinzer, Stephen. *All the Shah's Men: An American Coup and the Roots of Middle East Terror.* New York: John Wiley & Son, 2003.
Kiyani, Ghashia. "Coup-Proofing and Political Violence: The Case of Iraq." *Middle Eastern Studies* 57, no. 6 (2021): 1–17.
Knights, Michael. "The Military Role in Yemen's Protests: Civil-Military Relations in the Tribal Republic." *Journal of Strategic Studies* 36, no. 2 (2013): 261–88.
Koehler, Kevin. "Officers and Regimes: The Historical Origins of Political-Military Relations in Middle East Republics," in *Armies and Insurgencies in the Arab Spring*, edited by Albrecht, Holger, Aurel Croissant, and Fred W. Lawson, 34–53. Philadelphia: University of Pennsylvania Press, 2016.
Krieg, Andreas "The UAE's 'Dogs of War': Boosting a Small State's Regional Power Projection." *Small Wars & Insurgencies* 33, nos. 1–2 (2022): 152–72.
Kuran, Timur. *The Long Divergence: How Islamic Law Held Back the Middle East.* Princeton, NJ: Princeton University Press, 2011.
Kurkeu, Ertugrul. "The Crisis of the Turkish State." *Middle East Report* 199 (April–June 1997): 2–7.
Lahav, Pnina "A Small Nation Goes to War: Israel's Cabinet Authorization of the 1956 War." *Israel Studies* 15, no. 3 (2010): 61–86.
Lasswell, Harold D. "The Garrison State Hypothesis Today." In *Changing Patterns of Military Politics*, edited by Samuel P. Huntington, 51–70. New York: The Free Press, 1962.
Lawson, Fred H. "Armed Forces, Internal Security Services, and Popular Contention." In *Armies and Insurgencies in the Arab Spring*, edited by Holger Albrecht, Aurel Croissant, and Fred H. Lawson, 54–70. Philadelphia: University of Pennsylvania Press, 2016.
———. "Why Foreign Military Interventions Prolong Civil Wars: Lessons from Yemen." *International Politics* (2021). https://doi.org/10.1057/s41311-021-00357-6.
Lebovic, James H., and Ashfaq Ishaq "Military Burden, Security Needs, and Economic Growth in the Middle East." *The Journal of Conflict Resolution* 31, no. 1 (1987): 106–38.
Lenze, Paul E., Jr. *Civil-Military Relations in the Islamic World.* Lanham, MD: Lexington Books, 2016.
Lesch, Ann M. "Egypt's Spring: Causes of the Revolution." *Middle East Policy* 18, no. 3 (2011): 35–48.
Lesch, David W. *The New Lion of Damascus: Bashar al-'Asad and Modern Syria.* New Haven, CT: Yale University Press, 2005.

Lewis, David A. "Diversification and Niche Market Exporting: The Restructuring of Israel's Defense Industry in the Post-Cold War Era." In *From Defense to Development: International Perspectives on Realizing the Peace Dividend*, edited by Ann Markusen, Sean DiGiovanna, and Michael C. Leary, 121–50. New York: Routledge, 2003.

Lister, Charles. *Dynamic Stalemate: Surveying Syria's Military Landscape*. Doha: Brookings Doha Center, 2014.

Lord, Ceren. *Religious Politics in Turkey: From the Birth of the Republic to the AKP*. Cambridge: Cambridge University Press, 2018.

Lowi, Miriam R. *Oil Wealth and the Poverty of Politics: Algeria Compared*. Cambridge: Cambridge University Press, 2009.

Lust-Okar, Ellen. *Structuring Conflict in the Arab World: Incumbents, Opponents, and Institutions*. Cambridge: Cambridge University Press, 2005.

Lutterbeck, Derek. "Arab Uprisings, Armed Forces, and Civil-Military Relations." *Armed Forces & Society* April 2021. http://afs.sagepub.com/content/early/2012/04/11/0095327X12442768.full.pdf+html.

Maghraoui, Abdeslam. "Monarchy and Political Reform in Morocco." *Journal of Democracy*. 12, no. 1 (2001) 73–86.

Maher, Mohamed, and Yanji Zhao. "Do Political Instability and Military Expenditure Undermine Economic Growth in Egypt? Evidence from the ARDL Approach." *Defence and Peace Economics* (2021): 1–14. https://www-tandfonline-com.aufric.idm.oclc.org/doi/full/10.1080/10242694.2021.1943625.

Maniruzzaman, Talukder. *Military Withdrawal from Politics: A Comparative Study*. Cambridge, MA: Ballinger, 1987.

Maoz, Zeev. *Defending the Holy Land: A Critical Analysis of Israel's Security and Foreign Policy*. Ann Arbor: University of Michigan Press, 2006.

Marcus, Abraham. *The Middle East on the Eve of Modernity: Aleppo in the Eighteenth Century*. New York: Columbia University Press, 1989.

Marsot, Afaf Lutfi Al-Sayyid. *A History of Egypt: From the Arab Conquest to the Present*. Cambridge: Cambridge University Press, 2007.

Marshall, Shana. "Jordan's Military-Industrial Complex and the Middle East's New Model Army." *Middle East Report*, no. 267 (Summer 2014): 42–45.

———. "Jordan's Military-Industrial Sector: Maintaining Institutional Prestige in the Era of Neoliberalism." In *Businessmen in Arms: How the Military and other Armed Groups Profit in the MENA Region*, edited by Elke Grawert and Zeinab Abul-Magd, 119–34. Lanham, MD: Rowman & Littlefield, 2016.

Masri, Safwan M. *Tunisia: An Arab Anomaly*. New York: Columbia University Press, 2017.

Matei, Florina Christiana. "A new Conceptualization of Civil-Military Relations." In *The Routledge Handbook of Civil-Military Relations*, edited by Thomas C. Bruneau and Florina Christiana Matei, 26–39. Oxfordshire: Routledge, 2013.

Martini, Jeff, and Julie Taylor. 2011. "Commanding Democracy in Egypt." *Foreign Affairs* 90, no. 5 (2011): 127–37.

Massad, Joseph. *Colonial Effects: The Making of National Identity in Jordan*. New York: Columbia University Press, 2001.

Mbaku, John Mukum. "Military Coups as Rent-Seeking Behavior." *Journal of Political and Military Sociology* 22 (winter 1994): 241–84.
McDougall, James. *History and the Culture of Nationalism in Algeria*. Cambridge: Cambridge University Press, 2006.
McGerty, Fenella, and Tom Waldwyn "Middle East Defence Spending Showing Signs of Stabilising." *Military Balance* (blog), International Institute for Strategic Studies, November 18, 2021. https://www.iiss.org/blogs/military-balance/2021/11/middle-east-defence-spending-showing-signs-of-stabilising.
McManus, Allison. "The Egyptian's Military's Terrorism Containment Campaign in North Sinai." Carnegie Endowment for International Peace, June 30, 2020. https://carnegieendowment.org/sada/82218.
McQuinn, Brian. "Assessing (In)security after the Arab Spring: The Case of Libya." *PS: Political Science & Politics* 46, no. 4 (2013): 716–20.
Meng, Anne. *Constraining Dictatorship: From Personalized Rule to Institutionalized Regimes*. Cambridge: Cambridge University Press, 2020.
Michael, Kobi. "Military Knowledge and Weak Civilian Control in the Reality of Low-Intensity Conflict: The Israeli Case." *Israel Studies* 12, no. 1 (2007): 28–52.
Miller, Susan Gilson. *A History of Modern Morocco*. Cambridge: Cambridge University Press, 2013.
Mintz, Alex, and Michael D. Ward, "The Political Economy of Military Spending in Israel." *The American Political Science Review* 83, no. 2 (1989): 521–33.
Moreau, Odile. "Ottoman Military Reforms on the Eve of World War I." *Perceptions* 20, nos. 2–3 (2015): 59–73.
Moran, Theodore H. "Iran's Defense Expenditures and the Social Crisis." *International Security* 3, no. 3 (1978–1979): 178–92.
Moaz, Zeev. *Defending the Holy Land: A Critical Analysis of Israel's Security & Foreign Policy*. Ann Arbor: University of Michigan Press, 2006.
Mortimer, Robert A. "Islamists, Soldiers, and Democrats: The Second Algerian War." *Middle East Journal* 50, no. 1 (1996): 18–39.
Moskos, Charles. "Towards a Postmodern Military?" In *Democratic Societies and Their Armed Forces: Israel in Comparative Context*, edited by Stuart A. Cohen, 1–26. London: Frank Cass, 2000.
Nada, Garrett, and Mattisan Rowan. "Part 2: Pro-Iran Militias in Iraq." The Wilson Center, April 27, 2018.
Narang, Vipin, and Caitlin Talmadge. "Civil-Military Pathologies and Defeat in War: Tests Using New Data." *Journal of Conflict Resolution* 62, no. 7 (2018): 1379–405.
Narlı, Nilüfer. "Civil-Military Relations in Turkey." *Turkish Studies* 1, no. 1 (2000): 107–27.
Nasr, Vali. *The Shia Revival*. New York: W. W. Norton, 2006.
Nassif, Hicham Bou. "Turbulent from the Start: Revisiting Military Politics in Pre-Ba'th Syria." *International Journal of Middle East Studies* 52, no. 3 (2020): 469–88.
Noble, Paul C. "The Arab System." In *The Foreign Policies of Arab States: The Challenge of Change*, edited by Bahgat Korany and Ali E. Hillal Dessouki, 49–102. Boulder, CO: Westview Press, 1991.

Norton, Augustus Richard, and Ali Alfoneh. "The Study of Civil-Military Relations and Civil-Society in the Middle East and North Africa." In *Developments in Civil-Military Relations in the Middle East*, edited by Carsten Jensen, 7–28. Copenhagen: Royal Danish Defense College, 2008.

O'Donnell, Guillermo, and Philippe C. Schmitter. "Part IV: Tentative Conclusions about Uncertain Democracies." In *Transitions from Authoritarian Rule: Prospects for Democracy*, edited by Guillermo O'Donnell and Phillippe C. Schmitter, 3–73. Baltimore, MD: Johns Hopkins University Press, 1986.

Okruhlik, Gwenn. "Rentier Wealth, Unruly Law, and the Rise of Opposition: The Political Economy of Oil States." *Comparative Politics* 31, no. 3 (1999): 295–315.

Oren, Michael. "The Revelations of 1967 New Research on the Six Day War and Its Lessons for the Contemporary Middle East." *Israel Studies* 10, no. 2 (2005): 1–14.

Orkaby, Asher. "The North Yemen Civil War and the Failure of the Federation of South Arabia." *Middle Eastern Studies* 53, no. 1 (2017): 69–83.

Osman, Tarek. *Egypt on the Brink: From Nasser to Mubarak*. New Haven, CT: Yale University Press, 2010.

Ostovar, Afshon. *Vanguard of the Imam: Religion, Politics, and Iran's Revolutionary Guards*. Oxford: Oxford University Press, 2016.

Ottoway, David, and Marina Ottoway. *Algeria: The Politics of a Socialist Revolution*. Berkeley: University of California Press, 1970.

Panchon, Alejandro. "Loyalty and Defection: Misunderstanding Civil-Military Relations in Tunisia during the 'Arab Spring.'" *Journal of Strategic Studies* 37, no 4 (2014): 508–31.

Parkinson, Brian R. "Israel's Lebanon War: Ariel Sharon and 'Operation Peace for Galilee.'" *Journal of Third World Studies* 24, no. 2 (2007): 63–84.

Pelletiere, Stephen C. *The Iran-Iraq War: Chaos in a Vacuum*. New York: Praeger, 1992.

Peri, Yoram. "Civil-Military Relations in Crisis." In *Military, State, and Society in Israel*, edited by Daniel Mamam, Eyal Ben-Ari, and Zeev Rosenhek, 107–36. New Brunswick, NJ: Transaction Publishers, 2001.

Perkins, Kenneth J. *A History of Modern Tunisia*. Cambridge: Cambridge University Press, 2004.

Perlmutter, Amos. "The Israeli Army in Politics: The Persistence of the Civilian Over the Military." *World Politics* 20, no. 4 (1968): 606–43.

———. "The Praetorian State and the Praetorian Army: Toward a Taxonomy of Civil-Military Relations in Developing Polities." *Comparative Politics* 1, no. 3 (1969): 382–404.

———. *Egypt: The Praetorian State*. New Brunswick, NJ: Transaction Publishers, 1974.

Perthes, Volker. "A Look at Syria's Upper Class: The Bourgeoisie and the Ba'th." *Middle East Report* 170, May–June (1991): 31–37.

———. "The Syrian Economy in the 1980s." *Middle East Journal* 46, no 1 (1992): 37–58.

———. "*Si Vis Stabilitatem, Para Bellum*: State Building, National Security, and War Preparations in Syria." In *War, Institutions, and Social Change in the Middle*

East, edited by Steven Heydemann, 149–73. Berkeley: University of California Press, 2000.

Pion-Berlin, David. "Military Relations in Comparative Perspective." In *Armies and Insurgencies in the Arab Spring*, edited by Holger Albrecht, Aurel Croissant, and Fred H. Lawson, 7–33. Philadelphia: University of Pennsylvania Press, 2016.

Pollack, Kenneth M. *Armies of Sand: The Past, Present, and Future of Arab Military Effectiveness*. New York: Oxford University Press, 2019.

———. *Arabs at War: Military Effectiveness, 1948–1991*. Lincoln: University of Nebraska Press, 2002.

Provence, Michael. *The Last Ottoman Generation and the Making of the Modern Middle East*. Cambridge: Cambridge University Press, 2017.

Pusane, Özlem Kayhan. "The Role of Context in Desecuritization: Turkish Foreign Policy Towards Northern Iraq (2008–2017)." *Turkish Studies* 21, no. 3 (2020): 392–413.

Quandt, William B. *Revolution and Political Leadership: Algeria, 1954–1968*. Cambridge, MA: The MIT Press, 1969.

Quinlivin, James T. "Coup Proofing: Its Practices and Consequences in the Middle East." *International Security* 24, no. 2 (1999): 131–65.

Al-Rasheed, Madawi. *A History of Saudi Arabia*. Cambridge: Cambridge University Press, 2002.

Reiter, Dan, and Allan C. Stam III. 1998. "Democracy and Battlefield Military Effectiveness." *The Journal of Conflict Resolution* 42, no. 3 (1998): 259–77.

Rivlin, Paul. *Arab Economies in the Twentieth Century*. Cambridge: Cambridge University Press, 2009.

———. *The Israeli Economy from the Foundation of the State through the 21st Century*. Cambridge: Cambridge University Press, 2011.

Roberts, David B. "Bucking the Trend: The UAE and the Development of Military Capabilities in the Arab World." *Security Studies* 29, no. 2 (2020): 301–34.

Roberts, Tyson, and Lisa Mueller. "Does Charisma Affect Survival in Office for Leaders Who Take Power via Military Coup?" *Studies in Comparative International Development* 56, no. 4 (2021): 485–510.

Robins, Philip. *Suites and Uniforms: Turkish Foreign Policy Since the Cold War*. Seattle: University of Washington Press, 2003.

———. *A History of Jordan*. Cambridge: Cambridge University Press, 2004.

Rogan, Eugene. *The Arabs: A History*. New York: Basic Books, 2010.

Rome, Henry. "Iran's Defense Spending." *The Iran Primer*. United States Institute for Peace, June 17, 2020. https://iranprimer.usip.org/blog/2020/jun/17/iran%E2%80%99s-defense-spending.

Rosato, Sebastian. *Intentions in Great Power Politics: Uncertainty and the Roots of Conflict*. New Haven, CT: Yale University Press, 2021.

Rosenhek, Zeev, Daniel Maman, and Eyal Ben-Ari. "The Study of War and the Military in Israel: An Empirical Investigation and a Reflective Critique." *International Journal of Middle East Studies* 35, no. 3 (2003): 461–84.

Roy, Olivier. *Secularism Confronts Islam*. New York: Columbia University Press, 2007.

Rundell, David. *Vision or Mirage: Saudi Arabia at the Crossroads.* London: I. B. Tauris, 2021.
Russett, Bruce M. *What Price Vigilance? The Burdens of National Defense.* New Haven, CT: Yale University Press, 1970.
Rustow, Dankwart A. "The Army and the Founding of the Turkish Republic." *World Politics,* 11, no. 4 (1959): 513–52.
Rutherford, Bruce K. *Egypt after Mubarak: Liberalism, Islam and Democracy in the Arab World.* Princeton, NJ: Princeton University Press, 2008.
———. "Egypt's New Authoritarianism under Sisi." *Middle East Journal* 72, no. 2 (2018): 185–208.
Sadiki, Larbi. *Rethinking Arab Democratization: Elections without Democracy.* Oxford: Oxford University Press, 2009.
Saikal, Amin. *The Rise and Fall of the Shah: Iran from Autocracy to Religious Rule.* Princeton, NJ: Princeton University Press, 1980.
———. *Iran Rising: The Survival and Future of the Islamic Republic.* Princeton: Princeton University Press, 2019.
Sakallioğlu, Ümit Cizre. "The Anatomy of the Turkish Military's Political Autonomy." *Comparative Politics* 29, no. 2 (1997): 151–66.
Samuel, Annie Tracy, *The Unfinished History of the Iran-Iraq War: Faith, Firepower, and Iran's Revolutionary Guards.* Cambridge: Cambridge University Press, 2022.
Sarihan, Ali. "A New Theory of Military Behavior in the Arab Uprisings: 'Pro-State' and 'Pro-Regime.'" *Journal of International Studies* 14, no. 1 (2021): 9–23.
Sassoon, Joseph. *Saddam Hussein's Ba'th Party: Inside an Authoritarian Regime.* Cambridge: Cambridge University Press, 2012.
Sassoon, Joseph, and Alissa Walter. "The Iraqi Occupation of Kuwait: New Historical Perspectives." *Middle East Journal* 71, no. 4 (2017): 607–28.
Satana, Nil S. "Transformation of the Turkish Military and the Path to Democracy." *Armed Forces & Society* 34, no. 3 (2008): 357–88.
Sayigh, Yezid. "The Tunisian Army-a New Political Role?" *Cairo Review of Global Affairs,* November 14, 2011. http://www.aucegypt.edu/gapp/cairoreview/pages/articleDetails.aspx?aid=97.
———. "Egypt's Military Now Controls Much of its Economy. Is that Wise?" Carnegie Middle East Center, November 25, 2019. https://carnegie-mec.org/2019/11/25/egypt-s-military-now-controls-much-of-its-economy.-is-this-wise-pub-80281.
———. *Owners of the Republic: An Anatomy of Egypt's Military Economy.* Washington, DC: Carnegie Middle East Center, 2019.
Schiff, Rebecca L. *The Military and Domestic Politics: A Concordance Theory of Civil-Military Relations.* London: Routledge, 2009.
Schwartz, Rolf. *War and State Building in the Middle East.* Gainesville: University Press of Florida, 2012.
Seal, Jeremy. *A Coup in Turkey.* London: Chatto and Windus, 2021.
Seale, Patrick. *The Struggle for Syria: A Study of Post-War Arab Politics, 1945–1958.* New Haven, CT: Yale University Press, 1986.
———. *Asad: The Struggle for the Middle East.* Berkeley: University of California Press, 1988.

Sentek, Zeynep. "Turkey: Strengthening Personalized Political Control." In *Civil-Military Relations: Control and Effectiveness Across Regimes*, edited by Thomas C. Bruneau and Aurel Croissant, 175–90. Boulder, CO: Lynne Rienner Publishers, 2019.
no. Seidman, Guy. "From Nationalization to Privatization: The Case of the IDF." *Armed Forces & Society* 16, no. 4 (2010): 716–49.
Seitz, Adam C. "Patronage Politics in Transition: Political and Economic Interests of the Yemeni Armed Forces." In *Businessmen in Arms: How the Military and Other Armed Groups Profit in the MENA Region*, edited by Elke Grawert and Zeinab Abul-Magd, 157–74. Lanham, MD: Rowman & Littlefield, 2016.
Sela, Avraham. "Civil Society, the Military, and National Security: The Case of Israel's Security Zone in South Lebanon." *Israel Studies* 12, no. 1 (2007): 53–78.
Sezgin, Selami, and Jülide Yildirim. "The Demand for Turkish Defence Expenditure." *Defence and Peace Economics* 12, no. 2 (2002): 121–28.
Shaery-Eisenlohr, Roschanack. *Shi'ite Lebanon: Transnational Religion and the Making of National Identities*. New York: Columbia University Press, 2008.
Al-Shazly, Saad. *The Crossing of the Suez*. San Francisco: American Mideast Research, 1980.
Shiffer, Zalman F. "The Debate over the Defense Budget in Israel." In *Militarism and Israeli Society*, edited by Gabriel Sheffer and Oren Barak, 213–37. Bloomington: Indiana University Press, 2010.
Shlaim, Avi. "Jordan: Walking the Tightrope." In *The 1967 Arab-Israeli War: Origins and Consequences*, edited by William Roger Louis and Avi Shlaim, 99–125. Cambridge: Cambridge University Press, 2012.
Simon, Reeva Spector. *Iraq between the Two World Wars: The Militarist Origins of Tyranny*. New York: Columbia University Press, 2004.
Singh, Naunihal. *Seizing Power: The Strategic Logic of Military Coups*. Baltimore, MD: Johns Hopkins University Press, 2014.
Skocpol, Theda. "Rentier State and Shi'a Islam in the Iranian Revolution." *Theory and Society*,11, no. 3 (19820: 265–83.
———. "Social Revolutions and Mass Military Mobilization." *World Politics* 40, no. 2 (1988): 147–68.
Sohrabi, Hadi. "Clerics and Generals: Assessing the Stability of the Iranian Regime." *Middle East Policy* 25, no. 3 (2018): 34–46.
Sorenson, David S. "Why the Saudi Arabian Defense Binge?" *Contemporary Security Policy* 35, no. 1 (2014): 116–37.
———. "Civil-Military Relations in North Africa." *Middle East Policy* 14, no. 4: (2007): 99–114.
Sørli, Nils Petter Gleditsch, and Håvard Strand. "Why Is there so much Conflict in the Middle East?" *Journal of Conflict Resolution* 49, no. 1 (2005): 141–65.
Sprecher, Christopher, and Karl DeRouen, Jr. "Israeli Military Actions and Internalization-Externalization Processes." *The Journal of Conflict Resolution* 46, no. 2 (2002): 244–59.
Springborg, Robert. *Mubarak's Egypt: Fragmentation of the Political Order*. Boulder, CO: Westview Press, 1989.

———. "Economic Involvement of Militaries." *International Journal of Middle East Studies* 43, no. 3 (2011): 397–99.

———. "Egypt: An Ineffective Military Beyond Control." In *Civil-Military Relations: Control and Effectiveness Across Regimes*, edited by Thomas C. Bruneau and Aurel Croissant, 191–206. Boulder, CO: Lynne Rienner Publishers, 2019.

Springborg, Robert, and F. C. "Pink" Williams. "The Egyptian Military: A Sleeping Giant Awakens." Carnegie Middle East Center, February 2019.

Stookey, Robert W. *Yemen: The Politics of the Yemen Arab Republic*. Boulder, CO: Westview Press, 1978.

Sunar, Ilkay, and Sabri Sayari. "Democracy in Turkey: Problems and Prospects." In *Transitions from Authoritarian Rule: Prospects for Democracy*, edited by Guillermo O'Donnell, Philippe C. Schmitter, and Laurence Whitehead, 165–86. Baltimore, MD: Johns Hopkins University Press, 1986.

Szarejko, Andrew A. "The Soldier and the Turkish State: Toward a General Theory of Civil-Military Relations." *Perceptions* 19, no. 2 (2014): 139–58.

Tabaar, Mohammad Ayatollahi. *Religious Statecraft: The Politics of Islam in Iran*. New York: Columbia University Press, 2018.

Tabatabai, Ariane M. *No Conquest, No Defeat: Iran's National Security Strategy*. New York: Oxford University Press, 2020.

Tabatabai, Ariane M., and Annie Tracy Samuel. "What the Iran-Iraq War Tells Us about the Future of the Iran Nuclear Deal." *International Security* 42, no. 1 (2017): 152–85.

Tachau, Frank, and Metin Heper. "The State, Politics, and the Military in Turkey." *Comparative Politics* 16, no. 1 (1983): 17–33.

Takeyh, Ray. *Guardians of the Revolution: Iran in the World in the Age of the Ayatollahs*. New York: Oxford University Press, 2009.

Talmadge, Caitlin. "The Puzzle of Personalist Performance: Iraqi Battlefield Effectiveness in the Iran-Iraq War." *Security Studies* 22, no. 2 (2013): 180–221.

———. *The Dictator's Army: Battlefield Effectiveness in Authoritarian Regimes*. Ithaca, NY: Cornell University Press, 2018.

Tarbush, Mohammed. *The Role of the Military in Politics: A Case Study of Iraq to 1941*. London: Routledge, 1982.

Tekeoglu, Ertugrul. *Defense Expenditure and Economic Growth: Empirical Study on Case of Turkey*. Monterey, CA: Naval Postgraduate School, 2008.

Terrill, W. Andrew. "The Political Mythology of the Battle of Karameh." *Middle East Journal* 55, no. 1 (2001): 91–111.

Tessler, Mark, and Ebru Altınoğlu. "Political Culture in Turkey: Connections Among Attitudes Towards Democracy, the Military, and Islam." *Democratization* 11, no. 1(2004): 21–50.

Thompson, Eric V. "The Iraqi Military Re-enters the Gulf Security Dynamic." *Middle East Policy* 16, no. 3 (2009): 28–40.

Tishler, Asher, and Gil Pinchas. "Challenges of the Israeli Defense Industry in the Global Security Market." In *Israel's Defense Industry and US Security Aid*, edited by Sassan Haddad, Tomer Fadlon, and Shmuel Even, 33–50. Tel Aviv: Institute for National Security Studies, July, 2020.

Töngür Ünal, and Adem Yavuz Elveren. "The Impact of Military Spending and Income Inequality on Economic Growth in Turkey." *Defence and Peace Economics* 27, no. 3 (2016): 433–52.

Toronto, Nathan W. *How Militaries Learn: Human Capital, Military Education, and Battlefield Effectiveness*. Lanham, MD: Lexington Books, 2018.

Torrey, Gordon H. *Syrian Politics and the Military*. Columbus: Ohio State University Press, 1964.

Tracy Samuel, Annie. *The Unfinished History of the Iran-Iraq War: Faith, Firepower, and Iran's Revolutionary Guards*. Cambridge: Cambridge University Press, 2022.

Tripp, Charles. *The Power and the People: Paths of Resistance in the Middle East*. Cambridge: Cambridge University Press, 2013.

Turam, Berna. *Between Islam and the State: The Politics of Engagement*. Stanford, CA: Stanford University Press, 2007.

Uyar, Mesut and Edward J. Erickson. *A Military History of the Ottomans: From Osman to Atatürk*. Santa Barbara, CA: Praeger Security International, 2009.

Van Dam, Nikolaos. *The Struggle for Power in Syria*. London: I. B. Tauris, 1996.

Vandewalle, Dirk. *A History of Modern Libya*. Cambridge: Cambridge University Press, 2006.

Vatikiotis, P. J. *The Egyptian Army in Politics*. Bloomington: Indiana University Press, 1961.

Ward, Steven R. *Immortal: A Military History of Iran and its Armed Forces*. Washington, DC: Georgetown University Press, 2009.

Waterbury, John. *The Commander of the Faithful: The Moroccan Elite—A Study in Segmented Politics*. New York: Columbia University Press, 1970.

———. *The Egypt of Nasser and Sadat: The Political Economy of Two Regimes*. Princeton, NJ: Princeton University Press, 1983.

Wedeen Lisa. *Ambiguities of Domination: Politics, Rhetoric, and Symbols in Contemporary Syria*. Chicago: University of Chicago Press, 1999.

Wenner, Manfred W. *Modern Yemen, 1918–1966*. Baltimore: Johns Hopkins University Press, 1967.

White, Jenny. *Muslim Nationalism and the New Turks*. Princeton, NJ: Princeton University Press, 2013.

Whitman, Elizabeth. *The Awakening of the Syrian Army: General Husni al-Za'im's Coup and Reign, 1949*. Senior Thesis, Columbia University, 2011.

Wilford, Hugh. *America's Great Game: The CIA's Secret Arabists and the Shaping of the Modern Middle East*. New York: Basic Books, 2013.

Willis, Michael J. *Politics and Power in the Maghreb: Algeria, Tunisia, and Morocco from Independence to the Arab Spring*. New York: Columbia University Press 2012.

Winter, Stefan. *A History of the "Alawis: From Medieval Aleppo to the Turkish Republic*. Princeton, NJ: Princeton University Press, 2016.

Woods, Kevin B., Williamson Murray, Elizabeth A. Nathan, Laila Sabara, and Ana M. Venegas. *Saddam's General: Perspectives of the Iran-Iraq War*. Washington, DC: Institute for Defense Analysis, 2011.

Wright, Claudia. "Journey to Marrakesh: US–Moroccan Security Relations." *International Security* 7, no. 4 (1983): 163–79.

Wuthrich, F. Michael. "Factors Influencing Military-Media Relations in Turkey." *The Middle East Journal* 66, no. 2 (2012): 253–72.

Yaniv, Avner. "A Question of Survival: The Military and Politics Under Siege." In *National Security and Democracy in Israel*, edited by Avner Yaniv, 81–103. Boulder, CO: Lynne Rienner Publishers, 1993.

Yolcu, Furkan Halit. "The Democratizer Army Paradox: The Role of the Algerian Army in Impeded Democratization." *Journal of Asian and African Studies* 54, no. 7 (2019): 1033–47.

Zartman, I. William. "The Algerian Army in Politics." In *Soldier and State in Africa*, edited by Claude E. Welch Jr., 224–50. Evanston, IL: Northwestern University Press, 1970.

Zeraoui, Zindane. "Algeria: Army, Revolution, and Political Power." *Language and Intercultural Communication* 12, no. 2 (2012): 133–45.

Index

al-Abadi, Haider, 196
Abraham Accords, 210
Abullah I, 168
Abdullah al-Faris Company for Heavy Industries, 140
Abu Zaʿbal Tank Repair Factory, 109
Adalet ve Kalkınma Partisi (AKP), 20, 31–32, 75, 115, 178.
    See also Justice and Development Party
al-Ahmar, Mohammed Saleh, 90, 198
Ali, Salam Rubayi, 82–83
Amir, ʿabd al-Hakim, 89, 176, 190, 288n116
Ammar, Rachid, 97
Arens, Moshe, 182
Armed Islamic Group, 71
al-ʿAsad, Bashar, 92, 104, 166, 202
al-ʿAsad, Hafiz, 66, 86, 91, 92, 175, 202
al-ʿAsad, Rifat, 92
Arif, Abdel Rahman, 80
al-Ahdab, Aziz, 78
al Ahmar, Ali Mohsen 106, 152, 187
Artesh, 46, 52–53
Atatürk, Kemal, 37, 73, 203
al-Auqaili, Taher Ali, 107
al-Attayah, Hamad bin, 90
Âoun, Michel, 52, 79

Balyoz (Sledgehammer), 77
Al-Badr, Mohammad, 70
al-Bakr, Hassan, 80
Bani-Sadr, Abolhassan, 168, 169
Bar-Lev, Haim, 182
Barak, Ehud, 182, 193, 258n30
Baʿth Revolutionary Command Council (RCC), 80
Başbuğ, İker, 77, 178
Bayraktar TB2 drones, 115, 127, 145, 179
Begin, Menachim, 193
Ben Bella, Ahmed, 70
Ben Ali Zine Abidine, 21, 96
Ben Gurion, David, 44, 50, 181, 191, 192
Bensalah, Abdelkader, 72
Benjedid, Chadli, 71, 102
al-Bitar, Salah al Din, 66
Black September incident, 228n161
Boumediene, Houari, 70
Bourguiba, Habib, 96
Bouteflika, Abdelaziz, 8, 87, 102
bully praetorian states, 10
bully single party republics, 11
bunker states, 10

Central Intelligence Agency:
    role in Iran coup, 84

Chehab, Fouad, 78
Comite d'Etat-Major Operationnel Conjoint (CEMOC), 173
Committee for Union and Progress, 229n165
conservative monarchies, 12
Constructions Organization (Mu'assatat al-Iskan al-'Askari), 146
coup d'état:
  defined, 57;
  frequency, 57;
  Middle East, frequency, 63
coups for the nation:
  defined:
  Algeria, 70–71;
  Jordan, 72–73;
  Iraq, 79–81;
  Lebanon, 78–79;
  Morocco, 81–82;
  Turkey, 73–78;
  Yemen, 69–70
coups "with a little help from our friends":
  Iran, 84;
  Syria, 82;
  Yemen, 82–84
coup proofing:
  defined, 85;
  Egypt, 89;
  military effects of, 164;
  Syria, 91–
  Yemen, 90–91
Cyrenaica Defense Force, 68

Davutoglü, Ahmet, 88
Demirel, Süleiman, 74
Diyant, 32, 225n108
Druze, 44, 50, 67, 199, 226n127, 22
Dayan, Moshe, 191

Elbit Systems, 146
El-Nasr Company for Services and Maintenance, 137
Egyptian Directorate of Military Intelligence, 90

Egyptian Sovereign Wealth Fund, 138
Erbakan, Necmitten, 74, 75, 194
Ergenekon Affair, 38, 223n89;
  alleged assassination attempt, 241n165
Erdoğan, Recep Tayyip, 11, 12, 32, 75, 87, 88, 115, 178, 179, 194, 195, 209
Eshkol, Levi, 182, 191, 192
Evren, Kenan, 87

F-35 "Joint Strike Fighter," 127
Fahd bin Turki bin Abdulaziz, 185
Faisal I of Iraq, 79
Farouk I, 64
Food Security Division, Egyptian armed forces, 136
fragmented democracies, 10, 12
Free Officers, 33, 135, 176, 206, 288n114
Free Syrian Army, 49
Freedom House, 85, 94–95, 215n30
Front de Libération Nationale, (FLN), 11, 70

Gamasy, 'abd al-Ghani, 177
Gantz, Benny, 193
Gemayel, Amin, 79
Gemayel, Bashir, 79
al-Ghashmi, Ahmad, 82
Ghazala, 'abd al-Halim Abu, 137
Globalizing monarchies, 10
Gülen, Fethullah movement, 76, 77, 241n167
Gürsel, Cemal, 42, 73

Hadi, 'abd Rabbo Mansour, 83, 90
Haftar, Khalifa, 69, 174, 179, 209, 237n102
Hamrouche, Mouloud, 71
Hamza, Prince of Jordan, 72
Hassan II, 7, 16, 21, 81, 86, 228n161, 244n207
Hezbollah:
  Lebanese, 22, 156, 193, 199;
  Turkish, 76

Hoss, Selim, 79;
    Al-Houthi, 107, 143, 153\, 166, 184,
        187, 198, 209
Huneiti, General Yousef, 72
al-Hinnawi, Sami, 66
Hrawi, Elias, 79
Hussein I, 49, 72, 88
Hussein, Saddam, 22, 23, 80, 86, 93,
    160, 166, 170. 195

İnönü, İsmet, 74
Islamic Republican Guard Corps, 16,
    46, 52, 118, 168, 208, 256n10;
    business interests, 141–42, 203
Islamic State of Iraq and al-Shams
    (ISIS), 172
Israel Aerospace Industries (IAI), 146

Jabotinksy, Vladimir Ze'ev, 194
Joint Comprehensive Plan of Action
    (JCPOA), 118, 169
Jordanian Aeronautical Systems
    Company, 138
Jumblatt, Walid, 199
Justice and Development Party, 78, 201

al-Kailani Rachid 'Ali, 79
Kale Industries–Pratt and Whitney
    engine plant
Kamal, Hussein, 104, 171
Khamenei, Ali, 23
al-Khasawneh, Awn Shawkat, 216n46
Khomeini, Ruhollah, 169
Al-Kurdi, Mahmud, 155
Kurdish PKK, 166, 178, 195
King Abdulaziz City for Science and
    Technology:
    development of laser guided
        bombs, 140
King Abdullah II Design and
    Development Bureau
    (KADDB), 139

Lapid, Yair, 115
League of Arab States, 213n3

liberal monarchies, 12
Libyan Government of National Accord,
    69, 174, 199, 209
Libyan National Forces, 174

Mahmoud, Ali Habib, 105
al-Maliki, Nuri Kamel, 81, 169, 171,
    172, 268n184
Mansour, Adly. 65
Medbouh, Mohammed, 81

Golda Meir, 191
Menderes, Adnan, 73, 240n143
middle East militaries, public approval
    of, 35–40
military cohesion, 48–52
military corruption;
    defined, 150–51;
    Egypt, 154–55;
    Saudi Arabia, 153;
    Syria, 155–56;
    Turkey, 155;
    Yemen, 152–153
Military, definition of, 15
Military Intelligence Service
    (*Mukhabarat*), 91, 92
military Keynesian, 119
Ministry of Military Production
    (MMP), 109
Middle East military spending, 113–114;
    Egypt, 117–118;
    Iran, 118–119;
    Israel, 115–116;
    Syria, 116–117;
    Turkey, 114–115
moderator model of civil-military
    relations, 94
Mofaz, Shaul, 126, 193
Morsi, Mohammed, 33, 65, 101, 117,
    150, 197, 202
Mubarak, Hosni, 33, 36, 65, 89, 137,
    177, 197, 202
Mubarak, Gamal, 98, 198
Muslim Brotherhood;
    Egyptian, 33, 101

Muslim Brotherhood;
    Syrian, 67, 104

al-Nadha Party, 97
al Nahyan, 186
al-Nahyan, Mohammed bin Zayed, 186
Nasr, Turki bin, 153
Nasser Gamal 'abd, 43, 86, 138, 176
National Security Council (*Milli Güvenlik Kurulu*, or MGK), 74
National Service Projects Organization (NSPO), 135
Nawwar, Ali Abu, 72
Netanyahu, Benyamin, 45, 116, 126, 193, 258n30

Operation Straggle, 82
Oufkir, Mohamed, 81
Özel Harp *Dairesi* (Special Warfare Unit, or ÖHD), 76

Pahlavi Mohammad Reza, 84, 86, 141, 198, 204, 284n47
People's National Army" (PNA), 172
Peshmerga, 50
Phalangist militia, 79
Popular Mobilization Front, 203
Popular Mobilization Units (*Hashd al-Shaabi*), 196
Popular National Army, 71
Prince, Erik, 186

Qaddafi, Muamar, 22, 68, 86, 104, 173
abd al-Karim Qasim, 202
Quds Force, 46
al-Qudsi, Nazim, 66
al-Quwatli, Shukri, 65, 82

Rabin, Yitzhak, 182, 191
Rafael Industries146
Republican Guards:
    Iraqi, 87, 170
Revolutionary Guard militia (*Pasdaran*), 168

republican bully personalist, 11
rent-seeking, 17;
    Egypt, 135;
    Middle East, 134–35
rentier states, 123–24
Rohani, Hassan, 118, 142
Royal Jordanian National Defense College, 168
Royal Saudi Arabian Air Force, 184

Sadat, Anwar, 33, 43, 166, 177, 190
al- Sadr, Muqatada196
al-Said, Nuri, 80
al-Said, Qaboos, 201
Salah, Ahmed Gaid, 103, 104
Saleh, Ali Abdullah, 83, 106, 152, 178
Saleh, Tariq Mohammed Abdullah, 90
al-Sallal Abdullah, 70
Salman, Mohammed bin, 91, 140, 184, 185, 216n46, 279n357
al-Sanusi, King Idris, 68
al-Saud Abdul-Aziz, 91, 93
Saudi Arabia;
    support for 1948 Yemen civil war, 70;
    role in Yemen, 91;
    control of military, 86
Saudi Arabian Military Industries (SAMI), 140
SAVAK (*Sazman-I Ettela'at va Amniyat-I Keshwar*), 21, 84
security assistance:
    civil-military implications of, 196–199
Shabiha, 93, 113, 156, 175, 249n288
Shafiq, Ahmed, 98, 101
al-Shallal, Abdul Aziz Jassem, 105, 166
Shamkhani, Ali, 169
Shamir, Yitzhak, 193
Sharon, Ariel, 180, 182
al-Shater, Khairat, 102
Shazli, Saad, 165, 177
Shishakli, Adib, 66.
Sidqi, Bakr, 79

al-Sisi, Abdel Fattah, 33, 65, 89, 102, 117, 128, 139
Southern Transitional Council, 83
strategic assessment, 157, 188–189;
  Egypt, 189–91;
  Iraq, 195–196;
  Israel, 191–194;
  Turkey, 194–195
Suleiman, Omar, 98
Suleimani, Qassim, 169, 227n144
Supreme Council of the Armed Forces (SCAF), 65, 99, 101
Syrian Army Fourth Armored Division, 147, 175, 255n380
Syrian Ba'ath Party, 67, 235n83
Syrian Higher Military Academy, 175
Syrian Organization of Military Factories, 146

Tahrir Square, 98
Tantawi, Mohamed, 101, 190
Tebboune, Abdelmadjid, 104
al-Thani, Hamad ibn Khalifa, 90
Tlas, Mustapha, 105, 155, 292n371
Al-Tohamy General Mohamed Farid, 154
Tripolitania Defense Force, 68
Troupes Spéciales du Levant, 174
Turkish Armed Forces Trust and Pension Fund 143
Turki bin Bandar bin Abdulaziz, 185;
  Army Mutual Aid Association, 144

Turkish War College (*Harp Akademileri Komutanlığı*), 41

United Arab Emirates:
  military performance of, 149
Ulusu, Bülend, 75

velvet shove:
  definition of, 62–63;
  Algeria, 102–104;
  Bahrain, 106;
  Egypt, 98–102;
  examples, 95–96;
  Syria, 104–106;
  Tunisia, 96–98;
  Yemen, 106

Weizman, Ezer, 182

Yaalon, Moshe, 115–16, 126
Yahya, Hamid ad-Din, 69
Al-Yamamah arms purchase, 153
Yekîneyên Parastina Gel (YPG), 178, 194
Yemen Economic Corporation (YECO), 143
Yemen Military Economic Corporation, 142

Zadari, Asif Ali, 7
Za'im, Husni, 66, 82
Zeroual, Liamine, 87

About the Author

David S. Sorenson is professor of international security studies at the US Air Force's Air War College. He has previously authored seven books, co-edited or edited four additional books, and published numerous journal articles. His PhD is from the Korbel School of International Relations at the University of Denver.

www.ingramcontent.com/pod-product-compliance
Lightning Source LLC
Chambersburg PA
CBHW032031300426
44117CB00009B/1020